Our Fa
in Heav

Other books by John Cooper

Body, Soul, and Life Everlasting: Biblical Anthropology and the Monism-Dualism Debate
Cause for Division? Women in Office and the Unity of the Church

Our Father in Heaven

*Christian
Faith and
Inclusive
Language
for God*

John W. Cooper

Baker Books

A Division of Baker Book House Co
Grand Rapids, Michigan 49516

Published by Baker Books
A division of Baker Book House Company
P.O. Box 6287, Grand Rapids, MI 49516–6287

Printed in the United States of America

Library of Congress Cataloging-in-Publication Data

Cooper, John W., 1947–
    Our Father in heaven : Christian faith and inclusive language for God / John
W. Cooper.
        p.   cm.
    Includes bibliographical references and index.
    ISBN 0-8010-2188-X
    1. Nonsexist language—religious aspects—Christian Reformed Church.
2. Sexism in liturgical language. 3. Christian Reformed Church—Liturgy.
I. Title.
BX6825.C66   1999
231′.01′4—dc21   98-40633

For information about academic books, resources for Christian leaders, and all new releases available from Baker Book House, visit our web site:
                    http://www.bakerbooks.com

To my Mother and Father,
both of whom have imaged for me
Our Father in Heaven.

Contents

Acknowledgments

I am particularly grateful to a number of people for their help, encouragement, and contributions to this book.

It is a much better book than it would have been without the intense dialogue I had from 1994 to 1996 with the other members of the Christian Reformed synodical committee to study inclusive language for God. Serving with me on this committee were Mirth Vos, a family counselor from Barrie, Ontario; Lee Christoffels, a CRC minister then in Preakness, New Jersey; Jai-Sung Shim, a CRC minister and recent Ph.D. graduate of Calvin Seminary; Lorna Van Gilst, an English professor at Dordt College in Sioux Center, Iowa; Al Wolters, a biblical scholar and professor at Redeemer College in Ancaster, Ontario; and Bill Vande Kopple, professor of English at Calvin College. Only some of their contributions have been acknowledged in notes.

I am also grateful to my faculty colleagues in the Theological Division of Calvin Seminary. For years they patiently discussed inclusive language for God with me and have commented on several chapters of the book, offering important correctives and clarifications.

My sincere thanks go to Joel Kim, a very promising Calvin Seminary Ph.D. student, who read two entire drafts of the book, made dozens of important suggestions and corrections, and prepared the indexes.

Finally, I wish to thank the Seminary board of trustees for sabbatical time, the Seminary for a computer and workplace, and the good people at Baker Book House for their patience and expertise.

Introduction

Why This Book Was Written

It has been almost ten years since I first heard God addressed as "Our Father and Mother in Heaven." It was at an ecumenical service I attended with friends. I can still recall the sensation of spiritual shock and recoil. I was appalled. It was as though I had just witnessed blasphemy or the invocation of a pagan god. This sense of uncleanness made it impossible for me to worship during the rest of the service. "This is not the God I serve," I thought to myself.

After the service, of course, our conversation immediately turned to the innovative invocation of God. To my surprise, not all of my friends shared my reaction to it. A couple of them thought it was perfectly legitimate. "After all," they argued, "God is neither male nor female. And both men and women are created in his image, so both masculine and feminine language can image him. In fact, the Bible itself contains feminine language for God, although traditional Christianity has largely ignored it. So there is nothing wrong with calling God 'Father and Mother.' In fact, it's about time we do. We no longer live in a male-dominated society the way they did when the Bible was written. If the Bible were written today, it would use inclusive language for God as well as for humans." Obviously my friends had been thinking about gender-inclusive language for God and were persuaded that it is a good thing.

I was taken off guard and somewhat lost for words. All I could do was mumble something about "Father and Mother" not being the way God revealed himself in Scripture or the way the church has spoken of him for nineteen hundred years. But my friends had a pretty plausible argument based on what sounded like some true and orthodox premises. And their argument in favor of the new way of addressing God moved from the same Scripture and tradition that I appealed to. Though not persuaded, I was unable to counter their position effectively.

15

This incident is what moved me to begin serious consideration of feminist theology and its influence in North American church life. In just two minutes my friends had summarized the formidable case for inclusive language for God that has been built by feminist theologians, biblical scholars, liturgists, and clergy in the past two decades. Inclusive language for God is not just a theological position; it is increasingly the practice of individual Christians and churches alike.

My study of feminist theology and inclusive language for God was not motivated merely by personal discomfort. I am a minister of the Christian Reformed Church and a professor who teaches apologetics (the intelligent defense of the Christian faith) at Calvin Theological Seminary. I was interested in understanding the trend toward inclusive language for God, developing the response that I was unable to offer my friends, and helping my students prepare to deal with it honestly in their own ministries. So I developed an elective course on feminist theology. Further reading, reflection, and dialogue led to publication of several articles on inclusive language for God and eventually to the writing of this book.

Work was fairly well along—I had a detailed outline and much of the reading completed—when in the providence of God it was side-tracked for two years. The Synod of the Christian Reformed Church decided in 1994 to appoint a committee to study inclusive language for God, an issue that had received increasing attention in the CRC since 1991. I was appointed to that committee with six other people of diverse kinds of expertise (see *Acknowledgments*). The result of our work, which I wrote as a report, was adopted overwhelmingly by the Synod of 1997.

Those who read that report and this book will recognize that many of their arguments and conclusions are very similar. That is because I brought the work I had done previously, especially for the book, to the denominational study. I did so with the knowledge of the general secretary of the CRC and the members of study committee. At that time I reserved the right to publish this book. While there are obvious similarities between the report and this book, each is an original piece of writing. Not so much as a sentence was taken from the report. The book contains much that the report does not, and vice versa. However, the book is much better than it would have been without the input of my colleagues on the study committee, whose contributions I acknowledge here and elsewhere. The book has also benefited from discussions and criticisms of the report after its publication. For better or worse, the book is completely my own position, whereas the report expresses the consensus of a committee, which inevitably requires nuancing and yielding of one's own preferred ways of putting things.

How This Book Approaches the Debate

This book attempts a comprehensive presentation and evaluation of inclusive language for God. It is intended for pastors, college and seminary students, and thoughtful members of the church. It is not a professional academic treatise, although it is based on a great deal of scholarly research and deals with some very complicated theological and linguistic issues. It attempts to address the complexities that engage scholars in ways that are accessible to more general readers. At the same time I trust that professional theologians will find it useful and engaging.

Although it is largely a critical response to inclusive language for God, the book seeks an honest encounter. It attempts as clearly and accurately as possible to present and analyze the various arguments that are given in favor of inclusive language, referring regularly to major participants in the debate. It seeks to acknowledge what is true in these arguments and to recognize the legitimate concerns they raise about sexism and its harmful emotional, social, and spiritual effects on people. It attempts no gain by misrepresenting and demonizing opponents or by constructing "straw persons."

Having expressed commitment to intellectual honesty, I must inform readers of my religious and theological allegiances. (All scholars have basic worldview beliefs and commitments.) I am a minister of the Christian Reformed Church and a professor at Calvin Seminary. More specifically, I am a committed follower of the Jesus Christ presented in the Bible and proclaimed by the historic Christian faith. I believe Scripture itself is the inspired Word of God and without error in all that it teaches. I affirm the truth of Christian doctrine as professed in the Apostles' and Nicene Creeds and elaborated in the confessional statements of the CRC. In short, I am a biblical, evangelical, Reformed Christian.

This commitment does not require close-mindedness, however. The church is always to be reforming in the light of Scripture. While I think it takes a lot to overturn a traditional reading of Scripture or a doctrinal statement, I believe that honest, open, intelligent reflection can lead to a modification or abandonment of a traditional position. Accordingly, I recommend that Christians begin using feminine language for God according to the pattern of Scripture, but not according to the gender-inclusive pattern.

Further, commitment to Scripture does not require avoidance of modern biblical scholarship. While I reject the naturalistic assumptions of higher criticism and any hermeneutics (i.e., method of interpretation) that conflicts with the historic Reformed view of Scripture, I think much can be learned from modern scholarship about Scripture's composition and meaning that can be appropriated according to the principles of Reformed hermeneutics. New insights must not be ignored but appropriated within a proper approach to Scripture.

Finally, I believe that Scripture requires us to promote justice and the full humanity of women. Although I affirm a biblical view of men, women, marriage, and family, I believe there are many ways in which traditional social patterns have wrongly hindered women. I support many of the legal rights and opportunities for women that have developed in the past two decades. I have defended the hermeneutical and theological integrity₁ of arguments for the ordination of women in my own denomination. I therefore invite feminist and theologically progressive Christians to consider my analysis seriously. My views do not follow from any form of sexism or fear of intellectual engagement, as far as I can tell.

The Conclusion

In the end the book concludes that gender-inclusive language for God and the biblical-historical Christian faith are incompatible. I can find no successful way to combine a high view of Scripture, sound exegesis, standard linguistics, doctrinal orthodoxy, and good logic to justify inclusive language for God. (I do not address the question of inclusive language for humans, although I am open to it in moderate forms.)

While I realize that more progressive Christians may not find my conclusion surprising or compelling, I hope that Christians committed to the historic biblical faith will be persuaded to avoid gender-inclusive language for God or, if they are already using inclusive language, to abandon it.

Nevertheless, I recognize the significant elements of truth in the case for inclusive language. So I follow a number of other biblically orthodox Christians in recommending that the church bring the language of faith more fully into conformity with the language of Scripture by incorporating feminine imagery for God within its traditional, biblically based pattern of speech. This means retaining the primacy of God as Father, Lord, King, and He, but sometimes using figures of speech that compare God to a mother or another female, as Scripture itself does. Our heavenly Father does have a motherly touch. Recovering the biblical feminine imagery for God is not capitulation to the women's liberation movement. It is an example of continuing reformation in the light of the Word of God.

1. John Cooper, *A Cause For Division? Women in Office and the Unity of the Church* (Calvin Theological Seminary, 1991).

A Survey of the Contents

Chapter 1 introduces the movement for inclusive language for God, identifies its goals, and surveys the reaction that has generated the current debate. Chapter 2 surveys the standard biblical, theological, and linguistic arguments used to justify inclusive language. It summarizes the case to which the rest of the book responds.

Chapters 3 through 5 closely examine gendered language for God in the Bible. Chapter 3 discusses Scripture's feminine language for God and chapter 4 treats the Bible's masculine language. Chapter 5 then compares the Bible's gendered language for God with inclusive language to pinpoint their crucial differences.

Chapter 6 discusses divine revelation, Scripture, and various ways that defenders of inclusive language have approached Scripture in order to justify the right to revise the biblical names for God. Chapter 7 treats the difficult matter of the limits of human language for God and the doctrine that God has no gender, which are frequently combined to validate inclusive language. Chapter 8 inquires whether inclusive language can communicate the truth of the biblical presentation of God and provide orthodox statements of the doctrines of God's relation to creation, the Trinity, and the deity of Jesus Christ.

Chapter 9 points out the spiritual dangers inherent in the promotion of inclusive language for God. Chapter 10 addresses charges that the God of the Bible and his expressed will for women are sexist. It concludes the critical response to inclusive language. Chapter 11 appropriates the elements of truth in the case for inclusive language and proposes ways of using feminine language for God that are consistent with biblical Christianity.

The Controversy over Inclusive Language for God

The Growing Trend toward Inclusive Language for God

Jesus taught his disciples to pray "Our Father in heaven" (Matt. 6:9). According to Virginia Mollenkott, however, "Jesus' cultural surroundings made 'Our Father and Mother in heaven' an impossibility; our cultural surroundings make it not only possible but necessary."[1] Mollenkott's widely read book, *The Divine Feminine*, is just one of a host of recent works advocating gender-inclusive language for God, language that treats masculine and feminine references to God equally.

In fact, gender-inclusive theology and language for God are currently among the most powerful forces in mainline Christianity. This trend is viewed by many as a natural outcome of the full recognition of women's equality. Traditional masculine language for God reflects traditional patriarchal society, they say. Affirmation of the equal rights and dignity of women in contemporary society requires an expression of the Christian faith that equally validates "the Divine feminine," as Mollenkott puts it. Thus influential hymn-writer Brian Wren argues that "the systematic and almost exclusive use of male God-language, in a faith in which God is revealed as incarnate in a male human being, gives a distorted vision of God and supports male dominance in church and society."[2] Sensitive to these concerns, Rosemary Ruether, a leading American feminist theologian, refers to the Deity as "God/ess, a written symbol intended to combine both the masculine and feminine forms of the word for the divine while preserving the Judeo-Christian affirma-

---

1. Virginia Mollenkott, *The Divine Feminine: The Biblical Imagery of God as Female* (New York: Crossroad, 1983), 61.
2. Brian Wren, *What Language Shall I Borrow? God-Talk in Worship: A Male Response to Feminist Theology* (New York: Crossroad, 1989), 4.

tion that divinity is one."[3] Hundreds of current publications, both scholarly and popular, contain statements like these, advocating inclusive, nonsexist language for God to reflect and reinforce the liberation and equality of women in our society.

Inclusive language is not merely being advocated. It is steadily being introduced into the sources that shape the faith of Christians and the ministry of the church. Scripture itself is being rendered gender-correctly. In 1983 the National Council of Churches began publishing *An Inclusive Language Lectionary* for use in worship.[4] It translates *Father* as *God* or *Father* [*and Mother*]. Its version of John 3:16 reads: "For God so loved the world that God gave God's only Child," scrupulously avoiding the masculine terms *he*, *his*, and *Son*. *The Gospels and the Letters of Paul*, published by the United Church of Christ (1992), translates the Great Commission (Matt. 28:19) this way: "Go therefore and make disciples of all nations, baptizing them in the name of God the Father and Mother and of Jesus Christ the Beloved Child and of the Holy Spirit." *The Inclusive New Testament* provides yet another version of the triune name in Matthew 28:19, *Abba God, Only Begotten, and Holy Spirit*.[5] *The Inclusive Language Bible* begins the Lord's Prayer, "Our heavenly Parent."[6] Oxford University Press has recently produced *The New Testament and Psalms: A New Inclusive Translation*, which is not only sensitive to gender, but also to race, color, religion, and disability.[7] It translates *Father* as either *God* or as *Father and Mother*. Advocates of inclusive language are well aware that the Bible is the source and standard of the Christian faith. By producing gender-balanced versions of Holy Scripture, they aim to re-shape the Christian view of God from the foundation up.

In addition to the Bible, the language of worship is a powerful influence on the formation of the faith and piety of Christian believers. Inclusivists have launched major efforts in this area as well. A prime example is *The New Century Hymnal*, produced and promoted by the United Church of Christ.[8] Its orders of worship, litanies, and prayers use language for God that avoids masculine nouns and pronouns. Its Lord's Prayer comes in two versions: either *Our Father* or *Our Father-*

3. Rosemary Ruether, *Sexism and God-Talk: Toward a Feminist Theology* (Boston: Beacon, 1983), 46.

4. *An Inclusive Language Lectionary*, prepared by a committee appointed by the National Council of Churches (Atlanta: John Knox: New York: Pilgrim; Philadelphia: Westminster, 1983).

5. *The Inclusive New Testament* (Hyattsville, Md.: Priests for Equality, 1994).

6. *The New Testament of the Inclusive Language Bible* (Notre Dame, Ind: Cross Cultural, 1994), Matt. 6:9.

7. *The New Testament and Psalms* (New York and Oxford: Oxford University Press, 1995), "General Introduction," viii.

8. *The New Century Hymnal* (Cleveland: Pilgrim, 1995).

Mother. Its several hundred hymns and versification of the Psalms do not come in two versions. They are thoroughly gender-inclusive, carefully deemphasizing masculine words for God. Thus the great hymn "Come Thou, Almighty King," for example, has been rephrased as "Come Now, Almighty God." God is no longer *Lord* and *King*. He is rarely *Father*, even in the hymns devoted to the Trinity. "Of the Father's Love Begotten" is now "Of the Parent's Heart Begotten." Hymns that do sing of God as *Father* always carefully preserve gender balance by also invoking God as *Mother*. Brian Wren's "Bring Many Names," the theme-song of the inclusive-language movement, is a clear example.[9] It addresses "strong mother God" and "warm father God" with precise parallelism. Some hymns, such as "By Whatever Name We Call You," actually promote gender-inclusive theology by emphasizing God's transcendence and the inadequacy of all language (including traditional biblical language) for speaking of the Mystery.[10]

The trend toward inclusive-language hymnody is not limited to the *New Century Hymnal*. It is followed by most hymn-writers for mainline Christian churches, as evident from scanning a volume like *Holding in Trust*, a collection of contemporary hymns published by the Hymn Society in the United States and Canada.[11] While a number of compositions do refer to God as *Father* without an offsetting *Mother*, the large majority are gender-inclusive. They avoid the primary traditional masculine terms for God, *Father* and *King*, and the masculine pronouns that naturally accompany them.

The doctrinal standards of the Christian church have not been exempted from correction by inclusivists. The *New Century Hymnal* provides both traditional and alternative versions of the Apostles' and the Nicene Creeds. The inclusive-language versions confess God as *the Father-Mother almighty* and Jesus Christ as *God's only Child*. Thus the third part of the Nicene Creed now begins: "We believe in the Holy Spirit, the Sovereign, the giver of life, who proceeds from the Father-Mother, and from the Child."

I have not made a study of devotional literature or Sunday school and church education materials, but I assume that inclusivism has had a significant impact on these media as well. In any case, the movement toward gender-inclusive and gender-free language for God is not just an academic topic in institutions of higher learning. It is being promoted intentionally and vigorously in ways that fundamentally shape the religious perspectives of ordinary Christians.

9. Wren, "Bring Many Names" (Carol Stream, Ill.: Hope, 1989).
10. Dosia Carlson, "By Whatever Name We Call You" (Cleveland: Pilgrim, 1994).
11. *Holding in Trust* (Carol Stream, Ill.: Hope, 1992).

Both among church members and the general public, awareness of this trend was heightened and focused by the Re-Imagining God Conference, held in November 1993. Sponsored by several major denominations,[12] this event was attended by more than two thousand women of various backgrounds and theological orientations. While some of what took place was consistent with standard mainline Christianity, the focus of the conference was on celebration of God as *Mother* and *Sophia* (*Sophia* is the Greek term for *Wisdom* and is said to be a feminine aspect of deity). Some of what was re-imagined about God, Jesus Christ, and salvation elicited strong reactions even from within the sponsoring denominations.[13]

The trend toward inclusive language for God is not an insignificant development or a passing fad. In fact, the national media have treated it as a major development and significant alteration of historic Christianity. The Re-imagining God Conference received national television news coverage in November 1993, including extended discussion on ABC's *Nightline* and PBS's *McNeill/Lehrer Newshour*. Even before this conference, however, a feature on "Feminism and the Churches" in *Newsweek* magazine pointed out that an increasing number of women are not only demanding equality in church and synagogue, but are also insisting that masculine ways of presenting God be thoroughly revised according to current standards of gender-inclusiveness.[14] *Time* magazine's cover story on the ordination of women and inclusive language for God was entitled "The Second Reformation," reflecting how profoundly significant both supporters and opponents consider these trends.[15] Women clergy and feminine language for God were also given front-page coverage by the *Wall Street Journal*, which noted the movement's growing strength and the fact that the revisions in religious language reach as deep as the doctrine of the Trinity at the very heart of the Christian faith.[16]

Clearly the movement toward nonsexist language for God, with all its theological and ecclesiastical implications, is a major force in contem-

---

12. Among them were the Presbyterian Church (USA), the United Church of Christ, the Evangelical Lutheran Church in America, the United Methodist Church, the American Baptist Churches, and two Roman Catholic orders.

13. Kathryn Teapole Proctor, "Re-Imagining Conference Causes Church Stir," *Faith and Freedom*, Spring 1994, 4–5.

14. Kenneth Woodward, "Feminism and the Churches," *Newsweek*, 13 February 1989, 58–61.

15. Richard Ostling, "The Second Reformation: Cover Story," *Time*, 23 November 1992, 53–58.

16. Gustav Niebuhr, "The Lord's Name," *Wall Street Journal*, 27 April 1992, 1, 4. The article's subheadings identify key issues: "Image of God as 'He' Loses Its Sovereignty in America's Churches"; "More Worshipers Challenge Language That Describes Supreme Being as Male"; "What Happens to the Trinity?"

porary North American Christianity. In fact, it extends beyond North America[17] and involves Judaism as well as Christianity.[18] Traditionalists may wish to ignore or repudiate this trend. But it will not go away. It is tied to a broad and powerful dynamic in our culture—the movement toward full recognition of women's dignity and rights and the equality of women in all aspects of society and culture. Advocates believe that a gender-inclusive view of humans requires a gender-inclusive view of God and that the traditional presentation of God inevitably perpetuates a sexist, male-dominated hierarchy in both family and society.

What Exactly Is Inclusive Language for God?

Defining the Term

The general meaning of the term *inclusive language for God* is already somewhat apparent. It has to do with downplaying masculine language for God and employing more feminine language to promote gender equality in religious language and in our view of God. Nevertheless, it is important to move beyond impressions and to define the term precisely at the outset of our study. For people who use the term *inclusive language* or who advocate feminine language for God do not all share the same understanding of what it means or implies. Unless we define our terms clearly at the beginning, subsequent discussions will become confusing.

The definition of *gender-inclusive language* we work with in this book is *language that treats the genders equally either by using both masculine and feminine terms equally, or by avoiding gendered language altogether, or by a combination of using and avoiding terms of both genders equally.* How this definition applies to language for God is elaborated and illustrated below. It is easier to appreciate the significance of this definition if we contrast it with other approaches that use the term *inclusive language for God* somewhat differently.

Some people who wish to speak of God more inclusively merely want to use feminine language for God as part of the wide variety of Scripture's references to God, instead of limiting the Christian vocabulary almost exclusively to constant repetition of *God, Lord, Father,* and *he.* They point out that in the Bible God is called *a rock, a fortress, a con-*

17. See *The Motherhood of God: A Report by a Study Group Appointed by the Woman's Guild and the Panel on Doctrine on the Invitation of the General Assembly of the Church of Scotland,* ed. Alan Lewis (Edinburgh: Saint Andrew, 1984); and Manfred Hauke, *God or Goddess? Feminist Theology: Where Does It Lead?* trans. David Kipp (San Francisco: Ignatius, 1995), which reflects the situation in Germany.

18. See Samuel Dresner, "Goddess Feminism," *Conservative Judaism* 46 (1993): 3–23; and Matthew Berke, "God and Gender in Judaism," *First Things,* June/July 1996, 33–38.

suming fire, light, a friend, a potter, the desire of the nations, and that Scripture occasionally also uses feminine and maternal imagery for God. By including all the ways the Bible speaks of God in our religious language, they conclude, Christians will sometimes refer to God as *Mother* or use feminine imagery for God to augment the traditional language of God as *Father, Lord*, and *King*. This, for example, is the position of *The Motherhood of God*, a study done for the Church of Scotland. It concludes that "the motherly Father" is "well-attested by and fully in keeping with the biblical witness."[19] Thus when some people speak of *inclusive language for God*, they mean the use of feminine language as part of the whole pattern of biblical language for God. This position could therefore be called *biblical inclusivism*. To avoid confusion, however, we avoid the term *inclusivism* and refer to it as *the biblical pattern of gendered language for God*. In fact, a version of this position is what we defend in this book. Since this definition of *inclusive* does not require that masculine and feminine terms be used equally, it differs from the meaning identified above.

Another understanding of *inclusive language* also differs from the standard definition. Some who affirm inclusive language actually consider feminine terminology most adequate for speaking of God. They may not completely reject *Father, Lord*, and *King*, because these titles are at the heart of Scripture and Christian tradition. But they are persuaded that the vocabulary of *Mother* and *she* expresses who God is most adequately and effectively. They understand masculine language for God in terms of the more basic feminine language. Rosemary Ruether's theology culminates in this position. While her usual written term for the Deity is *God/ess*, a symbol intended to include both genders, she ultimately defines *God/ess* as *the Primal Matrix* of the world. *Matrix* is from the Latin *mater* (*mother*). Elizabeth Johnson also makes feminine language primary, at least as a tactic until true gender equality among humans is realized. While stating her ultimate hope for equal use of masculine and feminine imagery for God, she strategically promotes feminine terminology as more religiously available and translates the specially revealed name *Yahweh* as *She Who Is*.[20] While these theologians advocate inclusive language for God, their practice actually privileges feminine language for God as most appropriate and adequate. Thus the meaning of the term *inclusive*, taken within their overall approach, is different than ours.

19. *The Motherhood of God*, 45.
20. Elizabeth Johnson, *She Who Is: The Mystery of God in Feminist Theological Discourse* (New York: Crossroad, 1992). Yahweh is derived from "I AM," the name God revealed to Moses at the burning bush (Exod. 3:14).

However, most people who promote inclusive language for God do adopt the definition we have identified: complete gender equality, equivalence, equity, parity, balance, and mutuality. When femininst theologians in prestigious seminaries and liturgical revisionists in major denominations invoke *inclusive language for God*, this is what they typically mean—language that equally affirms both genders and slights or excludes neither. The examples with which the chapter began illustrate this position.

Let's look at this definition more closely. Inclusive language for God precisely parallels inclusive language for humans in form and in motivation. Inclusive language for humans has developed because gender equality and mutuality, widely embraced in the women's liberation movement, are increasingly influential values in our democratic society. These values allow recognition of some differences between males and females, but they do not permit regarding one gender as better or more important than the other. Thus gender-inclusive language avoids any suggestion that one gender is more privileged, prominent, valuable, desirable, normative, powerful, or gifted than the other. It is language that implies the equality, though not necessarily the sameness, of men and women.

The very same criteria are applied to language for God. Many who affirm egalitarian gender-inclusiveness for humans insist that our language for God must follow the same pattern.[21] This therefore is the standard meaning of *gender-inclusive language for God: speaking of God as equally masculine and feminine, or as ungendered, or as both ungendered and equally masculine and feminine.*

Another comparison further sharpens this definition. In contrast to *inclusive* language for God are two patterns that are regarded as *exclusive* because they use terminology of only one gender to represent the Deity. An example of one is obviously the Christian tradition, which has employed uniformly masculine language for God. An example of the other pattern is radical feminist spirituality, which has adopted feminine language for God almost exclusively.[22]

This book keeps an eye on the whole variety of inclusive and exclusive patterns of gendered language for God. But our primary focus is the mainstream approach to inclusive language for God, which treats both genders equally. Throughout the book we refer to this position as *inclusivism* and to those who promote it as *inclusivists*.

21. Johnson, "Basic Linguistic Options: God, Women, Equivalence," chap. 3 of *She Who Is*, is a full development of the arguments for this position.

22. See, for example, Carol Christ and Judith Plaskow, eds., *Womanspirit Rising: A Feminist Reader in Religion* (San Francisco: Harper & Row, 1979); and Aída Besançon Spencer et. al., *The Goddess Revival* (Grand Rapids: Baker, 1995).

It is apparent that not all who use feminine language for God are inclusivists. Some who do so may be consistent with the biblical pattern of gendered language for God. It is also evident that not all feminists are inclusivists, and that not all inclusivists are feminists. For these reasons it is not accurate simply to identify feminism, feminist theology, or feminine language for God with gender-inclusive language for God, or vice versa. We attempt to remain clear and consistent throughout the book regarding the use of these categories.

Means of Achieving Inclusive Language

How exactly does one achieve inclusiveness in practice? As already suggested, gender-inclusive language for God is achieved in ways that precisely parallel inclusive language for humans.[23] There are two different strategies, usually combined into a third. The first uses masculine and feminine terms equally. In the jargon of the trade this pattern is called *gender-egalitarian, gender-equivalent,* or *gender-balanced.* The second strategy avoids gendered terminology altogether, so it is usually labeled *gender-neutral* or *ungendered.* The third and most common practice combines gender-equivalent and gender-neutral language for God in various proportions. All of these patterns are subsumed under the general heading *inclusive language for God.* The rest of the book uses this terminology consistently to avoid confusion.

The first strategy, gender-egalitarian or gender-equivalent language, is quite straightforward. Obviously it intends to achieve equality of quantity, the number and frequency with which gendered terms are used. As often as we call God *Father* and use the pronoun *he,* we must also call God *Mother* and *she.* Balance can be maintained by juxtaposing these terms whenever we use them, as, for example, in *our Father and Mother in heaven,* and *His/Her Child.* But gendered terms need not always be immediately paired. Equality can also be achieved more generally by employing roughly equal numbers of masculine and feminine references throughout the pattern of religious language as a whole. Thus in Scripture readings, prayers, hymns, and sermons sometimes *Father* and *he* are used; elsewhere *Mother* and *she* are featured. However realized, overall balance in the quantity of masculine and feminine language is the goal.

But gender equality is also qualitative. There must be parity in the ways that gendered terms are used. They must share the same linguistic

---

23. A standard work on language for humans is Francine Wattman, Frank Treichler, and Paula Treichler, *Language, Gender, and Professional Writing: Theoretical Approaches and Guidelines for Nonsexist Usage* (Modern Language Association of America, 1989).

status, function, and importance. Terminology of one gender cannot be considered definitive while language of the other is figurative or supplemental. *Father* cannot be considered a divine name and *mother* only a metaphor, for example. *Father* must be balanced by a use of *Mother* that has the same linguistic and theological status. Only then is genuinely gender-egalitarian language for God achieved.

The second strategy for maintaining inclusiveness is to use ungendered or gender-neutral language. Instead of *Father* and *Mother*, *Parent* is preferred. In place of *King* and *Lord*, one would use *Monarch, Ruler,* or *Sovereign*. *Son of God* becomes *Divine Child*. *Creator, Redeemer, and Comforter* replaces *Father, Son, and Holy Spirit*. Gendered pronouns like *he* and *himself* are avoided. *Godself* or *God's own self* might replace *God himself*. Instead of *God . . . he* one might simply repeat *God . . . God . . . God* without ever using a pronoun. The point of this strategy is to choose terms that do not imply gender whatsoever.

The third strategy, combining gender-equivalent and gender-neutral language, is most typical among promoters of inclusive language for God, as can be seen from browsing in *The New Century Hymnal*.[24] Gender-neutral terms like *God, Holy One, Creator, Light of the World, Eternal Wisdom, Redeemer,* and *Ruler* far outweigh gendered words like *Father* and *Mother*. When masculine and feminine references to God do occur, they are carefully balanced in both frequency and status. *King* and *Lord* are not used because *Queen* and *Lady* are not regarded as appropriate correlations in language for God. Gendered pronouns are avoided altogether rather than paired as *he* and *she*.

All of these strategies fit within the broad category *inclusive language for God* as understood and promoted in mainline academic and ecclesiastical circles. Inclusive language for God in this sense is the primary focus of this book.

Inclusive Language for God and the Women's Liberation Movement

Feminism and Women's Liberation

Although inclusivism as we have defined it cannot simply be identified with feminist theology, there is obviously a strong link between the two. The current trend toward gender-inclusive language and theology in turn has largely been spawned by and is closely associated with the

24. While the combined strategy is generally employed, there may be a recently emerging trend toward using almost exclusively gender-neutral language. See, for example, Gail Ramshaw, *God beyond Gender: Feminist Christian God-Language* (Minneapolis: Fortress, 1995).

women's movement that has become widespead since the 1960s. While it is true that contemporary feminism and feminist theology have historical precursors, and although Christians throughout history have occasionally employed feminine language for God,[25] the revisions in religious language advocated by inclusivists leave historical precedent far behind. Thus the rationale for gender-inclusive language for God cannot be understood apart from contemporary feminism and the movement for women's liberation.

It is important to realize that feminism, the women's liberation movement, and feminist theology are not a single, monolithic force. They should not be lumped together and stereotyped, as both supporters and opponents sometimes do. While all feminists are committed to the full humanity of women, there are many different ideas about what the full humanity of women is and what must be done to promote it. In fact there are practically as many kinds of feminism as there are religious traditions, kinds of secularism, and political philosophies.[26]

Nevertheless, they also hold many views in common. The following paragraphs summarize positions that most feminists and advocates for women would affirm.[27] I present them rather than judge their truth or falsehood. But I am sympathetic to many of these concerns, especially those voiced by evangelical Christian feminists.

For over three decades feminists and the women's liberation movements have persistently challenged the ways in which they perceive gender relations and social patterns to harm and restrict women. Feminists charge that the structures and values of traditional society are sexist—favoring men at the expense of women. They point out that in the home as well as society at large, men have had the dominant and

---

25. Among them are Chrysostom, Augustine, Anselm, Julian of Norwich, a fourteenth-century abbess, and even John Calvin. See Mollenkott, *The Divine Feminine*, 8–10. For most, the practice was rare or infrequent. None elevated feminine imagery to the status of divine names and titles or used it nearly as frequently as biblical masculine language. This topic is treated in later chapters.

26. Helpful overviews of the women's liberation movement and feminism are Josephine Donovan, *Feminist Theory: The Intellectual Traditions of American Feminism* (New York: Ungar, 1986); Rebecca Merrill Groothuis, *Women Caught in the Conflict: The Culture War Between Traditionalism and Feminism* (Grand Rapids: Baker, 1994); Mary Kassian, *The Feminist Gospel: The Movement to Unite Feminism Within the Church* (Wheaton: Crossway, 1992); Francis Martin, *The Feminist Question: Feminist Theology in the Light of Christian Tradition* (Grand Rapids: Eerdmans, 1994), chap. 5; Ruether, *Sexism and God-Talk*, chaps. 4 and 9; and Elaine Storkey, *What's Right with Feminism* (Grand Rapids: Eerdmans, 1985). Groothuis, Kassian, Martin, and Storkey are orthodox Christians.

27. I am grateful to Mirth Vos, a family counselor and colleague on the Christian Reformed committee to study inclusive language for God, for her insights and contributions to my understanding of the ways women and men suffer because of sexism, in particular, the spiritual problems they experience.

advantageous positions. Women have often functioned as men's servants, cooking their food, cleaning their homes, and providing them sexual satisfaction and children, while men have kept most of the power, leisure time, and discretionary income for themselves. Women have been required to play subordinate, limited, and more self-sacrificial roles both in the private sphere of the family and in the public arenas of culture, economics, politics, and religious life. Feminists commonly label this social system *patriarchalism*, a male-dominated hierarchy that preserves the privilege and power of men.

Most feminists link patriarchalism with *androcentrism*, the cultural assumption that male ways of doing things—decision making, managing, learning, feeling, communicating, resolving conflicts, and the like—are normative for everyone. Androcentrism in the home means that women are judged by men's categories and standards and are made to feel inadequate if they do not measure up. Androcentrism in public life means that women have to think and do things like men to succeed in business, education, or politics.

Patriarchalism and androcentrism, the dual dynamics of sexism, have cooperated not only to make women subordinate, but also to *marginalize* them. This means that women have been kept on the sidelines when the important, culturally formative decisions are made, even about themselves. They do not occupy influential positions of leadership. Their opinions are not taken seriously. Their complaints are not adequately addressed. In fact they have not even been allowed to participate in many areas and levels of public life that have been regarded as "men's work," including leadership in the church. Or if they have been permitted to enter traditionally male vocations and activities, a sexist double-standard has hampered them. They have had to perform at a higher level, they have not been given equal pay for equal work, or they have not been given the same opportunities for advancement. In these ways the marginalization of women has perpetuated a variety of injustices. The women's movement has fought against all of these consequences of what is commonly called *sexism*, that is, stereotyping, prejudice, or unjust treatment due to a person's sex.

Sexism causes psychological harm as well as social injustice. People who do not fit the cultural stereotypes of masculinity and femininity often feel inadequate and "out of it." Women who internalize their subordinate social status easily acquire an inferior view of themselves. They become convinced that women in general are less capable than men, or at least that they as individuals are less gifted. Feelings of inferiority often lead to passivity: there is no point in trying to develop oneself if there is no ability or potential. Beyond passivity, inferiority sometimes leads to strong feelings of unworthiness. Inferior persons feel unworthy of love, respect, and equality. They believe that they deserve to be treated as subordinates, perhaps even to be hurt. Men, of course, are socialized to share these distorted views of women and to regard themselves with a correspondingly false sense of superiority.

Women who realize that they are endowed with the same basic rights, gifts, and dignity as men experience perpetual frustration at the ways in which gender stereotypes and the social order prevent their participation and contributions. They become righteously angry at this basic injustice. Their anger can become deep-seated and perpetual, turning into bitterness toward the whole social order and antipathy toward men in general. Obviously sexism has harmful emotional consequences for women. But feminists also frequently point out how men are damaged by sexist notions of male superiority, responsibility, and macho masculinity.

In addition to the detrimental consequences of sexism, social analysts (whether or not they are feminists) have exposed the more immediately harmful problems of neglect and abuse that women and children suffer, often from men. Millions of children have been abandoned by their fathers, who fail to give them the financial support they deserve and the loving nurture they crave. Untold numbers of other children have been physically, sexually, or emotionally abused by men—often their fathers, other male relatives, or family friends. Many women suffer harm and sometimes even death at the hands of men who claim to love them. The numbers suggest that there is an epidemic of abuse and neglect in our society. The problem is significant even among churchgoers, people who claim to be Christians. Conscientious men and women have pressed for the liberation of all people from the injustices and injuries of sexism and abuse.

Feminism and Inclusive Language for God

Of course it will take much more than changing religious language to reform gender roles and restore healthy relations between the sexes in society. But the links among women's liberation, feminism, and inclusive language for God are not hard to understand. Three important connections are regularly identified: pastoral concern for victims of sexism, justice and full participation by women in religion, and the far-reaching implications of theology for gender and social order.

Pastoral Concern for Victims of Sexism

Inclusive language for God is frequently promoted out of pastoral concern for people who are spiritually alienated from the all-male God of Scripture and the Christian tradition. Both males and females who have been abused, ignored, or abandoned by their fathers often have a difficult time relating positively to a Heavenly Father. Their entire experience of fathers or other powerful males has been either deeply traumatic or empty and meaningless. It may be emotionally impossible for such people to trust and love a God who is represented as an all-powerful masculine being, no matter how forcefully his attributes of love and goodness are preached. Similar difficulties may also be experienced by women who have suffered injustice and frustration because of the male-dominated patterns of traditional society. In addition, many people who are not themselves direct victims of sexism empathize deeply with those who are victims and so find themselves likewise alienated from a masculine God.

Advocates of inclusive language argue that it is religiously crucial for these people to be able to pray to God as *Mother, Lover, Friend,* or perhaps as *Parent,* rather than as *Father* or *Lord.* Their only emotionally viable alternative to inclusive language might be to abandon God altogether. According to this argument, then, inclusive language is necessary for many people's spiritual health. As liturgist Ruth Duck asserts: "One part of this healing ministry is questioning the patriarchal attitudes that keep 'father' predominant as a name for God in Christian worship."[28]

Equality for Women in Church, Theology, and Language for God

Sexism and patriarchy in the church and in the Christian community have historically excluded women from leadership in interpreting the Bible, constructing theology, and (except for some hymns) writing liturgy. Feminists point out that men have determined how to read Scripture and to extract doctrine from it. Men have formulated the Apostles' and Nicene Creeds, which define the Christian faith in terms of the Father, Son, and Holy Spirit. Males have written the treatises of theology that have enshrined and elaborated masculine language for God as essential Christian orthodoxy. Men have had a monopoly on ordination and authority in the church, both deciding the proper language for worship and then exercising exclusive leadership of it. It is no surprise to feminists that the doctrine and liturgy of the church are univocally masculine in their presentation of God.

For most feminists, the exclusion of women from participation and leadership in Bible interpretation, theology, and worship is an unjust consequence of partriarchalism. When this wrong is righted, they ar-

---

28. Ruth Duck, *Gender and the Name of God: The Trinitarian Baptismal Formula* (New York: Pilgrim, 1991), 49. Chap. 2, "Beyond the Father's Fearful Mask," surveys many reasons for alienation from a masculine God. See also Susan Thistlethwaite, *Sex, Race, and God* (New York: Crossroad, 1989), for a comprehensive exploration of this topic.

gue, women too will have the freedom to read Scripture, develop doctrine, and explore ways of worshiping. In the academic phraseology of Elisabeth Schüssler Fiorenza: "In reclaiming women's authority to shape and determine biblical religions, femininst theology attempts to reconceptualize the act of biblical interpretation as a moment in the global praxis for liberation."[29] Liberated women will be able to express their own experience of God and address their own needs as they read Scripture, just as men always have. What results will not necessarily reject Scripture or the entire tradition, but it will enrich faith and worship with language, ideas, and practices reflecting the fact that half the church is female. Feminist religious leaders conclude that the doctrine and vocabulary of the Christian community will be gender-inclusive rather than exclusively masculine. These reforms in the church, according to most feminists, are simply a matter of justice, which is not only a basic Christian virtue but an essential attribute of God.

The Ideology of Theological Patriarchalism

A third connection is more broadly a matter of worldview or ideology.[30] It pertains to the way human life and the whole world are perceived and patterned according to a comprehensive theological understanding of reality. In traditional Christianity, many feminists argue, reality is viewed as a great chain of being, a chain of command with God at the top, nature at the bottom, and between them the human race, with women subordinate to men. The subjection of women to men, according to this interpretation, directly follows from the fact that God as the Almighty Father and King is the source and support of the entire patriarchal hierarchy. Since the Supreme Being is thought to be masculine in this ideology, say feminists, it inevitably follows that primary authority on earth belongs to men, who are supposedly more like God in power and intellect. According to the frequently quoted quip of post-Christian feminist Mary Daly, "Since God is male, the male is God."[31] In other words, the injustice and oppression women have suffered are not just the results of male chauvinism, but are part of an en-

---

29. Elizabeth Schüssler Fiorenza, *But She Said: Feminist Practices of Biblical Interpretation* (Boston: Beacon, 1992), 8.

30. By *ideology* I mean an entire worldview or intellectual system based on a social or political program. Marxism and Nazism are examples. Feminists would add patriarchalism to the list. Feminism itself is an ideology when it takes commitment to women as its basic position, views all of reality from this standpoint, and subjects all of reality, including God and the Bible, to the demand for gender equality. Feminism that merely seeks justice for women in society is not an ideology in this sense, but a program for social reform.

31. Mary Daly, *Beyond God the Father: Toward a Philosophy of Women's Liberation* (Boston: Beacon, 1973), 19.

tire patriarchal worldview. Exclusive male leadership is not merely a social pattern, but a theological ideology that justifies the subordination of women to men and of nature to humans by defining this hierarchy as the divinely ordained structure of reality. The language of God the Father both expresses and reinforces the entire patriarchal worldview, according to this analysis.

The only way patriarchalism can be countered, say ideological feminists, is by replacing it with another view of reality. In the new worldview an inclusive God grounds inclusive and mutually affirming relations between men and women and between humans and nature. They believe it is not possible to treat women and men as equal image-bearers of God unless God is gender-inclusive: either equally masculine and feminine or wholly beyond gender. It is not possible to liberate women from injustice and oppression without eliminating the patriarchal view of God and his relation to creation. According to Rosemary Ruether, we "must rethink the whole Western theological tradition of the hierarchical chain of being and chain of command . . . that starts with non-material spirit (God) as the source of the chain of being."[32] Effecting this shift of perspective is a massive undertaking, and more than revised religious language is needed to bring it about. But inclusive language for God is an important part of the effort. Churches committed to the project should "begin not only to use inclusive language for humanity and God but also to transform liturgy to reflect the call to liberation."[33]

In sum, feminist theologians discern three general links between the well-being of women and inclusive language for God. Christians must avoid exclusively masculine language for God, they urge, because it is hurtful to those who have suffered from male domination, because it does not do justice to the religious experience and theological reflection of women, and most basically because the use of traditional male terminology for God actually maintains and supports male domination. Inclusive language for God both ministers to those who have been wronged and in some way contributes to changing the system that has hurt them.

Opposition to Inclusive Language for God

In spite of these powerful arguments, there has been vehement opposition to inclusive language for God from widely diverse points on the ecclesiastical spectrum. One might expect in advance that fundamentalist, evangelical, and theologically conservative churches would express

---

32. Ruether, *Sexism and God-Talk*, 85.
33. Ibid., 202.

the most negative reactions. Indeed, *Christianity Today* has run articles entitled "Does God Really Want To Be Called 'Father'?"[34] and "Why God Is Not *Mother*."[35] And in 1997 the theologically conservative Christian Reformed Church in North America condemned inclusive language for God as incompatible with Scripture, the confessions of the church, and healthy piety.[36]

Given the predictable conservative response, however, it is all the more surprising to learn that much of the criticism and opposition to inclusive language for God have been expressed by professional theologians, clergy, and lay members in mainline denominations and religious organizations. Perhaps the explanation is that since the conservative churches reject inclusivism out of hand and find so little attraction to it among their people, they can afford to ignore it. It is in mainline seminaries and churches where inclusive language is making great inroads and where people find it most compelling. Nevertheless, significant numbers of leaders and laity in most of these churches oppose it and feel the need to say so.

Consider examples from particular denominations. Even before the Evangelical Lutheran Church in America issued its *Guidelines for Inclusive Use of the English Language* in 1989,[37] *Lutheran Forum* editor Leonard Klein had urged "That God Is To Be Spoken of as 'He.'"[38] His subsequent evelation is direct: "The *Guidelines* are heretical."[39] Already in 1982 Lutheran theologian Robert Jenson was countering Mother-language for God in his book, *The Triune Identity*.[40] Carl Braaten, another ELCA theologian, has also spoken out against this trend.[41]

A number of members of the Presbyterian Church (USA) have likewise opposed inclusive language for God. Best known are Elizabeth

34. James Edwards, "Does God Really Want To Be Called 'Father'?" *Christianity Toda,y* 21 February, 1986, 27–30.

35. Elizabeth Achtemeier, "Why God Is Not Mother," *Christianity Today*, 16 August, 1993, 16–23.

36. *Acts of Synod 1997* (Grand Rapids: CRC Publications, 1997), 687–94. However, Synod did encourage the use of feminine imagery for God consistent with its use in Scripture.

37. *Guidelines for Inclusive Use of the English Language* (Chicago: Evangelical Lutheran Church in America, 1989).

38. Leonard Klein, "That God Is to Be Spoken of as 'He,'" *Lutheran Forum*, Spring 1988, 23–27. My thanks to Rev. James Culver, pastor of St. Peter's Church, Stendal, Ind., for information about the debate in the ELCA. See his "Is Schism Avoidable? Documenting the Crisis," *Lutheran Forum*, Spring 1990, 32–38.

39. Leonard Klein, "ELCA's Confessional Crisis Bottoms Out," *Lutheran Forum*, Fall 1990, 4–6.

40. Robert Jenson, *The Triune Identity* (Philadelphia: Fortress, 1982).

41. Carl Braaten, ed., *Our Naming of God: Problems and Prospects of Godtalk Today* (Philadelphia: Fortress, 1989).

Achtemeier, a retired seminary professor, and Roland Frye, a retired professor of English. Both have authored popular and academic articles criticizing the movement and its rationale.[42] Among Methodists Geoffrey Wainwright of Duke University has identified the new religious language as a threat to the church's confession of the Trinity and its presentation of the gospel.[43]

Even in the United Church of Christ, probably the most progressive American denomination on this issue, a vocal minority has consistently opposed inclusive language and feminist theology. *Uncloseting the Goddess* is the title of a pamphlet issued by the Biblical Witness Fellowship, a group that considers itself "a Renewal Movement in the United Church of Christ" and takes strong exception to the trend represented by the Re-Imagining Conference and its language for God.[44]

Alvin Kimel has led the opposition in the Episcopal Church. He is a signer of *The Baltimore Declaration*, a 1991 statement of clergy and laity against religious pluralism, including the new feminine language for God. He has not only challenged the inclusive language liturgies proposed for that denomination, but has also become a leading participant in the ecumenical debate.[45]

Kimel has edited *Speaking the Christian God*,[46] a collection of essays by scholars from a wide variety of ecclesiastical backgrounds: evangelical, Presbyterian, Lutheran, Episcopal, Methodist, Catholic, Orthodox, and other mainline denominations. All of them support promotion of the full humanity of women and the reform of church practice to include women more fully. Many but not all favor the ordination of

42. Elizabeth Achtemeier, "The Impossible Possibility: Evaluating the Feminist Approach to Bible and Theology," *Interpretation* 42, no. 1 (1988), "Exchanging God for 'No Gods': A Discussion of Female Language for God," in *Speaking the Christian God,* ed. Alvin Kimel (Grand Rapids: Eerdmans, 1992), and "Why God Is Not Mother," *Christianity Today,* 16 August 1993. Roland Frye, "Language for God and Feminist Language: Problems and Principles," *Scottish Journal of Theology,* 1988, 41: 441–69, reprinted in Kimel, ed., *Speaking the Christian God.*

43. Geoffrey Wainwright, "Trinitarian Worship," *New Mercersburg Review,* Autumn 1986, and "The Doctrine of the Trinity: Where the Church Stands of Falls," *Interpretation* 45 (1991).

44. *Uncloseting the Goddess: A Look at Emerging Feminist Neo-Paganism in the Church through the Open Door of Re-Imagining* (Candia, N.H.: Biblical Witness Fellowship, 1994).

45. Alvin Kimel, "A New Language for God?: A Critique of Supplemental Liturgical Texts" (Shaker Heights, Ohio: Episcopalians United, 1990); "The Holy Trinity Meets Ashtoreth: A Critique of the Episcopal 'Inclusive' Liturgies," *Anglican Theological Review* 71, no. 1 (1989): 25–47; and with Donald Hook, "The Pronouns of Deity: A Theolinguistic Critique of Feminist Proposals," *Scottish Journal of Theology* 1993 46: 297–323.

46. Alvin Kimel, ed., *Speaking the Christian God: The Holy Trinity and the Challenge of Feminism* (Grand Rapids: Eerdmans, 1992).

women. All recognize that Scripture contains some feminine imagery for God. They hold varying views of Scripture and specific doctrines such as the Trinity. But virtually all of these authors oppose inclusive language for God because they believe that it fundamentally conflicts with the Christian faith and the revelation of God on which it is based.[47]

Other academic defenses of the tradition are frequently mentioned as well. Vernard Eller published *The Language of Canaan and the Grammar of Feminism* in 1982, contending from Scripture against inclusive language for God (as well as for humans).[48] A couple of years later Donald Bloesch joined *The Battle for the Trinity*, a significant study arguing extensively that this essential Christian doctrine is undermined by inclusive language for God.[49]

These examples illustrate the fact that proponents and opponents of inclusive language and theology are not neatly divided along denominational lines. While there is little pressure for inclusive language in fundamentalist, evangelical, and traditional confessional churches, mainline denominations are divided over it. In fact vigorous advocates are only a minority in many of them, and there is significant opposition in most. Thus resistance to inclusive language for God cannot be written off simply as a knee-jerk reaction of the fundamentalist Christian right. The opposition is broad-based and crosses denominational lines.

In fact, criticism of this movement is found at the highest levels of ecumenical Christianity. The World Council of Churches recently commissioned Protestant, Roman Catholic, and Eastern Orthodox theologians to prepare an exposition of the historic Christian faith as set forth in the Nicene Creed. Their statement contains this warning, obviously alluding to inclusive language for God and its rationale: "We may not surrender the language of 'Father.' . . . 'Father' is not simply one amongst a number of metaphors or images used to describe God. It is the distinctive term addressed by Jesus himself to God. . . . We may not surrender the names Father and Son."[50]

The resistance movement also finds champions among world-class theologians and church leaders. Wolfhart Pannenberg, a German Luth-

---

47. I write "virtually all" because although Janet Soskice defends the use of *Father,* she does not explicitly reject inclusive language, and a couple of other authors do not specifically address inclusive language.

48. Vernard Eller, *The Language of Canaan and the Grammar of Feminism* (Grand Rapids: Eerdmans, 1982).

49. Donald Bloesch, *The Battle for the Trinity: The Debate over Inclusive God-Language* (Ann Arbor: Servant, 1985). He also wrote *Is the Bible Sexist?* (Westchester, Ill.: Crossway, 1982).

50. *Confessing the One Faith: An Ecumenical Explication of the Apostolic Faith as It Is Confessed in the Nicene-Constantinopolitan Creed (381)*, Faith and Order Paper No. 153 (Geneva: World Council of Churches, 1991), 31.

eran, is widely regarded as one of the most significant theologians since Karl Barth. Pannenberg emphatically rejects inclusive language for God and the theological arguments on which it is based. He recognizes the connection between God as Father and the patriarchal society of Israel. But this connection "does not justify the demand for a revision of the concept of God as Father. . . . Such a demand would be justified only if the idea of God were simply a reflection of the prevailing social relationships." He notes pointedly: "This applies especially to the demand that we should address God as Mother as well as Father."[51] His conclusion cuts to the heart of the Christian faith: "Where the word 'Father' is replaced by something else, there can be no warrant any more that we are talking about and addressing the same God as Jesus did."[52]

Perhaps a bit more gently, Willem Visser 't Hooft, long-time moderator of the World Council of Churches, argues that the Fatherhood of God should not be shunted aside as the church works for the liberation of women. While encouraging recognition of the feminine imagery and motherly qualities Scripture attributes to God, he asserts: "We call him Father because Jesus has taught us to do so, and to cease so to call him is to cease to pray as Jesus enjoined us. To refuse to use any reference to God as 'He' and to choose terms such as 'the divine being' or 'the Deity' is to depersonalize God."[53] On all levels of mainline Christianity there is strong resistance to inclusive language for God.

We must be clear about the deepest reason for this reaction. It is surely not a desire to subordinate and demean women. Some of the most articulate critics are women. It is not just attachment to a comforting tradition, such as Lutherans or Episcopalians might (legitimately) feel toward the historic language of the liturgy. In the final analysis it is not even theological orthodoxy, such as the doctrine of the Trinity. For many women and men who resist inclusive language for God, it is the Christian faith—the gospel itself—that is at stake. Retired theologian Leslie Zeigler is direct and succinct in her diagnosis: "most feminist theologians are presenting us *not* with the Christian faith but with a quite different religion."[54] Elizabeth Achtemeier concurs: "By attempting to change the biblical language used of the deity, the feminists have in reality exhanged the true God for those deities which are 'no gods,' as

51. Wolfhart Pannenberg, *Systematic Theology*, vol. 1 (Grand Rapids: Eerdmans, 1991), 262, including note 9. See also his "Feminine Language About God?" *Asbury Theological Journal* 48, no. 2 (1993).

52. Wolfhart Pannenberg, *An Introduction to Systematic Theology* (Grand Rapids: Eerdmans, 1991), 31–32.

53. W. A. Visser 't Hooft, *The Fatherhood of God in an Age of Emancipation* (Geneva: World Council of Churches, 1982), 133.

54. Leslie Zeigler, "Christianity or Feminism?" in *Speaking the Christian God*, 313.

Jeremiah would put it (2:11)."[55] The Ecumenical Coalition of Christian Women issued "A Christian Women's Declaration" in September 1997 in response to mainstream feminism. In it they affirmed that "We will worship no other god but the God and Father of our Lord Jesus Christ" and "We repudiate the assumption that Christian faith and teachings were first 'imagined' by men and now should be 'reimagined' by women."[56] For many opponents, the Christian faith itself is at issue.

The Debate Goes On

So the debate goes on. On one side are the inclusivists, who argue that the well-being of women and true religion demand inclusive language for God. On the other side are the traditionalists, who counter that faithfulness to divine revelation and to the gospel requires adherence to the historic language of the church, based in Scripture.

The purpose of this book is to summarize and evaluate the course of this debate. The main challenge for inclusivists is to defend the new representation of God against the formidable objections raised against it from Scripture, orthodoxy, and true piety. The tasks for those who oppose inclusivism are to show that their very serious allegations against it are valid and to answer the charge that traditional Christianity's language for God demeans women and even promotes injustice, harm, and abuse against them.

Our challenge is to track the debate honestly and carefully so that positions and arguments are clearly stated and fairly evaluated. That will minimize inappropriate generalizing and stereotyping of both sides. For as will become evident in the following chapter, inclusivism is not monolithic. Instead there is a variety of arguments for inclusive language for God grounded on a number of distinguishable views of revelation, Scripture, theology, and religious language.

A hint of the outcome may be helpful. In the end we find that fully *gender-inclusive language for God* as currently advocated cannot be warranted according to the standards of historical-biblical Christianity. However, there are enough elements of truth in the inclusivist position to require that traditional Christians become open to some feminine language for God and address legitimate issues of sexism in church and society. We defend the use of some feminine imagery within the *biblical pattern of language for God.*

---

55. Elizabeth Achtemeier, "Exchanging God for 'No Gods,'" in *Speaking the Christian God*, 3.

56. Republished as "Women of Renewal: A Statement," *First Things* 80 (1998): 36–40.

2

Theological Arguments for Inclusive Language for God

The Challenge: Must We Speak of God Exclusively as a "He"?

It is painfully apparent that the Christian tradition's affirmation of male primacy, in particular, its pervasively masculine language for God, is a stumbling block for feminists. According to theologian Elizabeth Johnson, the language of Scripture and the church suggests that "God is male, or at least more like a man than a woman, or at least more fittingly addressed as male than as female. . . . [T]his exclusive speech about God serves in manifold ways to support an imaginative and structural world that excludes or subordinates women."[1] Many feminists agree with this assessment, and some of them have repudiated their Christian faith because of it.[2]

There are many other feminists, however, who consider themselves committed Christians and seek to articulate their faith in terms of inclusive language. But how can they do this? If the Bible and Christian tradition are so heavily patriarchal—if God is a "He," a King, Father, and Lord—how is it possible to justify inclusive language for God? How is it possible to respond to the charge that nonsexist language is simply a feminist imposition and adulteration of the historic Christian faith?

Chapter 1 identified some powerful motives for adopting inclusive language for God—sensitivity to the victims of sexism, the desire to eliminate the sexism that hurt them, and the right of women to interpret Scripture, engage in theology, and develop their own expressions of faith. But these appeals for compassion and justice, compelling as

1. Johnson, *She Who Is*, 5.
2. Two examples are Mary Daly, *Beyond God the Father: Toward a Philosophy of Women's Liberation* (Boston: Beacon, 1973); and Daphne Hampson, *Theology and Feminism* (Oxford: Blackwell, 1990). Daly was Roman Catholic and Hampson was Anglican.

they are, are not sufficient to validate the new practice. What is necessary is a demonstration that inclusive language for God is consistent with and warranted by the authoritative standards of the Christian faith, Scripture and its doctrine, and that it is not just an extension of feminist ideology or "political correctness." It must be shown that a gender-inclusive view of God does not introduce doctrinal heresy or false religion, but is in fact faithful to the gospel. It is precisely at these points that the new practice has been challenged, as noted in chapter 1.

Inclusivists have responded to this challenge. They have gone well beyond demanding gender-inclusive language for the sake of compassion, justice, and women's well-being. They have offered a variety of arguments based on the study of Scripture, proper methods of interpreting Scripture (hermeneutics), theology, and linguistics. Inclusivist theologians have combined various of these arguments in different ways to construct a variety of cases for revising the vocabulary of the Christian faith. Thus there is no such thing as *the* case for nonsexist language for God. The theological defense of the new practice is complex, sophisticated, and pluralistic. Inclusivists are Protestant and Roman Catholic, representatives of different types of theology, and even count a few evangelicals in their ranks.

In this chapter we present a general survey of the main arguments typically invoked to justify inclusive language for God. They are collected under two main headings. The first section deals with a variety of arguments pertaining to God's revelation, Scripture, and their proper interpretation. The second group of arguments appeals to issues in theology and the nature of religious language. Each argument is summarized in the title of its subsection. Subsequent chapters assess the arguments in relation to the criticisms brought against them by opponents of the gender-inclusive view of God.

Arguments from God's Revelation and Its Interpretation

"The Bible Uses Inclusive Language for God"

No one disputes that Scripture uses almost exclusively masculine language for God. But many inclusivists argue that in spite of this the Bible itself justifies a gender-equal view of God. They point out that Scripture contains feminine allusions to God, such as the image of a nursing mother in Isaiah 49:15, where the Lord asks "Can a mother forget the baby at her breast and have no compassion on the child she has borne? Though she may forget, I will not forget you."[3] Scripture also

---

3. Chap. 3 examines the Bible's feminine references to God.

uses ungendered terms for God when it calls him *a rock, a fortress, our shield,* or a *light*. The whole argument goes like this: Since (as indicated in chapter 1) inclusive language is achieved by balancing masculine and feminine language and using gender-neutral language, and since the Bible uses masculine, feminine, and neutral terminology, it follows that the raw material for speaking of God inclusively is provided by Scripture itself. If the Bible speaks of God with language of both genders and with ungendered terms, inclusivists reason, then so may we.

Many inclusivists claim that the difference between Scripture and contemporary inclusive language for God is just a matter of quantity and balance. It is not a matter of quality or significance that would alter anything essential to our faith. They explain the gender imbalance in the language of Scripture as God's accommodation to the patriarchal cultures in which the Bible was written. The biblical truth about God, who is neither male nor female, should be restated in gender-equivalent terms for our more inclusive society and culture.

The argument that Scripture itself is inclusive is used by Johanna van Wijk-Bos, a Presbyterian seminary professor who is "concerned with exploring biblical images for God—in names, titles, and designations—that offer alternatives to exclusively male imagery."[4] Virginia Mollenkott also takes this approach: "the biblical authors did indeed move the feminine principle into the godhead . . . all three persons of the divine triad are depicted in feminine as well as masculine images."[5] In fact, she takes the presence of any feminine imagery for God in the Bible at all, given its patriarchal context, as evidence of the special divine inspiration of Scripture.[6] Paul Smith, a Southern Baptist minister and author of the book, *Is It Okay To Call God "Mother"?* likewise justifies gender-egalitarian language from its presence in the Bible. Noting that traditional Christians often subordinate women to men as well as view God as male, he writes: "A simple and biblically-based solution to both problems is to call God "Mother" while continuing to call God "Father."[7] Gordon-Conwell seminary professor Aída Besançon Spen-

---

4. Johanna van Wijk-Bos, *Reimagining God: The Case for Scriptural Diversity* (Louisville: Westminster/John Knox, 1995), ix.

5. Mollenkott, *The Divine Feminine*, 4. On p. 24 she appeals to her background "in a Protestant evangelical tradition where maternal images for God were totally repressed. Although we proclaimed our absolute devotion to the Bible (the *sola Scriptura* of the Reformers), obviously there was a great deal of imagery that we missed."

6. Ibid., 110–12. She writes, "because the biblical images of God as female run counter to any of the conscious concepts of males socialized patriarchally, they constitute a very strong argument for the inspired nature of the Hebrew and Christian Scriptures."

7. Paul R. Smith, *Is It Okay To Call God "Mother?": Considering the Feminine Face of God* (Peabody, Mass.: Hendickson, 1993), 3–4. He makes it clear that he is addressing "evangelicals and charismatics" and affirms "orthodox theology."

cer appeals to Smith as she urges avoidance of exclusively masculine language and endorses *Father* and *Mother*, *he* and *she* as equally legitimate terms for God. "I believe this practice in itself does not contradict the intentions of the biblical language," she writes.[8] Nancy Hardesty likewise proceeds from "Scripture, inspired by God . . . the authoritative word of God" in expressing her endorsement of inclusive language for God.[9] These advocates of inclusive language for God consider the Bible itself to be implicitly inclusive in its presentation of God.

While inclusivists of all theological persuasions make this point, it is most significant for those who wish to retain the Christian tradition's high view of the Bible as God's revealed Word. In fact, several advocates just quoted consider themselves to be orthodox, evangelical Christians. Furthermore, this appeal to the Bible is the argument for gender-equal God-language most likely to persuade other Christians from conservative traditions in which Scripture is "the only rule for faith and practice." For that reason subsequent chapters carefully analyze and evaluate the arguments that claim the justification of Scripture for inclusive language for God.

"God Accommodated Patriarchal Culture"

Inclusivists who have a traditional high view of Scripture must explain why the Bible's predominantly masculine language for God is not normative for Christians today. After all, they wish to affirm that the Bible is God's Word, the final authority for faith and practice. How is it permissible for us to depart from Scripture and change its way of speaking of God by adopting inclusive language?

A common answer to this question is the appeal to divine accommodation. Inclusivists point out that God chose to reveal himself to the Hebrews in the ancient Near East, to send Jesus Christ into first-century Jewish society, and to inspire the books of the New Testament in the context of Jewish and Greco-Roman culture. Patriarchalism—male domination—permeated all of these cultures. Thus, according to this explanation, it is understandable that God used the categories of patri-

---

8. Aída Besançon Spencer, Donna Hailson, Catherine Kroeger, and William Spencer, *The Goddess Revival* (Grand Rapids: Baker, 1995), 128. The fact that this book endorses inclusive language and some dubious arguments for it does negate its many fine insights about goddess religion and biblical theology.

9. Nancy Hardesty, *Inclusive Language in the Church* (Atlanta: John Knox, 1987), 9. Although she focuses mainly on language for humans, she does recommend language for God as found in the *Inclusive Language Lectionary*, 93, and approves the formula "in the name of the Father, Son, and Holy Spirit, the God and Mother of us all," attributed to William Sloan Coffin of Riverside Church in New York, 96.

archal society in order to reveal himself as the ultimate power and authority, the original source of love and justice. In cultures where fathers are absolute heads of their households and kings such as Pharaoh, Nebuchadnezzar, and Caesar are the ultimate authorities in the world, the categories of *Father* and *King* are obvious choices for divine self-revelation.

Since that is so, advocates of this position warn, we should not make these social categories into absolutes any more than we should make the Hebrew and Greek languages absolute merely because they are the media in which God revealed himself. Just as the Hebrew and Greek texts of the original Bible can and must be translated into other languages in order for God's revelation to be understood, so the masculine categories of biblical revelation must be translated into other terms so that people can really hear what God is saying through Scripture. The point of revelation is not the masculine categories, but what they mean—that God is all-powerful, authoritative, and lovingly intimate, and that we must worship, love, and serve him. It is understandable that masculine categories were necessary in a patriarchal society. But in our society, which recognizes the equality of men and women and where both men and women possess authority, have power, and show love, it is necessary to use gender-inclusive language to express the intent of the biblical revelation of God.

This notion of accommodation is not a modernistic distortion of the Bible, defenders of this approach point out. The Christian tradition has repeatedly recognized that Scripture uses cultural categories that are not normative for all times. One example is the ancient world's prescientific view of the universe. Other instances have to do with cultural customs, such the "holy kiss," the requirement that women's heads be covered, and the like. Furthermore, there are even instances of biblical accommodation to social patterns and institutions that are consequences of the fall, not just morally neutral cultural practices. Slavery is the prime example. Patriarchy, the exclusively male authority structure of society, is likewise a fallen institution, since male "rule" is a consequence of the curse recorded in Genesis 3:16. Gender-inclusivists argue that the time has come to recognize another example of a social practice in Scripture that is not permanently valid: the predominant, virtually exclusive use of masculine language for God. In this way they invoke the traditional notion of divine accommodation to explain how it is possible to affirm the Bible as the divinely inspired Word and yet to adopt gender-inclusive language for God.

This is the argument of Paul Smith, a Southern Baptist pastor: "If we can recognize the cultural influence in the early church practice of addressing one another with a holy kiss, why should we not also recognize the cultural influence in the New Testament practice of addressing God with almost exclusively masculine imagery?"[10] And further: "It was because of sin that culture came to value male over female, establishing patriarchy as the norm." "In a patriarchal society where only male was honored, to speak about God as female in any direct way would not be possible." Thus it was not possible for Jesus to address God as *Mother*, but only as *Father*. "It would have been too great a break with the existing culture. . . . But naming God more directly as Mother waited upon the results of Jesus' transforming model." So Jesus accommodated existing culture, but did not intend to teach for all times that *Father* is a special term for God. According to Smith, Jesus' long-term goal was just the opposite, eventually to make *Mother* equal in status.

Virginia Mollenkott also combines divine accommodation with "a very high view of biblical inspiration. . . . The biblical authors were socialized in a culture where . . . males held all honor and power in society. Nothing would seem more natural to them than to honor God by exclusively masculine references."[11] So she concludes: "Jesus' cultural surroundings made 'Our Father and Mother in heaven' an impossibility; our cultural surroundings make it not only possible but necessary." She, too, relies on a doctrine of divine cultural accommodation to argue that the masculine language of the Bible does not rule out gender-inclusive language for God.

"Scripture Is Not Identical with God's Word"

Thus far we have identified arguments promoting inclusive language for God that are consistent with the doctrine that the Bible is God's inspired Word, including the argument that God has accommodated his self-revelation to the language of patriarchal cultures.

However, other inclusivists are unable to accept and recast the Bible's patriarchal language so easily. New Testament scholar Sandra Schneiders is typical of many who consider Scripture itself to be a fundamental problem: "What many Christians believe to be in some sense 'the Word of God' is, in some important respects, very bad news for women because it legitimates and promotes male oppression of women."[12] According to Elisabeth Schüssler Fiorenza: "The Bible is not only written in the words of men but also serves to legitimate patriar-

---

10. Smith, *Is It Okay to Call God "Mother"?* 49. The next quotes are from pp. 110, 126, and 144.

11. Mollenkott, *The Divine Feminine*, 110. The next quotation is from p. 61.

12. Sandra Schneiders, "The Bible and Feminism," in *Freeing Theology: The Essentials of Theology in Feminist Perspective*, ed. Catherine Mowry LaCugna (San Francisco: Harper, 1993), 35.

chal power and oppression insofar as it 'renders God' male."[13] These inclusivists agree that the reason why biblical language for God is so overwhelmingly masculine is because it was written by men in male-dominated cultures.

But this is precisely why they cannot consider the biblical text itself to be God's true revealed Word. Because it oppresses women, Scripture cannot be infallible revelation. Brian Wren takes distance from the normativity of the Bible's "unquestioningly patriarchal" language for God by asserting that "all revelation is impeded by sin."[14] Schneiders holds that the biblical text "even though it is inspired (written and read under the influence of the Holy Spirit) is as capable of error, distortion, and even sinfulness as the church itself."[15] The oppressive aspects of Scripture as a whole mean that it must be distinguished from God's true revelation, although the Bible, or parts of it, may reflect, mediate, or witness to God's revelation. In this way the patriarchal language of Scripture is eliminated from God's permanently valid revelation.

Letty Russell drives the wedge between Scripture and revelation pointedly: *"the Word of God is not identical with the biblical texts."*[16] Ruth Duck makes a similar separation when she claims, echoing Karl Barth: "These writings are not, strictly speaking, revelation, but witness to revelation." Thus they "provide a starting point, not a limit, for our language about God."[17] Gail Ramshaw takes a similar approach when she rejects devotion to the very words of Scripture as "fundamentalism." She believes she is following Luther, who "urged the faithful to find the words that best reveal the Word." For Ramshaw, those words must be gender-inclusive or gender-neutral, appropriate to "the God beyond gender."[18] Elizabeth Johnson likewise moves away from "the very words of the Bible" as revealed truth toward "other models of revelation . . . among them revelation as historical event, or as inner experience, or as dialectical presence, or as new awareness, or as symbolic media-

---

13. Elizabeth Schüssler Fiorenza, *Bread Not Stone: The Challenge of Feminist Biblical Interpretation* (Boston: Beacon, 1984), xi.

14. Wren, *What Language Shall I Borrow?* 130–31.

15. Schneiders, "The Bible and Feminism," 49.

16. Letty Russell, *Feminist Interpretation of the Bible* (Philadelphia: Westminster, 1985), 17. Traditional Christianity has always recognized that the Bible is not identical with the Word of God in that the Word of God is more than the biblical text. Jesus Christ is the Word of God incarnate. And special communications from God given in extrabiblical form—his revelations to the prophets, for example—are the Word of God. But Scripture in its entirety is also considered the Word of God. The gender-inclusivists presented in this section deny that the text of Scripture is the Word of God and thus take a different position than historic Christianity. See chap. 6.

17. Duck, *Gender and the Name of God*, 23–24.

18. Ramshaw, *God beyond Gender*, viii, 4–5.

tion." Thus she no longer feels bound to "repeat the pattern of language for God in the metaphor of ruling men."[19] And Elizabeth Schüssler Fiorenza is open "not to *the* Bible as a whole but to the liberating Word of God finding expression in the biblical writings."[20] All of these feminist theologians separate the revealed Word of God from the biblical text as such.

Sally McFague is quite specific and vehement in rejecting identification of the Bible as the Word of God, the view of Scripture she attributes to "religious conservatism," which includes "evangelicals" and "fundamentalists." "The Bible, says this movement, is the Word of God; the Bible is inerrant or divinely inspired; the words and images of the Bible are the authoritative and appropriate words and images for God." For those who hold this perspective, she writes, "the Bible becomes an idol: the fallible, human words of Scripture are understood as referring correctly and literally to God."[21] Her view is that the Bible "is and is not" the Word of God; it is "a metaphor of the word or ways of God, but as metaphor it is a relative, open-ended, secular, tensive judgment."[22] It is not difficult to see how this doctrine of Scripture would allow her to propose gender-inclusive models of God.

"Revelation Occurs in Women's Experience"

Once divine revelation is separated from the Bible, it must be recovered. A variety of sources and strategies are recommended for this purpose.[23] The following three—women's experience, the liberating texts of Scripture, and the liberated reading of Scripture—are prominent examples, not an exhaustive list. Nor are they necessarily mutually exclusive.

At least since the time of Friedrich Schleiermacher, some theologians have considered the ongoing religious experience of humans in history to be the primary location of divine revelation.[24] They view Scripture as an important expression of the experience of God, but not as historically final or definitive.

19. Johnson, *She Who Is*, 77.

20. Fiorenza, *Bread Not Stone*, 3.

21. Sally McFague, *Metaphorical Theology: Models of God in Religious Language* (Philadelphia: Fortress, 1982), 4–5.

22. Ibid., 54.

23. Overviews of inclusivist methods of identifying "the word of God" are found in Elisabeth Schüssler Fiorenza, *In Memory of Her: A Feminist Theological Reconstruction of Christian Origins* (New York: Crossroad, 1983), chap. 1; Fiorenza, *Bread Not Stone;* Schneiders, "The Bible and Feminism," in Russell, ed., *Feminist Interpretation of the Bible*.

24. Friedrich Schleiermacher, *The Christian Faith*, ed. H. Macintosh and J. Stewart (Edinburgh: T. & T. Clark, 1948), sec, 4, located divine revelation in the human experience of absolute dependence. He interpreted the entire content of Scripture and Christian doctrine as an expression of this experience.

Many feminist and inclusivist theologians affirm and operate with this ranking of religious experience and Scripture.[25] Rosemary Ruether candidly identifies "revelatory experience" as the source of all religious truth and elevates women's experience of oppression and liberation from patriarchalism as "a basic source of content as well as critierion of truth" for feminist theology. "Scripture and tradition are themselves codified collective human experience," she asserts.[26] Her broad notion of experiential revelation enables her to claim revealed truth in sources other than the Bible: heretical or marginal Christian traditions, classical Christian theology, non-Christian traditional religions and philosophies, and modern post-Christian worldviews.[27] All of these sources must be subjected to criticism from the standpoint of women's experience, however, before their truth can be appropriated. Her criterion for true revelation is this: "what does promote the full humanity of women is of the Holy, it does reflect true relation to the divine, it is the true nature of things, the authentic message of redemption."[28]

More focused on Christian sources, Elizabeth Johnson also appeals to religious experience: "It is in this deeply personal-and-religious dimension that women are caught up in new experiences, which when articulated move toward new speaking about God."[29] Ruth Duck likewise appeals to ongoing revelation in experience: "God has been and continues to be revealed among humanity, and human beings use available language to respond and to describe that revelation."[30] For all these inclusivists, the experience of women is at least as normative a form of divine revelation and source of language for God as the Bible is.

"Revelation Is Located in the Liberating Texts of Scripture"

Although the Bible is thoroughly patriarchal, most inclusivists concede that it is not without value as a means or vehicle of divine revelation. In their opinion some parts and texts of Scripture do transcend patriarchal categories and clearly reveal God's identity and purposes. These are the texts that speak of love and justice for all, condemn oppression and exploitation of the weak and poor, and emphasize that God's salvation promises liberation from everything that impedes a full human life, not just the sin that merits condemnation in the afterlife.

---

25. Mary Catherine Hilkert, "Experience and Tradition—Can the Center Hold?" in LaCugna, ed., *Freeing Theology*, provides a survey.
26. Ruether, *Sexism and God-Talk*, 12–13.
27. Ibid., 21–22.
28. Ibid., 19.
29. Johnson, *She Who Is*, 66. She appeals to Roman Catholic theologian Karl Rahner.
30. Duck, *Gender and the Name of God*, 23–24.

By accepting these texts, inclusivists create a "canon within the canon," that is, a selection of certain parts or themes from the Bible that are regarded as true and normative while the others are relativized or rejected. Challenged on this strategy, inclusivists typically respond that all Christians tacitly operate with a limited canon.

Rosemary Ruether's criterion of revelation is the full humanity of women. "To the extent to which Biblical texts reflect this normative principle, they are regarded as authoritative. On this basis many aspects of the Bible are to be frankly set aside and rejected." Ruether does find revelation in the "prophetic-liberating" thrust of Scripture, which implicitly applies to women even when expressed in patriarchal terms.[31] Schüssler Fiorenza agrees: "A feminist hermeneutics cannot trust or accept the Bible and tradition simply as divine revelation. Rather it must critically evaluate them as patriarchal articulations." She goes on to stipulate that "*the* litmus test for invoking Scripture as the Word of God must be whether or not biblical texts and traditions seek to end relations of domination and exploitation."[32] The principle of liberation, derived from women's experience, is the criterion by which these theologians determine their "canon within the canon" of Scripture.

The principle of women's liberation is not the only critical framework through which inclusivists approach the Bible. Most adopt the standard higher critical assumptions and methods of interpreting Scripture that are commonplace in mainline Christianity. In the hands of some inclusivists these tools are wielded to undermine the authority of patriarchalism. The prime example is Jesus' use of *Father* as a regular term of reference to God and almost exclusive term of address in prayer, including the Lord's Prayer. Traditional Christians place a great deal of weight on the example and teaching of Jesus. New Testament scholar Joachim Jeremias is famous for his claim that Jesus' use of *abba* for *Father* expresses intimacy, not distance and subjection. Many inclusivists follow Jeremias in attempting to eliminate the negative connotations of the biblical term *Father* while they balance it with nonmasculine language. Some inclusivists, however, have used higher critical methods to argue that Jesus did not regard *Father* as an important term or use it regularly. They claim that the sayings of Jesus that give *Father* prominence were placed on the lips of Jesus by the patriarchalists who wrote the Gospels. Ruth Duck summarizes this line of scholarship: "Questions about the uniqueness, authenticity, exclusivity, and christological interpretation of Jesus' use of *abba* all throw doubt on Jeremias'

31. Ruether, *Sexism and God-Talk*, 23–24.
32. Fiorenza, *Bread Not Stone*, x, xiii.

thesis that the address of God as *abba* was central to Jesus' message."[33] Such doubts are intended to undermine traditional claims for the privileged status of God as *Father*.

"Revelation Occurs in Women's Reading of Scripture"

If the Bible itself is not God's definitive revelation, but revelation for women is located in their experience of liberation, then Scripture, or the liberating canon within Scripture, must be read by women according to this experience. When this happens, true revelation takes place. Thus revelation occurs in the proper interaction between the text and the reader.

This is the position of Sandra Schneiders. The locus of revelation, she says, is not in events behind the texts or in the theology of the authors of Scripture, but is "the texts themselves as language that involves the reader." "Through this dialogue reader and text are mutually transformed."[34] Notice that the text is also transformed, not just the reader. Ruth Duck takes a similar position: "God has been and continues to be revealed among humanity." Scripture is a prototype, touchstone, and starting point. When we read it properly, new ways of expressing the revelation of God will occur to the believing community. "By grace, revelation may occur through this human construction."[35] Elizabeth Johnson likewise prefers to view revelation as "dialectical presence, or as new awareness, or as symbolic mediation." She advocates language for God that arises from "reinterpretations of the text" by "communities . . . living in response to the covenanting God . . . in the struggle for emancipation from sexism."[36]

All of these writers attempt to create room for inclusive language for God by opening a gap between the text of Scripture and God's revelation. Using the liberation and full humanity of women as a criterion, they offer a variety of methods for locating true divine revelation. They conclude that the real meaning of God's revelation is better expressed by gender-inclusive language than by the patriarchal vocabulary used by the biblical writers. While most inclusivists adopt modern views of revelation and Scripture, the presence of evangelicals in the inclusivist camp prevents traditional Christians from simply dismissing the entire movement as result of modernism and higher criticism.

---

33. Duck, *Gender and the Name of God*, 69; see 59–72.

34. Sandra Schneiders, "Does the Bible Have a Postmodern Message?" in *Postmodern Theology: Christian Faith in a Pluralist World*, ed. Frederic Burnham (San Francisco: Harper & Row, 1989), 61–62. She adopts the reader–response approach to interpretation and locates revelation in the interaction.

35. Duck, *Gender and the Name of God*, 24.

36. Johnson, *She Who Is*, 77.

Arguments from Theology and the Nature of Religious Language

"Inclusive Language for God Is Part of the Christian Tradition"

The first argument we consider is actually an appeal to the language of the theological tradition. If a gender-egalitarian view of God is nothing more than a demand of ideological feminists, this argument goes, it would not be found in the Christian tradition. But in fact throughout history there have been Christians who have used feminine language for God. Some, such as the ancient Gnostics, were branded as heretics by the early church and suppressed.[37] But Clement of Alexandria, John Chrysostom, Gregory of Nyssa, Augustine, Bede, Anselm, Aquinas, and Bonaventure cannot so easily be dismissed.[38]

Julian of Norwich, a fourteenth-century English abbess with good standing in the Roman Catholic Church, used inclusive language for God extensively. In her *Showings* or *Revelations of Divine Love*, for example, she writes: "As truly as God is our Father, so truly is God our Mother."[39] "God almighty is our loving Father, and God all wisdom is our loving Mother, with the love and goodness of the Holy Spirit, which is all one God, one Lord."[40]

Such language can even be found in John Calvin.[41] His commentary on Isaiah 46:3, a verse he interprets as a maternal metaphor, is startling: "It is the intention of the Prophet to show . . . the Jews . . . that God, who has manifested himself to be both their Father and their Mother, will always assist them."[42] Conservative Protestants might dismiss Julian, but Calvin is a witness who must be taken seriously.

Inclusivists appeal to these examples to make the point that using maternal language for God is not just an item on the feminist agenda, rationalized with the resources of modern theology. This practice was followed by some of the greatest, most orthodox Christians of all time.

---

37. See, for example, Elaine Pagels, "What Became of God the Mother? Conflicting Images of God in Early Christianity," *Signs: Journal of Women in Culture and Society,* Winter 1976, 293–303.

38. Mollenkott, *The Divine Feminine*, 8–14. I simply repeat some of the names she lists and have not checked their authenticity.

39. Julian of Norwich, *Showings*, trans. Edmund Colledge, OSA, and James Walsh, SJ (New York: Paulist Press, 1978), 295.

40. Ibid., 293.

41. Jane Dempsey Douglass, "Calvin's Use of Metaphorical Language for God: God as Enemy and God as Mother," *The Princeton Seminary Bulletin* no. 8 (1987): 19–32. My thanks to Jai-Sung Shim for this reference.

42. John Calvin, *Commentary on the Book of the Prophet Isaiah*, trans. William Pringle, 4 vols. (Grand Rapids: Eerdmans, 1948), 3:436–37.

Thus, inclusivists contend, it is consistent with biblical Christianity and not just a dictate of current political correctness.

"Patriarchal Language Is Not Privileged: God Is beyond All Language"

A widely employed strategy for justifying gender-inclusive language proceeds from the theological doctrine of God's transcendence, that is, his being beyond creatures. It begins by pointing out that because of God's "otherness," no human words can adequately represent him. From this it concludes that the Bible's masculine language for God cannot be said to define God or to disclose his identify and nature in some special, "privileged" way. Such words as *father, lord,* and *he* do not have some unique capacity for revealing divine truth that other language lacks. Masculine language is on the same level as all human language—inadequate, partial, and not literally true when applied to God. At best our religious language is *analogical* or *metaphorical* or *anthropomorphic* (in human form),[43] that is, it uses humans (fathers, mothers, shepherds, kings) and other created entities (eagles, lions, rocks, light, wind) as pictures to give us some indication of what the infinitely great God who is beyond all experience is like. Using this line of reasoning, inclusivists strip the Bible's patriarchal language for God of its special status.

"God is wholly other, not like human beings, and beyond our comprehension in every way," Gail Ramshaw asserts. Because God is therefore beyond gender, she argues that we must not privilege language drawn from one human gender.[44] Elizabeth Johnson concurs: "there is basic agreement that the mystery of God is fundamentally unlike anything else we know of, and so is beyond the grasp of all of our naming." Thus "Women's refusal of the exclusive claim of the white male symbol of the divine arises from the well-founded demand to adhere to the holy mystery of God."[45] Rosemary Ruether offers the same argument: "If all human language for God/ess is analogy . . . then male language for the divine must lose its privileged place."[46]

"Exclusively Masculine Language Is Idolatry"

Privileging male terminology for God is not just bad theology, inclusivists warn. Ultimately it is idolatry or false religion. For if God is wholly beyond us and all language for the Deity is equally inadequate

---

43. These terms will be explained much more fully in chap. 7.
44. Ramshaw, *God beyond Gender,* 21.
45. Johnson, *She Who Is,* 117.
46. Ruether, *Sexism and God-Talk,* 68–69.

to name and describe him, then treating masculine language for God as privileged or definitive amounts to idolatry, according to inclusivist theologians. Idolatry is confusion of the Creator with a creature and thereby worship of the creature instead of the Creator. Giving exclusive status to masculine language treats it as literally true of God, and this is idolatry. So God ought not to be identified primarily as *King, Father,* or *He* any more than as *Mother, She,* or even *Rock* or *Light*. But inclusivists charge that in fact most of the people in the Christian church have come to think of God as an actual heavenly King and take *Father* as a literal name of God. Unwittingly these people are idolaters.

"Taking a particular human image [for God/ess] literally is idolatry," charges Ruether.[47] According to Sallie McFague, it is necessary "for many complementary models to intimate the richness and complexity of the divine–human relationship. If this criterion is not accepted, idolatry results."[48] Catherine LaCugna agrees: "no one image or name for God may be turned into an idol, and no one image or name expresses the totality of God's sacred mystery."[49] Mollenkott joins in making this allegation: "our almost exclusive focus on male God-imagery has resulted in an idolatry of the male."[50]

The charge that traditional Christian language is idolatrous is serious and powerful. For it not only alleges a theological mistake; it also raises the specter of false religion, the same allegation that traditionalists have made against inclusivists. The stakes are high.

"Both Male and Female Image God"

Inclusivists conclude that God's transcendence and the anthropomorphic character of language for God imply that God is beyond gender and thus that privileging masculine language is idolatry. Most do not think, however, that all language for God must be genderless. On the contrary, Scripture teaches that both human males and females image God (Gen. 1:27). Since both males and females image God, inclusivists argue that it is legitimate and necessary to represent or "image" God using language of both genders. Most of those who make this point are careful to remind us of the metaphorical or symbolic nature of religious terminology and to warn against literally projecting gender back into God.

---

47. Ibid.
48. McFague, *Metaphorical Theology*, p. 145. The charge that patriarchal language for God has been idolized in Christianity is a major thesis of this book, especially chap. 5, "God the Father: Model or Idol?."
49. LaCugna, "God in Communion with Us: The Trinity," in LaCugna, ed., *Freeing Theology*, 108.
50. Mollenkott, *The Divine Feminine*, 114.

Elizabeth Johnson articulates this position carefully: "If women are created in the image of God, then God can be spoken of in female metaphors in as full and as limited a way as God is imaged in male ones."[51] Johanna van Wijk-Bos is likewise cautious. She infers from the image of God in Genesis 1:26–27 that God is beyond gender, but she also concludes that "God can be referred to with feminine as well as with masculine pronouns. Both are equally accurate and inaccurate."[52] Brian Wren takes a similar line: "If male and female humans were really believed to be created as an equal partnership in the divine image, one would expect to find both feminine and masculine pronouns chosen for divine action."[53] Virginia Mollenkott also argues from the image of God. But she is less cautious about the figurative nature of language when she claims that "the biblical authors did move the feminine principle into the Godhead" and refers to "the female component in the divine nature."[54]

As a final example, consider Sally McFague's perspective. "The tradition says that we were created in the image of God, but the obverse is also the case, for we imagine God in *our* image."[55] The human persons we experience are both male and female, she reasons. Therefore we must use both male and female language in our attempts to communicate that God is person-like. But McFague stresses more strongly than the other theologians mentioned here that we imagine God in our image. Since God is so far beyond us, we really do not know the divine nature. She emphasizes that all our language for God is projected out of our human experience. In her later book, *Models of God*, McFague stresses the distance between our images and the reality of God so strongly that she is unwilling even to say that God is like a father, mother, lover, or friend. She can only say "it is *as if* God is like this."[56] Strictly speaking, the distance between Creator and creature puts all religious language, not just masculine language, in a hypothetical mode— maybe God is like this, maybe he is not.

Most inclusivist theologians, however, and even McFague in some contexts, posit or assume similarity as well as dissimilarity between God and humans. On this basis they appeal to the image of God in humans of both sexes as a basis for speaking of God in gender-inclusive language.

51. Johnson, *She Who Is*, 54.
52. van Wijk-Bos, *Reimagining God*, 25.
53. Wren, *What Language Shall I Borrow?* 118.
54. Mollenkott, *The Divine Feminine*, 4, 18.
55. McFague, *Metaphorical Theology*, 10. See also *Models of God: Theology for an Ecological, Nuclear Age* (Philadelphia: Fortress, 1987), 82.
56. McFague, *Models of God*, 70.

Furthermore, inclusivists point out that using exclusively masculine language for God implies that males bear the image of God more fully than females do. This consequence is not only unbiblical, they urge; it is also extremely hurtful to women. It has been a major theological support of sexism and patriarchalism in societies influenced by Christianity.

Thus Rosemary Ruether charges that although "classical orthodoxy never went so far as to completely deny women's participation in the image of God," it viewed them as "an inferior mix," who "can never as fully represent the image of God as man, who is seen as representing the rational and spiritual part of the self."[57] Mollenkott likewise identifies "the political effects of naming God as exclusively masculine: because God is husbandlike, husbands are godlike. Because God is fatherlike, fathers are godlike. The stage is set for exploitation of girls and women." But the fact that women image God gives her reason for hope: "the chances for exploitation are severely curtailed if we go further and recognize the biblical images that say God is womanlike and motherlike, so that women and mothers are in turn godlike."[58]

The doctrine that both genders image God implies for many inclusivists that God must be spoken of in language of both genders. Only then is the equality of males and females as image-bearers recognized, and only then is there a basis for healthy and just relations among men, women, boys, and girls.

"Father and Mother Are Equally Metaphorical"

As already noted, theologians commonly agree that all human language is incapable of literally defining or describing the transcendent God. At best, they say, our theological language is figurative or metaphorical—more unlike than like God in himself really is. According to inclusivists, this situation not only exposes exclusive use of masculine terms as idolatry; it also means that masculine words have no special linguistic status that feminine and ungendered language lacks. Since all terms for God are metaphorical, they conclude, feminine and ungendered language is just as adequate for speaking of God as masculine language.

Defenders of tradition often make a point of claiming that *Father*, *King*, and *Lord* are basic biblical names or titles of God and therefore are worthy of special honor. But inclusivists counter that at bottom these terms are just metaphors like all our other words for God. They

---

57. Ruether, *Sexism and God-Talk*, 94.
58. Mollenkott, *The Divine Feminine*, 5.

have no special status that cannot be shared by feminine and neuter terms for God.

Hymnodist Brian Wren gives extensive elaboration of this argument in *What Language Shall I Borrow?* In Chapter 4, "The Nature of God-Talk," he argues that all the ways in which God is revealed are metaphorical: "mother, father, son, friend, judge, rescuer, light, wind, fire, and even love."[59] He recognizes that the biblical names and titles for God, such as *Father* and *King*, are masculine. But in his chapter, "Dethroning Patriarchal Idols," Wren identifies these names and titles as part of "a metaphor system" that he labels "KINGAFAP (the King-God-Almighty-Father-Protector)" and "dethrones" it, that is, removes its privileged status. He then goes on in a subsequent chapter to recommend that we "Bring Many Names" to God, drawing from all sorts of biblical and extrabiblical imagery—masculine, feminine, and ungendered.[60] Thus Wren moves from the figurative-metaphorical nature of all our language for God to a very inclusive vocabulary for God. His "Many Names" approach accords equal status to words referring to masculine, feminine, and ungendered creatures as images for the Creator. Wren undercuts the fact that Scripture uses masculine but not feminine titles, names, and pronouns for God by appealing to the metaphorical nature of all language for God.

Parallels to Wren's argument are employed by virtually all inclusivists. It is the basic logic of Sally McFague's *Metaphorical Theology*, which argues that *Mother* and *Friend* are metaphors that should become models (i.e., basic or dominant metaphors) for God, as *Father* has been. "A truly metaphorical theology will encourage a variety of interpretive models. . . . If God is not seen to *be* 'father,' but 'father' is understood as *one* model, many people would feel comfortable about interpreting that relationship through other models as well, including a maternal model."[61] *Father* and *Mother* are equally valid because both are models—basic metaphors—for God, McFague concludes. They ought to be accorded equal status in our religious language.

The same approach is taken by Mollenkott. "If anyone needs any scriptural authorization to address the Lord's prayer to both Father and Mother," she writes, "Psalm 123:1–2, with its male-female parallelism concerning the divine, would seem to provide that sanction."[62] In one step she moves from correlate masculine and feminine figures of speech in a Psalm—similes that liken God to a master of servants and

---

59. Wren, *What Language Shall I Borrow?* 101.
60. Ibid., 123–36, 143–70.
61. McFague, *Metaphorical Theology*, 128.
62. Mollenkott, *The Divine Feminine*, 61.

mistress of maidservants—to naming God *Mother* on an equal footing with God as *Father*. Thus she assumes that feminine imagery justifies giving God feminine names and titles.

Johanna van Wijk-Bos affirms this strategy as she introduces *Reimagining God*: "I am concerned here with exploring biblical images for God—in names, titles, and designations—that offer alternatives to exclusively male imagery."[63] Apparently she assumes at the outset that names, titles, and designations of God are warranted by biblical imagery, which is female as well as male.

Consider similar statements by Ruth Duck: "Such terms as 'rock,' 'father,' 'mother,' or 'love' . . . when they refer to God . . . become metaphors." So *Father* is just one of many metaphors for God. Eventually she asserts: "All naming of God is necessarily metaphorical . . . The divine name 'Father, Son, and Holy Spirit' is metaphorical, as any alternatives will be." So she goes on to propose a number of inclusive alternatives.[64]

Aída Besançon Spencer also takes this line. "The term 'father' is no less a metaphor than 'light' or 'bread' or 'shepherd.'" This judgment, she believes, enables her to put *Father* on the same level as other biblical references to God, "images standing side-by-side with each other, rejected parent, rejected lover . . . and strong mother."[65]

The argument that we may refer to God with feminine as well as masculine names, titles, and pronouns because all our language for God—masculine, feminine, and ungendered—is metaphorical (figurative, imagery) is virtually universal among defenders of inclusive language for God.

"Women Experience God Differently Than Men"

The transcendence of God and the anthropomorphic nature of our language for God imply that our images for God are drawn from human experience. But while all human experience shares basic features in common, it is also true that factors like personality, culture, and gender can color or nuance experience. Thus it may be that some men and some women, whether for natural or cultural reasons, tend to experience life, including its deep, spiritual dimension, somewhat differently. To the extent that there is gender-relative diversity in spiritual experience, according to some inclusivists, the use of exclusively masculine language in religion is inadequate, especially for the experience of God. They urge that feminine language must be used to express how women experience God and the dimension of God's salvation that extends to their liberation from the sins of sexism and patriarchalism.

63. van Wijk-Bos, *Reimagining God*, ix.
64. Duck, *Gender and the Name of God*, 13, 154.
65. Spencer, *The Goddess Revival*, 113, 120.

Rosemary Ruether writes: "The uniqueness of feminist theology lies not in its use of the criterion of experience but rather in its use of *women's* experience." "Images of God/ess must include female roles and experience."[66] Elizabeth Johnson also makes this case. "Thus women's awakening to their own human worth can be interpreted at the same time as a new experience of God. . . . This theological interpretation of female identity is the center of gravity for feminist discourse about the mystery of God."[67]

Marchiene Vroon Rienstra appeals strongly to the differences in men's and women's religious experience. "The fact that the nature of our relationship to God, and therefore our spirituality, is grounded in gender is now beyond dispute," she writes. The factors that distinguish women from men "give their spirituality a shape different from that of male spirituality." Since there is both male and female religious experience, Rienstra argues, God "is as appropriately imaged and named in feminine ways as in masculine ways."[68]

"Humans Name God"

Underlying virtually all of these arguments for inclusivism is the assumption that we humans have the ability and right to name God. The rationale for that assumption goes something like this: God is wholly other and is therefore a Mystery beyond all human language. Nevertheless we humans bear God's image and are aware of God's presence, which motivate us to name that mysterious presence. We inevitably name God in terms of our own experience, conditioned by our cultural perspectives on gender. This, inclusivists reason, is the process which resulted in the Bible's language for God and the language of classical Christianity. It is the very same process that now generates gender-inclusive language for God. The universality of this process is a major reason why the language of Scripture cannot be regarded as definitive of God and binding for all times and places. The human ability and right to name God is an axiom that is crucial to the entire inclusivist project.

The basic assumption of the right to name God is apparent in the inclusivist arguments considered above. It is explicit in Sally McFague's advocacy of new models for God and in her claim that we humans inevitably imagine God in terms of our self-images. It is tacitly presumed by Marchiene Rienstra's invitation to men and women to select from

66. Ruether, *Sexism and God-Talk*, 13, 69.
67. Johnson, *She Who Is*, 62.
68. Marchiene Vroon Rienstra, "Grounded in Gender," *Perspectives*, November 1995, 8–11. This article is adapted from her book, *Come to the Feast: Seeking God's Bounty for Our Lives and Souls* (Grand Rapids: Eerdmans, 1995).

the divinely hosted smorgasbord of language for God what nourishes and appeals to our own spiritual experience. It is openly celebrated by the unofficial anthem of the inclusivist movement, Brian Wren's "Bring Many Names to God." It is invoked by Aída Besançon Spencer as a divinely granted privilege: "God allows humans to create names and titles for God."[69] Many other examples have already been cited. The prerogative of naming God is crucial to the entire inclusivist project.

"Traditional Language Is Dead"

A more practical reason inclusivists give for updating the vocabulary of the gospel is the fact that language tends to become stale and lose effectiveness through frequent and habitual usage. People often use words mindlessly without appreciating their significance. It was an astounding thing for the Israelites, a small and vulnerable people surrounded by ambitious monarchs like Pharaoh and Nebuchadnezzar, to exult in God as King (Ps. 145:1). It was a revelatory moment of intimacy with God when Jesus taught his Jewish disciples, who stood in awe of *The Holy One of Israel*, to pray "Our Father in heaven." But when the prayers, liturgies, and hymns of the church use *Father, Lord*, and *King* thousands of times with little variation and few alternatives for generations on end, these references to God become mere verbal labels, inclusivists contend. Christian worshipers simply repeat them over and over without experiencing much of the meaning and feeling that they had for their original users. According to this analysis, our once lively religious vocabulary has lost its vitality and has become a series of "dead metaphors." The point of religious language is to draw us to God and to make us profoundly aware of the gracious divine nearness to us. For this reason inclusivists urge us always to keep the language of faith fresh, always to seek new ways to speak of God. They insist that the adoption of feminine and gender-neutral language is necessary in this way for the spiritual vitality of the church in our culture.

This point is developed extensively in Sally McFague's *Metaphorical Theology*. Religious language, she asserts, is initially metaphoric—striking the user with insight, surprise, joy, or disbelief. But eventually, "the metaphor becomes commonplace, either dead and/or literalized."[70] Gail Ramshaw also follows this line. "Religious language begins in lively metaphor, babbling vision, exploding with ecstacy, nurturing human community. . . . Liturgical language is a communal repetition of such metaphoric texts." "When a metaphor no longer surprises, the lit-

---

69. Spencer, *The Goddess Revival*, 126. The quote continues: "God chooses attributes for self-description. . . ." Thus God chooses attributes and we are allowed to name them.

70. McFague, *Metaphorical Theology*, 41.

erary critic calls it a dead metaphor. Too many metaphors in Christian speech are dead, dead, dead."[71] Ruth Duck likewise follows McFague. "A dead, or literalized, metaphor has little power to evoke new perception because it has become so commonplace." She concludes that "'Father' is not a live metaphor" and proceeds to argue for gender-inclusive language for God.[72]

The motivation of these inclusivist theologians is to preserve and communicate the gospel to contemporary people with true spiritual impact. They are convinced that effective proclamation requires renovation of the language of Scripture and tradition because cultural change and habitual use have rendered the living language of the Bible writers meaningless to modern people. The assumptions behind this argument are that the gospel is separable from the words of Scripture and that new substitutions can fully preserve the meaning of the original language.

"The Gospel Must Be Proclaimed in Contemporary Language"

Missionaries and Bible translators have long recognized that the good news of salvation through Jesus Christ must be presented in language understandable by those who hear it.[73] Sometimes this requires departure from a word-for-word translation of Scripture and the use of different terminology in order to achieve "dynamic equivalence"—a presentation of the gospel that preserves its biblical meaning in the language of the hearers. Sometimes it is necessary to change words in order to keep the same meaning. This sort of cultural accommodation is apparent even in the New Testament. Paul is a Jew to the Jews, using the language and arguments of Judaism with them. When he writes to Greeks, he uses the vocabulary and rhetorical style of the Greeks. But he preaches the same message of salvation through the grace of Jesus Christ to both (1 Cor. 9:20–23).

Inclusivist Christians reason the same way. God's love for all people in Jesus Christ is what the Bible intends to proclaim. The masculinity of God and the normativity of patriarchal social institutions are not the message of the gospel, they say, but only the contextualized forms in which it was preached. In our inclusive, democratic culture the Christian gospel must be presented in nonsexist language. In fact, the predominantly masculine language of the Bible actually impedes communication of the gospel.

71. Ramshaw, *God beyond Gender*, 6, 99.
72. Duck, *Gender and the Name of God*, 16.
73. Eugene Nida, *Message and Mission: The Communication of the Christian Faith* (South Pasadena, Calif.: William Carey Library, 1975, reprint of Harper & Row, 1960), is a classic discussion of this issue.

"It seems natural to assume that Christian people, eager to transmit the Good News that the Creator loves each human being equally and unconditionally, would be right in the vanguard of those who utilize inclusive language," observes Virginia Mollenkott.[74] Gail Ramshaw's methodology explicitly separates the Gospel from the words of Scripture in order to restate it. She studies Scripture and tradition "to discover the most effective presentation of the gospel in the past." But then she follows this procedure: "edit out what obscures the Spirit, what no longer, to use Martin Luther's phrase, 'speaks the gospel.' . . . Reinterpret what is salvageable so that it more clearly 'shows forth Christ' . . . [and] Make necessary adaptations and write new material in the vernacular."[75] Since the vernacular today is gender-inclusive, the Christian faith must be expressed inclusively as well, which for Ramshaw means ungendered. The old story requires a new vocabulary.

Conclusion

This chapter has surveyed a variety of reasons commonly offered to justify the use of gender-inclusive language for God. Some of these reasons appeal to the Bible itself or are claims about the correct ways of identifying and interpreting God's revelation. Other reasons are more theological and linguistic, appealing to the transcendence or "otherness" of God, the image of God as male and female, and the metaphorical nature of the language we use to speak about God. These arguments are combined in different ways by inclusivists of different traditions and theological orientations. Even though there is a variety of defenses for inclusive language, however, they all tend to draw from a fairly standard set of arguments.

Taken cumulatively, these arguments appear to present a fairly formidable case for revising the way we speak of God. They may be forceful and persuasive enough to begin breaking down the intial resistance most Christians feel toward inclusive language for God. A cumulative case can seem especially powerful because many of the the reasons taken individually appear to be sound and orthodox. For example, the Bible does contain feminine language for God, there is cultural accommodation in Scripture, God is transcendent, both male and female do image God, and Christians can use biblical language out of habit without knowing its meaning. All these claims are true.

One reservation traditional Christians typically raise at the outset is the final authority of Scripture. The adoption of inclusive language for

---

74. Mollenkott, *The Divine Feminine*, 1.
75. Ramshaw, *God beyond Gender*, viii.

God seems on the face of it to abandon the Bible for the gender-egalitarian ideology of contemporary culture. But in fact evangelical Christians are among those who promote inclusive language for God. These are Christians who affirm the Bible as the inspired and authoritative Word of God and who base their arguments on Scripture itself.

For this reason Christians who defend traditional language cannot simply dismiss inclusivism as a form of liberalism or modernism. It is necessary to examine carefully all the arguments to determine whether the several cumulative cases are as formidable and persuasive as they initially appear. The rest of this book considers all of the attempted justifications of inclusive language presented in this chapter. Since the role of Scripture is basic, we begin with an examination of the Bible to test claims that it actually contains or implies inclusive language for God.

3

The Bible's Feminine and Maternal References to God

Many traditional Christians are surprised to learn that there actually are feminine references to God in Scripture. I was more than thirty years old before I noticed them even though I was raised a Christian, read Scripture regularly, and attended public worship every Sunday. In fact, it was encountering feminist theology that really brought these texts to my attention. So it may be true that by and large traditional Christianity has overlooked or ignored the Bible's feminine representations of God, as inclusivists often allege.

But where are these texts, and what do they mean? Inclusivists frequently and eagerly appeal to them to defend the claim that Scripture itself contains gender-inclusive language for God, or at least the raw material for it, as observed in chapter 2. Some inclusivists imply that there are many such texts and that the gender-biases of modern translations have obscured or eliminated a significant number of them.[1] Clearly a great deal in the debate about inclusive language depends on a proper account of this material, especially for Christians who believe that Scripture is the highest authority for the faith of the church.

This chapter therefore carefully examines the Bible's feminine language for God to determine whether it really does provide a foundation for gender-inclusive religious discourse. The analysis addresses two basic issues: which biblical terms and texts are genuine feminine refer-

---

1. For example, Phyllis Trible, "Feminist Hermeneutics and Biblical Studies," in *Feminist Theology: A Reader*, ed. Ann Loades (Louisville: Westminster/John Knox, 1990), 25, complains: "Over centuries, however, translators and commentators have ignored such female imagery, with disastrous results for God, man and woman." The validity of this complaint is the major premise of Virginia Mollenkott's *The Divine Feminine: The Biblical Imagery of God as Female*.

65

ences to God, and what parts of speech (names, metaphors, etc.) they represent.[2]

One task, then, is to identify the data—the actual instances of feminine language for God that Scripture contains. This must be done because inclusivists appeal to a wide variety and significant number of references, some of which are questionable. Thus, although a somewhat laborious undertaking, we consider all the texts and terms commonly claimed to be feminine references to God, classifying them into four categories: clear cases, plausible but debatable cases, possible but unlikely cases, and mistakenly claimed cases.

The other task is to determine the linguistic structure and function of these references: Are they names, titles, pronouns, metaphors, or other parts of speech? This classification is necessary because crucial inclusivist arguments move very easily from feminine imagery to feminine names and pronouns for God, as documented in chapter 2. Recall Virginia Mollenkott's claim, for instance: "If anyone needs any scriptural authorization to address the Lord's prayer to both Father and Mother, Psalm 123:1–2, with its male–female parallelism concerning the divine, would seem to provide that sanction."[3] Psalm 123 contains masculine and feminine figures of speech, not titles or names for God. Is Mollenkott's leap warranted by the way language works? Such inclusivist appeals to Scripture cannot be evaluated without determining what parts of language the feminine references to God actually represent. This issue becomes pressing, because it turns out that all the feminine references to God in Scripture are figures of speech. They are not names or titles for God. And in language for human beings, figures of speech do not usually warrant or function as names or titles.

Once we have a handle on the Bible's feminine references to God, we turn to its masculine language in chapter 4. That enables us to compare Scripture's masculine and feminine language for God in chapter 5 to determine whether they support gender-equivalent language, as inclusivists claim.

Clear Feminine References to God

If we apply standard methods of exegesis to the original languages of Scripture, it is fairly certain that the texts considered in this section

2. Much of this chapter was completed before the Christian Reformed study committee began its work. However, it also owes much to Al Wolters of Redeemer College, who corrected, sharpened, and added to my analysis of many of the biblical texts and to the formulation of appropriate linguistic categories. I am also grateful to William Vande Kopple of Calvin College for help in defining linguistic categories and applying them properly. If my analysis is mistaken, however, it is not because of their contributions.

3. Mollenkott, *The Divine Feminine*, 61.

contain genuine feminine references to God. According to standard linguistic classifications that fit the original languages as well as English, all of them turn out to be various types of imagery or figures of speech: similes, analogies, metaphors, and personification.[4] They are classified under these headings.

A crucial clarification must be made before proceeding: In one sense all human language for God may be metaphorical or analogical, because the nature of God far transcends our creaturely limitations. This point, as noted in chapter 2, is frequently made by inclusivists. In another sense, however, not all references to God are metaphors or analogies, which are imagery or figures of speech. Proper names and titles are not imagery or figures of speech, even if they have metaphorical meaning. Most discussions of inclusive language confuse metaphor as a part of speech with the metaphorical nature of all language for God. The following analysis avoids this confusion. This chapter classifies feminine references to God according to the parts of speech they represent. Chapter 7 discusses the significance of the fact that all language for God is metaphorical or analogical.

Similes

A simile is a figure of speech that describes a specific feature of one thing by comparing it with something different that shares a similar feature.[5] Examples are "life is like a dream" and "though your sins are as scarlet, they shall be as white as snow." Similes contain verbal cues which make clear that different things are being compared. In English *like* and *as* are the usual indicators. Identification of one thing with the other is explicitly excluded. Life is *like* a dream; it is not said *to be* a dream. Sin is compared to scarlet and white snow; it is not said to be scarlet and white snow. Further, similes are limited comparisons. They illustrate particular features, not broad similarities. The whiteness of the snow, not its wetness, coldness, or beauty, is what our sins will be like. Many of the Bible's feminine references to God are similes. They do not identify God as feminine but use a female creature to illustrate what specific attitudes and acts of his are like. Gender is not the point of comparison in the feminine (or masculine) similes for God.

Psalm 123:2. "As the eyes of slaves look to the hand of their master, as the eyes of a maid look to the hand of her mistress, so our eyes look to the LORD our God, till he shows us his mercy."

4. See William Harmon and C. H. Holman, *A Handbook to Literature*, 7th ed. (Upper Saddle River, N.J.: Prentice-Hall, 1996), 263, for the definition of imagery as figure of speech. Specific linguistic categories are defined in this section as the need arises.
5. See ibid., 483, for a definition of simile.

In this verse we find a simile indirectly comparing God to both a master and a mistress, that is, a woman in a position of authority. Strictly speaking, it does not explicitly state that God is like a master and a mistress. The explicit comparison is between our eyes and the eyes of servants. But the structure of the simile suggests that the master and mistress are both like God in having the power and inclination to show mercy to subordinates. Thus it is reasonably classified as an implicit feminine simile for God. It is worth noting that this image is not maternal but connotes authority and power.

Psalm 131:2. "But I have stilled and quieted my soul; like a weaned child with its mother, like a weaned child is my soul within me."

Here, too, is an indirectly implied maternal simile for God. The direct comparison is between the repose of the psalmist's soul and the security of a small child with its mother. It already begins to stretch the precise point of the simile to say that the soul is likened to a child. It stretches the point even further to infer that God, who is the source of the psalmist's comfort, is like a mother. But the comparison of God and the mother is suggested by the image as a whole, even if that is not its point. So this qualifies as an implied maternal simile for God.

Isaiah 31:5. "Like birds hovering overhead, the LORD Almighty will shield Jerusalem."

This is an explicit simile that compares the Lord's protection of Jerusalem with birds hovering over their nests. The participle form *hovering* is feminine although the generic plural of birds is masculine, which provides probable cause for concluding that these are mother birds.[6]

Isaiah 42:14. "But now, like a woman in childbirth, I cry out, I gasp and pant."

This expression is a straightforward birth simile for the Lord, who is the speaker of these words. The precise point of comparison is crying, gasping, and panting; it is not giving birth. But God directly likens his effort to redeem his people to that of a woman in labor.

Isaiah 66:13. "As a mother comforts her child, so will I comfort you; and you will be comforted over Jerusalem."

This verse contains an explicit simile for God in which maternity is not merely in the background of the comparison, but a mother's comfort is the central focus. This is possibly the clearest, most direct maternal image for God in the Bible.

Hosea 13:8. "Like a bear robbed of her cubs, I will attack them and rip them open."

---

6. Edward J. Young, *The Book of Isaiah*, 3 vols. (Grand Rapids: Eerdmans, 1960), 2:378.

This expression is a simile likening God to a bear, but it does not depict God's love and nurture for his children. In fact, ungrateful, faithless Israel is the object of divine wrath and punishment. God's honor and right to Israel's love are the cubs of which he has been robbed. Curiously, *bear* is grammatically masculine in Hebrew. But Hebrew words for kinds of animals, whether grammatically masculine or feminine, often include both males and females. So *bear* can stand for *mother bear*. In this case it most likely does because father bears take no parental responsibility for their offspring. Thus this probably is a maternal simile for God. However, the gender of the bear is incidental to the meaning of the simile. The point is God's anger at being robbed, not his mother-likeness.

Matthew 23:37 (and Luke 13:34). "O Jerusalem. . . , how often I have longed to gather your children together, as a hen gathers her chicks under her wings, but you were not willing."

In this simile Jesus explicitly compares himself to a chicken mothering her offspring. This is not a feminine reference to God as distinguished from the incarnate Jesus Christ. However, it is reminiscent of Old Testament imagery of wings and mother birds representing the protecting presence of God, discussed below.

1 Peter 2:2–3. "Like newborn babies, crave pure spiritual milk, so that by it you may grow up in your salvation, now that you have tasted that the Lord is good."

This is another indirect or implied simile. The explicit comparison is between those whom Peter is addressing and nursing babies, the precise focus being the desire for nourishment. Further, *spiritual milk* is a metaphor for the Word of God, which is mentioned three times just prior to this image in 1:23–25. Neither the simile nor the metaphor actually states that God is a mother or even is like one. However, both the simile and the metaphor indirectly suggest that God, who provides his Word and feeds us with it, is like a nursing mother. The literary intention of the text suggests a maternal image of God.

Analogies

Two texts use human females to depict God but are neither similes nor metaphors. Thus we simply list them here as analogies. Analogies are like similes in that they use one thing to model, image, or illustrate something about another without linguistically identifying the two. The comparison is usually made by simple juxtaposition.

Isaiah 49:15. "Can a mother forget the baby at her breast and have no compassion on the child she has borne? Though she may forget, I will not forget you!"

Here the Lord directly compares himself to a nursing mother (literally, *woman nursing the son of her womb*), assuring us that his love is even stronger and more reliable than what is arguably the strongest and most self-giving of human bonds. Actually, the stress of the comparison is on the *dissimilarity* between God and the mother. However, this is possible only on the basis of the explicit comparison. God is even more faithful than a nursing mother.

Luke 15:8–10. "Or suppose a woman has ten silver coins and loses one. Does she not light a lamp, sweep the house and search carefully until she finds it? And when she finds it, she calls her friends and neighbors together and says, 'Rejoice with me; I have found my lost coin.' In the same way, I tell you, there is rejoicing in the presence of the angels of God over one sinner who repents."

In this parable there is an implicit comparison of God and the woman. The precise hinge of the image is the rejoicing of the woman with her friends and the rejoicing of the angels in the presence of God. If the friends represent the angels, then the woman represents God. This, too, is an implied feminine figure of speech, inasmuch as parables are extended images.

In sum, all of the above texts figuratively employ creaturely females to illustrate what particular attitudes or actions of God are like. But none identifies God as a mother or any other female figure. Metaphors, however, come closer to making some kind of identification.

Metaphors

A metaphor is a figure of speech that describes or highlights a feature of one thing by directly but nonliterally identifying it with another thing or attributing the characteristics of something else directly to it.[7] Examples are "the Word is a two-edged sword," "her smile makes the sun shine," and "the earth will give birth to her dead" (Isa. 26:19). Each of these metaphors has the linguistic form of a direct, literal predication but is meant figuratively, using one thing to illustrate or highlight something about another. The Word is not literally a two-edged sword, but is like a sword in that it cuts to our spiritual hearts just as a sword can cut to the physical heart. The earth will not literally give birth to the dead, but the final resurrection of the dead will be as though they are being born from the figuratively pregnant womb of the ground in which they are buried.

There are various forms of metaphors. Some use a predicate noun to identify one thing with another while focusing their similarity: "the earth is the mother of the dead." Others do not identify one thing with

---

7. Harmon and Holman, *A Handbook of Literature*, 315–16.

another but use verbs or adjectives to attribute a specific action or particular quality of one thing to another: "the earth will give birth to her dead." Both of these are maternal metaphors, but only the former explicitly identifies the earth as mother. With respect to the Bible's feminine metaphors, God is never identified as a mother or any other female person, but only with feminine roles or activities, most frequently with giving birth.

Numbers 11:12. "Did I conceive all these people? Did I give them birth? Why do you tell me to carry them in my arms, as a nurse carries an infant?"

In frustration Moses fires a series of rhetorical questions at God which imply that God, not Moses, is the one who conceived and gave birth to the people of Israel and carried them as a nurse. His question is metaphorical, not literal. He is asking whether he, a male, conceived and gave birth to Israel, functions only females are capable of. In Hebrew *conceived* and *gave birth* refer to maternal functions, although *yalad*, the word for *give birth*, can also mean male procreation. Interestingly, *nurse* is not a feminine but a masculine noun.[8] But though Moses asks explicitly about himself, the rhetorical force of the question implies that God is the one who has figuratively conceived and borne his people. This is therefore an indirect birthing metaphor for God's action of making Israel his people.

Deuteronomy 32:18. "You deserted the Rock, who fathered you; you forgot the God who gave you birth."

Here is an explicit birth metaphor for God's making Israel his people. *Gave you birth*, a verb that usually refers to a woman bearing a child (*ḥil*), is directly predicated of God.[9] There is little room for debate about this.

More controversial is the first clause. The word translated as *fathered* here is *yalad*, which can mean the procreational role of either parent. *Begotten* is thus an accurate, though old-fashioned translation. It is possible that *yalad* reflects maternal connotations from the parallel expression, *gave birth*. But *Rock* and *God* are masculine. Thus the term might well bear the connotations of fathering. It is not possible to argue conclusively one way or the other. For this reason it may be appropriate to question translations that render it *fathered* instead of something more neutral. But it is too much to charge that *fathered* is "inadmissible."[10] In any case, *gave birth* is an explicit maternal metaphor for God in relation

---

8. The significance of the masculine and feminine grammatical genders in Hebrew is discussed as needed. It should also be noted here that even though "conceive" and "give birth" are maternal functions, these verbs are grammatically masculine in this text because their subject is God, who is linguistically masculine.

9. And thus its grammatical gender is masculine in spite of its maternal meaning.

10. Phyllis Trible makes this charge in *God and the Rhetoric of Sexuality*, 62.

to his people, Israel. However, the grammatical form of *gave birth* is masculine because it refers to *God*. The significance of this fact cannot be explained until chapter 5.

Job 38:8, 28–29. "Who shut up the sea behind doors when it burst forth from the womb? . . . Does the rain have a father? Who fathers the drops of dew? From whose womb comes the ice? Who gives birth to the frost from the heavens?"

In chapter 38 God confronts Job with a series of questions designed to make him realize that he cannot begin to comprehend divine power and wisdom. These questions from the mouth of God himself contain both maternal and paternal reproductive metaphors for his creation of the watery parts of the world. The word translated *gives birth* could also be gender-neutral or paternal. But in conjunction with *womb* it seems obviously maternal. These metaphors are not direct assertions that God has a womb and gives birth. However, they are in rhetorical questions whose implied answers would be in the form of direct metaphors: "I, God, am the one from whose womb the frost was given birth."

Psalm 90:2. "Before the mountains were born or you brought forth the earth and the world, from everlasting to everlasting you are God."

This is clearly an explicit maternal metaphor for God's activity of creation. The word for *were born* is not necessarily maternal. But *you brought forth* is a standard term for a woman giving birth, which justifies reading the parallelism *were born* as likewise maternal. This does not imply that God is a feminine person, however, for the grammatical gender of *you brought forth* is masculine, corresponding to the grammatical gender of *Lord* and *God*.[11]

Proverbs 8:1, 22–25. "Does not wisdom call out? Does not understanding raise her voice? . . . 'The Lord brought me forth as the first of his works [or, 'The Lord possessed me at the beginning of his works']'[12] . . . I was appointed from eternity, from the beginning, before the world began. When there were no oceans, I was given birth, when there were no springs abounding with water; before the mountains were settled in place, before the hills, I was given birth.'"

This is a complex passage of Scripture that actually contains two different kinds of feminine imagery: the personification of God's wisdom as a woman and God giving birth to wisdom. Personification is treated in the next subsection. Here we attend to the birth metaphor.

11. In chaps. 4 and 5 it is demonstrated that all the personal references to God are masculine and therefore all the feminine imagery for God is predicated of a masculine person, that is, cross-gender imagery. An example is "Bill gave birth to a great idea."

12. Different editions of the NIV have different wordings, but each offers the other wording in the footnotes.

I was given birth in verses 24 and 25 clearly means a child being brought forth by a mother. It is an implied birth metaphor for God, since being born is predicated explicitly of wisdom, whereas identification of God as the mother is the clear though unstated implication. This meaning may very well also nuance verse 22 as a birth metaphor. The word in 22 translated as *possessed* in one version of the NIV and *brought forth* in another does have the primary sense of *acquisition* or *ownership*. But its secondary sense is *originating* or *creating*, especially when used of God.[13] In the context of Proverbs 8:24–25, there is a reasonable case for supposing that *brought forth* is the primary meaning. And if that is so, the birth images of verses 24 and 25 may well nuance *brought forth* as a parallel birth metaphor. However, it is also possible that the main idea in verses 22–25 is a gender-neutral picture of God producing wisdom and that the birth metaphors of verses 24 and 25 are a maternal nuancing of that general idea. In any case, *I was given birth*, occurring twice, clearly suggests the metaphor of God birthing Lady Wisdom.

Isaiah 45:10–11. "Woe to him who says to his father, 'What have you begotten?' or to his mother, 'What have you brought to birth'? 'This is what the LORD says—the Holy One of Israel, and its Maker: Concerning things to come, do you question me about my children, or give me orders about the work of my hands?'"

This text contains indirect or implied metaphors of God as both father and mother. It does not directly state that God is the father or mother of his children. But given the fact that God explicitly speaks of *my children*, the rhetorical questions about the reader's challenging his father or mother clearly suggest that God is metaphorically the father and mother of his children.

John 3:3–8. "In reply Jesus declared, 'I tell you the truth, no one can see the kingdom of God unless he is born again.' 'How can a man be born when he is old?' Nicodemus asked. 'Surely he cannot enter a second time into his mother's womb to be born!' Jesus answered, 'I tell you the truth, no one can enter the kingdom of God unless he is born of water and the Spirit. You should not be surprised at my saying, 'You must be born again.' . . . So it is with everyone born of the Spirit.'"

The Greek word translated as *born* in this most beloved passage of Scripture is *gennao*, which can mean gender-neutral reproduction or the procreative role of either parent.[14] What tips the interpretation in

13. Francis Brown, S. Driver, and C. Briggs, *A Hebrew and English Lexicon of the Old Testament* (Oxford: Clarendon, 1907, 1977), 888–89.
14. W. Bauer, *A Greek-English Lexicon of the New Testament and Other Early Christian Literature*, ed. and trans. W. Arndt and F. Gingrich (Chicago: University of Chicago Press, 1957, 1964), 154–55.

favor of a maternal metaphor in this passage is Nicodemus' mention of a mother's womb in verse 4. Jesus does not challenge that understanding of the metaphor, but continues to use it in speaking of the role of the Spirit. So although we do not have a direct and explicit identification of the Holy Spirit as mother, the suggestion of the text is that regeneration by the Spirit is like being born from one's mother. Christians often call it "new birth." In the background there may well be an echo of the life-producing power of God's Spirit, for which, as noted below, there may be maternal imagery in the Old Testament.

Personification

Personification, like simile, analogy, and metaphor, is a figure of speech.[15] It can be understood as an extended metaphor because it linguistically identifies something that is not a person as a person. Examples are justice personified as a blindfolded woman or the United States as *Uncle Sam*. In languages that have grammatical gender, the gender of the personification usually reflects the grammatical gender of the word for what is being personified. In Latin *justitia*, *justice*, is feminine. So *Justitia* is personified as female. The same is true of wisdom (*ḥokmah*) in Hebrew.

Proverbs 8:1. "Does not wisdom call out? Does not understanding raise her voice?"

The entirety of Proverbs 8 is a monologue of God's wisdom personified as a woman or female figure.[16] She calls out, ultimately revealing herself to be the wisdom by which God created the world, and offers herself as the way of life and well-being to all who follow her. It is important to identify precisely what is being personified. The wisdom in this chapter belongs to *Yahweh* (v. 22). Wisdom is neither identical with God nor is it a personification of God.[17] It is one of God's attributes or powers, like his glory and holiness. Thus Lady Wisdom is a personification of God's wisdom. *Sophia* (Greek for wisdom) is not God.[18]

This completes consideration of those passages of Scripture that seem quite plainly to contain maternal and other feminine representations of God. All of them are figures of speech of one kind or another, and many of them are implicit and suggestive rather than explicitly stated.

15. Harmon and Holman, *A Handbook to Literature*, 385–86.

16. Ibid., 386, specifically lists Wisdom in Prov. 8 as an example of personification.

17. Johnson, *She Who Is*, 91, does claim that this is "a female personification of God's own being." van wijk-Bos, *Reimagining God*, 84, correctly identifies wisdom as "a divine aspect disclosed in female form."

18. This point is significant because of the Sophia-worship widespread in inclusivist Christianity and other religions.

Plausible But Debatable Feminine References to God

The following texts can reasonably be construed as feminine references to God. But they are ambiguous or indeterminate enough to prevent them from being identified as feminine with confidence because there are equally reasonable or plausible alternatives.

Genesis 1:2b. "and the Spirit of God was hovering over the waters."

Inclusivists frequently take this phrase as depicting God's Spirit as a mother bird hovering over her nest.[19] There is a good case to be made for bird imagery. The verb form translated *hovering* is also found in Deuteronomy 32:11, where the Lord's care for Israel is likened to an eagle hovering over its nest.[20] It is more difficult to make the case that the hovering bird is female, however. As indicated in the next section, the gender of the eagle is indeterminate. In fact, the image may be of a bird hovering and fertilizing—the Spirit preparing to inform the watery void—in which case the imagery is male.[21] Furthermore, it is doubtful that *Spirit of God* has the connotations of a female person, as shown in the next part of this chapter. On the other hand, the fact that *spirit* is grammatically feminine in Hebrew may imply that the hovering entity, whatever it is, is female.[22] In the end the evidence is inconclusive whether this metaphor is distinctively maternal.

Ruth 2:12b. "May you be richly rewarded by the LORD, the God of Israel, under whose wings you have come to take refuge." (Pss. 17:8 and 91:4 also attribute wings to the Lord.)

Many inclusivists interpret all references to God's wings or God's hovering as maternal images.[23] This inference is based on several associations. One is with eagles (Deut. 32:10–11). Another appeals to mother birds hovering, as in Isaiah 31:5. A third link is with the Spirit of God, understood as a mother bird, hovering over the waters in Genesis 1:2. Finally, Jesus clearly uses an image of maternal wings in Matthew 23:37, as noted above. Clustered together, these texts suggest an association of wings and mother birds. It is tempting to generalize this association for all references to the wings of God.

But this generalization cannot be made with confidence. For it is uncertain whether the hovering image of God's Spirit in Genesis 1:2 is

---

19. Mollenkott, *The Divine Feminine*, 89–90; Johnson, *She Who Is*, 134; and van Wijk-Bos, *Reimagining God*, 72–73.

20. Leon Wood, *The Holy Spirit in the Old Testament* (Grand Rapids: Zondervan, 1976), 30; Wilf Hildebrandt, *Old Testament Theology of the Spirit of God* (Peabody, Mass.: Hendrickson, 1995), 30–37.

21. Brown, *Hebrew and English Lexicon of the Old Testament*, 934.

22. The distinction between grammatical and personal gender in relation to the Spirit of God is discussed more fully in the next section.

23. Mollenkott, *The Divine Feminine*, chaps. 15 and 16.

feminine. Further, it will be shown that the gender of the eagle in Deuteronomy 32:11 is unknown. Finally, although the birds in Isaiah 31:5
and the hen in Jesus' lament are mothers, this does not imply that all
winged or hovering birds mentioned in Scripture are female. Father
birds also have wings and in many species they tend their young. So
each text must contain sufficient evidence to justifiy the claim that the
birds it mentions are female. Otherwise we are only entitled to claim
ungendered avarian parenting imagery.

Furthermore, birds are not the only creatures in Scripture that have
wings. The angels surrounding the throne of God in Isaiah 6 are
winged, but they are anthropomorphically and grammatically masculine in the Hebrew Bible. Perhaps having wings in the imagery of the
Old Testament is a characteristic God shares with heavenly beings such
as these. Thus allusions to the Lord's wings do not necesssarily suggest
birds at all, let alone mother birds.

For all these reasons, the claim that all the hovering and wing images
of God in Scripture are distinctively maternal is tenuous. It is possible
but far from certain that God's wings in Ruth and the Psalms are feminine imagery.

Psalm 22:9–10. "Yet you brought me out of the womb; you made me
trust in you even at my mother's breast. From birth I was cast upon you;
from my mother's womb you have been my God."

Phyllis Trible and Elizabeth Johnson identify this text as a maternal
symbol for God.[24] Virginia Mollenkott, with most of those who see feminine imagery here, understands it as the figure of a midwife.[25] So there
is a debate about the content of the image. But a prior question is
whether this verse even contains any imagery at all.

It may not. For the Bible often speaks of God's actions in generic personal language without using figures of speech.[26] For example, *God
cares for his people* expresses God's providence nonfiguratively in basic,
generic personal language. However, *God shepherds his people* speaks of
his care in an identifiable figure of speech, a metaphor that depicts it
specifically in the role of a shepherd, not merely as generic divine action. Given this distinction, we can see that the Psalmist may simply be
stating, without a figure of speech, that God has taken care of him ever
since he was born. There is no terminology or linguistic structure here
which must be interpreted as imagery. In fact the Psalmist is speaking

24. Johnson, *She Who Is*, 101.
25. Mollenkott, *The Divine Feminine*, 33–34. van Wijk-Bos does not include this text
in her list of feminine references to God.
26. This assertion does not deny that all language for God is *analogical* or *metaphorical* because of God's transcendence. The distinction between figures of speech and the
metaphorical character of all language for God is discussed in chaps. 5 and 7.

of his actual birth, not a metaphorical birth. Nevertheless, it may be that this is an image involving God in the Psalmist's birth.

If so, what is the image? Is it the mother who *brought me out of the womb* and the one upon whom the newborn was cast? The major problem with this reading is that God is addressed directly as *you*, whereas the mother is referred to as a third person: *from my mother's womb you have been my God*. Thus God is not the mother but another person who is attending the birth. This conclusion is also supported by the expression *you brought me out of the womb,* which does not express the activity of giving birth but of someone assisting in the delivery of the baby. Of course it is conceivable that the mother delivered the baby herself. On the whole, however, the figure addressed in this text is more plausibly a birth-assistant than a mother.

Is the birth assistant a midwife, a female figure? Customary in Israel, a midwife is the obvious candidate, since midwives attend birth, deliver babies, and lay them on their mothers' breasts. However, there are biblical examples of men attending birth, as in the case of Joseph at the birth of Jesus. It is likely but not certain that if there is the image of a birth-attendant, it is a woman.

In the end, then, this text remains unclear. It may or may not contain imagery. If it does, the image is a metaphor that attributes birth-assisting actions to God, more likely those of a midwife than a mother.

Isaiah 46:3b–4a. "Listen to me, O house of Jacob, all you who remain of the house of Israel, you whom I have upheld since you were conceived,[27] and have carried since your birth. Even to your old age and gray hairs I am he, I am he who will sustain you."

Like Psalm 22, the major question is whether there is any imagery for God here at all. It is perfectly possible that the Lord is speaking to his people in nonfigurative language, simply asserting that he is the one who upholds them all of their lives, from conception to old age. The verbs *uphold, carry,* and *sustain* are generic actions and do not necessarily elicit specific figurative associations as *shepherd* or *give birth* do. Perhaps this text contains no imagery.

However, it could very well be that Isaiah 46:3 implies a maternal figure for God. For elsewhere in Isaiah God is compared to a mother, and other texts of Scripture use the image of birth for God's electing his people. Further, the text can be read straightforwardly as the Lord likening himself to a mother who carries and upholds her baby after its birth. A number of exegetes, including John Calvin, have understood it this

27. The Hebrew means literally *carried from the belly*. It does not clearly speak of conception and perhaps not even of pregnancy but only of the time since birth. Thus the RSV reads *from your birth, carried from the womb*.

way.[28] Nevertheless, a mother does not sustain her children until they are old and gray, which counts against this being a maternal image. Though debatable, there is a reasonable case to be made for maternal imagery in Isaiah 46:3. If this is imagery, it is a metaphor attributing maternal holding and carrying to God.

Isaiah 66:7–9. "'Before she [Zion] goes into labor, she gives birth; before the pains come upon her, she delivers a son. Who has ever heard of such a thing? Who has ever seen such things? Can a country be born in a day or a nation be brought forth in a moment? Yet no sooner is Zion in labor than she gives birth to her children. Do I bring to the moment of birth and not give delivery?' says the LORD. 'Do I close up the womb when I bring to delivery?' says your God."

Although there is obviously a birth metaphor here, it is not of God but of Jerusalem. If there is imagery for God, it is a metaphor of God attending the birth of his people from mother Jerusalem, perhaps as a midwife.

Like Psalm 22 and Isaiah 46:3, this passage can be read as not containing any imagery for God at all. The metaphor of birth depicts Jersualem and her people. But God is the one who non-figuratively brings to birth and either gives delivery or closes the womb. For although presence at birth is surely suggested, a moment's reflection reveals that midwives do not have the power to bring to birth, give delivery, or close the womb. These eventualities are in the hands of God alone and have no human analogue. So although an implied metaphor of God as a birth-attendant or midwife is possible, there are also good reasons against it.

Possible But Unlikely Feminine References to God

Ruah is the Hebrew word for *spirit*. Of the forty-three instances in the Old Testament where the grammatical gender of *ruah* in the phrase *Spirit of God* can be determined, thirty-six are feminine and seven are masculine.[29] The feminine instances typically govern feminine verb and adjective forms as well. Inclusivists often infer from this that the Spirit of God is primarily feminine, and many take this as a compelling reason not only for using feminine language for God, but also for regarding God as personally feminine.[30]

28. Calvin, *Commentary on Isaiah*, 3:436: "This is a very expressive metaphor, by which God compares himself to a mother who carries a child in her womb."

29. I gratefully acknowledge Al Wolters as a source of much of the careful linguistic and theological analysis of *ruah* in relation to God and gender reported in this section.

30. Mollenkott, *The Divine Feminine*, 36; Johnson, *She Who Is*, chap. 7 "Spirit-Sophia"; and van Wijk-Bos, *Reimagining God*, 71–77.

There is no debate about the mixed grammatical gender of *ruaḥ*. The disagreement is whether the grammatical gender of this term implies personal gender of God. This dispute in turn usually involves two issues. One is whether *Spirit of God* refers to God himself or only to an aspect, attribute, or power of God. For if *Spirit* is feminine and refers to God himself, then we have a significant feminine term for the person of God.[31] But if *spirit* refers to an attribute or power of God, like his glory, mind, or will, then it is not a feminine personal term for God himself. The other question is whether the grammatical gender of *ruaḥ* reflects personal gender in the Hebrew language: Is *spirit* a distinctly feminine attribute because it is grammatically feminine?

First, does *Spirit of God* refer to the divine personhood of God? Some theologians understand the term this way, among them apparently the translators of the NIV, who capitalize *Spirit of God* in about seventy-five cases. One way it would be a personal term is if it were equivalent to the Holy Spirit, the Third Person of the Trinity. But most theologians recognize that the Holy Spirit is not fully revealed as a distinct divine person until the New Testament. It may be legitimate from the perspective of the New Testament to see hints of the Trinity and the Holy Spirit in the Old Testament, but claiming them as clear references to the Third Person is regarded by most scholars as explicating what is at best only implicit in the text.[32] So *Spirit of God* probably does not refer to a divine person in this way.

The other way that *Spirit of God* could refer to divine personhood is if it referred to God himself and not merely to an aspect or attribute of God. While some theologians take it this way, there are reasons for caution. Old Testament scholars point out that the Hebrew word *ruaḥ* can mean the wind, the breath or vital energy of a living thing, various human emotional dispositions and moods, and the intellectual, moral, and spiritual power of a human being. Thus the spirit of a person can be said both to act and react. Pharaoh's spirit was troubled (Gen. 41:8 RSV). Mary's spirit rejoiced in God her Savior at the announcement that she would be the mother of the Messiah (Luke 1:47). But this way of speaking about a person's spirit does not intend to either make the spirit itself a personal agent or literally to equate the person with the spirit. It is a figure of speech—synecdoche—where the part figuratively

31. We have not yet discussed the relationship between personal gender and grammatical gender in the biblical languages or the analogical/metaphorical nature of all language for God. The significance of both topics for God and gender is elaborated in subsequent chapters.

32. See Herman Bavinck, "The Holy Trinity," in *The Doctrine of God*, trans. William Hendricksen (Grand Rapids: Baker, 1951, 1977), 255–56; and John Rea, *The Holy Spirit in the Bible* (Lake Mary, Fla.: Creation House, 1990).

stands for the whole (example: "all hands on deck"). *Spirit* is something a person has; it is rarely if ever the person as such.[33]

The Old Testament speaks of God's spirit the same way. Most modern biblical scholars, including evangelical and orthodox scholars who affirm the doctrine of the Trinity, agree that in the Old Testament *spirit* is a power of God and not the person of God himself.[34] Not until the New Testament is the Lord the Spirit (2 Cor. 3:17). Yves Congar asserts: "In the Jewish Bible, the Breath-Spirit of God is the action of God."[35] And according to Walther Eichrodt, "'Spirit' is the inexhaustible power of the divine life, in which all life takes its origin."[36] Just as Mary's spirit is said to act, so God's spirit is said to act. Given the consistency of this pattern in the Old Testament, it is unlikely that *Spirit of God* is a term that is equivalent to *God* as such. Even if *ruaḥ* is feminine, therefore, it is probably not a term for God, but for an aspect or power of God.

But this raises the second question: Even if it is a personal term for God, does the feminine gender of *ruaḥ* imply that God is feminine? The answer is negative, given that language for God parallels language for humans. God is anthropomorphically said to have spirit (*ruaḥ*), as well as heart (*leb*, e.g., Gen. 6:6) and soul (*nephesh*, e.g., Isa. 1:14).[37] But none of these crucial categories reflects personal gender in the case of human beings. So it probably does not for God either.

To work through this argument one must distinguish between personal and grammatical gender.[38] Personal gender refers to the sexual and gender identity of persons: male or female, masculine or feminine, boy or girl. Grammatical gender is a way certain languages classify nouns, pronouns, and other parts of speech: masculine, feminine, and sometimes neuter. In some languages there is a natural correlation of personal and grammatical gender so that masculine words refer to males, feminine words to females, and genderless things have neuter terms. In other languages there is no regular correlation at all.

---

33. See Hans Walter Wolff, *The Anthropology of the Old Testament* (Philadelphia: Fortress, 1974), 32–39; and Hildebrandt, *An Old Testament Theology of the Spirit of God*, chap. 1, "The Semantic Range of *Ruah* in the Hebrew Canon."

34. *"Pneuma,"* in *Theological Dictionary of the New Testament*, ed. G. Kittel and K. Friedrich, trans. G. Bromiley (Grand Rapids: Eerdmans, 1968) 6:332–451, esp. 359–67, "Spirit in the O.T." Victor Hamilton, *The Book of Genesis: Chapters 1–17* (Grand Rapids: Eerdmans, 1990), 114, is unsure about Gen. 1:2: "there is no way to tell from the Hebrew whether one should read 'spirit' or 'Spirit.'"

35. Yves Congar, *I Believe in the Holy Spirit*, 3 vols., trans. D. Smith (New York: Seabury, 1983), 1:12.

36. Walther Eichrodt, *Theology of the Old Testament*, 2 vols., trans. J. Baker (Philadelphia: Westminster, 1961), 1:215; also 2:48–60, "The Spirit of God."

37. Wolff, *Anthropology of the Old Testament*, 32, 40.

38. This topic is discussed more fully in chap. 4.

In Hebrew all nouns are either masculine or feminine, governing gendered verb forms, adjective endings, and pronouns. Words for male persons are usually masculine. Words for female persons are usually female. The problem is that words for things that have no sex, like rocks and wisdom, are also grammatically masculine or feminine. So the question arises: Does the fact that *ruah* is usually grammatically feminine somehow imply that God is personally feminine?

The evidence is negative. There do not seem to be gender implications in the case of humans. All humans, both male and female, are equally animated by grammatically feminine *ruah*. But this does not suggest that all humans are somehow feminine. The fact that Pharaoh has *ruah* does not imply that he is female. Furthermore, if *ruah* refers to an aspect or power of persons, it is not a distinctively feminine quality. Pharaoh's *ruah* does not represent a feminine side of his personality.[39] The same pattern holds for the other anthropological terms. *Leb* (heart) is grammatically masculine, but males and females alike have hearts. *Nephesh* (soul, living being) is grammatically feminine, but it applies to male and female persons equally. Possessing grammatically feminine characteristics does not make men more feminine.[40] Conversely, no one supposes that masculine terms project masculine qualities on females. Consider the fact that the Hebrew words for womb, *rehem*, and breast, *s'ad*, are grammatically masculine.

Given the fact that the Old Testament speaks of God's *heart, soul,* and *spirit* in the same linguistic patterns that it speaks of humans, we can conclude that *Spirit of God,* though usually grammatically feminine, implies nothing at all about the personal gender of God. Thus even if *Spirit* were a personal term for God, it would not indicate that God is feminine. And if *spirit* refers to an aspect of God, it does not imply that it is a feminine aspect.

Denying that *Spirit* is a feminine personal term for God does not rule out the possibility that Genesis 1:2 or other particular texts contain feminine imagery, as discussed above. However, it is unwarranted to generalize the claim that in the Old Testament God's Spirit is personally feminine.[41] This common inclusivist assertion is doubtful.

39. In the same way, a Hebrew speaker does not attribute femininity to a male by saying "Pharaoh has wisdom" even though *wisdom* (*hokmah*) is grammatically feminine. Some inclusivists make this mistake when they take God's wisdom in Prov. 8 as a feminine quality.

40. On this matter Hebrew is like German, in which many abstract nouns are grammatically feminine but do not bear any meaning for personal gender. My favorite example is *die Männlichkeit* (masculinity). Germans do not consider masculinity to be a feminine characteristic because the word is grammatically feminine.

41. The language for the Holy Spirit in the Greek New Testament is discussed in chap. 4.

Deuteronomy 32:10b–11. "He [the Lord] shielded him and cared for him; he guarded him as the apple of his eye, like an eagle that stirs up its nest and hovers over its young, that spreads its wings to catch them and carries them on its pinions." (Exod. 19:4 also likens God to an eagle caring for its young.)

Inclusivists often assert that the eagle in this text is a mother. Some even chide translators who fail to make that clear.[42] In fact, however, the Hebrew word for eagle is grammatically masculine, as are all the verb forms and pronouns. Typical of words for animals, it can stand for birds of both genders (recall the mother bear of Hosea). Furthermore, we know from observation that eagle parents of both genders share in the care of their young. It is therefore impossible to conclude that this text contains distinctively maternal imagery for God. The gender of the eagle is indeterminate and irrelevant to the meaning of the simile. It is possible that it is a maternal image, but there is no clear evidence for this claim.[43]

Psalm 103:13. "As a father has compassion on his children, so the LORD has compassion on those who fear him." (There are a number of other texts that contain Hebrew words for *compassion, pity,* or *love* that are related to the root *rhm*.)

Although this text seems to be a simple father simile for God, Phyllis Trible has popularized the notion that *compassion* must be understood as *mother love.* More precisely, she argues that the terms for compassion, pity, and parental love that come from the Hebrew root *rhm* actually connote maternal love because the noun *rehem* means *womb.*[44]

There can be no doubt of a linguistic connection between these words. Although we have no way of determining whether *compassion* was actually derived from *womb,* or *womb* came from *compassion,* or their meanings developed together, there is almost surely some original association of these terms.

This link does not imply, however, that the word *compassion* continues to have maternal connotations in the actual use of the language. James Barr has alerted us to the etymological fallacy, that is, defining the meaning of a word solely on the basis of its linguistic derivation.[45] For as languages develop, words can lose original meanings and take on

42. Mollenkott, *The Divine Feminine*, chap. 15, esp. 89.

43. This is recognized by van Wijk-Bos, *Reimaging God*, 70, who nevertheless interprets it maternally because of an alleged (but obscure) allusion to *suckling* in Deut. 32:13.

44. Trible, "Journey of a Metaphor," *God and the Rhetoric of Sexuality* (Philadelphia: Fortress, 1978), 31–59. Many inclusivists hold this maternal interpretation of *compassion*.

45. James Barr, *The Semantics of Biblical Language* (Philadelphia: Trinity Press International, 1961).

new ones. Consider the word *gay* since the 1960's, for example. In addition, people may be wholly unaware of original meanings when they use words and thus not intend to express them. Many people have no idea that the surname *Cooper* means *barrelmaker*.

By the same dynamics, a word that originally had specific sex or gender connotations may have lost them, partially or completely. The word *mammal* is a good example. It derives from the Latin word for *breast* and refers to the class of animals who suckle their young. It is probably also related to *Mama*, Mother. But when most people use the word *mammal*, they are unaware of these connections. And even if they do know this meaning, they do not intend to imply that John is breasted, feminine, or Mama-like if they say "John is a mammal."

This illustrates the problem with Trible's definition of *compassion* as *mother-love*. An original connection in no way determines that the maternal connotation is intended by the Psalmist or is echoing in the linguistic background of the father's compassion in Psalm 103:13. This claim would be plausible in a text that explicitly contained mother or birth imagery. But in the texts where compassion is predicated of God and of human kings, conquerors, and children, without overt maternal connotations, there is scant evidence that the word bears any specifically maternal meaning or womb nuance. It may function just like "John is a mammal." Therefore the claim that this word is a feminine reference to God is without much foundation.

Matthew 13:33 (and Luke 13:20–21). "The kingdom of heaven [Luke: "the kingdom of God"] is like yeast that a woman took and mixed into a large amount of flour until it worked all through the dough."

This parable is an extended simile in which the kingdom of heaven is directly compared to yeast. What the woman represents is not clear; it must be extrapolated. In Matthew it could be God, although it is more likely to be the angels or the Son of Man, who are the agents in other parables in this chapter, whereas God is beyond the picture as the one who sends them. In Luke there simply is nothing that the woman represents, God or anything else. The simile is between the kingdom and the yeast, just as the simile is between the kingdom and the mustard seed in the preceding parable, with no significance given to the man who planted it. It is therefore not very likely that this parable contains feminine imagery for God.[46] Seeing the woman as a figure for God is literally a free association—not impossible, but without support.

John 1:13. "children of God—children born not of natural descent, nor of human decision or a husband's will, but born of God."

46. Mollenkott, *The Divine Feminine*, devotes a whole chapter to "Bakerwoman God."

It is tempting to list this verse as a maternal reference to God by association with the birth metaphor for regeneration by the Holy Spirit in John 3, already considered. However, the Greek term *gennao*, rendered *born* here does not carry gender-specific connotations. It can refer to generation, reproduction, or begetting by either parent. In fact, John 1 mentions a husband, so the explicit gender image is masculine. Since husband implies wife, background maternal nuances cannot be ruled out. But this verse is not an obvious instance of feminine imagery for God.[47]

1 John 4:7b. "Everyone who loves has been born of God and knows God." (*Born of God* also occurs in I John 5: 1, 4, 18.)

The same Greek word is used in these verses as in John 1, so the same point applies. In 1 John 4:7 and 5:4, 11 no human parent is mentioned, so a gender-neutral understanding of *born* as *begotten* is most accurate. In 5:1 a human father and child are mentioned, so if there is parental symbolism in that verse, it is paternal. The association of mother with *born* is not impossible, but has no explicit warrant and is therefore an argument by suggestion.

Mistakenly Claimed Feminine References to God

The texts discussed in the previous section were classified as possible but unlikely feminine references to God because, although there is little evidence supporting them, they could not be completely ruled out. The terms and texts we now consider can virtually be ruled out on standard exegetical grounds.

Genesis 17:1 and all other Old Testament texts in which *Shaddai* or *El Shaddai* occurs as a name of God.

Inclusivists are fond of claiming that *El Shaddai* actually means *Breasted God* or *The God with Breasts*.[48] For if this interpretation were correct, they could point to a feminine name for God that shared the same status as *El* (a basic name for God discussed in chapter 4), thereby identifying a biblical precedent for the practice of giving feminine names to God.

The case for rendering *El Shaddai* as *Breasted God* is usually a simple appeal to the fact that *s'ad* is the Hebrew word for breast. A more sophisticated version is that *El Shaddai* may mean *God of the Mountains*, as in other ancient Near Eastern religions, but that the word for mountains evolved from *shadu*, the Akkadian word for breast, and retained

---

47. Mollenkott, *The Divine Feminine*, 18, enlists John 1 and the verses from 1 John treated next.

48. Phyllis Trible, "God, Nature of, in O.T.," in *Interpreter's Dictionary of the Bible*, Supplemental Volume, 368; Mollenkott, *The Divine Feminine*, 57–59; Smith, *Is It Okay?* 66–69; van Wijk-Bos, *Reimagining God*, 26–28.

these nuances. The evidence that this divine name actually had mammary connotations in the Old Testament is its connection with fertility blessings in Genesis.[49]

Against this line of argument is the fact that both *El Shaddai* and *Shaddai* are always treated as masculine names in the Old Testament.[50] Furthermore, they have been translated as *God Almighty* and *the Almighty* without any feminine connotations by the entire Judeo-Christian theological tradition at least since the Septuagint, the Greek Old Testament produced by Jewish scholars more than two centuries before Christ. Inclusivists counter that the feminine meaning was lost or suppressed. So we examine the evidence.

In the first place, the etymology of *Shaddai* remains unclear. Scholars debate whether it derives from the word for *mountains*, from the word for *plains*, or from the verbal root *sdd*, which means *to destroy* (*Shaddai* occurs in several texts that speak of divine destruction). The origin of the name cannot be established with any certainty. However, no expert on this topic believes that *El Shaddai* was understood as *The Breasted God* by any Old Testament writer.[51] Of those who think that *Shaddai* is associated with mountains, some speculate that the word for *mountain* may have derived from the term for *breast*, sharing the connotation of a mound or peak. But this derivation would have occurred long before the writing of the Old Testament, and any maternal nuances of *Shaddai* would long since have evaporated.[52] *El Shaddai* is a God of unsurpassed power in the Old Testament, *The Almighty*. Even when *Shaddai* occurs without *El*, it is always a linguistically masculine name. In sum, since the word origin of *Shaddai* is only a matter of conjecture and any connection with *breast* is archaic, there is no reason whatsoever to suppose that the accurate translation is *Breasted God*. The traditional case is much stronger.

---

49. David Biale, "The God with Breasts: *El Shaddai* in the Bible," *History of Religions* 20, no. 3 (1982): 240–56, is the most thorough scholarly treatment of this topic. Harriet Lutzky, "Shadday as a Goddess Epithet," *Vetus Testamentus* 48 (1998): 15–36 argues the same position. Thanks to my colleague in Old Testament, Carl Bosma, for the Lutzky article.

50. This claim is documented in chap. 4.

51. Even Biale, who eventually defends *God with Breasts*, agrees with the majority "that the meaning given to Shaddai in the sixth century was of a storm and war god and that this meaning was part and parcel of the image of Yahweh in the exilic and postexilic period." "The God with Breasts," 245.

52. Frank Cross, *Canaanite Myth and Hebrew Epic: Essays in the History of the Religion of Israel* (Cambridge, Mass.: Harvard University Press, 1973), 52–56. Tryggve Mettinger, *In Search of God: The Meaning and Message of the Everlasting Names* (Philadelphia: Fortress, 1988), 69–72. Recall the etymological fallacy, the mistake of determining the meaning of words simply by appeal to their origins.

Hints of a possible connection of meaning are allegedly found in the six fertility blessings of Genesis, where *El Shaddai* promises to greatly increase Abraham, Isaac, and Jacob. But five of these texts make no mention of breasts or anything female. Given the religious-historical context, it is a real stretch to claim that God must be implicitly maternal and breasted in order to make a great nation of the patriarchs. In fact, the father God *El* was considered to be the giver of children.[53] Possible evidence is found in Genesis 49:25 in Jacob's blessing to Joseph: "the Almighty [*Shaddai*] blesses you . . . with the blessings of the breasts [*s'adayim*] and womb." This *Shaddai-breasts* connection is claimed to be direct evidence that this name of God means *The Breasted One*.[54] However, it is more likely a play on words with different meanings, a pun that turns on the similar sound of the words, which in turn may result from a common ancient root.[55] So even if the Genesis 49 connection is correct, there is still no reason to translate this name *The Breasted God*, as though that is the meaning that Jacob had in mind.

Nevertheless, Biale defends his title, "The God with Breasts." Since his article has almost canonical status among inclusivists, it is worth noting what he actually says. He reads Genesis as definitely attributing breastedness to *Shaddai* and goes on to offer a hypothetical reconstruction of how this might have come about, since it is absent from the rest of the Old Testament. Biale admits that he is speculating on the basis of circumstantial evidence. His thesis is such an ingenious product of scholarly imagination, it must be read to be appreciated:

> [T]he Priestly author was concerned to assimilate all of the patriarchal gods, including the Canaanite El, to Yahweh. It would make sense that he would have wanted to give Yahweh the fertility functions of El's consort, Asherah, who was so venerated by the Israelites. Hence, it is possible that, just as El was assimilated to Yahweh, so Asherah was adopted into Priestly Yahwism by a surreptitious sex change: the Canaanite "wet nurse of the gods" was reincarnated as El Shaddai, the God with breasts.[56]

Having presented this startling scenario, which includes a theological sex-change operation, Biale goes on to endorse "androgynous monotheism" and to interpret it as a precursor of the Father-Mother God of the Christian Gnostics in the second century A.D.

---

53. Mettinger, *In Search of God*, 67, notes a Canaanite text in which "El is the one who gives a child to the childless king Keret."
54. Biale, "The God with Breasts," 247–49.
55. Cross, *Canaanite Myth and Hebrew Epic*, 55–56 note 44.
56. Biale, "The God with Breasts," 254. Lutzky also stresses the Asherah connection.

Biale's research is scholarly and his hypothesis is ingenious. But it must be recognized for what it is: wholly speculative. Furthermore, orthodox Jews and Christians will take exception to his baptism of Asherah worship, utterly condemned in the Old Testament, and his promotion of heretical Gnosticism. This article, although frequently invoked as validating *The God with Breasts*, is highly problematic. It deserves to be exposed as a scholarly myth that has acquired canonical status among inclusivists. Given the strong traditional case for *God Almighty*, it is almost surely false.

Hosea 11:1–4. "When Israel was a child, I loved him, and out of Egypt I called my son. . . . It was I who taught Ephraim to walk, taking them by the arms . . . I led them . . . I lifted the yoke from their neck and bent down to feed them."

This text is widely claimed as a maternal image for God. The reason is that the activities it mentions are ways mothers care for their children. As Paul Smith puts it, "These are all tasks that a mother, not a father, performed in the Hebrew society of that day."[57]

Three reasons jointly imply that this reading is almost certainly wrong. First, the argument for it is not based on any explicit textual evidence, but only on an assumption about gender roles in ancient Israel. Even if these activities were usually mothers' work, however, there is historical and biblical evidence that fathers sometimes participated, as in Luke 11:12, where Jesus asks fathers if they feed their children snakes instead of fish. Smith's argument amounts to gender-role stereotyping read back into the text: mothers always, fathers never.

Second, the major image throughout Hosea is of God as husband and father.[58] Hosea marries a prostitute and fathers children in order to illustrate God's relation to Israel. Unless there are explicit indications to the contrary, standard exegesis requires that the parental imagery of Hosea 11 be read as a continuation of the basic theme of the book as a whole. There is nothing except gender stereotyping that stands in the way of the natural reading of God as father.

Finally, there is clear textual evidence that the imagery is paternal. *Out of Egypt I called my son* recalls Exodus 4:22–23, where God identifies Israel as his son in warning Pharaoh: either release my son, or I will kill your son. This text strongly implies, although it does not explicitly state, that God is the father of Israel as Pharaoh is the father of his son

---

57. Smith, *Is It Okay?* 68; see also Mollenkott, *The Divine Feminine*, 27; van Wijk-Bos, *Reimagining God*, 60; and many others.

58. An excellent treatment of Hosea focused on the metaphorical nature of biblical language for God is Nelly Stienstra, *YHWH Is the Husband of His People* (Kampen: Kok Pharos, 1993).

and his people.[59] In addition, God's parental care for Ephraim is paralleled in Jeremiah 31:9, where he is explicitly said to be a father: *I am a father to Israel and Ephraim is my firstborn.* The only sound exegetical conclusion is that God is represented as a father in Hosea 11, not as a generic parent, and surely not as a mother. This text is falsely enlisted by inclusivists.

Acts 17:28. "'For in him we live and move and have our being.' As some of your own poets have said, 'We are his offspring.'"

This passage is widely understood as containing womb and birth imagery.[60] In fact, it is taken as suggesting that we live in the divine womb, in *the Primal Matrix*, even after we are born.

In the absence of any clear textual evidence to the contrary, this expression could be interpreted as a womb-birth image for God. It does speak of *offspring*; and *in him we live and move and have our being* can be taken as suggesting a baby in its mother's womb. This interpretation would be speculation, however, for there is nothing in the text that requires it.

But in fact there is definitive textual evidence, and once again it indicates a masculine reference. Most good commentaries on Acts identify the poems from which Paul is quoting. The line about living and being in God is from Epimenides the Cretan and the allusion to offspring is from Aratus. Both poems are about Zeus. In the first he is ruler of the mythical Greek pantheon and in the second he is probably the Supreme Being of Greek philosophy.[61] So if Paul intends gender imagery for God at all, it is masculine, not feminine. But most likely the language implies divine omnipresence and complete human dependence on God, not divine gender. In either case, inclusivists are mistaken to claim it as a feminine reference to God.

Conclusion

This chapter has examined the alleged feminine references to God in the Bible, since they are a major premise in the argument from Scripture to inclusive language for God. Our analysis aimed both at validating these references and at classifying them according to their linguistic type.

There surely are a number of texts of Scripture that refer to and represent God with feminine language. This result may come as a surprise

---

59. This claim is defended in chap. 4.

60. Johnson, *She Who Is*, 134; Mollenkott, *The Divine Feminine*, 15–16; Smith, *Is It Okay?* 57.

61. F. F. Bruce, *The Book of Acts* (Grand Rapids: Eerdmans, 1977), 359–60. See also *"pater,"* in *Theological Dictionary of the New Testament*, ed. G. Kittel, trans. G. Bromiley (Grand Rapids: Eerdmans, 1967), 5:952–53, "Zeus the Father and Ruler."

to many traditional Christians who almost instinctively react negatively to the idea of feminine language for God. Since Scripture itself speaks of God with feminine imagery, it is surely permissible for Christians to do so. But this conclusion does not automatically validate inclusive language for God.

The number of genuine feminine references to God turns out to be significantly smaller than is often claimed. Reading the original languages according to standard exegetical methods, we have identified about twenty texts that quite surely contain feminine references[62] and another half dozen or so for which a reasonable but debatable case can be made.[63] However, a number of other examples regularly invoked by inclusivists are judged unlikely because a tenable case cannot be made.[64] And some claims are almost surely mistaken.[65]

Linguistically, all the clear and plausible instances of feminine reference to God are imagery or figures of speech: similes, analogies, metaphors, and personification. Excluding the unlikely reading of *Spirit* in the Old Testament as a feminine personal reference to God, there are no cases in which feminine terms are used as names, titles, or invocations of God, and thus there are no feminine pronouns for God. There are no instances where God is directly identified by a feminine term, even a metaphorical predicate noun. In other words, God is never directly said to be a mother, mistress, or female bird in the way he is said to be a father, king, judge, or shepherd.

In fact, there is a noticeable indirectness in many of the feminine references to God. All the metaphors are verbs, not predicate nouns. They do not identify God as such but image some of his actions as birthing wisdom, the world, and his people, and as mothering his people. Many of these metaphors are indirect, implied by rhetorical questions or parallelisms but not directly asserted of God. The similes and analogies are even more limited and indirect. Since their linguistic structure compares specific features of different things, they never even appear to identify God with a female role, much less with a female person. Additional indirectness is reflected by the fact that many of the feminine

62. In biblical order: Num. 11:12; Deut. 32:18; Job 38:8, 29; Pss. 90:2; 123:2; 131:2; Prov. 8:1, 22–25; Isa. 31:5; 42:14; 45:10; 49:15; 66:13; Hos. 13:8; Matt. 23:37 (of Jesus in distinction from God); Luke 13:34; 15:8–10; John 3:3–8; and 1 Peter 2:2–3.

63. Maternal hovering or wings in Gen. 1:2; Ruth 2:12; Ps. 17:8; and Ps. 91:4; maternal or midwife imagery in Ps. 22:9–10; Isa. 46:3; and Isa. 66:7–9.

64. *Spirit* as a feminine personal term for God in the Old Testament; the eagle of Deut. 32:10–11, Exod. 19:4, and elsewhere; human *compassion* as *mother-love* in the Old Testament, God as a bakerwoman in Matt. 13 and Luke 13; and *born of God* in John 1 and 1 John 4 and 5.

65. *El Shaddai* throughout the Old Testament; Hos. 11:1–4; and Acts 17:28.

similes are not explicitly stated but implied by questions, parallelism, or context. Scripture is very cautious and reserved in its use of feminine imagery to illustrate God's attitudes and actions.

A third observation regards the distribution of the feminine images for God throughout Scripture. They are greater in number and directness in the Old Testament than in the New Testament. In other words, as the Bible progressively reveals God as Father, Son, and Holy Spirit and Jesus as the Messiah, the Son of God, the feminine imagery for God does not increase but recedes into the background.[66]

The Bible uses feminine language for God, but does so only infrequently and figuratively. Whether this practice provides an adequate basis for gender-inclusive language cannot be determined until we compare it to Scripture's masculine language for God.

66. This is also true of *Spirit* (*ruah*), even if it is a feminine noun for God. In the Greek translation of the Old Testament and in the New Testament it is no longer grammatically feminine.

4

The Bible's Masculine Language for God

Chapter 3 examined Scripture's feminine references to God to determine their number and linguistic structure. This chapter undertakes a similar analysis of the Bible's masculine language for God. The point of these studies is eventually to evaluate arguments that Scripture provides justification for inclusive language for God.

For as we saw in chapter 2, many inclusivists do argue that in principle the Bible itself supports their position by its use of masculine, feminine, and gender-neutral language for God. They claim that the difference between Scripture and fully inclusive language is largely a matter of quantity. Whereas the Bible's masculine references to God vastly outnumber the others, all that is required to make our language inclusive, they argue, is to balance the frequency of their use, employing masculine, feminine, and neuter terminology in equitable proportions.

Most of these advocates are aware of the linguistic distinctions among images, titles, and names, but do not think that these differences are impediments to inclusive language. Masculine titles and names are just metaphors, they say. And feminine figures of speech count as names for God. Recall, for example, Johanna van Wijk-Bos's approach in *Reimagining God: The Case for Scriptural Diversity*: "I am concerned here with exploring biblical images for God—in names, titles, and designations—that offer alternatives to exclusively male imagery."[1]

Arguments of this sort cannot be evaluated until we are as clear about the quantity and linguistic structures of the Bible's masculine references to God as we are about its feminine references—the purpose of this chapter.

---

1. Van Wijk-Bos, *Reimagining God*, ix.

Given the massive amount of masculine language for God in Scripture, it is impossible to consider every instance. Instead we examine the various kinds of masculine references, classified according to the linguistic structures they represent, indicating the frequency with which they occur, and providing illustrative examples of each. The chapter has three main divisions. The first treats masculine figures of speech—similes and metaphors—some of which parallel Scripture's feminine references to God. The second and most extensive section examines the masculine names, titles, and common nouns that identify God. The third division explores how the masculine grammatical forms of the Hebrew and Greek languages anthropomorphically imply personal gender of God.[2]

Perhaps a hint of the outcome will provide helpful orientation: Although the original languages of the Bible never speak of God as a sexual being, they almost always speak as though he is a masculine person. In other words, the gender language of Scripture applies to God the same ways that it applies to Moses, David, and Jesus. Without qualification, therefore, the linguistic structure of Scripture's presentation of God would lead toward the conclusion that God is a masculine person. What lead away from that conclusion are the analogical-metaphorical nature of language for God and the biblical-theological affirmation that God is neither male nor female, discussed in chapter 7. In anticipation of those discussions we are careful in this chapter to claim that Scripture speaks of God *as though* he is masculine or as *anthropomorphically* masculine. Furthermore, in speaking of gender for God we use the term *masculine*, which refers to a personal characteristic, but never *male*, which has biological-sexual meaning.[3]

Figures of Speech

A number of Scripture's masculine references to God are figures of speech—similes and metaphors. Some of them are the same kinds as the feminine references to God. In fact, a few even occur in parallel with feminine figures of speech. Examples of parallels are found in Isaiah 42:13–14, where the Lord is "like a mighty man" and "like a woman in

2. I am indebted to Al Wolters for helpful insights on the linguistic analysis of the biblical languages and William Vande Kopple for suggestions about appropriate linguistic categories and their applications.

3. It is common among contemporary academics to distinguish between *sex* and *gender*. Sex—male and female—is usually regarded as biological and reproductive, whereas gender—masculine and feminine—is more psychological, social, and cultural, that is, the set of personality characteristics and styles of expression typically associated with human persons who are biologically male and female. Given this distinction, it is possible to speak (analogically) of God as a masculine person even though he is not male, since he does not have a body.

childbirth," and in Job 38:28–29, where God fathers the drops of dew and gives birth to the frost. These examples are evidence that some masculine and feminine references to God are linguistically equivalent.

Masculine similes[4] are found throughout Scripture. "As a father has compassion on his children, so the LORD has compassion on those who fear him," Psalm 103:13 assures us. Isaiah 42:13 prophesies that "the LORD will march out like a mighty man, like a warrior he will stir up his zeal." Interestingly, in Jeremiah 14:9 we find God compared to the same male figures as in Isaiah 42 but with virtually opposite meaning: "Why are you like a man taken by surprise, like a warrior powerless to save?" In all these similes, God is explicitly compared to human males in order to highlight features of his attitudes, actions, and even his inaction toward his people. However, God is not thereby identified as a male being, and masculinity is not the point of these similes any more than femininity is the point of the feminine similes.

Masculine metaphors[5] also occur in Scripture. Some of them attribute male functions to God parallel to how feminine metaphors predicate female functions of him. Consider the paired procreative imagery in Deuteronomy 32:18: God is the Rock who both fathered and gave birth to Israel. Job 38:28–29 likewise juxtaposes fathering and birthing as parallel metaphors for God's creative activity. An exclusively masculine example is found in Psalm 99:1, where God as King (4) "sits enthroned between the cherubim." The Bible contains a number of metaphors that use verbs and predicate adjectives to attribute paternal and other masculine actions and attitudes to God. Though far fewer in number, there are also feminine metaphors of this kind.

A difference between the Bible's masculine and feminine language for God begins to emerge when we consider metaphors that linguistically identify God himself and do not merely describe an attitude, attribute, or activity. The Bible never uses a predicate noun to assert figuratively or nonfiguratively that God is a woman, mother, midwife, female ruler, or any other female person. However, Scripture is full of assertions that God is a king, ruler, creator, maker, father, husband, judge, redeemer, savior, shepherd, and other masculine figures.[6] Some of these designations, such as God the King, are so frequent, basic, and significant that they actually have the status of standard titles, as indi-

---

4. Recall that similes explicitly compare two different things, using *like* or *as*. See Harmon and Holman, *A Handbook to Literature*, 483.

5. Recall that a metaphor figuratively identifies one thing with another thing or with an attribute or activity of another thing. See Harmon and Holman, *A Handbook to Literature*, 315–16. Examples: life is a bowl of cherries; an explosive idea. Metaphor has the linguistic structure of literal predication, but not a literal meaning.

6. A more complete list is found in Bavinck, *The Doctrine of God*, 86–88.

cated below. Others are relatively unusual, for example, God as a potter (Isa. 64:8), a builder (Heb. 11:10), and a gardener (John 15:1), and probably function as typical metaphors. The point of comparison of these metaphors is not gender but the kind of authority, action, function, or relationship portrayed. Nevertheless, there are no counterparts in the Bible that figuratively identify God as a female person.

The claim that these identifications of God are masculine requires further explanation. It is obvious in English that terms like *father, husband,* and *king* indicate male persons. Such words are gender-specific or gender-marked. However, words like *shepherd, ruler, teacher, judge,* and *savior* are not gender-specific in English. Teachers, rulers, and judges may be male or female. These terms are gender-neutral, not indicating the sex of the person. In biblical Hebrew and Greek, however, almost all words that refer to human persons, vocations, positions, and functions are explicitly gender-marked. One way gender is indicated is by means of distinct terms for male and female persons in parallel positions, as in the English cases of *father* and *mother, king* and *queen,* or *nephew* and *niece.* But gender is also indicated by grammatically masculine and feminine endings on a common word-root. English examples are *actor* and *actress, steward* and *stewardess,* or *waiter* and *waitress.* In the Hebrew and Greek Bible words like *judge, savior, teacher, redeemer, maker, creator,* and *potter,* which are gender-neutral in English, are all gender-specific.[7] And all such words used as predicate nouns that figuratively identify God with a human position or vocation are masculine. This is a clear and exceptionless pattern that is significantly more pronounced in the original languages of Scripture than in English translations.

Nonfigurative Designations of God[8]

Appellatives, Titles, Names

Thus far in considering gendered language for God we have been dealing with figures of speech, such as similes and metaphors. The

7. In Hebrew there are occasional apparent exceptions, like *qoheleth, teacher,* which is feminine in form. However, these words function as masculine nouns when referring to males in that they take masculine verbs, pronouns, and adjectives. See Bruce Waltke and M. O'Connor, *An Introduction to Biblical Hebrew Syntax* (Winona Lake, Ind.: Eisenbrauns, 1990), 109.

8. In chap. 7 we discuss the fact that, whereas all language for God is analogical (and in that sense "metaphorical"), not all linguistic references to God are figures of speech. This issue is much-confused in discussions of inclusive language for God. In this section we consider references to God that are nonfigurative in the sense that linguistically they are not figures of speech.

Bible also identifies God by common nouns, titles, and names which, although they may contain figurative elements, are not linguistically classified as figures of speech. The Explanations and illustrations of these linguistic categories are necessary before considering the biblical references to God.

Figures of speech are illustrative or comparative. They are not intended and do not function to identify or classify things in the literal or primary meaning of the language. If my students say of me that I am *as mean as a junkyard dog* or that I am *a real bear*, they are attempting to assert something descriptive about my demeanor and temperament, but they do not wish to be understood literally. They do not mean that I am a canine or that I belong to a species of animals that hibernate in the winter.

However, if my students say that I am a *teacher*, a common noun, or refer to me by the title *Professor*, or call me by the name *John*, they are identifying who I am in nonfigurative language. Consider each of these categories.

Classifying me as *a teacher* identifies me as a member of a group of people who have a specific vocation. The students are using an *appellative* (designation by a common noun). This identification has the same formal structure as when they call me *a bear*, but they do not mean it figuratively.[9] Calling me *a teacher* refers to me with a term that links me directly and literally with all other persons who are teachers. It implicitly attributes to me everything characteristic of being a teacher. Identifying me in this way is different than saying *life is a teacher*, a metaphor that is comparative, figurative, and limited in meaning.

If my students call me *Professor*, they now identify me by a *title*. Labeling me *a teacher* is using a general appellative or common noun to identify me with a group of people. But calling me *Professor* refers to me as an individual. There are lots of teachers who are professors, but *Professor* indicates a particular position I have at Calvin Seminary and thus points to me in distinction from all others. Titles are words or phrases that designate specific persons in terms of their positions, vocations, or relationships and which therefore have special status as terms of identification, reference, and address. Examples are *Mother*, *Uncle*, *Captain*, *Pastor*, and *Queen*. Descriptions, called *epithets*, can also be titles, such as (William) *the Conqueror* and (Peter) *the Great*. Some titles are used as regular and primary terms of personal identification, as *Queen* in reference to Elizabeth. Others, such as her title *De-*

---

9. The possibility that some predicate nouns identifying God are figures of speech and some are more literal (although analogical in the sense that all language for God is analogical) is considered in chaps. 5 and 7.

fender of the Faith, are used infrequently and secondarily, and therefore function less readily as widely understood means of identification.

My students may also refer to me as *John Cooper*. Here they use my *proper name*. There are other John Coopers in the telephone book. But my name picks me out from all other people because it refers to me as a unique individual. That is the job of a name. It may have other meanings and functions as well. John means *God is gracious*; Cooper means *barrelmaker*. Names may even have figurative or metaphorical meanings: *Snow White, Sitting Bull,* and Richard *Lionheart* (a description that became a title and then a surname). But what makes these words names is their role as basic terms of reference and address whose primary function is identifying a particular person in distinction from all others.

In what follows we consider the masculine terms for God found in the Hebrew and the Greek Bible as they appear in our English translations and analyze them according to the linguistic categories of names, titles, and appellatives.

God

EL AND ELOHIM

According to the *Theological Dictionary of the Old Testament,* "The OT uses three different words for 'God,' viz. *'el, 'eloah,* and *'elohim.* In general these words are interchangeable."[10] Each of them is used as a name, as part of various divine titles, and as a general appellative or common noun.

The word *el* is a common noun for a god or supernatural being in various ancient Semitic languages, including Hebrew.[11] But *El* is also the name of the high God, the head of the Canaanite pantheon. In fact, *El* is the name by which God revealed himself to the patriarchs before Moses (Exod. 6:3). The altar of Jacob at Shechem is called "El is the God of Israel" in Genesis 33:20. As a proper name it sometimes stands on its own, most often in the book of Job and in the Psalms. It also functions as a title (like *King*) designating the one true God: "my God and my King" (Ps. 68:24).

Most regularly, however, the term occurs in combination with descriptive terms (epithets) that connote God's greatness: *El Shaddai (God Almighty), El Elyon (God Most High), El Olam (Everlasting God),* and

10. Helmer Ringgren, *"'elohim,"* in *Theological Dictionary of the Old Testament,* ed. H. J. Botterweck and H. Ringgren, trans. John Willis (Grand Rapids: Eerdmans, 1974), 1:267–84, 272.

11. Frank Cross, *"'el,"* *TDOT,* 1:242–261; "God, Names of," *International Standard Bible Encyclopedia* (Grand Rapids: Eerdmans, 1982), 2: 504–509; Mettinger, *In Search of God,* 65–68; Werner Schmidt, *The Faith of the Old Testament,* trans. John Sturdy (Philadelphia: Westminster, 1988), 15–20.

others. Theoretically these combinations could be understood as a general appellative with the name of a deity: *the god Shaddai, the god Elyon.* In the actual usage of the Old Testament and other ancient semitic texts, however, it is likely that most of these cases use *El* as a divine title with an epithet (*the Almighty God, the Most High God, the Everlasting God*) or as the name *El* with an epithet title (*El the Almighty, El the Most High, El the Everlasting*).[12] In sum, the word *El* is used as an appellative, a divine title, and a name.

There is no doubt that the term *El* has masculine connotations. In ancient Semitic religion El is the universal father God who has female consorts and fathers the other gods, including Baal. The biblical authors retained the linguistic masculinity of El even though they believed that the true God transcends sexuality and procreation. Consequently, the gender roles appellatively attributed to El in the Old Testament are all masculine. He is a king, father, warrior, shepherd, and judge. Grammatically, *el* is masculine in gender and invariably takes masculine verb, adjective, and pronoun forms. As a generic plural term, *gods*, it can include female deities. When it is a title and a proper name, however, it functions grammatically exactly as it would if it were a title or name of a human male.[13] The point here is not that the God of Israel was thought to be male but that the original language bears unmistakable connotations of personal masculinity.

Elohim is the most common word for *God* in the Old Testament, occurring over 2,500 times.[14] It is plural in form. As a common noun or appellative it can refer to the gods of the nations (Exod. 20:3; Josh. 24:16; Jer. 5:7) and even to angels or superhuman beings (Pss. 8:5; 82:1). But these uses are exceptional compared to the hundreds of instances in which, though plural in form, it functions as a singular noun meaning *God.* "In the beginning God created the heavens and the earth" (Gen. 1:1). Here it is a proper noun referring to the true God. When it stands alone and functions this way, *Elohim* looks very much like a name for God.[15] It simply identifies him.

However, *Elohim* also frequently functions as a title for the only true God. This is evident when it is used as a designation of who Yahweh is: "I am the Lord your *God* . . . have no other *gods* before me" (Exod. 20:2–

---

12. Cross, "*el*," 256; Mettinger, *In Search of God*, 65, labels them "special proper names."

13. We postpone until chaps. 7 and 8 our discussion of the meaning of masculine language for God and whether it actually attributes gender to God.

14. "Elohim," in *International Standard Bible Encyclopedia*, 5 vols. (Chicago: Howard-Severance, 1930), 2:505–6; Ringgren, "*'elohim*," *TDOT*, 1:267–84.

15. T. E. McComisky, "God, Names of," in *Evangelical Dictionary of Theology*, ed. W. Elwell (Grand Rapids: Baker, 1984), 467.

3); "the LORD, your *God* is *God* of *gods* and Lord of lords" (Deut. 10:17). In these texts *God* (*elohim/elohe*) indicates the status of Yahweh as compared to other pretenders to his position. Thus it seems to function as a title of Yahweh rather than as another name for him. This function is even more apparent when the expression *my God* is considered as parallel to other titles, for example, *my Lord and my God.* This expression indicates God's status or relationship to the speaker. Thus *Elohim* is a frequent Old Testament word that functions as a basic name and definitive title for the true God, in addition to being a common noun.

There is no question that *Elohim* is a masculine term. It is grammatically masculine in form. It always takes masculine verbs, adjectives, and pronouns, whether it functions as a generic plural term (*gods*) or as a singular proper noun for God. In its generic plural use it is not exclusively masculine in meaning, for in one text its reference includes a female god, Asherah (1 Kings 11:5, 33). Among *the gods of the nations* are goddesses. Here it functions as a generic masculine term used for both sexes, as the English word *men* was used until recently to mean *human beings.* However, the singular use of *Elohim* as a name and title for God, like *El,* has masculine meaning as well as grammatical form. Without exception, in hundreds and hundreds of cases it functions as a title-name for a masculine person, and the only gendered appellatives (king, father, husband, warrior, etc.) it takes are masculine. Linguistically the infrequent gender-inclusive meaning of the generic plural *elohim* cannot be read into *Elohim* as a proper noun for God in order to make it an inclusive term.[16]

THEOS[17]

Theos is the word for *God* used in the Septuagint, the Greek translation of the Old Testament, to render *El, Elohim,* and their variations. The New Testament follows this practice, using the term hundreds of times. *Theos* is infrequently used as a generic appellative for false gods (Acts 14:11; 17:23). But it is almost always a proper noun for the true God. Occasionally it occurs with a definite article, *ho theos,* and is used as a definite appellative, as when Paul addresses the Athenian philosophers in Acts 17:24: "The God who made the world and everything in it." But often it is a title-name referring to the Deity as *Theos, God.* Used this way, it occurs both with and without the definite article, "with no

---

16. I do not deal separately with *'eloah,* which is either the singular form of *'elohim* or is derived from *'elohim.* Its linguistic functions are the same. Smith, *Is It Okay to Call God "Mother"?* 55, identifies *Eloah* as "an ancient Semitic female god." I was unable to find any scholarly corroboration of this claim in Smith or any other work on Old Testament terms for God.

17. *"Theos,"* in *Theological Dictionary of the New Testament,* ed. Gerhard Kittel, trans. G. Bromiley (Grand Rapids: Eerdmans, 1965), 3:65–119.

discernable distinction."[18] To illustrate, when the self-righteous Phari-see prays in Luke 18:11, he addresses God as *ho theos*. This is properly translated as *God* or *O God*, but not as *The God*. *Theos* is also used to retain Old Testament compound titles, such as *the Lord God Almighty* (Rev. 4:8). In sum, *theos* generally has the same meaning and linguistic functions as *El* and *Elohim*.

Theos also preserves the masculinity of *El* and *Elohim*. The Greek language has three grammatical genders: masculine, feminine, and neuter. *Theos* is masculine, having the masculine form of the article, *ho*, and the masculine ending *-os*. It invariably takes masculine pronouns and adjectives. *Theos* is also masculine in meaning. Admittedly its plu-ral form is a masculine term that can be used generically to include fe-male deities, as the English word *men* until recently could include women. But this gender-inclusiveness does not carry back to the singu-lar. For Greek distinguishes *god* and *goddess*. In Acts 19:27 the word for the goddess Artemis is *he thea*, a feminine counterpart of *theos* with a feminine article. In Acts 19:37 she is *he theos*, the masculine form of the noun with the feminine article. Thus New Testament Greek has the ca-pacity to be gender-inclusive with respect to *God*, but it never avails it-self of the opportunity. In hundreds of instances without exception, the word *God* is masculine in grammatical form and in meaning. It is the word that is used for *Zeus* but not for *Artemis*. The claim that God's na-ture is genderless is a legitimate theological inference from the Bible as a whole, but not from a linguistic analysis of *theos*.

LORD, Lord

Y AHWEH[19]

Yahweh is the special proper name of God revealed to Moses in Exo-dus 3:15: "God also said to Moses, 'Say to the Israelites, '*Yahweh*, the God of your fathers—the God of Abraham, Isaac and Jacob—appeared to me.'"" And again in Exodus 6:2–3: "I am *Yahweh*. I appeared to Abra-ham, to Isaac and to Jacob as God Almighty [*El Shaddai*], but by my name *Yahweh* I did not make myself known to them." God himself iden-tifies *Yahweh* as his name. It is used almost seven thousand times in the Old Testament and never has any other linguistic status than a proper name. It is often combined with other divine names and titles, as in *Yahweh elohenu*, *The Lord our God*.

---

18. Ibid., 92.

19. Mettinger, "The God Who Says 'I AM': The Riddle of the Name YHWH," *In Search of God*, 14–49; G. H. Parke-Taylor, *Yahweh: The Divine Name in the Bible* (Waterloo, Ont.: Wilfred Laurier University Press, 1975). Walter Brueggemann, *Theology of the Old Testa-ment* (Minneapolis: Fortress, 1997), chaps. 4–7.

With respect to its meaning, scholars have ranged from *I Am What I Am* as God's disclosure of his Absolute Being to *I Will Be What I Will Be*, which emphasizes God's dynamic, historical, and future-oriented involvement with his people. Whatever its nuances, most scholars agree that this name denotes the everlasting God's covenantal faithfulness toward his people and not primarily his ontological immutability.

More important for our purposes is the linguistic analysis of *Yahweh*. Scholars are generally agreed that the tetragrammaton *YHWH* is derived from or in some other way is related to an archaic form of the verb *haya*, to be. They disagree about the precise analysis, whether it is a participle or verb form, whether it is assertive (*Who Is*) or causative (*Who Causes to Be*), and whether it is combined with other words (*ya* as a word for God or *hu* as a pronoun).[20]

But what about *Yahweh*'s gender? Most scholars conclude in one way or another that the name is masculine. If it contains the pronoun *hu*, it is masculine because that it is the third masculine singular pronoun, *he*. If it is a participle, it is masculine in form. And if it is a form of the verb *to be*, it is third masculine singular—*He Who Is* or *He Who Will Be*. In the words of Mettinger, "The Hebrew divine name *YHWH* is to be understood as a form of the verb *haya*, 'to be.' More precisely, we have a form of the main stem of this verb; it means 'He Is.'"[21] In other words, God introduces himself in first-person language, *I Am*, which is not gender-specific in Hebrew. But *Yahweh*, the proper name he gives his people by which to address and refer to him, is the third-person masculine form of *I Am: He Is*.

This is the most personal, intimate and frequently used term for God in the Old Testament. It is his special personal name. Although there is not absolute consensus among scholars about the masculine linguistic form of *Yahweh*, this conclusion is widely accepted. There is no plausible alternative. We can speculate about why God chose this masculine name, whether the Israelites "heard" its masculinity when they spoke it, and whether they somehow attributed or denied masculinity to the divine nature in their theological reflections.[22] But it is difficult to deny that the name *Yahweh* has masculine meaning.

---

20. Parke-Taylor, *Yahweh*, 46–62, provides a detailed survey of these debates.

21. Mettinger, *In Search of God*, 36; also Barry Bandstra, *Reading the Old Testament: An Introduction to the Hebrew Bible* (Belmont, Calif.: Wadsworth, 1995), 120: "When the first-person verbal form *ehyeh* is transformed into the third-person form it becomes *yahweh*, which can be translated as 'he is.'"

22. Erhard Gerstenberger, *Yahweh the Patriarch: Ancient Images of God and Feminist Theology*, trans. Frederick Gaiser (Minneapolis: Fortress, 1996), 6, claims: "For the orthodox believers represented by . . . Third Isaiah, Yahweh was incontrovertibly a single, male deity."

For this reason the attempt of Elizabeth Johnson to render *Yahweh* as *She Who Is* founders badly.[23] Her analysis begins with the Hebrew *ehyeh asher ehyeh* in Exodus but leaves it prematurely for Thomas Aquinas's treatment of the Latin rendering of *Yahweh*: *Qui est*. In Latin *Deus*, the masculine word for God, is the antecedent of *Qui* (*who*), and thus *Qui est* is properly translated *He Who Is*. But Johnson points out that *qui est* by itself is not gender-marked and could also be translated as *the one who is* or *she who is*. She goes on to make a liberation-theological case for the feminine rendering. The fatal flaw in her argument is her failure to notice that the Hebrew name, unlike the Latin, is explicitly masculine. *Yahweh* is certainly not *She Who Is*.[24]

Something intriguing happens as we move toward the New Testament. The special proper name *Yahweh* is translated by the title *Lord*, the Greek word *kurios*. This shift began with the Septuagint, the Greek translation of the Old Testament made by Jews after the Old Testament era ended. The standard explanation is that Judaism was becoming hesitant even to utter the divine name for fear of violating its holiness. So faithful Jews substituted the Hebrew term *Adonai, My Lord*, for *Yahweh*. This word was translated straightforwardly into Greek as *kurios*, a masculine noun meaning *lord*.[25]

ADONAI

Adon is a Hebrew title and term of respectful address which also refers to human lords and masters. It is a masculine term. Its most common use in the Old Testament is as a title for God, *Adonai, my Lord*, and occurs most frequently as a form of address to God. It can stand alone, as in Psalm 62:12: "you, O Lord, are loving." But more often it is combined with *Yahweh* into *Adonai Yahweh*, as in Genesis 15:2, where Abram addresses God by this name-title.

KURIOS

Because *Adonai* came to be substituted for *Yahweh* in Judaism, and because *kurios* is the Greek translation of *adon*, the Septuagint translates both terms as *kurios*.[26] The New Testament, which follows this pattern, never uses *Yahweh* but regularly refers to God as *Kurios*. Thus *Kurios* continues to have the meaning that both *Yahweh* and *Adonai* had as Old Testament words for God.

23. Johnson, *She Who Is*, 241–45.
24. Johnson is virtually alone in making this point. Thus we did not consider it in chap. 3 with *El Shaddai* and other mistakenly claimed feminine references to God.
25. Parke-Taylor, *Yahweh*, 100.
26. It is interesting to note that some English translations follow this practice. The NIV distinguishes them by translating *Yahweh* as LORD and *Adonai* as Lord. The RSV translates *adonai Yahweh* as *the Lord GOD* and *Yahweh Elohim* as *the LORD God*.

This is especially significant because the New Testament uses *Kurios* more frequently to refer to Jesus than to God as such. This practice is a major indication that the New Testament presents Jesus as God. For example, Philippians 2:6–11 hymns his humiliation and exaltation, climaxing with the proclamation that "Jesus Christ is Lord, to the glory of God the Father." Jesus is *Lord*, the title-name that belongs originally to God the Father. *Kurios* is rarely if ever used as a general appellative, as in "Jesus is a lord." Rather, he is *the Lord of lords* (Rev. 17:14, 19:16). *Lord* is such a basic term for God that some scholars consider it "almost like a personal name" in texts where it occurs as a proper noun without the article.[27] This makes sense if *Kurios* has the same status as *Yahweh* in the Old Testament. However, it is also possible that *Kurios* is a nonequivalent substitution and that the New Testament, following the Septuagint, leaves *Yahweh* behind as the unexpressed Name of God. This issue is discussed further below. In any case, *Lord* generally has the same linguistic status and function as *God*, whatever their differences in nuance. *Lord, Father,* and *God* are the basic terms of reference and address to the Deity in the New Testament.

The Greek term *kurios* preserves the grammatical masculinity of *Yahweh* and *Adonai*. This is clear both from the definite article *ho* and the suffix *-os*. The corresponding feminine term is *he kuria, the lady* or *the mistress*.[28] The possibility of gender-equivalance for God as *Kurios* is thus available to the Greek New Testament, but it absolutely never occurs.

In conclusion, the biblical words for *God* exhibit an overwhelmingly consistent pattern. All function mainly as basic titles and names and all are masculine in linguistic form and meaning.

Other Titles and Appellatives

King: The Basic Title

Lord is directly associated with the divine title *King*. In the New Testament Jesus Christ is *King of kings and Lord of lords* (Rev. 17, 19) and *King of the Jews* (Luke 23:3, 37, 38). Jesus is *King* because he is the Messiah, the promised son of David who is to rule God's kingdom forever (2 Sam. 7:12–16). David and his messianic son are kings because they are sons of God, who himself is King. "Who is he, this King of glory? The LORD Almighty—he is the King of glory" (Ps. 24:10). Quickly skimming the Psalms and prophets reveals how frequently and definitively the Old Testament speaks of *Yahweh* and *Elohim* as

27. Bauer, Arndt, and Gingrich, *Lexicon*, 460.
28. Ibid., 459.

King.[29] "The Lord, the King" writes the Psalmist (Ps. 98:6). "I will exalt you, my God the King" (Ps. 145:1). Isaiah is troubled, for he says "my eyes have seen the King, the Lord Almighty" (6:5).

So basic and pervasive is the notion of God as King that many scholars consider it the definitive idea in the Old Testament. Mettinger identifies it as the "root metaphor" for God.[30] A root metaphor is "a basic analogy or model; it is used to describe the nature of the world. It is a way of seeing 'all that is' through a specific key concept." God's Kingship is manifest, for example, in the central Old Testament themes of creation, the Exodus, the messianic kingdom, and God's universal rule. As King of creation God creates heaven and earth by commanding and judging from his heavenly throne. In the Exodus the Lord is a greater King than Pharaoh, whose armies he defeats and whose royal son he kills. He is King of Israel, whose earthly throne is in the temple in Jerusalem, the capital of his earthly kingdom, ruled by his messianic son, David. And the Lord is the King of the kings of all the earth, whose kingdom is even greater than that of Nebuchadnezzar and his imperial successors (Dan. 2). Practically all the great themes of the Old Testament elaborate the kingship of God.

Linguistically, *King* functions as a term for God exactly the same ways that it does for human kings. Nowhere is this clearer than in the appointment of Saul as king of Israel. Samuel admonishes the people afterwards: "you said to me, 'No, we want a king to rule over us'—even though the Lord your God was your king" (1 Sam 12:12). *King* is not just a metaphor or even a general appellative, but the basic title that defines who God is in relation to all creation and especially to his people, the citizens of his earthly kingdom. As such it also functions as a term by which God is regularly addressed: "O Lord Almighty, my King and my God" (Ps. 84:3). The Greek word *basileus* continues the Old Testament uses into the New Testament, extending them to Jesus Christ as well.

The fact that *king* is masculine needs little comment. Both Hebrew and Greek have feminine forms of the same word-root to indicate *queen*. But they are never used of God.

Related Titles and Appellatives

The idea of God as King is basic to many other biblical designations of God. According to Mettinger, "A root metaphor feeds a whole family of extended metaphors; it comprises the genetic code for a broad com-

---

29. Mettinger, *In Search of God*, 116–17, lists many occurrences.

30. Ibid., 92; and chaps. 6 and 7, "'The Lord as 'King': The Battling Deity" and "'The Lord of Hosts':The Regnant God." See also Marc Z. Brettler, *God Is King: Understanding an Israelite Metaphor* (Sheffield, England: Journal of the Study of the Old Testament, 1989).

plex of ideas. . . . The kingship of the Lord, then, provides an organizational matrix for a whole cosmos of ideas. This understanding of God lies beneath the surface of numerous texts, even of some that do not use 'king,' 'to rule,' 'throne,' and so forth."[31]

Thus many of the other titles, appellations, and descriptions of God in the Old Testament are related to divine kingship as understood in the ancient Near East. Because God is King he is also *Judge* of the nations (Gen. 18:25). He is the *warrior* who defends his people and defeats his enemies (Exod. 15:3). He is therefore *Yahweh sabaoth, Lord of Hosts* (the armies of heaven and earth) (Isa. 6:3, 5) and *Savior* (Ps. 65:5) of his people, their *fortress, refuge* (Ps. 31:2), and *shield* (Ps. 7:10). He is the *Creator, Maker, Lord,* and *Ruler* of the heavenly bodies and of nature, not just of human beings (Ps. 95–99). But he is especially close to his people. He is their *Shepherd* (Ps. 23; 80:1), a title likewise held by ancient kings.[32] He is also a *father* to his people, as Pharaoh was a father to his own son and to the Egyptian people (Exod. 4:22–23). This is the connection between God as King and God as Father, of which more is said below.

The kingship of God is even associated with other designations of God whose connections are less obvious. God the King is the *Holy One of Israel*, set apart by his royal glory and majesty (Isa. 6). *El Elyon, God Most High*, expresses his royal elevation or enthronement.[33] He is also the *Rock*, a term that means something more like a *fortress* (Ps. 18:2) on Gibralter (actually, Mount Zion) than a mere stone or boulder, thus connoting God's status as royal defender. These are some of the many titles and appellatives of God in the Old Testament that take their meaning from the basic idea of God as King.[34]

Another intimate relationship is God as the *husband* of his people Israel, who are to remain faithful as a wife to him (Hosea).[35] Whereas *Baal* and the Canaanite *El* are divine kings who have female consorts, *Yahweh* does not. He is married faithfully and exclusively to Israel.

These divine titles and appellatives vary in status and frequency of use. Obviously *King* is a basic title used regularly. In contrast, God is

31. Mettinger, *In Search of God*, 92–93.

32. "Shepherd," in *The New Bible Dictionary*, ed. J. D. Douglas (Grand Rapids: Eerdmans, 1962), 1175–76.

33. Mettinger, *In Search of God*, 122.

34. Elizabeth Achtemeier, an Old Testament scholar, asserts that "the God of the Bible has revealed himself in five principal metaphors as King, Father, Judge, Husband, and Master, and finally, decisively, as the God and Father of our Lord Jesus." See "Exchanging God for 'No Gods,'" in *Speaking the Christian God*, 5.

35. Nellie Stienstra, *Yahweh Is the Husband of His People: Analysis of a Biblical Metaphor with Special Reference to Translation* (Kampen: Kok Pharos, 1993). This book has an excellent discussion of the nature of all language for God as well as the nature of metaphors.

said to be *a potter* (Isa. 64:8) only rarely and as a predicate metaphor. Some terms have multiple functions. They are used as figures of speech, appellatives, and divine titles. *Shepherd* is a good example. Ezekiel 34 uses the human shepherd–sheep relationship as an extended simile for God's care of his people. Psalm 23 strengthens the term to a predicate noun, "the LORD is my shepherd." And in Psalm 80:1 God is actually addressed as *Shepherd*: "Hear us, O Shepherd of Israel." In this case the term is used as a divine title, as it was for human kings of that time. These uses constitute the Old Testament background for Jesus' self-designation: "I am the good shepherd" (John 10:11, 14).[36] The term *rock* is another example of a word that functions as an image and also as a divine title. But even as titles, *Shepherd* and *Rock* do not share the basic, definitive status that *King* and *Father* have.

Admittedly, it is sometimes difficult to determine whether a predicate noun is an appellative or a metaphor. In the Old Testament *God is king* is an appellative. *The Lord is my shepherd* is a metaphor. But *the Lord is a mighty warrior* is harder to classify. The hard cases do not invalidate the linguistic distinctions, however. In sum, the Bible's masculine terms for God have different ranks of frequency and importance, and some terms have more than one function.

All the personal titles and appellatives for God in Scripture are without exception masculine. There are ungendered impersonal titles, appellatives, and predicate metaphors for God, such as *fortress, shield*, or *rock*. "The LORD is my light and my salvation," confesses the Psalmist (27:1). But there simply are no feminine personal terms of this type. Given that all the basic personal names and titles of God are masculine, the secondary and derivative titles and appellatives naturally follow suit, given how language works. Taking the thousands of examples together as they function in the text, it is difficult to avoid the conclusion that the linguistic pattern of Scripture intentionally presents God as though he is a masculine person.

Father: The Distinctive New Testament Title-Name[37]

The most definitive multiple-status masculine term for God in Scripture is *Father*. We have already encountered it above among the figures of speech, a status that has feminine parallels. However, it has other signficant functions and meanings that *mother* does not share.

---

36. The *I am* is Jesus' self-identification with *Yahweh*, who said *I Am*.

37. *"Pater,"* in *Theological Dictionary of the New Testament*, 5:945–1014; Robert Hamerton-Kelly, *God the Father: Theology and Patriarchy in the Teaching of Jesus* (Philadelphia: Fortress, 1979); and "God the Father," *International Standard Bible Encyclopedia* (1982) 2:509–15.

Given its prominence in the New Testament, it is surprising that *father* is used directly of God only about twenty times in the Old Testament. In addition, there are two dozen human names that contain references to God as father (*ab*): Abraham means *the (divine) father is exalted*; Abimelek means *my (divine) father is king*; and Abigail (a woman's name) means *my (divine) father is joy*.[38]

Above we encountered God as father in connection with God the King. But some texts simply identify God as a father without this explicit association. The Song of Moses asks, "Is he not your Father, your Creator, who made you and formed you?" (Deut. 32:6). The fatherhood of God is connected here with the election and salvation of his people. Similarly, Psalm 68:5 calls God "a father to the fatherless." In Jeremiah 31:9 God identifies himself as a father: "I am Israel's father," and in Malachi 1:6 he asks, "Am I not your father?" Isaiah 63:16 and 64:8 directly identify God as *Father* while addressing him: "you, O Lord, are our Father." In Jeremiah 3:19 we see God himself suggesting *Father* as a term of address, that is, as a kinship title: "I thought you would call me 'Father' and not turn away from following me."

Other instances are explicitly connected with God as King. This association is focused centrally in the messianic covenant made with David (2 Sam. 7; I Chron. 17). God promises David that one of his sons will always reign over the kingdom that God will establish forever. The Lord pledges, "I will be his father, and he will be my son" (2 Sam. 7:14a). Here God reveals his relation to the Davidic dynasty in terms of the ancient Near Eastern notion of the divine father-king. In those religions, the king was believed to be the earthly son of God the King, and the king's sons are also therefore sons of God. David is the divinely chosen anointed one, *messhiah* in Hebrew. The son of David who reigns forever is therefore the Messiah. The messianic covenant is a central theological theme in the Old Testament, celebrated in the Psalms and heralded by the prophets. Psalm 89:26 predicts that the messianic son of David "will call out to me, 'You are my Father, my God, the Rock, my Savior.'" The best-known messianic prophecy is Isaiah 9:6b–7: "And he [his name] will be called Wonderful Counselor, Mighty God, Everlasting Father, Prince of Peace. . . . He will reign on David's throne and over his kingdom . . . forever." Here we find the divine-father relationship being passed on to the messianic son.[39] So although *father* is not used frequently of God in the

38. I am grateful to John Stek, professor of Old Testament emeritus, Calvin Theological Seminary, for pointing out these names to me.

39. We also see an example of the biblical meaning of the term *name*. It does not refer to a proper name but to a series of titles. The meaning of *name* is discussed in the next chapter.

Old Testament, it acquires special significant as an integral part of a central theological theme, God's promise of the Messiah's kingdom.

The fulfillment of this promise in Jesus Christ is the basis for the frequent use and definitive significance of *Father* in the New Testament. With respect to quantity, it is used over two hundred times, occurring in every book except 3 John. As a term for the Deity it is second only to *God*, being used more frequently than *Lord* and *King*. This reverses the Old Testament emphasis, although God as Father, King, and Lord remain interrelated as they were in the Old Testament.[40] We first consider *Father* linguistically, then theologically.

As to its linguistic status, the New Testament includes and expands the Old Testament functions of *father*. There are figurative uses, as in the parable of the Prodigal Son (Luke 15), which portrays God as a father. And there are instances where *father* is a general predicate noun, an appellative. Both 2 Corinthians 6:18 and Hebrews 1:5, which borrow the language of the messianic covenant of 2 Samuel 7, are examples.

But in the vast majority of cases, *Father* is the standard kinship title that specifies the identity of God. In 1 Corinthians 8:6 Paul writes: "There is one God, the Father." Having distinguished the true God from idol gods, he then identifies who the true God is—*the Father*. In the Gospel of John and throughout the New Testament, God is simply identified as *the Father*, with the definite article and in the absence of the word *God*. Thus *the Father* is functionally equivalent to *God*. In John 14:8 Philip asks Jesus, "Show us the Father."

The unique, intimate personal relationship between Jesus and God is highlighted in Jesus' use of the personal pronoun, *my Father*, a common locution in John and elsewhere. Jesus asks his earthly parents in Luke 2:49, "Didn't you know I had to be in my Father's house?" This intimate relationship with God is also available through Jesus to his disciples. He says to Mary in John 20:17, "I am returning to my Father and your Father, to my God and your God." We too may call God *abba, Father* through the Spirit of Jesus the Son (Gal. 4:6–7). Nowhere is this privilege more clearly granted than in the Lord's Prayer: "Our Father, who art in heaven." This is an instance of using the most intimate sort of kinship title as a form of address.

Even more intimate, if possible, is Jesus' use of *Father* as a term of address without the article, as he often did in prayer. "Father, forgive them, for they do not know what they are doing," he prayed, and again six hours later: "Father, into your hands I commit my spirit" (Luke 23:34, 46).[41] It is this very personal use of *Father* without the definite ar-

---

40. *"Pater,"* in *TDNT*, 5:995–96.

41. Other places where Jesus prays, *Father . . .* , are Matt. 11:25, Mark 14:36 [*Abba, Father*], Luke 24:42, and several times in John 17.

ticle or possessive pronoun, the familial intimacy of the Aramaic *abba*, that many scholars are inclined to classify functionally as a personal name for God.[42] They do so by analogy with a child's use of *Mommy* and *Daddy* as personal names, not just kinship titles, for her parents. This topic is revisited below.

In sum, *Father* exemplifies a broad range of linguistic categories in the New Testament: it is a figure of speech, general appellative, divine title, intimate kinship title and term of address, and possibly even a name. In contrast, *mother* always occurs as a figure of speech.

Theologically, the New Testament uses *Father* to identify God in distinct, though importantly related ways. The first refers to God as in the Old Testament, without any trinitarian distinction of persons. We have already encountered an example of this in 1 Corinthians 8:6, where Paul proclaims, "yet for us there is but one God, the Father, from whom all things come." Here he seems to echo the great Old Testament confession in Deuteronomy 6:4, "Hear, O Israel, the LORD our God, the Lord is one." He connects the fatherhood of God with his status as creator of all things. Similarly, in Ephesians 4:4 Paul confesses "one God and Father of all, who is over all and through all and in all." God as such is Father in some New Testament texts, without overt trinitarian or redemptive role distinctions. As Herman Bavinck notes, "the real N.T. equivalent for Yhwh is Father."[43]

The vast majority of cases of *Father* in the New Testament are more specific, however, identifying God particularly in relation to Jesus as the Messiah, the Son of David who reigns over God's people in his kingdom forever (Luke 1:32–33). This is the second use of *Father*.[44] The messianic covenant is fulfilled in Jesus Christ, the Messiah, the Anointed One.[45] In 2 Samuel 7 God promised to be the father of this son. So God is the Father and Jesus is the Son (Heb. 1:5). The divine royal sonship of Jesus is reiterated in relation to his baptism (Matt. 3:17), transfiguration (Matt. 17:5), crucifixion (Matt. 26:63), resurrection (Acts 2:32–33), and exaltation (Phil. 2:6–11). He is "King of kings and Lord of lords" (Rev. 19:16). In all these events he is the messianic Son and God is his royal Father. Most of the scores of occasions when Jesus speaks of *my Father*, or *the Father*, or addresses God as *Father*, therefore, ought

42. *"Pater,"* in *TDNT,* 5:1007, for example, asserts that "omission of the article . . . gives 'father' almost the appearance of a proper name." On page 1009 it does identify *Father* as a name.

43. Bavinck, *The Doctrine of God,* 263.

44. Oddly, Hamerton-Kelly, *God the Father,* pays little attention to the messianic father-son relationship.

45. *Xristos,* Christ, is the Greek translation of the Hebrew word, *messiah,* anointed one.

to be read as allusions to the royal father–messianic son relationship that has deep roots in the Old Testament. Thus the God of Scripture is not merely the universal *Father*, an idea found in other religions. He is the Father of Jesus Christ, the Son. This is what distinguishes New Testament faith from all other religions.

The messianic father–son relation is the basis for the more robust and explicit New Testament references to the Father and Son as God—the basis for references to distinct divine persons. This is the third way in which *Father* is used. The messianic relationship on its own could be interpreted as a bond between God and a merely human descendant of David, whom God chose, specially empowered, and even raised from the dead to a heavenly throne. A merely human Son could call God *Father*. But it becomes clear from some texts that Jesus Christ is the incarnation of the Son who was with the Father before creation: "Father, glorify me in your presence with the glory I had with you before the world began" (John 17:5). The *Son* is the *Word* who is God and by whom all things were made (John 1:1–3; Col. 1:15–16; 1 Cor. 8:6). He did not originate as a human being but emptied himself to take on our humanity (Phil. 2:6–8). So the kinship title *Son of God* in the New Testament begins to disclose the deity of Jesus Christ. This was perfectly obvious to the Jews who wanted to kill Jesus the Son because "he was even calling God his own Father, making himself equal with God" (John 5:18–19). Thus designations of God as *Father* in texts like these refer to the one whom theologians later called the first person of the Trinity. And so it becomes apparent in the New Testament that God is *Father, Son, and Holy Spirit*. Jesus in Matthew 28:19, the Great Commission, quite clearly invokes the "triune name" of God: "Therefore go and make disciples of all nations, baptizing them in the name of the Father and of the Son and of the Holy Spirit." Here God is identified by one complex name constituted by the conjunction of the title-names of the three divine persons: Father, Son, and Holy Spirit. *Father* is the title-name of the first person.

These three theological meanings of *Father* map the progress of revelation from the Old Testament to the New. The first refers to God as father in the way the Old Testament did. The second builds on the specific Old Testament role of God's fatherhood in the messianic covenant and makes *Father* a primary term in relation to the revelation of Jesus as the messianic Son. The third meaning, *Father* as first person of the Trinity in relation to *Son* as second person, is disclosed on the basis of the messianic relationship, but goes beyond anything revealed in the Old Testament.

The second and third meanings of Father are central and distinctive in the New Testament. They are definitive of the Christian faith and cannot be revised or superceded. In the words of Dutch Reformed theologian Herman Bavinck, *Father* "is the highest revelation of God. . . . There is a gradual unfolding of the fulness which from the beginning was in Elohim, and this fulness has become most gloriously manifest in God's trinitarian name."[46] This definitive revelatory status of the trinune name and the fact that Jesus commanded the church to baptize and disciple the world in terms of that name are two of the most compelling reasons why biblical Christians are reluctant to adopt inclusive language for God. *Father, Son, and Holy Spirit* is the final form of God's self-revelation in history and in Scripture.

Holy Spirit[47]

We include the Holy Spirit in this chapter because *spirit of God*, although grammatically feminine thirty-six times in the Hebrew Old Testament, is masculine at least seven times. As indicated in chapter 3, if *Spirit* is a proper noun for God himself, it might well attribute personal gender to God. In that case there would be thirty-six cases where God is presented as a feminine person and seven where he is masculine—an extremely odd situation. However, if *spirit* is not who God is but something he has—like his love, power, soul, or mind—then it does not linguistically imply personal gender of God. We concluded that *spirit* is most likely not a personal term for God in the Old Testament.

In the New Testament the distinct personal nature of the Holy Spirit is more obvious. The Spirit is *Paraclete* or *Counselor* in John (14:16), who engages in personal actions and even refers to himself with the first-person pronoun: "the Holy Spirit said, 'Set apart for me Barnabas and Saul'" (Acts 13:2). Taken in conjunction with the triune name, texts such as these indicate the distinct personhood of the Holy Spirit. Linguistically *the Holy Spirit* is an epithet-title that functions as the name of the third person of the Trinity.

Since *pneuma* is neuter in Greek, all the alleged feminine personal qualities of *Spirit* based on the feminine grammatical gender of *ruaḥ* are abandoned by the Septuagint (the Greek Old Testament).[48] Since the New Testament adopts the neuter term *pneuma* from the Septuag-

---

46. Bavinck, *The Doctrine of God*, 109–10.

47. *"Pneuma,"* in *TDNT*, 6:332–451. Relevant pages are 359–72 and 396–451.

48. There are postbiblical strands of Judaism that hypostatize *Spirit, Wisdom,* and the glory of *Shekinah* as quasi-personal feminine manifestations of God. But this view is not found in the Greek Old Testament or in the New Testament. It is a mistake to read these Jewish traditions into the New Testament, which speaks of the Holy Spirit in relation to God the Father and the Son. The Spirit as understood in Judaism is quite different from the Holy Spirit in Christianity. Mollenkott, *The Divine Feminine,* chap. 7, mistakenly confuses them.

int, it suggests that the person of the Holy Spirit is neither feminine nor masculine.

However, a few exceptions further justify consideration of *Holy Spirit* with the Bible's masculine language for God. In John 14:26 and 16:13–14 there are three masculine associations, perhaps echoing the Old Testament's masculine cases of *ruah*. In these texts, the Holy Spirit seems to be referred to by a masculine pronoun. In each case, however, the masculine word *parakletos* is also in the context. So grammarians debate whether the antecedent of the pronoun is the Paraclete, who is the Holy Spirit, or the Holy Spirit, who is Paraclete.[49] Either way, the Holy Spirit is identified by a masculine personal term.

Another consideration is the fact that the Holy Spirit is the power by which the Virgin Mary miraculously becomes pregnant with Jesus (Luke 1:35). Of course, all crude analogies with human impregnation must be avoided. But the fact is that the Holy Spirit supernaturally substitutes for the role of the human father. Caution is appropriate here, but if it is plausible to find a maternal image in the Spirit's hovering over the waters in Genesis 1, it is equally plausible to see a paternal analogy in Luke 1.

In the final analysis, however, four debatable references to *Holy Spirit* do not make a strong case for claiming it as a masculine term for God.[50] The New Testament, like the Old, gives us little basis for conclusions about the anthropomorphic gender of the Spirit. In fact, *Holy Spirit* is as close as we get in the Bible to a gender-neutral personal reference to God.

Grammatical Forms

Thus far in this chapter we have considered the linguistic status and function of masculine words and phrases that refer to God. In the biblical languages masculine grammatical forms and syntax also frequently appear to attribute personal masculinity to God in the same ways that they attribute masculinity to humans.[51]

We have already encountered grammatical gender in words for God. Hebrew has noun endings that are masculine and feminine, and Greek

49. This claim reflects comments of Al Wolters of Redeemer College and Richard Wevers of Calvin College, the latter relayed to me by Margo Houts.

50. The strong tradition in Western Christianity that speaks of the Holy Spirit as masculine probably results from two factors: by extension from the general biblical presentation of God as masculine; and the use of the masculine Latin term *Spiritus* by the Roman Catholic Church.

51. Recall that we will deal with the meaning of the Bible's gendered language for God in later chapters. Here we are analyzing only its linguistic functions.

has masculine, feminine, and neuter noun endings, as well as articles. We must be careful in linking grammatical and personal gender, however. For in some languages there is no significant correlation between grammatical gender and the gender of persons.[52] For example, *the girl, die Mädchen*, is neuter in German. In French a female professor is *le professeur*, referred to by the masculine article. In both Hebrew and Greek, however, there is a highly regular if not absolute correlation between grammatical and personal gender in words that refer to persons.[53] We have already explored this correlation with respect to the various terms for God.

In addition to the grammatical gender of nouns, Greek has gendered articles, adjective endings, and pronouns. We saw, for example, that the masculine article *ho* goes with *theos* when it means *God*, but the feminine article *he* goes with *theos* (or *thea*) when it means *goddess* (Acts 19:37). Adjectives also typically reflect the gender of the persons they describe. Thus *axios* would indicate that the worthy person alluded to is male, whether explicitly mentioned or not, and *axia* would indicate that she is female. The demonstrative personal pronoun *ekeinos* indicates that *that one (person)* is masculine, whereas *ekeina* signals that *that person* is a *she*. Except in the case of the Holy Spirit, which is neuter, all adjectives and articles for God are masculine, just as they would be for a male human being. The hundreds and hundreds of these words in the New Testament must be added to the masculine terms for God in order to calculate the massive amount of masculine language for God in Scripture.

In Hebrew there are gendered verb forms as well as pronouns and adjectives, but no gendered articles. Hebrew verbs typically have masculine and feminine forms in the second and third persons. In other words, *you* (masculine) or *you* (feminine) is indicated by the verb ending. And we saw above in discussing *Yahweh* that third-person verbs themselves indicate whether the personal subject is a he or she. Hebrew has masculine and feminine pronouns in the second-person singular and plural and the third-person plural, in addition to the third-person

52. See Waltke and O'Connor, "Gender," *Introduction to Biblical Hebrew Syntax*, chap. 6, for a helpful overview of grammatical and personal gender in general linguistics as well as in Hebrew.

53. Hebrew has a few terms for males that appear grammatically feminine in form, a classic case being the plural form *abot, fathers*. However, these words function syntactically as masculine in the appropriate personal sense: *fathers* takes masculine verbs, adjective, and pronouns. There are also epicene nouns, like *elohim, gods*, the plural of which includes both males and females. This is the case mainly with animals, less so with humans. But as we have seen, these exceptions do not counter the claim that the terminology for God in Hebrew is overwhelmingly masculine.

singular forms that are also found in English (*he* and *she*). Only the first person (*I* and *we*) is not gender-specific. Thus when Psalm 28 begins, *To you I call, O Lᴏʀᴅ*, the pronoun *you* is masculine because it refers to *Yahweh*. Even if *Yahweh* was not mentioned, the form indicates that the person whom the psalmist is addressing is masculine. In addition, Hebrew has gendered pronoun suffixes that attach to nouns: *dabareka* in Psalm 119:9 means *your word*, and indicates that God, to whom *your* refers, is masculine. Finally, Hebrew adjectives are virtually infallible in indicating the gender of the person they modify. In other words, even if the grammatical form of a noun for a male is occasionally feminine, the adjective reflects the person's maleness. An example is *the teacher is wise*. In Hebrew *teacher* has feminine form but *wise* is masculine if it refers to a male teacher.[54] It turns out that all of the thousands and thousands of Hebrew verbs, pronouns, and adjectives that reflect personal gender when used of human persons are masculine when used for God.[55] Hebrew grammatical gender is additional evidence for the thesis that the Bible intentionally speaks of God as though he is a masculine person.

Conclusion

This chapter set out to determine both the quantity and linguistic functions of the Bible's masculine language for God. Linguistically, the biblical text utilizes masculine language for God in the same wide spectrum of ways it does for humans. It uses masculine figures of speech—similes, metaphors, and extended comparisons in parables. But Scripture also employs masculine language to speak of God in the ordinary modes of identification and address. It uses masculine nouns to identify the roles of God: *warrior, shepherd, judge*. It uses masculine words as titles and terms of address indicating both his greatness—*God Almighty, King*, and *Lord*—and his nearness—*Father*. Even the names of God are masculine: *Yahweh* and the broader sense in which *God* and *Father* are title-names. In addition to the wide range of linguistic functions served by masculine terms for God, the grammar and syntax of the biblical languages refer to God as though he is a masculine by the verb forms, articles, pronouns, and adjectives used in speaking of him.

The sheer quantity of this language is as overwhelming as it is exceptionless. There are thousands and thousands of masculine words and

---

54. Waltke and O'Connor, *An Introduction to Biblical Hebrew Syntax*, 109.
55. The word for *spirit* has feminine verbs and adjectives in those cases where it is feminine. No feminine pronoun ever occurs in these cases, however. So not even the Old Testament language of God's Spirit provides precedent for referring to God as *she*.

phrases that refer to God. The additional grammatical and syntactical markers that reflect masculinity upon God are even more numerous.

The only reasonable conclusion is that the intended practice of Scripture as a whole is to speak of God as though he is a masculine person. That is to say, the way in which Scripture uses gendered language for God is precisely parallel to how it does so for human males, with the crucial exception that it never speaks of God as a sexual being. Without more information, in other words, it would be possible to conclude from how Scripture speaks of God that he is a non-bodily masculine person. But in that case, how do the feminine references fit in?

The Essential Difference between Biblical and Gender-Inclusive Language for God

In chapter 3 we found that the Bible's feminine language for God consists of about two dozen figures of speech that illustrate some of God's ways with creation and his people. Scripture contains no feminine names, titles, common nouns, pronouns, or other grammatical forms that refer to God as a feminine person. In contrast, chapter 4 reported literally thousands of instances of maculine names, titles, common nouns, figures of speech, and grammatical constructions that present God in language appropriate for a masculine person. Whatever this means theologically, it is obvious that the Bible does not use masculine and feminine language for God equivalently. The difference is not only quantitative—a proportion of thousands to one—but also qualitative: All the identifying terms are masculine, none are feminine. Since inclusivism requires both quantitative and qualitative equality of masculine and feminine language for God, its significant difference from the biblical pattern is obvious.

It is therefore surprising to discover that inclusivists of all theological perspectives claim the Bible as a source of gender-egalitarian language for God. "I endorse the ideal of language for God in male and female terms used equivalently," writes Elizabeth Johnson.[1] She is among those, including Rosemary Ruether and Elizabeth Schüssler-Fiorenza, who find most of Scripture's presentation of God oppressively patriarchal and adopt nontraditional approaches to the Bible in order to salvage parts of it.[2] Inclusivists with more positive views of

---

1. Johnson, *She Who Is*, 56.
2. Recall "Arguments from God's Revelation and Its Interpretation" in chap. 2.

Scripture are understandably more eager to appeal to the Bible in support of their cause. Johanna van Wijk-Bos's *Reimagining God* is subtitled *The Case for Scriptural Diversity*. Virginia Mollenkott's *The Divine Feminine* is billed as *The Biblical Imagery of God as Female*. The inclusivists with the highest view of Scripture are evangelical. Paul Smith, a Southern Baptist minister who professes a strong view of biblical inspiration and affirms orthodox theology, believes that Scripture requires the use of gender-egalitarian language: "I . . . call God Mother and Father because I want to be faithful to the meaning and the message of the Bible."[3] In spite of very different attitudes and approaches to Scripture, virtually all inclusivists claim its support for gender-egalitarian language for God.

But how can they make this appeal when the biblical and gender-egalitarian patterns are so different? Their main strategy is a series of linguistic arguments that downplay the differences among names, titles, appellatives, and figures of speech. This line of reasoning typically treats all references to God equally as "metaphors" that "name" him and thus as equally attributing or not attributing linguistic personal gender to God. The first section of this chapter therefore reflects on various parts of speech and their relation to personal gender in order to recognize the insights and pinpoint the fallacies in the appeal to Scripture in support of gender-equivalent language for God. (The diverse inclusivist views of the nature and authority of Scripture are treated in chapter 6.)

Once the insights and mistakes of the gender-egalitarian analysis of biblical language have been identified, we look more closely at how the linguistic structure of Scripture's gendered language for God ought to be understood. The concept of *cross-gender imagery* is introduced to characterize the biblical pattern, which occasionally uses feminine images while speaking of God with language that on the human level is appropriate for a masculine person. Cross-gender images are figures of speech that linguistically juxtapose features of one gender with a person of the other. In a final section, the chapter acknowledges that some defenses of biblical-traditional language for God also rely on inadequate linguistic analysis.

It is crucial to bear in mind throughout this chapter that we are speaking about language and the ways it indicates personal gender. We are not drawing conclusions about the meaning of this language, whether it implies that God himself has gender, and what its theological significance is. Those topics are addressed in chapters 7 and 8.

---

3. Smith, *Is It Okay to Call God "Mother"?* 129.

The Gender-Egalitarian Appeal to Scripture: Metaphors and Names for God

As we saw in chapter 2, inclusivists share a common approach in moving from the Bible's feminine imagery to an equally *Father-Mother* God in spite of the fact that they hold diverse views of Scripture. The crucial strategy is to treat *metaphors*, which are figures of speech, and *names*, which are not figures of speech, as synonyms and to slip back and forth between them.[4] Hymnwriter Brian Wren, for instance, uses the terms *metaphor* and *name* as having practically the same meaning. He classifies the Bible's central terminology, God as King-Almighty-Father-Lord-Protector, as "a metaphor system," urges that it be "dethroned," and then encourages us to "Bring Many Names to God," including both *Father* and *Mother*.[5] Thus metaphors and names are functionally equivalent for Wren. In the same way Ruth Duck asserts that "all naming of God is necessarily metaphorical." She then identifies both *father* and *mother* as metaphors for God, and on that basis claims to be justified in revising "the strong name of the Trinity," *Father, Son and Holy Spirit*, with feminine language.[6]

This sort of argument, which slides between metaphors and names, between figures of speech and non-figures of speech, is deployed by almost all inclusivists. It boils down to this: since the Bible's masculine and feminine terms for God are all metaphors that name God, both masculine and feminine terms ought to have equal status and functions in Christian language for God. Language of both genders is equal in linguistically attributing or not attributing personal gender to God. God is equally *Father* and *Mother*, *He* and *She*.

This approach allows inclusivists to take feminine figures of speech (which, as we will show, do not disclose the personal gender of their subjects) and make them into titles and names (which do linguistically disclose personal gender). Thus, for example, they regard the nursing mother analogy of Isaiah 49:15 as functionally equivalent to naming God *Mother*. At the same time their approach enables them to neutralize the exclusively masculine linguistic gender of God: they treat the divine names and titles as metaphors (figures of speech). Thus the masculine titles and names are no different than the feminine figures of speech in attributing or not attributing linguistic personal gender to God. *Father* and *He* are no more significant than *Mother* and *She* or *Parent* and *That One* as a reference to God.

4. See chap. 2, "*Father* and *Mother* Are Equally Metaphorical."
5. Wren, *What Language Shall I Borrow?* chaps. 5 and 6.
6. Duck, *Gender and the Name of God*, 13, 154, 163–66.

This attempt to derive inclusive language for God from Scripture is seriously flawed. It ignores significant differences between parts of language, generating bad arguments and illegitimate category leaps. These result in the unwarranted and false conclusion that feminine names and pronouns for God are implied by the language of Scripture and that the terms *Father* and *Mother* are linguistically equivalent references to God.

In order to demonstrate precisely how the inclusivist argument is linguistically confused and fallacious, it is necessary to compare the relevant parts of speech more closely—names, titles, appellatives, and images—and to determine how they relate to personal gender. We begin by showing that each of these parts of speech can be considered a *name*, as inclusivists claim, but only because the term *name* has several distinct meanings. The subsequent section exposes how the inclusivist argument from feminine imagery to feminine titles, names, and pronouns for God illegitimately shifts among these different meanings.

Four Meanings of Name

The term *name* has different meanings in discussions about language, meanings that are perfectly legitimate as long as they are not confused.[7] It can mean (1) *proper name* (e.g., Jesus), (2) *any proper noun or specific designation* (e.g., Lord), (3) a *common noun* or *general appellative* (e.g., a true human being), and (4) *any linguistic reference*, including figures of speech. These categories are not arbitrary, but are found in all languages, including the biblical languages. They are part of the structure of language itself. The problem with inclusivism is not its broad definition of *names*, but its confusion of this definition with the other meanings.

The first meaning to consider is the very narrow sense of *proper name*. A proper name is distinct from a title and a general appellative. My name, *John*, is not a title like *Professor*, which states my particular position. It is not a general appellative like *teacher*, which classifies me with others who do what I do. As my name, *John* is surely not a figure of speech, for example, a slang term for *toilet* or *customer of prostitutes*. The defining linguistic function of a proper name is to identify a particular person as such, not to specify someone's status, role, or relationship, or to describe that person (although it may also have those functions). It is the basic, primary linguistic label attached to a person,

---

7. Technical discussions are found in John Searle, "Proper Names and Descriptions," in *The Encyclopedia of Philosophy*, ed. P. Edwards (New York: Macmillan and Free Press, 1967, 1972), 6:487–91, and E. J. Lowe, "Names," in *The Oxford Companion to Philosophy*, ed. T. Honderich (New York: Oxford University Press, 1995), 602–3.

enabling us to pick him or her out from all other persons. *John Cooper, Richard Lionheart, Sitting Bull, Jesus,* and *Yahweh* are proper names, whatever their origins and meanings may be. They function primarily as basic terms of identification and address for individual persons, not as descriptions of them.

Chapter 3 demonstrated that there are no feminine proper names for God in Scripture. In the previous chapter we saw that *Yahweh* is God's special personal name in the Old Testament. *El, Elohim,* and *theos* (*God*) may also sometimes function as proper names, even though they are also used as common nouns. (*Kitten* is a common noun, but a child can give her pet the proper name *Kitty.*) We wondered whether *Father* on the lips of Jesus (paralleling *Daddy* expressed by a child) functions as a proper name for God. In the end the debate over inclusive language does not turn on whether *Father* and *God* are proper names, however, for this is not the most important meaning of *name.*

The second meaning is a somewhat broader, *name* as *proper designation* or *specific identification,* that is, any term that refers to an individual in distinction from all others. This category obviously includes proper names, since they identify individuals, but it also includes titles and epithets (descriptions), which designate specific individuals in terms of their status, role, functions, relationship, accomplishments, and characteristics. This category of *name* has the same scope as *proper nouns and definite descriptions* (in distinction from *common nouns and general descriptions*). To illustrate, there may be many fathers, queens, people who defend the faith, and warriors who conquer enemies. These are common or generic terms. But when I speak of *my Father, the Queen* (Elizabeth), *Defender of the Faith,* and (William) *the Conqueror,* I am using proper nouns and epithets that refer to specific persons. These examples are titles, which both identify specific individuals and state their particular status, roles, relationships, or other signficance. Interestingly, *King, Cooper, Freeman,* and *Johnson* are terms that, like titles, connote status, role, or relationship, but have actually become proper surnames and no longer convey the descriptive meaning that titles do. The distinction between proper name and title is finally unimportant in this definition of *name,* as suggested above regarding *Elohim* and *Father.*[8] This is the meaning of *name* that is crucial in the debate about inclusive language.

The reason for its importance is that this definition—proper designation—is the primary meaning of *name* used in the Bible and in the theological tradition. In the Old Testament *hashem, The Name,* most funda-

---

8. We identified these terms as title-names in chap. 4 in order not to prejudice their classification before this more thorough analysis was provided.

mentally stands for God himself in all his glory and in all his dealings with his creatures, not just for words used to refer to him (Lev. 24:11; Isa. 30:27).[9] But almost always *name* includes words as well. *Yahweh* is the special personal name revealed to Moses. *Yahweh Almighty* is *the Name* (2 Sam. 6:2). *El* and *Elohim*, whether technically proper names or proper nouns, are regularly used as names of God in this sense. They are likewise often paired with *Yahweh*, as in *Yahweh eloheka*, *the Lord your God*, the name sanctioned by the Third Commandment. In Genesis 21:33 the divine name is *Yahweh El Olam*, *the Lord God Everlasting*. Thus the Old Testament includes among *names* what we would classify technically as *titles*. Probably the most famous example is celebrated in Handel's *Messiah*: "his name will be called 'Wonderful Counselor, Mighty God, Everlasting Father, Prince of Peace'" (Isa. 9:6 RSV). These titles are explicitly identified as his *name*. The New Testament follows suit. Consider the names of our Lord. In addition to the obvious cases, such as *Jesus* and *Immanuel*, which are names given him by the Holy Spirit, the epithets *Faithful, True,* and *Word of God* and the title *King of king and Lord of lords* are explicitly identified as *names* (*onoma*) of Jesus (Rev. 19:11, 13, 16). The Bible contains no feminine names for God in this sense.

The theological tradition follows the biblical understanding of *name*. In the *Summa Theologica* 1.33.2, Thomas Aquinas asserts that "the proper name of a person signifies that whereby the person is distinguished from all other persons. . . . Hence this name *Father*, whereby paternity is signified, is the proper name of the person of the Father."[10] The term translated as "proper name" is actually *nomen propria*, a term more like *proper noun* than what we above have called a *proper name*, such as *John* or *Mary*. Thomas's term fits exactly the meaning of *name* we have identified as *proper designation*, a category that includes both proper names and titles. He asserts that *Father* is a name because it is the proper noun that uniquely distinguishes the first person of the Trinity. Thomas is quite aware that *Father* is a relational term and that it is not a name in the same sense as *I AM*.[11] But using this definition, he nevertheless considers *Father* the name of the first person of the Trinity. It is interesting and instructive but not surprising that the theological tradition follows the biblical understanding of *name* in dealing with language for God.[12]

9. Bavinck, "God's Names," in *The Doctrine of God*, 83–85.

10. Thomas Aquinas, *The Basic Writings of Thomas Aquinas*, 2 vols., ed. Anton Pegis (New York: Random House, 1945), 1:326.

11. Aquinas, *Summa Theologica* 1.13.11 in *Basic Writings*, 1:131–32.

12. Bavinck, *The Doctrine of God*, 98, is using this definition when he identifies God's names as "those appellatives by which we designate God and by which we address him" and gives as examples *El, Elohim, El Shaddai, Yahweh,* and *Father*.

Given this definition, there is no question that *Father, Son, and Holy Spirit* is the triune name of God.[13]

A third meaning of *name* is *classification or general designation*. In this sense naming something is assigning it a common noun or general appellative, thereby identifying it as an instance of a certain kind or class of thing. As a hypothetical illustration, suppose that when Adam named the animals in Genesis 2, he called the lion *a lion* but did not give it a proper name like *Leo* or a title, such as *King of the Beasts*. Since the designation *lion* applies equally to all the members of this species, it does not uniquely identify individual lions and is therefore significantly different than a proper name or proper designation, the first two kinds of naming. It is a general or common name rather than an exclusive identification. When I identify a tree as *a black oak*, a feeling as *anxiety*, or a gesture as *a greeting*, I am naming them according to this third definition.

Scripture names God in this way when it identifies him as a *judge, king, shepherd, potter, warrior, husband,* and *father*. Used in this manner, these words are common nouns for human positions and vocations that are predicated of God. They are not titles, proper names, or terms of address (although some of them have these other functions as well). But all of them are *names* defined as general appellatives, designations, or identifications by means of common nouns.[14] As indicated in chapter 4, Scripture identifies God using a variety masculine names in this sense.

The Bible never uses feminine language to name God in this way. Its feminine imagery compares God to females, such as nursing mothers. Biblical feminine metaphors sometimes predicate female functions of God, such as giving birth. But there is no passage in Scripture that predicates a female personage or role of God. There is not a single text that contains a feminine appellative for God. The Bible never, even as a metaphor, makes statements like "God is a mother" or "God is a woman

13. There are interesting debates about whether *Father* is a proper name or a title. See, for example, Alvin Kimel, "The God Who Likes His Name: Holy Trinity, Feminism, and the Language of Faith," in *Speaking the Christian God*, esp. 190–95. Although this question is significant, it is not crucial to the refutation of inclusive language. For feminine imagery does not justify naming God with proper names or titles, as shown below.

14. The issue of the metaphorical nature of such predication should not be allowed to obscure this point. In one sense all language for God is metaphorical because God transcends human categories, a topic treated in chap. 7. But since the Bible does speak of God as though he is a masculine person, using masculine names, titles, and grammatical forms, such masculine appellatives should be read the same way as when predicated of humans. "The Lord is a king above all kings" should be read as a designation like "David is king" and not as figure of speech like "David is a mother to Judah." The metaphorical nature of all language for God does not change the linguistic function of appellatives into sheer imagery.

householder." Since there are no feminine personal nouns ever predicated of God, there are no feminine names for God in the third meaning of *name*.

Finally, there is a very broad sense in which *name* is equivalent to "verbal reference to." In this sense all human language that alludes to God names him. In this category there is no relevant distinction among names, titles, general designations, pronouns, and figures of speech. To refer to God as *Light* or the *Keeper of Leviathan*, as *the Necessary Being* or *my Co-Pilot*, as *He*, or even as *The Unnameable* is to name him just as much as calling him *Father* or *Yahweh*. According to this definition, metaphors, similes, and all images are names for God simply because they are forms of language that refer to him.

There is precedent in the theological tradition for this broad definition. Since all of creation reveals God, any linguistic expression that conveys how any creature reflects "God's invisible qualities—his eternal power and divine nature" (Rom. 1:20) names God.[15] References to God derived from female creatures in creation's general revelation and repeated in the feminine imagery of the Bible are included in this broad sense of *name*.

In summary, *name of God* can mean (1) a proper name in distinction from all other references, including titles; (2) a proper designation, whether name, title, or epithet; (3) a general noun, appellative, or description designating who or what God is; and (4) any verbal reference to God.

The Fallacies of Gender-Inclusive Arguments from Biblical Imagery

Equipped with this analysis of *name*, we can now pinpoint the fallacies of the inclusivist argument that uses the Bible's feminine imagery for God as warrant for the full range of feminine language for God. In deploying their arguments, inclusivists equivocate or illegitimately slip between the fourth meaning of *name* and the other three. Moreover, these slips lead them to make other mistakes about language and gender. By transforming figures of speech into titles and names, they attribute anthropomorphically feminine gender to God in ways not linguistically warranted by the biblical text. And by reducing names and titles to metaphors, they deny anthropomorphically masculine gender to God in ways that are warranted by biblical language.

We substantiate the case against this line of reasoning by comparing images or figures of speech (the fourth meaning of *name*) with appella-

---

15. Bavinck, *The Doctrine of God*, 88: "In order to give us an idea of the majesty and exalted character of God, names are derived from every kind of creature, living and lifeless, organic and inorganic." This topic is discussed in chap. 6.

tives, titles, and proper names (the other three meanings). Figures of speech are not linguistically equivalent to the other parts of speech, they do not of themselves linguistically generate the other parts or the pronouns they require, and they do not attribute personal gender as the other parts do.

Let's begin by comparing metaphors, which are figures of speech, and appellative predicate nouns, which are not. My students might complain that "Professor Cooper is a real bear." I might lament that "I brought forth a stillborn child" if I "labor hard" on this book but no one reads it. But these figures of speech are not and do not generate appellatives. They do not name me by classifying me as a hairy mammal who hibernates or by identifying me as a mother. In the same way, birth images and other feminine figures of speech simply are not and do not generate appellatives for God as a mother or as any female person.

Confusion on this point is possible because both predicate metaphors and appellatives have the same form. "John is the mother of his book" and "Sylvia is the mother of her child" have the same linguistic structure, but the first is figurative and the second is not. Although the Bible itself contains neither feminine appellatives nor predicate noun metaphors for God, it is linguistically appropriate, I believe, to move from a birth image for God to a predicate noun metaphor. This is what John Calvin does when he writes that "God . . . has manifested himself to be both their Father and their Mother" in commenting on Isaiah 46:3, noted above.[16] What is illegitimate is to turn a predicate metaphor into an appellative. Let me illustrate. It seems linguistically natural to gloss the maternal depictions of God's love in Isaiah 49:15 and 66:13 by saying, "The Lord is a mother to us." But this assertion must be understood as a predicate metaphor parallel to "King David is a mother to his people." It has the same linguistic status as the simile "God is like a mother to us." Thus it is not an appellative parallel to "Deborah is a mother because she has a child."[17] To conflate metaphors and appellatives is a linguistic category mistake, an illegitimate slide from the fourth to the third meaning of name. Scripture's feminine language for God never extends metaphors into appellatives.

This is a slide, furthermore, that involves unwarranted attribution of personal gender. For appellative predicate nouns that are gender-marked reflect the gender of their subjects: "David is a king." But predicate metaphors do not necessarily correspond to the gender of their subjects. In fact it is not only possible to say "David is a father to his

---

16. Calvin, *Commentary on Isaiah*, 3:436.

17. Recall that we do not discuss the general metaphorical/analogical nature of language for God, including figures of speech, appellatives, titles, and names, until chap. 7.

people," but also "David is a mother to the motherless." The latter is a *cross-gender image*, the figurative attribution of something of one gender to a person of the other. (Cross-gender imagery is discussed later in the chapter.) This expression is possible because gender imagery does not disclose the gender of its subject. To confirm this rule, compare three metaphorical assertions: "John is bull-headed," "she is bull-headed," and "that child is bull-headed." It is obvious that the first person is male and the second is female, but the gender of the third is not indicated. Although "bull-headedness" is a figuratively male characteristic, it does not reveal the gender of the unfortunate person who manifests it.

In conclusion, it is illegitimate to conflate figures of speech, including predicate noun metaphors, and appellatives. And it is linguistically inappropriate to attribute gender to a personal subject from the gender of a figure of speech.

Figures of speech and titles follow the same pattern. As figures of speech, metaphors are not titles and do not by themselves generate titles. My daughter might say, "Dad, you're a grumpy old bear." But she would not consequently use *Bear* as a title for reference or address. She would not use it to introduce me to her friends: "Jane, I'd like you to meet my Bear. Bear, this is Jane." This point is even more obvious in cross-gender imagery. My daughter once complimented my housekeeping efforts by saying, "Dad, you sure do make a good mom." But she would have found it silly to call me *Mom*. Figures of speech are not and do not naturally imply titles.

In the same way, the Bible's feminine images and birth metaphors for God are not equivalent to titles and do not linguistically generate feminine titles. This is surely the case where the names and titles of God are masculine. Thus the fact that God (*El*) gives birth to the waters in Job 38 does not make *Rain Mother* a divine name. And the Lord's (*Yahweh*, a masculine name) self-comparison with motherly love in Isaiah does not imply that he should be addressed as *Our Mother*, a name in the second sense.

Imagery is certainly not equivalent to a proper name. My students may consider me a bear, but that does not linguistically warrant augmenting the name *John Cooper* with *Bear*, much less *Smoky*, *Yogi*, or *Pooh*. It surely creates no right for them to give me such a nick-name or to address me with one. (The *right* to name God is considered in chapter 6.) In the same way, the Bible's feminine imagery adds no divine names to *Yahweh*, *El*, and *Elohim*. It provides no linguistic right at all, much less a spiritual right, to give God new proper names.

The invalidity of inclusivist arguments from feminine imagery to feminine names can be highlighted by testing them. If figurative language warranted titles and names, eagle imagery would entitle us to call God *Big Bird* and rock imagery would invite us to bring *Rocky* as one of his many names. These parodies not only expose a certain irreverence in the inclusivist argument. They show its fallaciousness. In jumping from figures of speech to nonfigurative parts of language, inclusivists push language in ways it does not naturally go.

The same fallacy vitiates their argument for feminine pronouns. David may be "the mother of the motherless" and John may be "giving birth to a book," but these men do not become "shes" when feminine images are predicated of them. The appropriate pronoun is *he* because it is required by the masculine names. The same is true of *God—Yahweh, Elohim, theos*—who is *King, Lord,* and *Father.* God is *He* even when the subject of a maternal simile or metaphor, because the pronoun is governed by the divine name, title, or appellative, and not by the gender of the image. Thus giving birth to wisdom in Proverbs 8 does not make God *She.*[18]

The net result of our analysis is that none of the inclusivist attempts to validate feminine names, titles, appellations, and pronouns for God on the basis of the Bible's feminine imagery for God is linguistically legitimate. All of these efforts extend figures of speech and the attribution of personal gender in ways that are linguistically unwarranted. These fallacies are masked by imprecise and confused definitions of names and figures of speech. As a consequence, the relationship between personal gender and the several parts of speech are misunderstood and misapplied. The linguistic argument that gender-inclusive language for God is based on biblical language is fatally flawed.

The Figurative Meaning of Titles and Names

But aren't God's names and titles figurative or metaphorical, as inclusivists insist? In fact, there are two senses in which this claim can be made and there is truth to both. The important point, however, is that neither of them supports the case for gender-equal language. First, there is a general sense in which language for God is metaphorical or analogical (not literal) because God transcends creaturely categories. (This point is elaborated in chapter 7.)

Second, it is true both that figures of speech are sometimes used to form titles and names and that titles and names sometimes have figurative meanings. A metaphor would become a name, for example, if

---

18. Masculine pronouns have the same nongendered meaning as their antecedents. But they are linguistically necessary precisely because their antecedents are masculine. Chap. 7 and 8 discuss the nongendered meaning of Scripture's masculine language for God.

bear imagery caught on among my students to the point where I ended up with the nick-name *The Bear*. Likewise, *coeur de lion, lion-heart,* was a figure of speech honoring King Richard's bravery. But it became a proper epithet-title, *The Lionhearted*, and eventually his surname. *Snow White* and *Sitting Bull* are other names with figurative meanings.

Similarly, the biblical titles and names for God have meanings, many of them figurative. *Yahweh* means *He Is. El ro'i* (Gen. 16:13) means *God Who Sees*. Some of these terms originate as meaningful names. *Yahweh* and Jesus' name, *Immanuel* (*God with us*), are examples. Others may have developed from images into titles or names as revelation progressed through the Old Testament into the New. *Rock, shepherd,* and *father* are used as biblical images for God. But they also sometimes function as titles and forms of address. God is *the Rock, the Shepherd of Israel,* and our *Father*. Jesus is *the Lamb of God* (John 1:29), a designation that is both a title and a metaphor that continues its Old Testament sacrificial meaning. As title-names these terms retain their figurative meanings. They are not just linguistic labels but continue to have particular significance in disclosing God's attitudes, actions, and relationship with his people.

Thus inclusivists are correct when they claim that divine titles and names are frequently metaphorical in meaning. But this does not allow them to reclassify titles, names, and other appellations of God as metaphors or other figures of speech. A metaphor is not a name or title. And a name or title is not a metaphor even if its origin and meaning are metaphorical. The figurative aspects of language for God that inclusivists point out have always been recognized by traditional theology without the inclusivists' confusion of linguistic categories.

The Biblical Pattern of Gendered Language for God

Gender-inclusive language for God cannot be derived linguistically from the biblical pattern of language for God. The inclusivist attempt to link them fails. But what then is the proper linguistic analysis of Scripture's gendered language for God?

Chapter 3 concluded that there are about a couple dozen feminine references to God in Scripture and that all of them are figures of speech—similes, analogies, metaphors, and personification. In fact, it demonstrated that Scripture never speaks of God as though he is a feminine person. Chapter 4 concluded that the Bible speaks of God as though he is a masculine person: the names, titles, appellatives, and grammatical gender for God are masculine in the same way that they are for human males, such as Moses and David. (We do not conclude from this that God is a masculine person.) Combining these results, we conclude that Scripture speaks of God as though he is a masculine person, but occasionally uses feminine metaphors to describe particular divine attitudes and actions. We must analyze this pattern more precisely.

The Bible does not segregate the masculine and feminine references to God, as our study has done thus far. The text of Scripture integrates them, sprinkling occasional feminine images among the constant stream of masculine references, frequently using them in the very same phrases and sentences. The feminine figures of speech are predicated of the God whose names, titles, and appellatives are masculine. In other words, God is presented as though he is a masculine person even when feminine imagery is used. Therefore, a standard inclusivist claim is demonstrably false. It is not true that the Bible occasionally speaks of God as a feminine person while usually speaking of him as masculine.

Cross-Gender Imagery

The conceptual key to understanding the linguistic role of Scripture's feminine language for God is *cross-gender imagery*.[19] Cross-gender imagery is the use of something associated with one gender as a figure of speech for a person of the other gender. We might say, for example, that "Bill is mad as a wet hen" or that "Mary is bull-headed." Here are a simile and a metaphor in which creatures of one sex are associated figuratively with humans of the other. In like manner my writing this book can be described using a maternal metaphor: "John conceived the idea, let it gestate, and is now laboring painfully to deliver what he hopes is not a stillborn child." I am a male, but my literary effort is imaged maternally. This is a cross-gender metaphor. Similarly, Saddam Hussein has been parodied as "the mother of all dictators." And you may recall the humorous movie character, "Mr. Mom," a father who took the role of full-time parent and home-maker. In all of these examples a person of one gender is figuratively linked with a person, animal, role, or characteristic of the other gender.

Most personal imagery does not cross genders. We typically call George Washington "the father of his country," not "the mother of his country." We follow this pattern because the image is intended to shed light on its subject, not the other way around, and we find same-gender imagery most natural. But sometimes the point we wish to make about someone can be illustrated using an image of the opposite gender.

19. I owe my acquaintance with this important category to Al Wolters, who has done extensive work on it. His paper, "Cross-gender Imagery in the Bible," was presented at the Evangelical Theological Society meeting in Jackson, Mississipi, in November 1996 and has been published in *Bulletin for Biblical Research* 8 (1998), 217–28.

Cross-gender imagery, although unusual, is possible because figures of speech by definition juxtapose things that are both like and unlike in order to highlight a similarity. In cross-gender images, sex and gender are typically not meant to be included among the similarities. Just as the metaphor "John is a bear" does not intend to suggest that I am hairy or hibernate, so "John labored to give birth to this book" does not connote that I am a female person, but highlights my literary effort in an interesting way.

Consequently, cross-gender imagery creates no confusion at all about the gender of the image's subject. We are not suddenly uncertain about the fact that Mary is female when we describe her as bull-headed. The feminine images predicated of Bill, John, and Saddam Hussein do not make us wonder whether they are female or bisexual. In no way does the linguistic trajectory of these figures of speech incline us to refer to them with the pronoun "she."

There is no confusion about the gender of these subjects because personal gender is indicated by gender-marked names and other terms of identification, whereas figures of speech may or may not reflect the gender of their subjects. Thus we can tell the gender of Bob, Mary, Jane, and Bill from their names. Similarly, *king, queen, nurse-maid,* and *scoutmaster* are gender-marked titles or appellatives. *He* and *she* are pronouns that signal the gender of their antecents. But gender imagery does not disclose the gender of its subject. We cannot tell whether a "bull-headed" person is masculine or feminine simply from the attribution of this metaphorically masculine quality. Whether an image is same-gender, cross-gender, or gender-neutral depends on the gender of the subject. If the gender of the subject is indicated, it is by gender-marked terms of identification, not by figures of speech.

Cross-Gender Imagery for God

The Bible's gendered language for God conforms to this general pattern. The masculine names, titles, appellatives, pronouns, and other grammatical forms (in the original text) all refer to God as though he is masculine. (Recall that we are not concluding that God *is* masculine from this language as we would from masculine language about a human being.) The masculine figures of speech (e.g., "as a father . . . so the Lord . . .") do not cross gender and therefore reflect and amplify God's linguistic masculinity. The feminine references to God are all cases of cross-gender imagery and therefore do not linguistically imply, attribute, or suggest anthropomorphic personal gender. Thus, even when masculine and feminine images occur in parallel, they do not equally reflect the anthropomorphic gender of God. For example, in the statement that "God fathers and mothers his people," *fathers* reflects and reaffirms the linguistic masculinity of God in Scripture whereas *mothers* is a cross-gender image. Though parallel, they do not imply a Father-Mother God.

The feminine similes for God are clear cases of cross-gender imagery.[20] In Isaiah 66:13 the Lord says: "As a mother comforts her child, so will I comfort you." Taken out of context, this might sound like the expression of a female person: the "I" is grammatically ungendered in both English and Hebrew and thus might plausibly be translated in the third person as "she." In context, however, the speaker is *Yahweh*, whose name is masculine, and all the inflected verb forms, adjectives, and pronouns are masculine. In this cross-gender simile Yahweh, who is King of heaven and earth in Isaiah and throughout the Old Testament (whose throne is mentioned in 66:1), compares his care for his people to a mother's comforting her child. The same kind of imagery is found in Isaiah 42:14, where Yahweh likens himself to a woman in childbirth, and in 49:15, where the Lord says that he is more faithful than a nursing mother.

The feminine metaphors for God are also cross-gender images. Consider again Deuteronomy 32:18 in the Song of Moses, a text inclusivists frequently invoke as presenting a Mother God: "You deserted the Rock who fathered [begot/mothered?] you; you forgot the God who gave you birth." Since the sex of the procreative role in the first clause is debatable and the second clause could be read in English as a straightforward predication of birthing to God, one might conclude that God is here represented as an anthropomorphically feminine person. But these readings are impossible in the Hebrew text. For God is identified as *El* (18) and *Yahweh* (19). These are masculine names and are accompanied by exclusively masculine grammatical forms. Both *fathered/mothered/begot* and *gave you birth* are masculine verb forms, implying that their subject is a masculine person.[21] So the metaphor here is not portraying God as a feminine person, but as a masculine person figuratively giving birth. It is a cross-gender image of the same kind as "John gave birth to a book." The identical analysis fits Job 38:28–29, another image that parallels fathering and mothering. The one who is speaking is *Yahweh* (1), *El* (41), and the grammatical gender of the verb *gives birth* is masculine. There is no Mother God in Job 38.

20. Here we only illustrate cross-gender imagery in a few representative texts. A complete survey of feminine imagery was provided in chap 3.

21. The grammatical subject of the first clause is *Rock*, which is masculine, but not a personal term. So the verb *fathered/mothered/begot* may not directly indicate a masculine person. However, *The Rock* is a title of *Yahweh*, not just a metaphor. Thus it probably does reflect a masculine subject. The *El* of the second clause is unambiguously masculine.

The important personification of wisdom as a woman in Proverbs 8 likewise involves cross-gender imagery. For it is *Yahweh* (22) who *brought forth* or gave birth (24, 25) to wisdom. Predictably the birthing verb is masculine in form. The language of this text presents the Lord as an anthropomorphically masculine person who figuratively gives birth to wisdom, not as an anthropomorphically feminine person, the Mother of Wisdom.

Wisdom, a grammatically feminine term in Hebrew, is personified as a woman in Proverbs, following the usual pattern of personification in languages with grammatically gendered nouns. However, this feminine personification does not imply that wisdom is more characteristically a feminine than a masculine trait. The fact that the wisdom which is personified as female belongs to God does not imply that God is presented anthropomorphically as a feminine person.[22] Wisdom in Proverbs 8 is a feminine image of an attribute of God, who is written of as though he is a masculine person. This, too, is cross-gender imagery.

It is important in exegeting these texts to note that cross-gender imagery was also used of human kings in the ancient Near East. An inscription of King Azitawadda reads: "Baal made me a father and a mother to the Danunites." King Kilamuwa writes: "To some I was a father. To some I was a mother. To some I was a brother."[23] We also find a striking cross-gender image of this sort in Isaiah 60:16b: "you shall suck the breasts of kings" (NRSV).[24] In all of these cases, maternal (and paternal) roles are figuratively predicated of masculine persons—kings. Surely, however, no one who reads this imagery has any question about their gender or is inclined to address them as both King and Queen. No one supposes that they were androgynous or wonders whether these kings were expressing confusion about their gender identity. The meaning of cross-gender imagery is unambiguous. The Old Testament uses this same convention when it occasionally speaks of God using feminine imagery. The New Testament examples, far fewer than the Old Testament ones, are also feminine figures attributed to a linguistically masculine person.[25]

---

22. These points were made above in chap. 3.

23. *Ancient Near Eastern Texts Relating to the Old Testament*, ed. J. B. Pritchard (Princeton, N.J.: Princeton University Press, 1969), 653–54, quoted from Mettinger, *In Search of God*, 206. Mettinger discusses the significance of biblical gendered language for God in Appendix 24, but is unable to get beyond treating masculine and feminine as equally figurative and equally lacking attribution of gender to God. The concept of cross-gender imagery completely solves his puzzle.

24. Thus the name *El Shaddai* would not imply that God is anthropomorphically female even if it were true that *Shaddai* meant "Breasted," a claim we disputed in Chapter Three.

25. Even the Holy Spirit giving new birth in John 3 is technically a cross-gender image. For the Holy Spirit is neuter in Greek. The mothering activity is predicated of a linguistically genderless person.

In sum, the verifiable feminine references to God in Scripture are without exception cross-gender images. This is usually obvious from the gender of the terms contained within the images themselves. It is always clear from the context of the images.

This conclusion offers an alternative explanation of the Bible's gendered language for God, a conclusion that directly challenges a fundamental thesis of inclusivism. Gender-egalitarians as theologically diverse as Brian Wren, Rosemary Ruether, Ruth Duck, Elizabeth Johnson, Virginia Mollenkott, Paul Smith, and Joanna van Wijk-Bos claim that the Bible's feminine references speak of God as though he is a feminine person in order to justify naming God *Mother* and using the pronoun *She*. But since the feminine references are cross-gender images, they have no such implications. In fact, these images actually highlight the Bible's presentation of God in language appropriate for a masculine person for whom feminine names, titles, and pronouns are linguistically improper. Thus the strategic inclusivist argument which attempts to find support for gender-egalitarian language in Scripture is fundamentally mistaken.

Who God Is and What God is Like

We conclude our analysis of the biblical pattern of gendered language for God by making a commonsense generalization: most of the Bible's masculine language has the linguistic function of telling us both who God is and what he is like. In other words, it both identifies and describes God. Scripture's feminine language only has the linguistic function of telling us what particular attitudes and actions of God are like. This conclusion follows straightforwardly from the fact that the feminine language is imagery whereas most of the masculine language identifies God by name, title, or appellative. (Recall again that we are not inferring that God actually has gender.)

Figures of speech compare two different things in order to highlight particular features of one of them. The figure depicts what something about the subject is like. In the familiar feminine images of the divine, God's love is like the love of a mother. God's anger is like that of a mother bear. God's creating the mountains is like giving birth. God's eager effort to save his people is like that of a woman in labor. Thus elaborated, it is obvious that these figures of speech show what God, or more precisely, what God's love, anger, act of creating, and eager effort to save are like. Since they are images, they do not function to identify who God is.[26]

26. In the fourth meaning of *name* they do identify who God is in a general, figurative sense: he is the one whose love is like a mother's, whose anger is like a mother bear's, etc. But this does not alter the distinctions between images and the other kinds of *names*.

However, it is the function of proper names, titles, and appellatives to identify who God is. God tells Moses who he is by revealing *Yahweh* as his proper name. Who is *Yahweh*? The answer is given by another title and name: *the God of Abraham*, who is *El Shaddai* (Exod. 3 and 6). Again, who is Yahweh? The answer is given by another basic title: "Yahweh is King" (Ps. 98:6). A further answer is provided by an appellative, a predicate noun that says who God is by identifying him with a kind of person in relationship: the Lord is "a father to the fatherless" (Ps. 68:5). Unlike figures of speech, these ways of naming God state who he is.

However, they also disclose what he is like. They do so because they are not name-tags pinned to God with no intrinsic meaning. They are not proper names whose sole meaning is to refer to God. They all have meanings that state or describe things about God as they identify him. They are proper names—*names* in the first sense—that have inherent meanings (e.g., *Yahweh*) or *names* in the second and third senses: terms of identification and description. It is therefore misleadingly simplistic to say, as some do, that figures of speech tell us what God is like, whereas names and titles tell us who he is.

It may happen that we forget the descriptive biblical meaning of these names. We may not realize that *Yahweh* is related to *I Am*, the faithful God of the covenant, when we use that name of God. (The translation of *Yahweh* as *Lord* does not help us recover the biblical meaning.) We may not remember the redemptive, messianic meaning of *Father* when we use it to address God in prayer. We may even understand it as implying abusive patriarchalism. Thus inclusivists are right to point out the danger that these terms can become distorted or "dead metaphors."[27] But the biblical names and titles of God have meanings whether we know them or not. They tell us what God is like, as well as telling us in various ways who he is.[28]

A Traditionalist Confusion about Language?

Since we have criticized inclusivists' use of linguistic categories, fairness requires that we also acknowledge problematic linguistic arguments made by defenders of biblical-traditional language for God. A prominent example is the attempt to locate the qualitative difference between masculine and feminine language for God in the distinction between similes and metaphors.

Elizabeth Achtemeier and Roland Frye, on whom Achtemeier depends, are two defenders of traditional language who take this position.

27. Duck, *Gender and the Name of God*, 16–18.
28. Bavinck, "God's Names," in *The Doctrine of God*.

According to Achtemeier, "a simile compares one aspect of something to another." There is no linguistic identification of the two. "In metaphors, on the other hand, identity between the subject and the thing compared to it is assumed. God *is* Father, or Jesus *is* the Good Shepherd."[29] Frye applies this distinction to the inclusive language debate. "In feminist interpretation, simile and metaphor are confused and conflated so that a simile is assumed to do what a metaphor is in fact designed to do. In this way, occasional biblical comparisons of the divine to a mother are given the same force as if they were names or identifications."[30] Achtemeier and Frye classify all the feminine references to God as similes and argue that, since metaphors identify two things, the masculine metaphors, such as father and king, identify or name who God is, whereas the feminine similes do not.[31]

Traditionalists who take this approach have been criticized by defenders of inclusive language for making too much of the simile–metaphor distinction. Inclusivists counter that both similes and metaphors are figures of speech that compare different things. It is not true that metaphors intend to equate God with a father or king whereas similes merely intend to compare him, they say. Metaphors and similes are basically the same.[32]

There are several reasons why basing opposition to inclusive language for God heavily on the metaphor–simile distinction is a faulty strategy. First, not all maternal references are similes. In fact, there are birth metaphors for some of God's acts, as shown in chapter 3. God "brings forth" the mountains (Ps. 90:2) and figuratively gives birth to the frost from his womb (Job 38:29). It is important to point out, however, that these metaphors are not predicate nouns that figuratively identify God as a mother. They are surely not appellatives. Thus the point important to Frye and Achtemeier is still valid.

The second reason against too strong a metaphor–simile distinction is that both can be used in naming or giving titles. *Lamb of God* is a metaphor that is a title of Jesus. Occasionally similes also supply the material for a name. For example, Snow White's name was based on her

---

29. Achtemeier, "Exchanging God for 'No Gods,'" in *Speaking the Christian God*, 5.

30. Frye, "Language for God and Feminist Language," in *Speaking the Christian God*, 34.

31. Ibid., 36–43.

32. See, for example, Margo Houts, "Language, Gender, and God: How Traditionalists and Feminists Play the Inclusive Language Game" (Ph.D. dissertation, Fuller Theological Seminary, 1993), and "Is God Also Our Mother?" *Perspectives* 12 (1997): 8–12; also Aída Besançon Spencer, *The Goddess Revival*, 255, note 19, and "Father-Ruler: The Meaning of the Metaphor 'Father' for God in the Bible," *Journal of the Evangelical Theological Society* 39, no. 3 (1996): 433–42.

mother's observation that her skin was *white as snow,* which is a simile. In Isaiah 40:11 the Lord is *like a shepherd* (a simile), in Psalm 23 the Lord *is a shepherd* (a metaphor), and in Psalm 80:1 his title is *Shepherd of Israel.* Thus it is not true that metaphors can be turned into names whereas similes cannot.

There is third problem. Frye and Achtemeier stress the point that metaphors identify two things, whereas similes merely compare different things. But this claim does not acknowledge the fact that metaphors are often functionally equivalent to similes. "Bill is a clown" and "Bill acts like a clown" say virtually the same thing in slightly different ways. Metaphors (e.g. "John is a bear") do not intend to identify one thing as another the way appellatives do (e.g., "John is a teacher"). They too juxtapose different things.

Nevertheless, it is true that predicate noun metaphors share the same form as appellatives and thus do appear to identify different things figuratively, whereas similes are always explicitly comparative. So Achtemeier and Frye are correct when they chide inclusivists for treating similes as equivalent to identifications of God. And they are right that metaphors are formally suited for kinds of identification that similes cannot duplicate. Two of his titles identify Jesus as *the Good Shepherd* and *the Lamb of God.* These metaphorical titles are not equaled in meaning by similes stating that he is like a shepherd and like a lamb.

But this raises a fourth problem. In asserting that metaphors identify, Frye and Achtemeier do not recognize the difference between how appellatives and predicate metaphors identify. In other words, they do not distinguish between "David is the king of Judah" and "David is the lion of Judah." The former identifies David literally; the latter describes him figuratively. Similarly, we must be able to distinguish the appellative, "God is king" from the metaphor "God is light." Frye and Achtemeier do not leave room for this distinction in their concern to affirm that divine transcendence renders all language for God metaphorical (see chap. 7). As we saw, virtually all inclusivists make this same mistake in another way.

Fifth, in Scripture's presentation of God as Father, the key linguistic point is not so much that *Father* is a special metaphor, but that it is a title or name. Achtemeier and Frye speak of terms like *King* and *Father* as metaphors that are extended in use to identify or name God. But this classification is misleading and can play into the hands of those who regard the names of God as mere metaphors. The fact is that *King* and *Father* are primary title-names for God in the sense that they are proper designations. They are not metaphors, that is, figures of speech, even though they may have metaphorical meanings.

For these reasons it is better to locate the basic distinction within language for God between figures of speech on one hand and appellatives, titles, and names on the other. The figurative origin and meaning of some appellatives, titles, and names can be recognized without classifying them as extended metaphors. This approach is more linguistically accurate and avoids the misunderstandings and criticisms of inclusivists.

However, my criticisms of the approach of Achtemeier and Frye, some of which are also raised by inclusivists, touch only parts of their analysis, and do not undermine their main conclusions, which are based on biblical revelation as the ultimate source and norm for naming God. I therefore strongly disagree with those critics who infer that the problems in this approach vitiate its force against gender-inclusive language. Furthermore, even if Achtemeier and Frye were fundamentally mistaken, that would not repair the confusions and fallacies in inclusivist arguments from biblical imagery to feminine names, titles, and pronouns for God. Two wrongs don't make a right.

Conclusion

This chapter has shown that gender-inclusive language for God is significantly different from the gendered language of the Bible and that it cannot be linguistically derived from Scripture. We have located the confusions and fallacies in inclusivist claims that gender-egalitarian language—the regular use of feminine as well as masculine names, titles, appellatives, and pronouns—naturally arises from the presence of both masculine and feminine references to God in Scripture. As an alternative analysis, we noted that the consistent pattern of Scripture presents God as though he is a masculine person, using masculine names, titles, and appellatives to state who he is. Scripture never speaks as if God is a feminine person. The feminine references are cross-gender images, feminine figures of speech predicated of a linguistically masculine person.

This analysis yields a provisional conclusion for the debate about language for God: surely it is permissible for Christians who follow Scripture to use feminine language for God according to the biblical pattern. In other words, Christians are not required to reject all feminine language for God even though the use of gender-egalitarian inclusive language cannot be derived from the Bible. There are ways to refer to God with feminine terms that are found in Scripture or are consistent with the biblical pattern. (Specific guidelines for this practice are worked out in chapter 11.)

But the debate is not over. Rejection of gender-inclusive language is required at this point only if language for God must be validated by a strict reading of Scripture taken as the definitive source of our language for God. The scriptural pattern is normative for all times and places only if certain assumptions about the nature and proper interpretation of the Bible are true. Perhaps inclusive language can still be reconciled with Scripture if different assumptions are made. These issues are treated in the following chapters.

6

Revelation, Scripture, and Naming God

Inclusive Language Is Not Yet Refuted

It has become clear that gender-inclusive language cannot be derived directly from the Bible by balancing its feminine and masculine language for God. For Scripture does not speak of God as equivalently masculine and feminine. The feminine expressions are cross-gender images for a linguistically-anthropomorphically masculine person. Inclusivists who appeal to Holy Scripture to justify the current movement for gender-correctness in religious language have built a house of cards.

But is that the end of inclusive language for God? Is strict adherence to the biblical pattern of language the only way that Christians may speak about God? Is the Bible the only legitimate source of language for God? These are fair questions, because the Christian tradition has often used language for God that does not occur in the Bible. Why is gender-inclusive language not capable of the same validation? Let's explore the problem.

An obvious example of nonbiblical language in Christian tradition is the doctrine that the one God is three persons. This teaching is essential to the Christian faith as stated in the Apostles' and Nicene Creeds. But terms like *Trinity, person,* and *one substance (homoousios* in the Nicene Creed) are nowhere to be found in Scripture. They come from a vocabulary devised by the church's doctors and theologians. Furthermore, *the Absolute, Necessary Being, Final Cause,* and *Great Designer* are titles for God that come from philosophers, some of whom were not even Christians.

Poets and preachers have also taken liberties in speaking of God. Gripping sermon illustrations frequently liken God, his attitudes, and his actions to all sorts of things never mentioned in the Bible. As a boy

in the 1950s I heard a sermon on God's sovereign, irresistible grace delivered by a strictly orthodox Calvinist preacher who concluded by
reading from Francis Thompson's famous poem, "The Hound of
Heaven." This minister then had the audacity to follow the sermon with
a prayer beginning, "O Hound of Heaven." Worshipers were struck by
this image, but I recall no one expressing concern about the minister's
orthodoxy, loyalty to Scripture, or possible blasphemy, even though he
addressed God as a dog.

If referring to God as *Trinity, First Person, Necessary Being,* and
Hound of Heaven are legitimate, what is objectionable about calling
God *Mother*? For the Bible does contain the words *mother* and *give birth*
in its imagery for God, whereas these other terms are not found in
Scripture. Inclusivists can therefore argue that egalitarian feminine
language for God is an extension of biblical imagery. As we have seen,
some biblical images, such as *rock, shepherd,* and *father,* became titles
for God as written revelation progressed. Why is it wrong for Christians
to apply the same process to the feminine images, especially at a time
in the history of the church when the sins of sexism are finally being
recognized and addressed?

So the question legitimately arises, Why is it impermissible to adopt
feminine terms for God just as the other extrabiblical vocabulary of the
Christian tradition has developed? If our forebears in the faith, including Julian of Norwich and John Calvin, were not linguistically promis-
cuous in speaking of God as our Mother, why must we resist contemporary inclusivism?

A complete answer to these questions is complex and extends beyond
the scope of this chapter. The issue as a whole involves recognizing the
order among the various sources of language for God, such as the Bible,
God's revelation in creation, and the religious experience of faithful
Christians. Are all of these sources equally valid and definitive? Or is
Holy Scripture a special source and norm? If the Bible is the highest authority, then the legitimacy of language for God derived from other
sources depends on whether that language faithfully maintains the biblical presentation of God or confuses and undermines biblical revelation. These complex questions about revelation, biblical interpretation,
and theological elaboration will occupy us for several chapters.

The present chapter focuses on the basic issue—the role of Scripture
and other kinds of revelation in naming God. It has four sections. The
first presents a traditional Christian account of God's revelation in creation, Jesus Christ, Scripture, and the church. The second evaluates a
number of inclusivist approaches to revelation and Scripture in terms
of the first section. The third section confronts questions about the enduring normativity of Scripture's masculine language for God. For in-

clusivists, even those with a high view of the Bible, claim that its patriarchal language is merely God's accommodation of an ancient, sinful social system and is no longer binding on Christians in a gender-egalitarian culture. The fourth section explores what the Bible teaches about the significance and limits of the human act of naming God. The chapter concludes that Holy Scripture, although it is not our only source of language for God, is the enduring and definitive source.

God's Revelation: The Source of Our Knowledge of His Names[1]

Humans can rightly name God only if God reveals himself. As the Dutch Reformed theologian Herman Bavinck has pointed out, "God's name is . . . most of all God's revelation of himself whereby he actively and objectively makes himself known."[2] It stands to reason that if God did not make himself available to our experience and language, we humans could not know and speak of him. Thus the human possibility of naming God depends on our apprehending and rightly understanding divine revelation. But where and how exactly does God reveal himself? Most Christian traditions, no matter how high their view of Scripture, affirm that the Bible is not the only medium of God's revelation. In varying ways they also affirm creation, Jesus Christ, and God's continuing presence in the church as means by which God is known. We explore each means of revelation in relation to the others.

General Revelation

Most Christians follow Scripture in affirming that the first and broadest revelation of God is in his creation, the cosmos. Psalm 19:1 exclaims, "The heavens declare the glory of God" and Romans 1:20 asserts, "since the creation of the world God's invisible qualities—his eternal power and divine nature—have been clearly seen, being understood from what has been made." Of all God's creatures, human beings most clearly reveal him, for they have been made in God's own image and likeness, a status not granted other creatures (Gen. 1:26–28).

Theologians have called creation's disclosure of God *general revelation*.[3] It continues in God's providential maintenance and governance

1. An excellent classical Reformed acount of general revelation, special revelation, and Scripture is found in Herman Bavinck, *Our Reasonable Faith*, trans. Henry Zylstra (Grand Rapids: Baker, 1956, 1977), chaps. 3–7.
2. Bavinck, *The Doctrine of God*, 84.
3. In addition to Bavinck, see G. C. Berkouwer, *General Revelation* (Grand Rapids: Eerdmans, 1955); Bruce Demarest, *General Revelation* (Grand Rapids: Zondervan, 1982), and Wolfhart Pannenberg, *Systematic Theology* (Grand Rapids: Eerdmans, 1991), 1:107–18, "The 'Natural' Knowledge of God."

of his entire creation even after the fall. Thus all of creation, especially the human race, is a source of language for God. According to Bavinck, God's names "are derived from every kind of creature, living and lifeless, organic and inorganic." But since humans alone are made in God's image, "most of the names of the Deity, particularly the most exalted ones, are derived from man."[4] In this way traditional Christian theology affirms that general revelation does give us "many names for God."

The "names" implicit in general revelation include all four kinds of *name* identified in the previous chapter: proper names, specific titles, general appellatives, and the broad sense that includes figures of speech. For even the proper names and titles presented in Scripture are taken from things God created: kings, shepherds, and fathers. According to Bavinck, "all the names with which God names himself and by means of which he allows us to address him are derived from earthly and human relations."[5] Furthermore, the names taken from general revelation include both male and female language for God, because both human males and females bear his image, and because mother bears and mother birds reflect his divine nature as much as father birds and father bears do. Thus the biblical images of God as a woman and mother are grounded in God's general revelation. In the broadest sense they too are "names" of God.

Special Revelation

God's Involvement in History

Obviously God has not limited himself to general revelation. Even before the fall he condescended to commune and communicate with our first parents (Gen. 2). Although they were excluded from this fellowship after the fall, God continued to show himself and to speak with them and their descendants, Noah, Abraham, Isaac, Jacob, Moses, David, and the prophets, through whom he spoke to his people. God showed himself in blessing, instructing, admonishing, and even in punishing them. He was specially present in the particular natural, historical, and supernatural occurrences that shaped their history. All these events in which God acted, encountered, or verbally communicated with his people theologians call *special revelation*, because they reveal God in particular ways that general revelation does not. These events include God's revealing himself and his name to Abraham as *El*, to Moses as *I Am*, *Yahweh*, the God of the covenant, and to David as the father of his messianic son.

4. Bavinck, *The Doctrine of God*, 88, 89.
5. Ibid., 86.

Jesus Christ

The greatest, clearest, and most definitive special revelation of God is Jesus Christ. The Word, who created the world and who is true God, was made flesh (John 1). Thus Jesus Christ is rightly named *Immanuel, God With Us* (Matt. 1:23). And therefore he can say "Anyone who has seen me has seen the Father" (John 14:9). The incarnation, life, teachings, miracles, suffering, death, resurrection, and ascension into heaven—all of Jesus' earthly existence is the fullest presence and revelation of God to humans in history until the second coming. Since Jesus is the definitive revelation of God, his naming of God and the names that identify him and his relation to God his Father are the highest and most definitive revealed names of God.

Holy Scripture[6]

Meanwhile we live between Jesus' first and second comings. But God has not left himself without a witness. We have more than general revelation. The Holy Spirit, sent by the risen and exalted Jesus Christ (Acts 2), came to dwell in the hearts of God's people, the church. And the Holy Spirit has continued to guide Jesus' disciples into the truth (John 16:13). But we have even more than the apostolic tradition of the church. We have more to guide us than the church's memory of God's special revelation in the history of Israel and in Jesus' earthly life.

God the Holy Spirit has "breathed out" the Holy Scriptures for us (2 Tim. 3:16). The Bible is not the supreme revelation of God; Jesus Christ is. Jesus himself said: "These are the Scriptures that testify about me" (John 5:39).[7] Nevertheless, since the Ascension the Bible is the most reliable and definitive form of special revelation we have until Jesus' return. For the Holy Spirit has inspired the Scriptures in such a way that they are without error in all that they teach, assume, and imply. Thus they have a reliability and truthfulness that the pronouncements of the church and the religious experiences of individual Christians do not share.

6. See Bavinck, "The Holy Scriptures," in *Our Reasonable Faith* for an engaging classical Reformed view. Contemporary treatments of biblical revelation from a historic Christian point of view are William Abraham, *Divine Revelation and the Limits of Historical Criticism* (New York: Oxford University Press, 1982); Avery Dulles, *Models of Revelation* (Garden City, N.Y.: Doubleday Image, 1985); and Nicholas Wolterstorff, *Divine Discourse: Philosophical Reflections on the Claim That God Speaks* (Cambridge: Cambridge University Press, 1995).

7. Jesus and Paul are speaking specifically about the Old Testament Scriptures, but the church has considered the New Testament to share the status as Word of God because the apostles did so. For example, 2 Peter 3:15–16 considers the writings of Paul as Scripture.

In addition, the Bible is broader in scope than the revelation of God in the earthly presence of Jesus Christ. For it narrates the entire history of God's earthly kingdom from its creation, through the fall of our first parents into sin, recounting the redemption that God promised and fulfilled in Jesus Christ, and looking forward to the establishment of God's everlasting kingdom with the return of Jesus Christ. The Bible presents the history of the triune God's mighty acts in creation and redemption, the acts and communications that reveal who he is, what he has done, and what he wills. This self-revelation includes the divine names and titles from *El* to *Yahweh* to *Father, Son, and Holy Spirit*. It states definitively the meaning of God's general revelation in creation and providence, his special revelation in the history of his people, and his supreme self-revelation in Jesus Christ.

That is why the Christian church has always regarded the Bible as the definitive source of our knowledge of God, ourselves, and the way of salvation. In the Protestant Reformation tradition it is regarded as "the only rule of faith and practice." In the Roman Catholic and Orthodox communions, Scripture is also regarded as without error in its teaching, although the church's proclamation of the apostolic tradition and its interpretation of Scripture are given correlative authority.[8] All historic Christians agree that the church must continue to profess what Scripture teaches.

Scripture Interprets General Revelation

Since Holy Scripture provides the definitive interpretation of all revelation, it constitutes the definitive account of the names of God. The relationship between Scripture and other forms of revelation deserves fuller elaboration. For acknowledgment of the Bible's normative status is crucial in evaluating arguments for gender-inclusive language for God.

Scripture is necessary to illumine and correctly understand general revelation. The Athenian philosophers whom Paul addressed according to Acts 17 knew that there is a great Creator God. But they did not know who he is. Paul's sermon had the force of special revelation, informing them of the particular identity of the Unknown God. Special revelation is necessary to illumine general revelation for two reasons.

First, general revelation manifests God's attributes as creator and sustainer of the universe. But Scripture states much more clearly his personal identity as the God who involved himself with his people in the

8. See "The Relationship Between Tradition and Sacred Scripture" and Article 3, "Sacred Scripture," *Catechism of the Catholic Church*, 26–27 and 30–38.

history of their redemption, culminating in the Jesus Christ whom Paul proclaimed to the Athenians. The Bible is much richer, fuller, and more detailed than general revelation in answering the question, Who is the God creation reveals? And so the names of God disclosed in Scripture are more specific and personal than those derived from general revelation. To use a human analogy, my neighbors may know me as "the middle-aged man who lives in that house" from observing me (general revelation). But if I introduce myself to them or if they read of my name and occupation (special revelation), they will know that I am John Cooper, professor at Calvin Seminary. Special revelation in Scripture provides a lot of detailed information, including God's particular names and titles, that general revelation does not.

Second, Scripture is necessary to overcome the effects of sin on the human perception and interpretation of general revelation. Although God's eternal power and divine nature are manifest in creation, human beings "suppress the truth by their wickedness" so that "their thinking became futile and their foolish hearts were darkened" and "they exchanged the truth of God for a lie, and worshipped and served created things rather than the Creator" (Rom. 1:18, 21, 25). Human religious experience, the world's religions, and the great philosophical systems always mix and distort the truth of general revelation with sinful human misinterpretations. Human notions of God may contain elements and fragments of truth, but their positive namings and interpretations of God are human inventions—distorted pictures that they worship instead of the Creator. Confronted with the true interpretation, as the philosophers of Athens were by Paul, many reject it. They claim to want a relationship with the true God, but when he is explicitly named, they turn their backs on him. Scripture is necessary for rightly understanding the revelation of God in nature and human nature. To continue the illustration, my neighbors may have many false ideas about "the guy who lives in that house." Introducing and explaining myself to them not only identifies who I am, but clears up a lot of misinformation as well.

Thus appeals to the world's religions and philosophies as sources from which we can "bring many names to God" are at best dubious. While there may be glimpses of truth about God in them, these sources are mixed with and distorted by falsehoods. *The Absolute, Brahman, The Great Spirit, The Supreme Being,* and *The Great Mother*[9] may in one way or another reflect the general revelation of the true God. But the meanings of these terms in their religious and philosophical contexts are different from and often incompatible with the God of Scripture.

9. See James Livingston, *The Anatomy of the Sacred: An Introduction to Religion*, 2nd ed. (New York: Macmillan, 1993), 174–81 for an account of mother gods in world religions.

Only in the light of biblical revelation can the true and false representations of God be sorted out. Therefore the biblical names for God may
not be relativized by mixing them with other human namings of God.
For that would amount to embracing religious pluralism, the view that
all human religious symbols in different ways validly name God.[10]

Scripture Interprets Christian Experience

Scripture is likewise necesssary for understanding the continuing
presence and leading of God's people by the Holy Spirit. Jesus promised
to send the Counselor, the Holy Spirit, to lead the church. He has kept
his promise, empowering and leading the church ever since Pentecost.
The Spirit has led the church to evangelize the world, to live the gospel
in the many cultures in which it took root, to develop forms of worship,
organization, discipling, evangelism, and cultural engagement not explicitly found in Scripture, and indeed to understand the teaching and
meaning of Scripture itself more fully. God has been present in the history of the church, whatever differences Protestants and Catholics have
on the authority of Christian tradition. Furthermore, the Holy Spirit
continues to dwell in the heart of each believer, nurturing, empowering,
and leading every one into fuller Christlikeness. Obedience to Scripture
therefore does not mean doing only what is specifically enjoined in its
pages as a legalistic repetition of the letter of the text. Spirit-led obedience can involve creativity and novelty for the whole church and for individual believers.

But all of this work of the Holy Spirit unfolds within the framework
laid out by the very same Spirit in Scripture. The Holy Spirit leads the
church to understand and obey Scripture in fuller and deeper ways, as
well as to develop novel applications of the teachings of Scripture in
new and different cultural situations. But the Spirit does not contradict
or annul the definitive teaching of the Bible. The Holy Spirit, who proceeds from the Father and the Son and who inspired and illuminates
Scripture, is not self-contradictory or inconsistent with the whole work
of the triune God. Scripture remains the rule of faith and practice for
the church, including each of its individual members, throughout history. Religious experiences and developments in doctrine or practice
that contradict, weaken, confuse, modify, or supplant the teaching of
Scripture must be judged by the church as contrary to the leading of the
Holy Spirit. This criterion also applies to the church's ways of speaking
and thinking about God.

10. See, for example, John Hick, *God Has Many Names* (Philadelphia: Westminster,
1982).

Scripture Interprets Jesus Christ

Finally, the Bible is the definitive presentation of Jesus Christ. We have accounts of Jesus from the ancient world and from modern higher critical scholars.[11] History presents us with hundreds of interpretations of his identity and signficance.[12] But the true presentation of who Jesus is, what he has done, and what he is still doing in human history is found in Holy Scripture. Jesus is who the Bible says he is.[13] To be a true follower of Jesus Christ, a true Christian, is not to reverence and emulate some human reconstruction of Jesus, but to worship the Jesus understood in terms of the whole of Scripture as Savior, Lord, and God. Jesus Christ is the full revelation of God. Scripture is the definitive account of Jesus Christ. Therefore Scripture is the definitive account of our understanding of God through Jesus Christ.

For all these reasons, the way we think and speak of God may never supplant or contradict the Bible. It is the definitive, unerringly reliable framework of interpretation for all of God's revelation. As the living word of God, it continues as the means through which God speaks to us. It is not merely a record of what God said millennia ago. Through Scripture God still testifies to the church and the world that he is Father, Son, and Holy Spirit.

Summary: Revelation and Naming God

To summarize our conclusions about revelation, Scripture, and naming God I can do no better than to quote Herman Bavinck: "the names which we use in mentioning and addressing God are not arbitrary: they are not the mere inventions of our mind. Rather it is God himself who in nature and in grace reveals himself consciously and freely, who gives us the right to name him on the ground of his revelation, and who has even made known to us in his Word the names which are based on that revelation."[14]

This position has clear implications for the linguistic structures with which we name God. Masculine, feminine, and ungendered language for God is available to religious experience from general revelation. Thus creation and Christian piety reveal to us that God is not only like

11. Josephus and Tacitus wrote of Jesus in the first and second centuries. Currently the infamous Jesus Seminar is confidently pronouncing on what Jesus did and did not say and do, basing its judgments on "the assured results" of historical-critical scholarship.
12. Jaroslav Pelikan, *Jesus Through the Centuries: His Place in the History of Culture* (San Francisco: Harper & Row, 1987).
13. C. Stephen Evans, *The Historical Christ and the Jesus of Faith: The Incarnational Narrative as History* (New York: Oxford University Press, 1996).
14. Bavinck, *The Doctrine of God*, 86.

a father, but is also like a mother. However, special revelation is the definitive source of the names of the God who shows himself in creation and to his people. The one who is like a mother has revealed himself as our Father through Jesus and the Bible.

To put the point more precisely, all four kinds of names distinguished in the previous chapter—proper names, titles, identification by common nouns (appellatives), and a broad category that includes figures of speech—are grounded in general revelation. But in special revelation God has chosen to use masculine language for his proper names and basic titles, as well as the common nouns that identify him. The biblical references derived from females are all figures of speech. If we recognize the definitive status of Scripture, we will adopt its pattern of language for God as the framework for speaking of God as known in creation and in our religious experience.

Revelation and Naming God Inclusively

Given the nature of Scripture and its relationship to other revelatory sources of language for God, many inclusivist approaches introduced in chapter 2 are inadequate or mistaken. The following approaches are typical and significant, though treated briefly.

Equalizing Special and General Revelation

Any practice of egalitarian inclusivism inevitably levels out the hierarchical order of special and general revelation. In general revelation both fathers and mothers, both kings and queens in some way show us what God is like. But in special revelation God declares himself to be Father and King, not Mother and Queen. Taking the feminine imagery for God derived from general revelation and found in Scripture and giving it a status equal to the basic biblical names and titles for God inevitably relativizes the Bible to general revelation. Either the experience of general revelation is elevated to the level of Scripture, or Scripture is relegated to the level of general revelation. The inclusivist attempt to "bring many names to God" inevitably contravenes the final authority of Holy Scripture as the source of our knowledge of the names of God.

Some inclusivists relativize the biblical presentation of God by emphasizing divine transcendence.[15] God is so far beyond human concepts and language, they say, that none of our terminology is adequate. The Bible's masculine language therefore should not be privileged, but balanced with language from females and other creatures in representing God. According to Elizabeth Johnson, "Women's refusal of the exclusive

---

15. Chap. 2, "Patriarchal Language Is Not Privileged: God Is Beyond All Language."

claim of the white male symbol of the divine arises from the well-founded demand to adhere to the holy mystery of God."[16] In effect, this approach, like the previous one, relativizes the special revelation of the Bible to God's general revelation in creation, which in turn is considered an inadequate reflection of the hidden, wholly other God. (Inclusivist appeals to divine transcendence are considered more fully in chapter 7.)

Reducing the Authority of Scripture

Inclusivists reduce the authority of the Bible itself in a variety of ways. One is to separate the Bible from divine revelation. Letty Russell asserts: *"the Word of God is not identical with the biblical texts."*[17] Ruth Duck follows suit, claiming that Scripture is not revelation but "witness to revelation."[18] Similarly, Elizabeth Johnson and Gail Ramshaw reject as "fundamentalism" identification of the text of Scripture as revelation.[19] This inclusivist strategy is discussed more fully in the next section, "The Words of Scripture." Here we only point out that it contradicts the traditional Christian confession, which does affirm Scripture as the most definitive form of revelation for the church in history, although it does not limit revelation to the Bible or claim that the Bible is God's fullest revelation, which is Jesus Christ.

Some inclusivists relativize Scripture by denying its infallibility, especially because they regard it as accommodating the sin of patriarchalism. For this reason Brian Wren asserts that "all revelation is impeded by sin" and Sandra Schneiders claims that the biblical text "is as capable of error, distortion, and even sinfulness as the church itself."[20] But in so doing they deny the basic Christian confession that the Bible is without error in all that it teaches, reveals about God, and requires of human beings.

Still other inclusivists minimize Scripture by accepting only parts of it. They isolate a "canon-within-the-canon." Rosemary Ruether adopts this approach. She makes it clear that she regards only the "prophetic-liberating texts," those that criticize hierarchical authority and elevate the poor and oppressed, as the Word of God. "Feminist readings of the Bible can discern a norm within Biblical faith by which the Biblical texts themselves can be criticized. To the extent to which Biblical texts

16. Johnson, *She Who Is*, 117; also Ramshaw, *God beyond Gender*, 21; Ruether, *Sexism and God-Talk*, 68–69.

17. Russell, *Feminist Interpretation of the Bible*, 17.

18. Duck, *Gender and the Name of God*, 24.

19. See chap. 2, "Scripture Is Not Identical with God's Word."

20. Wren, *What Language Shall I Borrow?* 130–31; Schneiders, "The Bible and Feminism," in *Freeing Theology*, C. LaCugna, ed., 49.

reflect this normative principle, they are regarded as authoritative. On this basis many aspects of the Bible are to be frankly set aside and rejected."[21] Inclusivists who take this canon-within-the-canon approach toward Scripture openly reject the principle, *tota Scriptura*: the Bible as a whole is the Word of God and normative for the church.

Another means of setting aside the privileged status of *Father* as a basic biblical term for God is through the use of higher criticism. This strategy is evident among those who challenge the historical veracity of the Gospels' accounts of Jesus teaching about God as Father and his exclusive use of *Father* to address God. They argue that Father-language is not basic to the teaching of Jesus but was placed in his mouth by the patriarchalist writers of the Gospels. They conclude from this that privileged Father-language is not binding on the church today. Thus they hold that the lost words of Jesus would be normative if we had them, but that the biblical text is not normative. According to Ruth Duck, "Most New Testament references calling God 'Father' probably reflect early Christians' experience of prayer more than the actual words of Jesus, who may also have addressed God as Mother."[22] In this way the speculative conclusions of higher criticism are used to eliminate the definitive status of the Bible. The historic Christian church uses biblical scholarship to illuminate the meaning of Scripture, not to deny what it teaches.

Some inclusivists relativize the Bible by treating it as just one of several representations of God. Rosemary Ruether, for example, draws her theology from the liberating texts of the Bible, heretical Christian traditions, classical Christian theology, non-Christian religion and philosophy, and post-Christian worldviews.[23] Obviously Scripture is not the definitive interpretation of revelation for her. The Christian tradition recognizes that there can be elements of truth in religious experience apart from special revelation. But it insists that the glasses of Scripture are necessary to discern what is on track in the theologies of nonbiblical worldviews from what "exchanges the truth of God for a lie" (Rom. 1:25).

The Appeal to Religious Experience

Ruether and other inclusivists also relativize Scripture to "revelatory experience," especially women's experiences of repression and liberation as "a basic source of content as well as criterion of truth" for feminist Christianity.[24] They hold that God continues to manifest himself in the Spirit-guided experience of women and in women's interpreta-

---

21. Ruether, *Sexism and God-Talk*, 23.
22. Duck, *Gender and the Name of God*, 69.
23. Ruether, *Sexism and God-Talk*, 21–22.
24. Ibid., 12–13.

tions of Scripture, so that the human dialogue with Scripture, not Scripture itself, is the location of revealed truth. Ruth Duck holds that "God has been and continues to be revealed among humanity" so that in reading Scripture, "new ways of expressing the revelation of God will occur to the believing community." She affirms "continuing revelatory presence of God among men and women."[25] Schüssler-Fiorenza makes the same point in scholarly jargon: "A feminist critical interpretation of the Bible cannot take as its point of departure the normative authority of the biblical archetype, but must begin with women's experience in their struggle for liberation."[26] Historic Christianity also affirms that God continues to work in the church and in the individual lives of his people. But it does not use postbiblical Christian experience to contradict the revelation of God in Scripture or to set parts of it aside.

The most extreme appeal to experience is made by those like Sally McFague, who hold that all language for God is largely a projection of human experience. Being made in the image of God, she says, "inevitably means that we imagine God in our own image."[27] This completely anthropomorphic view of language for God is typically correlated with a strong appeal to divine transcendence, which supposedly renders impossible any true propositional assertion about God. However, this is a reversal of the biblical perspective on the relationship between God and experience-based human language for God. For we image God, not he us. Thus Paul writes: "For this reason I kneel before the Father, from whom his whole family in heaven and on earth derives its name" (Eph. 3:14–15). Father-language comes from God, not from human families.

In conclusion, none of these attempts to reconcile gender-inclusive language with the Bible treat Holy Scripture as the definitive source and final authority for faith and practice. Therefore Christians who affirm the church's historic view of revelation and the Bible must reject cases for inclusive language for God based on them. It is not possible here to argue for the truth of the historic position, but only to point out the fact that most inclusivists depart from it.[28]

25. Duck, *Gender and the Name of God*, 24.
26. Fiorenza, *Bread Not Stone*, 13. See also Johnson, *She Who Is*, 77, who moves away from "the very words of the Bible" to "other models of revelation . . . among them revelation as historical event, or as inner experience, or as dialectical presence, or as new awareness, or as symbolic mediation."
27. McFague, *Models of God*, 82, and "Symbolic Theory of Language for God" in chap. 7.
28. Most arguments against inclusive language for God, including most of the essays in *Speaking the Christian God*, ed. Alvin Kimel, finally rest on the definitive authority of Scripture. Virtually all arguments for inclusive language devise ways of relativizing the language of the Bible. The status of Scripture in our knowledge and naming of God is the basic issue in the debate.

The Words of Scripture: Mere Accommodation?

Although some inclusivists do not regard Scripture as the supreme source and norm of revelation, others do confess the Bible as inspired and authoritative. They nevertheless deny that its patriarchal language is normative for the church today. They argue that God merely tolerated exclusively male language, but does not endorse it. As indicated in chapter 2, three distinct strategies are employed to justify this view. The first distinguishes between the message and the words of Scripture. The second and third arguments affirm the words of Scripture but claim that they are an accommodation to patriarchalism, either as an alternative social order or as sinful.

Nonverbal Inspiration

The first approach takes distance from the verbal inspiration of Scripture. It holds that God inspired and guided the writers and editors of the Bible so that its content is true, but the actual words writers used to express its truth are theirs, not God's. The vocabulary, linguistic structures, and literary genres of the biblical text are regarded as the results of human choices from among culturally available materials. The patriarchal terminology and metaphors for God found in Scripture are therefore not understood as God's own self-introduction, but as human namings of God that reflect ancient Near Eastern male-dominated culture. In the words of Ruth Duck, who appeals to Karl Barth, "These writings are not, strictly speaking, revelation, but witness to revelation."[29] Thus we are not tied to the words of Scripture, but to the ideas it expresses: that God is loving, that he acts in history and in Jesus Christ to save his people, and that he wants love, justice, and peace for all his children. If inclusive language can be used to proclaim this gospel, it is argued, there is no reason not to use it. In fact inclusive language may be necessary in an egalitarian, nonhierarchical society to express truly the Bible's message.

This view of Scripture must be judged as inadequate by those who confess that the Holy Spirit inspired the words and literary forms of the Bible, the full verbal inspiration of Scripture.[30] This traditional view of inspiration is not necessarily tied to crude mechanical or dictation theories of inspiration, an association frequently made by those who wish to discredit verbal inspiration.[31] All it affirms is that the Holy Spirit

---

29. Duck, *Gender and the Name of God*, 23.

30. Bavinck, *Our Reasonable Faith*, 95–102, is a fine summary of the view of inspiration defended here. On p. 96 Bavinck rejects the view that "the Holy Scripture *is* not the Word of God, but that the Word of God is *contained* in the Holy Scripture."

31. In some Reformed circles it has been called "organic" inspiration in contrast to "mechanical" inspiration.

brought it about that the texts themselves, not merely the ideas they express, are how God willed to reveal himself. This view does not deny that the personalities, minds, cultural and social categories, and religious experiences of the writers were involved in their composition. It does not deny that processes of editing oral and written tradition were involved in the formation of the biblical books. It does not deny the activity of the human authors of Scripture and compilers of the canon. In fact it gives no simple explanation of the processes, both natural and supernatural, by which the Bible was formed. It simply asserts that the Holy Spirit providentially worked before, in, and through all these human factors and "carried along" (2 Peter 1:21) the writers to bring it about that the texts of Scripture as written are what God willed that they be. This view of inspiration, therefore, both acknowledges the various processes scrutinized by modern biblical scholars and affirms the historic Christian belief that the words of Scripture themselves are the results of the work of the Holy Spirit.[32] It concludes that the biblical vocabulary for God is not just the choice of human males who were socialized in a patriarchal culture, but also the intention of God.

Accommodation to Patriarchal Culture

But does verbal inspiration automatically make the words, including the language for God, universally true and binding on the church for all time? Isn't it possible to believe that the very words of Scripture are inspired and at the same time to hold that the Holy Spirit does not mean them all to stay the same forever? We must consider this question.

Most believing Christians acknowledge that the language and contents of the Bible are culturally embedded and historically dynamic, and that not everything in Scripture is intended by God as normative for all times. The Old Testament laws regarding clean and unclean practices no longer apply to Christians. The holy kiss is a cultural custom not binding on modern Westerners. Even the special divine name *Yahweh* is left behind by the New Testament. Thus the church has recognized that not all the words and teachings in Scripture are everlastingly unchangeable just because they have been inspired by the Holy Spirit.

32. Currently available are are excellent accounts of the nature of Scripture and how to read it written by evangelical-orthodox scholars who are fully competent academics. Among them are William Klein, Craig Blomberg, and Robert Hubbard, *Introduction to Biblical Interpretation* (Dallas: Word, 1993), Walter Kaiser and Moisés Silva, *An Introduction to Biblical Hermeneutics: The Search for Meaning* (Grand Rapids: Zondervan, 1994), Grant Osborne, *The Hermeneutical Spiral: A Comprehensive Introduction to Biblical Interpretation* (Downers Grove: InterVarsity, 1991), and Moisés Silva, ed., *Foundations of Contemporary Interpretation* (Grand Rapids: Zondervan, 1996).

So it is legitimate for Christians committed to the verbal inspiration of Scripture to ask whether the Bible's pattern of speaking of God as though he is a masculine person is binding on the church for all times. Perhaps it is an accommodation to patriarchal culture that is not normative for those of us who live in a more gender-egalitarian society.

Promoters of inclusive language for God frequently appeal to divine accommodation, offering two different reasons. The first appeals to socio-cultural relativity: Old Testament culture was patriarchal, which may have been legitimate at that time, but now God wants us to express the gospel in our situation, which is egalitarian. The second reason is an appeal to the fallen nature of patriarchal culture. It claims that God accommodated male domination in revealing himself, just as he accommodated slavery, polygamy, and divorce in Scripture. But like these other cultural practices, male domination is a sin. Those who are redeemed in Christ must work to overcome the effects of sin, even in our language for God. Let's look at each of these arguments in turn.

Accommodation of Sociocultural Diversity

Margo Houts is one inclusivist who uses the sociocultural accommodation argument. "Given the patriarchal context of God's self-revelation, one would expect the very prevalence of masculine terminology one finds in the Bible," she writes.[33] After all, the Hebrew people valued the masculine above the feminine, so it was tactically necessary for God to present himself as masculine to them. Furthermore, they were in danger of worshiping female deities such as Asherah and Astarte. So God manifested himself as exclusively masculine in Scripture. But Houts concludes that these divine acts of historical accommodation do not make privileging the masculine normative for us. The same sort of appeal to cultural diversity is made by Paul Smith: "If we can recognize the cultural influence in the early church practice of addressing one another with a holy kiss, why should we not also recognize the cultural influence in the New Testament practice of addressing God with almost exclusively masculine imagery?"[34]

This sort of argument is much too quick and easy, however. In the first place, the cultural and religious environments of the Old and New Testaments did not make it necessary for God to reveal himself as a masculine person, a fact that numerous scholars on both sides of the debate have pointed out.[35] For although almost all the cultures of the ancient

33. Margo Houts, "Is God Also Our Mother?" *Perspectives*, June/July 1997, 12.

34. Smith, *Is It Okay To Call God "Mother"?* 49.

35. See, for example, Elizabeth Achtemeier, "Exchanging God for 'No Gods,'" in A. Kimel, ed., *Speaking the Christian God*, esp. 7–11; and Ruether, "The Goddess in the Ancient Near East," *Sexism and God-Talk*, 47–52.

world were patriarchal in social structure, they worshiped both male and female deities. The female deities were not necessarily inferior in power and importance to the male deities. Baal and Asherah were equally important as the male and female sources of fertility. In fact, some patriarchal cultures worshiped a goddess such as Ishtar, Athena, or Diana as their highest deity. So "the divine feminine" was a lively cultural possibility for Scripture. It is demonstrably false that God found it necessary to take on a masculine persona for the sake of historical acceptance.

Inclusivists are correct that the Old Testament polemicizes against female deities. Asherah worship is condemned. Yahweh does not have a wife or girlfriends like the other masculine deities do. (He is "married" to Israel.) However, worship of the male gods Baal, Molech, Chemosh, and Dagon worship is also condemned. Gender privilege is not the basic problem in the Old Testament; idolatry and false gods are. Inclusivists misidentify the fundamental issue.

On the other hand, if God's choice of gender language were merely temporary polemic against ancient Near Eastern religion, why does he choose to "assimilate" the divine masculine, especially if the male gods were more important and thus more likely to be rivals to God? As noted in chap. 4, *El* with its various epithets (*Shaddai, Elyon, Olam*) and *Elohim* were masculine names of the high God known to Melchizedek and the ancestors of Abraham before the Lord, *Yahweh*, announced his (masculine) name to Moses and identified himself as the God known by these other names. The Old Testament certainly moves away from conceiving of Yahweh as a quasi-sexual, procreative male god in the sense that Baal and El were. But it internalizes the divine masculine, engraving it permanently in the special divine name, *Yahweh*, the King, while it rejects the divine feminine with the false gods it condemns.

A similar argument can be made from the New Testament. Male and female deities abound in Greco-Roman civilization. A gender-inclusive presentation of God was an obvious religious-cultural possibility. It would have been easy for the New Testament to move in the direction taken by later Gnosticism: a deity who ultimately transcends gender yet who in relation to creation is both masculine and feminine. But the God of Jesus Christ is exclusively Father.

The fact that God could easily have chosen a gender-inclusive self-presentation in terms of ancient culture and did not do so is a strong reason for supposing that the exclusively masculine language for God in Scripture is not merely a temporary accommodation. In fact it is a good indication that God is not interested in promoting gender-inclusive language for himself.

Those who believe that the biblical pattern of language is intended to be permanent do not deny that the categories of Scripture are aimed at the religious-cultural situations in which they took shape. In fact, we affirm that these categories arose in those cultures. But this contextuality does not make them culturally relative, limited, and temporary. The inclusivist appeal to the necessity of cultural accommodation is insufficient to explain away the depth and consistency of the masculine language for God as a passing phase of divine revelation.

The real issue is how we can tell whether something taught in Scripture is meant by the Holy Spirit to apply for a limited time and place or more universally and permanently. Consider covenants, law codes, and the clean–unclean distinction as examples. These existed in Near Eastern religions long before they were incorporated into the Old Testament. But some are permanent, others temporary. God's covenant of redemption is everlasting and the Ten Commandments state his universal intentions for human life. However, many Old Testament laws, including the distinction between clean and unclean animals, were not retained after Jesus Christ. So some biblical content remains in effect while other themes are fulfilled or abrogated. How do we know which is which?

In the final analysis we know from Scripture, the final authority. Scripture itself makes clear what is provisional and what is enduring. With respect to covenants, laws, and the clean–unclean distinction, Scripture presents the origin and history of God's covenants and promises, culminating with the new and eternal covenant in the blood of Jesus Christ, which is still in effect for us. Scripture presents the Ten Commandments and teaches us that God's law is good, still holding for us, although Jesus Christ has freed us from the necessity of keeping the law in order to become acceptable to God. In the same way Scripture shows us that the ceremonial law and the clean–unclean distinction of the Old Testament no longer hold since they have been fulfilled in Christ. These examples illustrate one important criterion we have by which to sort out what the Holy Spirit intends to be permanent in distinction from what is merely temporary in Scripture: whether the teaching endures, whether it is reaffirmed as constant, important, and effectual as revelation progresses from the Old Testament into the New Testament. Theologians call this criterion *the analogy of faith* or the *analogy of Scripture*, what Scripture repeatedly and consistently teaches, presupposes, or implies.[36]

It is not illegitimate for inclusivists to ask whether the religious-cultural embeddedness and relevance of the Bible's masculine language for God means that it is of temporary validity. But it is irresponsible for

---

36. See Louis Berkhof, *Principles of Biblical Interpretation* (Grand Rapids: Baker, 1950, 1990), 160–66; and Osborne, *The Hermeneutical Spiral*, 11, 271–74.

them to conclude that it is temporary simply because of its historical embeddedness and relevance. It is foolish to deny the enduring validity of biblical language without applying the usual criteria for distinguishing the enduring from the temporary contents of Scripture. Failure to apply this criterion is to practice cultural relativism or historicism, the assumption that everything culturally situated is temporary and changeable. This position in turn implies that nothing in the Bible is enduring, because all of it comes in particular cultural categories and language. But historicism is false, and so therefore is any method of biblical interpretation that implies or presupposes it. Inclusivists must face up to this issue.

If the criterion of constancy is applied to the masculine language for God in Scripture, we must conclude that it is universally valid even though it is embedded in and relevant to ancient Near Eastern religious categories. Chapter 4 demonstrated at length that the progressive revelation of God throughout both Testaments, using three languages and spanning several cultural epochs, is massively and without exception in language appropriate for a masculine person. God's self-revelation moves from *El* through *Yahweh* to *the Father* of Jesus Christ, and culminates in *Father, Son, and Holy Spirit*. If the Bible is the definitive account of all God's revelation, as argued above, then this pattern cannot be relativized by invoking divine accommodation to patriarchal culture. In fact, the trajectory is just the opposite. Although the status of women is progressively raised in the Bible, there are proportionally fewer feminine images in the New Testament, where God is definitively Father.[37] The appeal to cultural accommodation fails according to the analogy of Scripture.

We are not wiser than God. Even if we have reason to wonder whether something is cultural accommodation, if we are not sure, the only pious and responsible thing to do is to give Scripture the benefit of the doubt and conform ourselves to its pattern. In fact even if we fully understood all the cultural-historical-religious reasons why God chose the language pattern he did, such lofty wisdom would still not authorize us to change it. Consider a human analogy. Knowing why my parents named me *John* or why I have the title *Professor* does not authorize you to change or add to my name and title. How much less does insight into the wisdom of God's revelation authorize us to change it. The normativity of the biblical presentation of God does not depend on the ability of theologians to defend it from challenges to its continuing validity.

---

37. Second Cor. 6:18 is most instructive. Here Paul continues the Father-language of the messianic covenant of 2 Sam. 7:14 but augments and applies it to include women: "I will be a Father to you, and you will be my sons and daughters, says the Lord Almighty."

Accommodation of Sin

The other kind of divine accommodation invoked by inclusivists is God's allowance for sin, the consequences of the fall. According to Brian Wren, "all revelation is impeded by sin, and one of the sins of the society through which our classic revelation came is that it was a patriarchal society."[38]

As Margo Houts elaborates, "Patriarchy is seen as arising not out of Creation but out of the Fall, subsequently redeemed by Christ."[39] Houts makes clear that she means several things by this statement. First, human patriarchy—the father as the highest authority in the family and males as controlling power in society—is not God's intention for creation, but only arises because of the fall. Second, this fallen condition has been redeemed in Christ (Gal. 3:28), so that Christian marriages, families, and all social relations should no longer be patriarchal but gender-egalitarian. Third, the fallenness and sinfulness of patriarchy not only applies to human relations; it is also reflected in the biblical terminology for God. In revealing himself, God accommodated fallen human social relations, but ultimately he wants the redeemed community to use inclusive language for him.

Other accommodationists argue that, just as God temporarily adapted to slavery, polygamy, war, and divorce—all consequences of the fall—so he accommodated patriarchy in Scripture. But just as he wants us to put away these sinful practices, they say, so he wants us to move beyond exclusively masculine language for God.

There is a plausible, gospel-liberating aura surrounding this line of argument. So why do defenders of God's Fatherhood reject it? Because they take Scripture in its entirety as their final guide, and Scripture does not support the claim that *Father* is a sin-stained term for God.

First let's put aside an ultimately irrelevant issue: whether some sort of human patriarchy is God's will for creation or entirely a consequence of the fall. Orthodox, evangelical Christians disagree over this.[40] Traditionally most Christians have believed that, although men and women equally image God and are equal in Christ, the headship of the husband and father in the family was intended by God from the beginning. Until recently, most Christians believed that male "headship" extended be-

---

38. Wren, *What Language Shall I Borrow?* 131.

39. Houts, "Is God Also Our Mother?" *Perspectives*, June/July 1997, 8. Recall the claim of Smith, *Is It Okay to Call God "Mother"?* 110: "It was because of sin that culture came to value male over female, establishing patriarchy as the norm." On this basis he argues for inclusive language.

40. Groothuis, *Women Caught in the Conflict*, chaps. 7 and 8. The debate between groups like Evangelicals for Biblical Equality and The Council on Biblical Manhood and Womanhood is well-known.

yond the family into church and society as well. On the traditional view, the fall led to abuse of patriarchal authority, but was not the cause of all forms of patriarchy. Recently some Christians, including evangelicals, have come to believe that all hierarchical, nonegalitarian human relationships, including marriage and the relationship of parents within the family, are consequences of the fall.

However this debate turns out, we must not confuse the Bible's treatment of humans with its presentation of God. Each must be taken on its own terms. It is perfectly possible that human patriarchy could be a consequence of the Fall and yet that God would reveal himself exclusively as our Father. Patriarchy involves two things: fatherhood and ultimate authority. Both are biblically possible for God in spite of the sinfulness of human patriarchy.

First, no Christian can argue that fatherhood in itself is a consequence of the fall. That notion is biblically false. It is not Christianity but Gnosticism that rejects procreation and thus fatherhood as inherently sinful. It is fully possible, therefore, that God chose to reveal himself as a perfect Father who suffers from none of the limitations and sins that cling to human fathers.

Second, no Christian can rightfully argue that God's having ultimate power reflects the fall. For he has power simply because he is God, quite apart from anything in creation or the fall. So God could be the perfectly good, loving, and just Father Almighty even if all human father-hierarchies are by nature sinful. These theological reflections demonstrate that appeals to the fallenness of patriarchy are finally irrelevant, a dead-end best avoided in discussions of appropriate language for God.

Thus we are back to what Scripture as a whole teaches about God's names in relation to creation, fall, and redemption. Here the case for God's Fatherhood as accommodation to sin does not stand up well. For Scripture explicitly links God the Father with creation, as noted in chapter 4. In Ephesians 3:14–15 Paul confesses: "I kneel before the Father, from whom his whole family [*patria:* fatherhood] in heaven and on earth derives its name." Surely one biblical meaning of God's fatherhood is his being Creator, as stated in the Apostles' and Nicene Creeds. Is this doctrine to be entirely reinterpreted as a concession to the fall? That would twist Scripture to fit a preconceived idea that actually contradicts Scripture.

Furthermore, if *Father* were the language of the fall, why would Jesus continue to use it for the redeemed? Why did he teach his own disciples, the nucleus of the church, to pray *Our Father*? Why would Paul, who knew that "in Christ there is neither male nor female" (Gal. 3:28) and taught that "the old has gone; the new has come" (2 Cor. 5:17), continue to speak of God regularly as Father and never as Mother? Jesus, Paul, and the other New Testament authors were speaking and writing to the new community of equals in Christ. They would not accommodate the old sinful patterns. It cannot seriously be maintained that sinful cultural patterns prevented them from using the inclusive language supposedly willed by God. Jesus and Paul did not refrain from denouncing other deeply rooted cultural evils they encountered. They did not soft-pedal the need for conversion or avoid calling people to radical repentance from other sins that were firmly embedded in their cultural contexts. New Testament writers worked hard to correct other misunderstandings of God among the various recipients of their books. Why is there not so much as a hint in Scripture in support of theological gender-inclusivism against God the Father?

It is on just this point that the parallel between masculine language for God and polygamy, slavery, and divorce breaks down. For although God does seem to accommodate or tolerate these practices for certain periods in redemptive history, it eventually becomes clear from Scripture itself that these patterns are consequences of the fall. The Bible itself indicates that they are out of line with God's will for our lives, and thus that they are accommodations evidencing God's patience and forebearance. Jesus rejects divorce. While Paul allows slavery, he also promotes freedom. He enjoins women to submit to their husbands but also teaches that they are equals in Christ. Historical accommodation and the final norm are both visible in Scripture taken as a whole.

There is no such testimony regarding gender-inclusive language, however. There is not so much as a hint that God wants to be called *Mother* as he is called *Father*. If anything, the movement is in the other direction. As demonstrated in previous chapters, there is less feminine imagery and far more clear, plentiful, and doctrinally central Father-language as revelation progresses from the Old to the New Testament.[41]

A final argument against the accommodation to sin view is this. It means that God in himself, apart from sin, is not *Father, Son, and Holy Spirit*. It implies that *Yahweh* and *Father* taken by themselves, noninclusively, are tainted by sinful sexism, since they are masculine terms. God would not have revealed himself as *Yahweh* and *Father* had humans not sinned. This position further implies that, after his ascension, Jesus in glory no longer considers God exclusively as his Father. It

---

41. Inclusivists such as Brian Wren argue that "the biblical tradition itself is marked by frequent self-criticism and innovation" (*What Language Shall I Borrow?* 131) to generate a kind of analogy of Scripture for changing the language of Scripture. But that amounts to using the authority of Scripture to deny the authority of Scripture. It is a fundamental difference between his approach and the one taken in this book.

means that we will not be singing the *Gloria Patri* ("Glory be to the Father . . . ever shall be . . .") in the kingdom of God. For sin will be no more and thus *Father* will no longer be the exclusive way God reveals himself to us. He will either be the Father-Mother or else will provide us a proper gender-neutral vocabulary with which to praise him forever. The most generous judgment about these implications is that they are groundless speculations.

If the Bible is the final framework of interpretation for all God's revelation, including the work of the Spirit in the life of the Christian church on earth until the return of Jesus Christ, then there is no basis at all for claiming that we are authorized to move beyond God as *Father* to the *Father-Mother* or the *Parent*. In making this move by appeal to divine accommodation, inclusivists wander far beyond what can be warranted from the teaching of Scripture. That they do so elicits legitimate questions about the meaning of their affirmations of biblical authority.

Who Can Name God?

The Human Activity of Naming God

Inclusivists presume that we humans can name God and that we may do so.[42] This is the explicit assumption of a favorite hymn of the movement, Brian Wren's "Bring Many Names."[43] The right to name God is a necessary presupposition if giving God feminine names and titles not found in Scripture is to be justified.

But this raises an obvious question: Must those who oppose inclusivism deny that humans may name God? How then can they refer to God as *the Trinity*, a title not found in the Bible? And if they do concede the right to name, do they thereby implicitly validate the inclusivist project? We must consider what it means to name God.

Defenders of the biblical pattern agree that humans may name God, but only by discovering and following the way God has named himself in revelation.[44] That is the crucial condition. Nothing we have argued in this chapter denies or undercuts the human activity of naming God, provided that this activity is rightly understood and practiced. We have insisted that naming God is dependent on the ordered content of God's

42. See chap. 2, "Humans Name God."
43. Wren, *What Language Shall I Borrow?* 137–38.
44. This basic point is regularly made by defenders of traditional language across the spectrum of the ecumenical community. See, for example, the essays of Achtemeier and Frye (Presbyterian), Kimel (Episcopal), Jenson (Evangelical Lutheran), Hopko (Eastern Orthodox), and DiNoia (Roman Catholic) in *Speaking the Christian God*.

entire revelation as its source and norm. Naming God correctly depends on accurate recognition of how God has revealed himself and on rendering that recognition accurately into language. Some of those names are given explicitly, such as *El, Yahweh,* and *Father,* and need only to be acknowledged. Others are implicit in Scripture, such as *Trinity,* or in general revelation, such as *Great Designer.* These need to be explicated.[45] God has granted humans the capacity to "name" him in these ways—to acknowledge and discover the names God has given himself in revelation.

It follows, therefore, that human naming of God is not an innovative, creative act—"arbitrary" or "the mere invention of our minds," to repeat Herman Bavinck. The legitimate human act of naming God neither creates new names nor rearranges the pattern of those God has given. It is not like naming a newborn child, who has no name until one is given. It is not like devising a name for a person whose actual name is unknown. It is not like naming a newly discovered planet or entitling a book one has written or labeling a new invention. In none of these cases are names pregiven, waiting to be discovered. It is up to the name-giver to make the determination. In contrast, rightly naming God is an activity in which humans truly recognize who God has identified himself to be in the various modes of special and general revelation.

There is room for novelty in the sense that some "naming" is still left to do. The givenness of divine names in revelation does not mean that Christians have already discovered them all. It took time for the church to explicate the language of the Trinity from biblical teaching and for theologians to accept the philosophical terms *Necessary Being* and *Great Designer* as legitimate references from general revelation to the Christian God. In the same way there may still be content in the Bible and in general revelation that has not been rendered into verbal references or forms of address to God. The definitive character of revelation does not preclude progress in the human discovery and understanding of the names of God.

Nevertheless, Scripture is the basic source and final norm for all of our naming of God, for reasons indicated earlier in this chapter: It is both divine revelation and the definitive interpretation of all God's other media of revelation. In the Bible the personal names, basic divine titles, and standard designations of God have been given explicitly and repeatedly. The church has been studying and using them for almost two millennia. Thus there is little likelihood of major new discoveries in standard Christian language for God.

45. Criteria for legitimate explication of implicit divine names are discussed in chap. 8.

This conclusion cuts against the position of those inclusivists, such as Ruth Duck, Gail Ramshaw, and Sally McFague, who argue strongly for inventiveness and innovation in the church's primary language for God.[46] They proceed from the view that all language for God is metaphorical, and couple it with the claim that metaphors are supposed to be surprising and provide new insight. Once religious metaphors cease to stimulate new awareness or are taken "literally," they become "dead" and fail to communicate God truly. New metaphors (among which they include titles and names) must therefore be found. According to gender-inclusivists, *Father* and *King* are dead or harmfully misunderstood, so they should be agumented or replaced. Defenders of the biblical pattern counter that the language of Scripture and its revelatory meaning are alive and well and remain relevant as the Christian church and community, animated by the Holy Spirit, continue to study, worship, proclaim the gospel, and live according to the Bible as the Word of God that still speaks.

The Biblical Understanding of Names and Naming

In addition to the theology of revelation outlined above, there are other biblical themes that speak directly to the permissibility of naming God: Scripture's view of names and naming. In modern culture we typically view language as an arbitrary cultural convention. This notion assumes two things. First, words have no meaning apart from what we humans give them. Second, we humans have the right to name and define everything we encounter. Both assumptions are dubious and inconsistent with the biblical perspective.

The first assumption regards words and names as labels that we arbitrarily attach to things, like verbal sticky notes. There is nothing inherent in an apple that would make calling it an *orange* inappropriate. As Shakespeare observed: "A rose by any other name is just as sweet." Similarly, there is no decisive reason why Mary couldn't just as well be called *Jane*. We modern people don't typically see any important connection between the nature of things and the words we use to refer to them. Consequently, we tend to think that words and their references are wholly up to our cultural conventions.

This brings us to the second assumption. Humans take it for granted that we are the masters of the world. One way we exercise this mastery is by mapping the world with our language, assigning names to things which in themselves have no definite order or meaning. In classical phi-

46. See chap. 2, "Traditional Language is Dead" and "The Gospel Must Be Proclaimed in Contemporary Language."

losophy this notion was called *nominalism*. In current postmodernist jargon, language is said to be a human "projection," a sociocultural system of meaning that we read onto the world or through which we give order to our experience. Some theologians, including Sally McFague, believe that we also project our language on God, suiting ourselves in the process, and they use this assumption as a major argument in favor of inclusive language.[47]

But Scripture clearly contradicts the first assumption, that words and their referents share no inherent meaning. In previous chapters we considered the biblical names and titles of God, noticing that all of them have meanings reflecting who God is and how he has related to his creation, especially his people. None is a mere verbal label that could be detached and replaced with something else without altering its meaning. God disclosed himself to Moses as *I Am Who I Am* and *Yahweh, He Who Is*. God said he was known by Moses' ancestors as *El Shaddai, God Almighty*. The name of the Promised One in Isaiah is *Wonderful Counselor, Mighty God, Everlasting Father, Prince of Peace*. He was named *Jesus* (*Joshua,* Hebrew: *Yahweh saves*) "because he will save his people from their sins." He was called "*Immanuel*, which means, 'God with us'" (Matt. 1:21, 23). His title *Christ* is Greek for the Hebrew term *Messiah*, both of which mean "Anointed One." Jesus gives Simon the name *Peter*, which means *rock*, for "on this rock I will build my church" (Matt. 16:18)

The point is clear: these biblical names are not mere labels. They have meaning that is integral to the identity, significance, status, and activity of the persons they name. Persons and the meanings of their lives—their "stories"—are expressed by their names. "In the ancient world a name was not merely a label but was virtually equivalent to whoever or whatever bore it. . . . The name and being of God are often used in parallelism with each other, stressing their essential identity."[48] This understanding of names is at odds with our modern arbitrary-label view.

Since names and things are meaningfully connected, changing biblical names and titles of God cannot be done. For that would be tantamount to changing God himself, or at least changing how he has involved himself in human history. The point is not first of all that we *may* not do this; in fact, we *cannot*. It is not possible for us to change our own history, much less the history of God's relation with the world. We can-

---

47. McFague, *Metaphorical Theology,* 10, writes: "The tradition says that we are created in the image of God, but the obverse is also the case, for we imagine God in *our* image. And the human images we choose for the divine influence the way we feel about ourselves, for these images are 'divinized' and hence raised in status."

48. R. Youngblood, "Names in Bible Times, Significance of," in *The Evangelical Dictionary of Theology,* 750.

not change the biblical names and titles for God precisely because they uniquely verbalize who he is and what he has been doing.

Furthermore, we have no right to name or rename God in the biblical sense. The second modern assumption—the basic human right to name and define reality—is false with respect to God. For in Scripture the right to name or rename presupposes a relationship of power and authority over the one named. "Giving a name to anyone or anything was tantamount to owning or controlling it, and changing a name signified promotion to a higher status . . . or demotion to a lower status."[49] Thus God legitimately names the parts of his newly created world in Genesis 1, and Adam is authorized to name the animals in Genesis 2. The Lord changes the names of Abram and Sarai (Gen. 17) and calls Jacob *Israel* (Gen. 32:28). Nebuchadnezzar changes the names of Daniel and his three friends. And Jesus renames Simon *Peter*. In all of these cases the act of naming is an exercise of authority over the one named.

This is precisely why in the Bible no one ever names God in the sense of assigning to him a term or label he has not already authorized. God names himself. He made himself known to Israel's ancestors as *El*, to Moses as *Yahweh* the God of the covenant, and in all the other variations of the divine names given to the writers of Scripture. In Jesus Christ God draws near to us, introducing himself as *our Father in Heaven*. God names *Jesus, the Messiah,* our *Immanuel*. He does not leave this up to Mary and Joseph to choose from their little book of currently popular names for children. Jesus discloses the name of God as *Father, Son, and Holy Spirit*. In the Bible God names himself.

For only God may name himself. No one has the right to name God, for no one stands as God's equal or superior. No one is in a position to give a name and identity to God. God has given humans dominion and authority, including the right to name, over creation. But we do not have the right, much less the ability, to name God.

This point is obvious even in analogous human situations. We can name our children and give titles to those over whom we have authority. My parents named me *John* and the seminary board of trustees gave me the title *Professor*. But other people do not have the right to give me names and titles or to change them. Nick-names are legitimate only if I accept and thereby authorize them. Otherwise they are rude, disrespectful, and cannot be used to address me. Likewise if someone introduces herself as *Dr. Smith*, it is out of place for me to call her *Mary* unless invited to do so. Those Americans who referred to President Nixon as *Tricky Dick* were not honoring him, but expressing disgust with his dishonorable behavior. These examples from our own culture illustrate

49. Ibid., 750.

that naming involves respect, rights, and authority. How much more do we dishonor God by renaming him when we do not have the right to do so.

So we conclude from Scripture that we neither may nor can name God in the sense of assigning him verbal references that are not explicitly given in or validly derived from God's self-revelation. We have neither the right nor the ability to "bring many names to God" in the modern sense of dictating the terms that we deem appropriate. Cultural understandings of names and naming may have changed since biblical times. But our relation to God and our fallen human capacities for knowing him have not changed. The biblical notion of the name of God, strange as it may seem to us initially, is still normative for us. In the pointed words of Bavinck, "Men do not name him; he gives himself a name."[50]

Conclusion

We began this chapter by recognizing that the Christian church throughout its history has spoken of God in ways not found in the Bible. Is it possible that gender-equal and gender-neutral language for God might likewise be justified in the same way? We began to address this question by demonstrating that Holy Scripture provides the definitive interpretation of God's revelation, even though revelation as the source of language for God is not limited to the Bible. A variety of inclusivist approaches to Scripture and appeals to extrabiblical revelation were therefore judged to be inappropriate. Next we argued that the normativity of biblical revelation extends to the very language it uses for God. Inclusivists cannot relativize the Bible's pervasive and consistent practice of speaking of God as though he is a masculine person as mere accommodation to ancient patriarchalism. Finally, we showed why God's self-designation in Scripture is authoritative for all human naming of God. We humans have neither the ability nor the right to name God otherwise than as he has revealed himself.

It is worth noting again that God's self-naming in Scripture and in creation includes females as likenesses of himself. Thus using feminine imagery for God according to the way he has revealed himself is legitimate. The problem is not with feminine imagery for God per se but with giving it the same status and functions as the Bible's divine names and titles, which happen to be masculine. The problem is with gender-inclusive language for God.

Chapter 5 demonstrated that gender-inclusive language for God cannot be derived from the language of the Bible. Chapter 6 has eliminated

50. Bavinck, *The Doctrine of God*, 84.

a number of other inclusivist arguments as incompatible with a proper understanding of divine revelation. But the door is still not closed. We have not yet shown why inclusive language is unacceptable by the criteria that allow us to refer to God as *Trinity, Great Designer,* and *Hound of Heaven.* And we have not yet dealt with a basic theological fact that is fundamental to the argument for inclusive language: God is not male.

7

But God Is beyond Gender!

Perhaps the previous chapter has persuaded some inclusivists that the biblical pattern of language for God remains the defining source and norm for Christians. Some might therefore agree that gender-inclusive versions of Holy Scripture are problematic. They might also agree that the Christian doctrine of God must be derived from the standard text of Holy Scripture. But they might still argue that fully inclusive language for God is legitimate as long as the meaning of Scripture is preserved. They might still urge that, except for the Bible, inclusive language be used throughout the rest of the Christian life—in the liturgy and hymnody of the church, in the religious education of children, and in the language of everyday Christian piety, witness, and ministry. They would probably do so for a simple, undeniable, and persuasive reason that we have not yet considered: God is not masculine but is beyond all gender.[1]

The argument goes something like this. Although the language of the Bible presents God as anthropomorphically masculine, Scripture also suggests that God in himself is beyond gender. Traditional theologians have taught that the gendered language of Scripture does not mean that God has gender. Thus calling God *Father* does not attribute maleness or masculinity to him. However, the argument continues, using only masculine language for God leaves the impression that God is masculine—in fact, that he is exclusively masculine. This language thereby obscures the Christian doctrine that God is neither masculine nor feminine. In the process it hurts both women and men. Furthermore, if gendered terminology such as *Father* does not attribute gender to God, it must also be possible to call God *Mother* without attributing gender. It must even be possible to use gender-neutral terms, such as *Parent*, without altering what *Father*-language really means in Scripture. Therefore, this line of

1. Chap. 2, "Patriarchal Language Is Not Privileged: God Is beyond All Language."

reasoning concludes, the practice of fully gender-inclusive and gender-neutral language for God is compatible with the normativity of the biblical text and with the doctrinal content of orthodox Christianity. In fact, it is necessary to preserve what the language of Scripture really means.

Evaluating this powerful argument requires examining several complex issues it involves. The first issue is the relation of language to God as he really is. The claim that God far transcends categories of creaturely existence and the meaning of human language is a key theological ground for the doctrine that God has no gender and thus for dealing with the Bible's masculine language for God. In fact many in the debate—gender-inclusivists and biblical-traditionalists alike—claim that theories of theological language are crucial to its outcome. Thus we consider the most significant theories about language for God invoked in these debates—the analogical, figurative/metaphorical, and symbolic theories—and their bearing on the debate about inclusive language for God.

The second issue involved is the relationship between Scripture and the doctrine of divine genderlessness. Inclusivists appeal to God's transcendence of gender to change the language of Scripture or at least to change the language of the Christian community. This appeal claims to accept the text of the Bible as its norm and starting point, concludes from Scripture (and philosophy) that God is ungendered, and then promotes a linguistic practice that cannot be derived from or rendered consistent with Scripture. This move in effect makes a theological-philosophical conclusion about God's nature more determinative of Christian language than the text and teaching of the Bible. It deserves critical scrutiny. The first and second issues are the substance of this chapter.

A third issue is taken up in the next chapter, the claim that gender-inclusive language for God does not change the meaning of biblical language for God. For it may be that even if masculine terms such as *Father* and *King* do not attribute gender to God, the biblical pattern of language does have religious and theological significance that is altered or undermined by regular substition of gender-egalitarian and gender-neutral terms such as *Mother* and *Parent*.

Divine Transcendence and Human Language

Both inclusivists and traditionalists recognize that the Bible's gendered language for God cannot be interpreted directly and literally, as if it were no different than language about human beings. In the words of Elizabeth Johnson, "there is basic agreement that the mystery of God is fundamentally unlike anything else we know of, and so is beyond the grasp of all of our naming."[2] When Scripture speaks of David as the king of Israel and the father of Solomon, it clearly implies that he is male. But when Scripture speaks of God as king and as father, the implication that he is male is only apparent. Other things Scripture says make this clear. For God is Spirit (John 4:24). Unlike humans, God has no body and no male sex organs. He does not procreate. And even as Spirit, God is not more a masculine spirit than a feminine spirit in any human sense, like Zeus but unlike Hera. For God is not like a man or a woman (Deut. 4:16). Thus the biblical language of God's masculinity must be figurative or anthropomorphic in some important way, just as the language about his arms, hands, eyes, and face.[3] On these assertions there is wide agreement between biblical-traditionalists and gender-inclusivists.

The consensus is short-lived, however. For inclusivists quickly conclude that God's transcendence of gender justifies egalitarian language. According to Johnson, "Women's refusal of the exclusive claim of the white male symbol of the divine arises from the well-founded demand to adhere to the holy mystery of God."[4] Rosemary Ruether makes the point this way: "If all human language for God/ess is analogy . . . then male language for the divine must lose its privileged place."[5] In stark contrast the biblical-traditionalist Thomas Hopko, an Eastern Orthodox theologian who emphasizes that God "is absolutely beyond all that creatures can know, think, and say," concludes just the opposite. "Orthodox Christians refuse to emend the trinitarian names of Father and Son and Holy Spirit apophatically because the 'nameless God' has personally revealed himself to them as Father through the person of Jesus Christ the Son, by the person of the Holy Spirit."[6] Both inclusivists and traditionalists affirm the transcendence of God, but they come to opposite conclusions about language for God. Apparently the connection between divine transcendence and gendered language is more complex than initially supposed. The topic needs to be explored.

2. Johnson, *She Who Is*, 117.

3. Although we have waited until now to discuss this issue, we have been very careful throughout the book to claim that the Bible presents or speaks of God "as though he is a masculine person" or "anthropomorphically as a masculine person." We have never claimed or assumed that Scripture's pattern means that God in himself is male or masculine. In fact this book assumes that the traditional position is correct: ontologically God is genderless.

4. Johnson, *She Who Is*, 117.

5. Ruether, *Sexism and God-Talk*, 68–69. Consider also Old Testament scholar van Wijk-Bos, *Reimagining God*, 11–12: "In our search for language about God that is other than masculine, we look first for models in Scripture that emphasize a God who transcends male and female."

6. Thomas Hopko, "Apophatic Theology and the Naming of God in Eastern Orthodox Tradition," in *Speaking the Christian God*, 161.

Theories of Language for God

Advocates for both sides of the debate almost always address the question of the adequacy of human language as such for communicating the truth about God. This question arises because Christians confess that God is not defined by or limited to human creaturely categories, but we also believe that he reveals himself truly in creation and in the language of the Bible. How can both be true? Let's explore the dilemma.

On one side is divine transcendence. Christian theology asserts that God is infinite, whereas we humans are finite in time, space, knowledge, power, ability, and accomplishment. He is self-sufficient; we are relative and dependent. He is perfectly good; we are fallible and sinful. He is pure Spirit; we are embodied. The contrasts could not be greater. But our human language is a creaturely instrument that bears creaturely meaning, derived from our experience in this world. Bavinck makes this point very strongly: "God uses human language to reveal himself and manifests himself in human forms. It follows that Scripture does not merely contain a few anthropomorphisms; on the contrary, *all* Scripture is anthropomorphic."[7]

On the other side is knowledge of God. Christians believe that God can reveal himself, has done so, and that this revelation can be communicated by human language. So this is the problem: if God transcends creaturely categories, how can merely creaturely language truly disclose who he is, what he is really like, and how he has actually involved himself in his creation? How can human language communicate anything truly meaningful about God as he really is? This is the question of language for God in general. It is an issue of particular significance for gendered language: If *Father, King,* and *He* do not mean that God is masculine, what do they mean? And if God is not really masculine, why are these terms so important?

Over the centuries thousands of pages have been written about religious language.[8] For our purposes I merely summarize three major theories and evaluate them with respect to their bearing on inclusive language for God. To keep things simple I call these theories the *analogical,* the *figurative/metaphorical,* and the *symbolic* theories. All of them at-

---

7. Bavinck, *The Doctrine of God,* 86.

8. A good introduction by Christian philosophers is "Religious Language: How Can We Speak Meaningfully of God?" in Michael Peterson, W. Hasker, B. Reichenbach, and D. Basinger, *Reason and Religious Belief: An Introduction to the Philosophy of Religion* (New York: Oxford University Press, 1991), 136–55. More advanced accounts are William Alston, *Divine Nature and Human Language* (Ithaca, N.Y.: Cornell University Press, 1989) and John Macquarrie, *God-Talk: An Examination of the Language and Logic of Theology* (London: SCM, 1967).

tempt to recognize divine transcendence and yet preserve the significance of our language for God. Some do a better job than others, and some are more helpful than others in approaching gendered language for God. It remains to be seen whether the outcome of the debate between traditionalists and inclusivists hinges more on theories of religious language or the final authority of God's special revelation.

The Analogical Theory

The analogical theory of language for God is the main approach of the theological tradition, presented in the Church Fathers, elaborated by Thomas Aquinas and Duns Scotus, and continued through twentieth-century theology.[9] The meaning of the term *analogical* can be clarified by contrasting it with *univocal* and *equivocal*. *Univocal* means *one meaning*. If human language for God were *univocal*, it would have exactly the same meaning for God as it does for us. But God's being, love, goodness, knowledge, and justice are different than ours because they far surpass ours in quantity and quality. Thus our language for God cannot be univocal, for that would deny God's transcendence.

However, if our language for God were *equivocal*, it would have an utterly different meaning than it does for us. The greatest, most perfect human love and justice would be nothing like God's love and justice. *Equivocal* means *having completely different meanings*. To illustrate, *love* as a human relationship and *love* as a score in tennis are equivocal; so are the *bark* of a tree and the *bark* of a dog. The words are the same, but their meanings are completely different because what they refer to is completely different. If this were true of our religious language, it would be impossible for anything we say to convey any truth about God whatsoever. Genuine revelation and any knowledge of God would be impossible. It would be impossible for us to relate to him at all.

But there is a third possibility, that language for God is *analogical*. This solution includes the strengths and avoids the weaknesses of univocal and equivocal language. It affirms that our talk of God can truly refer to and disclose him, but only in a manner that is finite and merely analogical—both similar and dissimilar—to God himself. Elizabeth Johnson explains how this works: "A word whose meaning is known and prized from human experience is first affirmed of God. The same word is then critically negated to remove any association with creaturely modes of being. Finally, the word is predicated of God in a

---

9. Helpful summaries of this approach are provided by traditionalist Joseph DiNoia, "Knowing and Naming the Triune God: The Grammar of Trinitarian Confession," in *Speaking the Christian God*, 162–87, and inclusivist Johnson, *She Who Is*, 113–17.

supereminent way that transcends all cognitive capabilities."[10] Other analogical theorists argue that Johnson's last phrase, "transcends all cognitive capabilities," ultimately closes off knowledge of God.[11] They affirm that there is a literal sense of language on which analogy depends. "It is possible to purify our concepts of love, knowledge, power, and so forth, by eliminating all features pertaining to temporality, embodiment, and other creaturely conditions, leaving a core of meaning that can be attributed to God. Thus purged, these terms can be literally applied to God and used to make statements that are true."[12] Although analogical theorists differ among themselves about the nature and proportion of similarity and dissimilarity of meaning, all agree that human language can express truth about God without being able to fully define or comprehend him.[13]

The analogical theory of religious language typically depends on the doctrine that there is some analogy between humans and God and that creatures reflect the nature of their Creator: God has created humans in his image and likeness (Gen. 1) and has made the whole world to reflect his eternal deity and power (Rom. 1).[14] Therefore creaturely language can give finite, limited expression of truth about God without denying that he is high and holy and lifted up, far beyond the existence and comprehension of humans. We are confident that words of God's love, forgiveness, justice, kingdom, fatherliness, and motherlikeness do truly tell us who God is and what God is like.

Although the analogical theory has been the standard position of traditional Christian theology, it is also embraced by inclusivists. Elizabeth Johnson gives it an extensive elaboration in *She Who Is*. Her fellow Roman Catholic theologian Catherine Mowry LaCugna employs it in her major work, *God for Us*.[15] We have noted it invoked by Rosemary Ruether. Adopting this theory apparently does not determine one's position on inclusive language for God.

10. Johnson, *She Who Is*, 113.

11. Francis Martin, *The Feminist Question: Feminist Theology in the Light of Christian Tradition* (Grand Rapids: Eerdmans, 1994), 262–63.

12. Peterson, Hasker, Reichenbach, and Basinger, *Reason and Religious Belief*, 150–51. This quote represents the view of Christian philosopher William Alston. It is the view I prefer. In the Middle Ages Duns Scotus made the same point in response to Aquinas: there must be some literal element of meaning in order for analogy to work and not slide into equivocation.

13. Bavinck, *The Doctrine of God*, 32–33, puts the result of the analogical theory this way. "He can be apprehended; he cannot be comprehended. There is a 'knowledge'; there is no 'comprehension' of God."

14. These doctrines were discussed in chap. 6 as general revelation.

15. Catherine Mowry LaCugna, *God for Us: The Trinity and Christian Life* (San Francisco: Harpers, 1991).

The Figurative/Metaphorical Theory

In many ways the figurative/metaphorical theory is similar to the analogical theory. (Hereafter I call it *the figurative theory*.) Most who hold this theory affirm the doctrine of humans as the image of God as well as divine transcendence and therefore conclude that humans are both like and unlike God. Since this is so, they argue, figurative language is well-suited for communicating truth about God, for figures of speech are both like and unlike their subjects. Most figurative theorists prefer their approach instead of the analogical theory because they are uncomfortable with some of the classical linguistic and philosophical positions often associated with the analogical theory. Among these positions is the assumption that language expressing clear, distinct, and literal ideas best corresponds to reality and thus that such language most adequately conveys truth. This assumption implies that figurative language is deficient for communicating truth. Figurative theorists prefer the idea, recently popularized by philosopher Paul Ricoeur,[16] that all language is originally and basically figurative or metaphorical and that words become literal only by losing their metaphorical meaning through common use in ordinary language.[17] If even the language through which we access creaturely reality is basically figurative, they reason, then surely language for the transcendent God must be figurative.

Roland Frye, the English professor whom we encountered in chapter 5 as a defender of the biblical pattern, takes this approach to language for God. He begins by affirming that "it is impossible for unaided human beings to discover on our own the mysteries of God's being and will for us" and follows Calvin in stressing that divine revelation is "God's accommodation to our human capacity and need." On this basis he asserts that "biblical language is pervasively figurative" and that "Scripture relies on figurative language for God . . . because it is the most effective mode for conveying God's self-disclosure."[18] Because a figure of speech is both like and unlike that of which it is predicated, he points out, figurative language for God can truly disclose God to us, but

16. Paul Ricoeur, *The Rule of Metaphor: Multidisciplinary Studies of the Creation of Meaning in Language*, trans. R. Czerny et al. (Toronto: University of Toronto Press, 1977). An excellent account of theories of metaphor in relation to language for God is Nelly Stienstra, *YHWH Is the Husband of His People: Analysis of a Biblical Metaphor with Special Reference to Translation* (Kampen: Kok Pharos, 1993), chaps. 1 and 2.

17. A standard example is the word *muscle*, which comes from the Latin *musculus*, "little mouse." Apparently someone thought muscles looked like mice under a blanket (of skin) and coined the word. But that association has fallen away and the word is now a literal noun.

18. Roland Frye, "Language for God and Feminist Language," in *Speaking the Christian God*, 31–32, 33.

cannot do so fully, literally, or definitively. Thus Frye's position ends up roughly similar to the analogical theory.

Frye is among those who defend traditional biblical and liturgical language for God.[19] Like the analogical theory, however, the figurative approach is employed in favor of inclusive language as well. Ruth Duck, Brian Wren, and the Sally McFague of *Metaphorical Theology* make their cases using the figurative/metaphorical theory of language for God.

The Symbolic Theory

Whereas the analogical and figurative theories typically affirm both the likeness and unlikeness of God and creatures, the symbolic theory more strongly emphasizes the transcendence of God and consequently the experience-bound, anthropomorphic nature of language for God. The philosopher Kant denied that our concepts have any correspondence to God at all, although our moral nature gives us sufficient reason to use language representing God as author of the world, moral lawgiver, and judge. Such concepts he labeled "symbolic anthropomorphisms."[20] The Romantic theologian Schleiermacher followed Kant's critique of the traditional understanding of conceptual knowledge of God and interpreted all religious language, including the language of the Bible, as expressing the human experience of absolute dependence. Our words and concepts of God express the contents of a feeling of unconditional relatedness to the Absolute. They refer to the Source of this feeling but do not in any way describe that Reality in itself.[21] Paul Tillich is a twentieth-century philosophical theologian who continues this line.[22] He holds that language about God is *symbolic*, somehow "participating

19. See the essays by Elizabeth Achtemeier, Garrett Green, and Colin Gunton in *Speaking the Christian God* for other figurative or metaphorical theorists who defend tradition. Janet Soskice's essay uses this approach to defend the legitimacy of feminists calling God *Father*.

20. Immanuel Kant, *Prolegomena to Any Future Metaphysics*, ed. L. W. Beck (Indianapolis/New York: Bobbs-Merrill, 1950), sec. 57. In *Religion Within the Bounds of Reason Alone*, trans. T. Greene and H. Hudson (New York: Harper & Row, 1960), 58–59, note, he makes it clear that while we may think of God in terms of human categories, "it is on no account permitted us to infer by this analogy that what holds of the former [the sensible] must hold of the latter [the supersensible]."

21. Friedrich Schleiermacher, *The Christian Faith*, trans. H. R. MacIntosh and J. S. Stewart (Philadelphia: Fortress, 1976), 194. The heading of section 50 reads: "All attributes which we ascribe to God are to be taken as denoting not something special in God, but only something special in the manner in which the feeling of absolute dependence is to be related to Him."

22. Paul Tillich, "Religious Symbols and Our Knowledge of God," *The Christian Scholar* 38, no. 3 (1955). See also the excellent essay by Dewey Hoitenga, "Tillich's Religious Epistemology," in *God and the Good: Essays in Honor of Henry Stob*, ed. C. Orlebeke and L. Smedes (Grand Rapids: Eerdmans, 1975), 140–49.

in" the transcendent reality to which it refers without bearing descriptive conceptual content about that reality. Religious symbols are derived from human experience and can refer to ultimate reality, but not convey propositional truth about it. Thus as soon as we take our language for God too literally, cognitively, or definitively, it becomes a "dead metaphor" and is no longer authentically religious. In fact a religious symbol can become an idol, a nonultimate substitution for the Ultimate.

Sally McFague is the most articulate representative of the symbolic theory among inclusivists, although she does not identify with it exclusively. While her important book, *Metaphorical Theology,*[23] occasionally invokes the analogical theory and seems mainly an articulation of the figurative theory, it sometimes drifts over into the symbolic view. Her *Models of God* tilts decidedly in the direction of the symbolic view.[24] What places her among the symbolic theorists is her almost exclusive stress on the dissimilarity between God and our metaphors for God: "We must not forget the crack in the foundation beneath all our imaginings and the conceptual schemes we build upon them. That crack is exemplified in the 'is not' of metaphor which denies any identity in its assertions." As a result of stressing the "is not," McFague concludes that religious language does not so much describe God as refer to, that is, symbolize him. McFague considers theology largely to be the human enterprise of devising ideas about God: "theology, at any rate my kind of theology, is principally an elaboration of a few basic metaphors and models. . . . As remythologization, such theology acknowledges that it is, as it were, painting a picture . . . theology is *mostly* fiction." McFague is not completely agnostic, however. She does affirm "the God on the side of life and its fulfillment."[25]

McFague uses her symbolic-anthropomorphic view of religious metaphors in support of inclusive language for God. She characterizes the traditional patriarchal model of God, founded in Scripture, as "our construction," something "we have reified into objective reality."[26] Other inclusivists also stress divine transcendence to justify revising religious language.[27]

---

23. McFague, *Metaphorical Theology.*

24. Sally McFague, *Models of God: Theology for an Ecological, Nuclear Age* (Philadelphia: Fortress, 1987).

25. These quotations are from *Models of God*, ix–xii. See *Metaphorical Theology*, 131–44, for an earlier discussion of "The Truth of Theological Models."

26. McFague, *Metaphorical Theology*, 150.

27. Duck, *Gender and the Name of God*, 12, and Johnson, *She Who Is*, 45–46, invoke the symbolic theory of Tillich although they also use other approaches. Martin, *Feminist Question*, 260–63, argues that Johnson as well as McFague articulate ambiguous theories and end up implying theological agnosticism in spite of their intentions.

An Evaluation of Theories of Religious Language

The Symbolic Theory Implies Agnosticism

If an adequate theory of religious language must acknowledge God's transcendence and the limits of language, on one hand, and at the same time affirm the truth content of God's self-disclosure, on the other, then the symbolic theory in general is less theologically and religiously adequate than the analogical and figurative theories.

The symbolic theory, since it stresses that God is Wholly Other and religious language is completely anthropomorphic, leaves us more with incredulity toward religious language than with awe for the God who in a real but superhuman sense loves us, speaks to us, hears us, and is closer than hands and feet. Roman Catholic theologian Avery Dulles describes this position as a form of *philosophical agnosticism*: "God, even if he exists, is held to be utterly incomprehensible, with the result that all statements about God and his actions are devoid of cognitive value. Revelation itself is viewed as a myth or metaphor that cannot be taken literally."[28] This judgment is valid quite apart from the question of inclusive language for God.

But it applies in particular to inclusivist theology, as Francis Martin points out: "The Kantian and Schleiermachian form of representationalism characteristic of feminism is to be found in the manner in which language for God is treated, either implicitly or explicitly, as expressive of the subject's experience but not of what is experienced. This gives rise to a very specific understanding of metaphor and models that is basically agnostic."[29]

McFague's theory of religious language surely merits this judgment.[30] She regards the God of Scripture as "our construction" and asserts that "theology is *mostly* fiction." "What can be said with certainty about the Christian faith is very little."[31] Nevertheless, she does say with apparent certainty that, "God is not a 'person' or 'personal' as such."[32] But this view of language for God is unacceptable because it fails to allow for the propositional truth content of divine revelation or human theology. It undermines religious confidence.

Figurative/Metaphorical Language for God: A Crucial Confusion

So the analogical and figurative theories are left as more adequate accounts of the fact that our language can communicate the truth of the

28. Avery Dulles, *Models of Revelation* (Garden City, N.Y.: Image, 1985), 6.
29. Martin, *The Feminist Question*, 166.
30. The essays of Garret Green and Colin Gunton in *Speaking the Christian God* contain extensive critiques of McFague's view of religious language.
31. Quoted above from *Models for God*.
32. McFague, *Metaphorical Theology*, 128.

transcendent God. But now we ask whether one of them is more helpful than the other in the debate about inclusive language for God. I believe that the analogical theory is more helpful because it promotes greater clarity and is therefore less easily misunderstood and misapplied than the figurative theory in these discussions. The figurative theory is prone to a major confusion about language for God that is almost universal among inclusivists. It is the failure to distinguish between the fact that all language for God is analogical/figurative/metaphorical and the fact that only some references to God are figures of speech or metaphors. Let me elaborate this complicated but important point.

An adequate theory of language for God must take account of at least two things. First, it must recognize the transcendence of God. We have seen that, in spite of their different theories, Christian theologians agree that human language does not have exactly the same meaning when referring to God as when it refers to humans. Language for God cannot be taken merely literally, but is to some extent analogical, figurative, or anthropomorphic. This is a principle that must be embraced and upheld to honor God's transcendence.

Second, an adequate theory must also recognize the different parts of speech and functions of language identified in chapters 3 through 5. Among them are figures of speech, such as metaphors, similes, and personifications. God is like a mother. God gives birth to the mountains. But there are also nonfigurative parts of speech, among them pronouns, verb forms, and other grammatical structures, as well as terms of identification, such as appellatives, titles, and names. The Lord is King. God is our Father. Any adequate theory of biblical, religious, and theological language for God must maintain these linguistic distinctions, as well as uphold the principle that all our language for God is analogical or figurative.

The problem is that most inclusivists and some traditionalists, especially those who embrace the figurative theory, fail on the second point. They fail to maintain the distinction between figurative and nonfigurative uses of language. That is, they do not consistently distinguish between two meanings of *figurative* or *metaphorical language*: (1) the figurative/metaphorical (or analogical) nature of all language for God, and (2) figures of speech, including metaphors, in distinction from names, titles, appellatives, and other parts of speech. Even worse, by failing to distinguish these meanings consistently, they almost unavoidably slide from the fact that all language for God is figurative-metaphorical to the false conclusion that all terms for God are metaphors or figures of speech. They conclude that *Father* is just a metaphor.

This mistake is almost inevitable for inclusivists because of their equivocation (illegitimate switch) of different meanings of *name of God* (identified in chapter 5). We saw that in order to make language for God fully gender-inclusive it is necessary to take *names* in the broad fourth sense that includes feminine figures of speech (similes and metaphors) and turn them into *names* for God in the other three senses—appellatives, titles, and proper names. This equivocation of *names* is directly implicated in the equivocation of the term *figurative–metaphorical*. For when inclusivists extend feminine figures of speech, which are *names* in the fourth sense of the term, into *names* in the other three senses, they thereby treat all language for God—including appellatives, titles, and names—as equivalent to figures of speech. Inclusivism holds that all terms for God are equally figures of speech or metaphors for God: *God is Light* and *God is our Father* are both metaphors. Thus inclusivism implicitly means two things when it asserts that *all language for God is figurative or metaphorical*. It means both that *all terms for God are figures of speech or metaphors* and that *all language for God is figurative or metaphorical* due to divine transcendence. Because they fail to appreciate the difference between these two meanings of *figurative/metaphorical language*, inclusivists overlook the fact that the masculine divine names and titles, though figurative in the sense that all language for God is figurative, are not figures of speech. The confusion and mistake are obvious as soon as they are pointed out. The problematic consequences of this confusion were indicated in chapter 5.

Inclusivists do not have a monopoly on inadequate linguistic theory, however. In chapter 5 we noted that some defenders of traditional biblical language for God also fail to distinguish sufficiently between figures of speech and other parts of language for God. And thus a significant liability of the figurative theory becomes apparent. It does not easily distinguish the two meanings of the term *figurative/metaphorical*, and thus it aids and abets the linguistic confusion pointed out above. Like inclusivism, the figurative theory needs to use the terms *figurative* and *metaphorical* in two senses. It uses them to characterize the nature of all language for God in relation to divine transcendence. But it also needs these terms to identify metaphors and other figures of speech in distinction from appellatives, titles, and names. If it uses these terms in both senses, it has no vocabulary with which to acknowledge the non-figurative parts of speech. The implication seems to be that all parts of speech are somehow figures or metaphors.

The inherent difficulty of the figurative theory to keep these things straight is why in my opinion Frye and Green, for example, end up considering *Father* to be a metaphor (figure of speech) that names God.[33] It

---

33. Other criticisms of the Achtemeier–Frye approach were offered in chap. 5, the section entitled "A Traditionalist Confusion about Language."

is more accurate, as we have done, to classify *Father* used in this way as a title-name that has metaphorical meaning. Strictly speaking it is not a metaphor. On this issue the figurative/metaphorical theory is more harmful than helpful in the debate about inclusive language for God.

The Analogical Theory

The terminology of the analogical theory helps keep us clear of this potential confusion and the fallacies that hide in it. This theory uses the term *analogical* for the limited way in which all human language can convey truth about God. It reserves the terms *figurative* and *metaphorical* for those linguistic entities that function as figures of speech and metaphors. Thus the analogical theory can affirm that, whereas all language for God is analogical, not all terms for God are figurative or metaphorical. Names (*Yahweh*), titles (*King, Father*), and generic designations or appellatives (*judge, redeemer*) are not figures of speech, although what they attribute to God must be understood analogically (figuratively or metaphorically in that sense) because of God's transcendence. The analogical theory can readily identify the fact that figures of speech for God are figurative in two senses: they are figurative in the sense that all language for God is figurative (analogical); they are also figurative in that they are similes, metaphors, or other nonliteral descriptions. Namings of God that are not figures of speech, such as *God is good* and *the Lord is God*, are figurative only in the sense of being analogical. This result conforms exactly to the linguistic analysis elaborated in chapter 5. On grounds of terminological and conceptual clarity, then, the analogical theory is best equipped to understand the complexities of gendered language for God.[34]

Why Theories of Religious Language Are Finally Irrelevant

But do theories of language for God have a decisive bearing on arguments for inclusive language for God? Does endorsing the analogical theory predispose one toward biblical language, for example, whereas taking the symbolic approach inclines one toward inclusivism? In spite of their uneven strengths and weaknesses, in the end the answer is "no." Let me explain.

Obviously there is some bearing of theories of religious language on the openness of their adherents to inclusive language. If, with the analogical and figurative theories, we are able to affirm that humans can

---

34. I recognize but do not here address all the other issues regarding the nature of God, the Creator–creature distinction, and philosophical positions regarding being, knowledge, and language that would have to be considered to judge that the analogical theory is superior to the figurative/metaphorical theory, all things considered.

truly say both who God is and what he is like,[35] though only partially, inadequately, and noncomprehensively, then we must ask seriously whether Scripture and historic Christianity have done so as definitively as possible. If, with the symbolic theory, we are inclined to regard all language for God as inadequate human projection, then we would probably be more inclined against taking Scripture and apostolic tradition as the final norm.

However, the analogical and figurative theories are employed by theologians on both sides of the issue. DiNoia and Johnson are Roman Catholics who use the analogical position of Thomas Aquinas, but he is a traditionalist and she is an inclusivist. Achtemeier and Frye are Reformed Christians (Presbyterians) who use the figurative theory to defend the biblical pattern, but Duck and Wren are hymnwriters in the Reformed tradition who use it to promote gender-egalitarian language.

Even the symbolic theory comes in versions that strongly endorse the language of Scripture. Whereas Sally McFague readily adopts new metaphors and models for God, Thomas Hopko, whom we quoted at the beginning of this section, reveres the revealed triune name.[36] The Eastern Orthodox tradition, influenced by Neo-Platonism, has always stressed the "wholly Otherness" or "supraessentiality" of God: "God's being is radically different from all other beings." Thus the "supraessential Godhead is unutterable and nameless." Human language cannot even relate to the divine nature. Yet in Orthodox liturgy and theology "the hypostases of Father, Son, and Holy Spirit are never transcended and/or negated."[37] Both Hopko's and McFague's views of language for God strongly emphasize the transcendence of God and the incapacity of human language and concepts for corresponding to the divine nature. Nevertheless Hopko considers the triune name to be absolutely definitive, whereas McFague discards it as worn-out, irrelevant, and harmful. Why this difference?

The Relation between Revelation and Theological Doctrine

What Is Finally Relevant

The difference becomes clear if we return to our first quote from Hopko: "Orthodox Christians refuse to emend the trinitarian names of Father and Son and Holy Spirit apophatically because the 'nameless God' has personally revealed himself to them as Father through the per-

---

35. See chap. 5, the section entitled "Who God Is and What God Is Like."
36. Hopko, "Apophatic Theology and the Naming of God in Eastern Orthodox Tradition," in *Speaking the Christian God*, 144–61.
37. Ibid., 149, 154, and 158.

son of Jesus Christ the Son, by the person of the Holy Spirit."[38] The difference between Hopko and McFague is that Hopko fully accepts the revelation of God in Jesus Christ and stated in Scripture as the genuine personal self-revelation of God, whereas McFague is very tentative about what Jesus Christ and Scripture reveal about God. In other words, what separates them is not the doctrine of divine transcendence and a theory of religious language but their view of the authority of the naming of God presented in Holy Scripture and witnessed by the historic church.

This is likewise the difference between the analogical theorists DiNoia and Johnson and between the figurative theorists Achtemeier and Frye in contrast to Duck and Wren.[39] Those who defend the enduring authority of the traditional pattern of language for God do so because they affirm God's self-naming or self-revelation in Jesus Christ and Scripture. Promoters of inclusivism invariably regard biblical revelation as in some way historically limited, fallible, imbalanced, nonpropositional, and in need of subsequent correction, as shown in chapter 6.

So we conclude that acceptance of divine special revelation as witnessed in Holy Scripture, not theories about the transcendence of God and the descriptive capacity of language for God, is finally determinative in the debate between defenders of the biblical pattern and gender-inclusivists. This may seem to be a fruitless or disappointing result, given the number of pages we have devoted to theories of language for God. Why did we waste so many words when it finally does not matter?

The presentation was necessary for two reasons. First, this topic is standard fare in practically all discussions of gendered language for God, too many of which on both sides of the debate suffer from misunderstandings, confusions, and fallacies. These issues needed to be sorted out. Second, there is a widely held assumption that theories of religious language are determinative of the outcome of the debate. Defenders of the biblical pattern sometimes argue as though elaborating the right theory of language will provide an impregnable defense against inclusive language. For their part many inclusivists are convinced that unpacking the proper view of religious language will convince all except incorrigible fundamentalists that our language for God must be gender-inclusive or gender-neutral. While it is true that theories of language do shape our understanding of Scripture and theology,

---

38. Ibid., 161.
39. DiNoia, "Knowing and Naming the Triune God," in *Speaking the Christian God*, 187, concludes: "No considerations of any kind can be advanced that would warrant the revision of the language in which the Father, Son, and Holy Spirit invite us to speak with them." The views of the others regarding the normativity of scriptural language have been quoted above in this chapter and in chap. 2.

including the meaning of the Bible's gendered language for God, it is not true that either biblical-traditionalism or inclusivism stands or falls with these theories. We have shown that one's view of the authority of revelation in Scripture is the best single predictor of one's views about gendered language for God.

Scripture, Doctrine, and God's Genderlessness

This chapter began with a strong argument for inclusive language: Scripture and the limitations of human language imply that God in himself is genderless. Thus using almost exclusively masculine language distorts our picture of God. Furthermore, if masculine language does not attribute gender to God, then neither does feminine language. Even gender-neutral language is adequate. Thus inclusivists conclude that all language for God is equally valid.

Given this argument, we observed that virtually all Christian theologians agree that God is genderless and proceeded to discuss various theories of human language for God. In the end it turned out that neither this doctrine nor theories of religious language settle the issue of inclusive language for God. One's views of the nature and authority of God's self-revelation in Jesus Christ and in Scripture determine one's position on gender language.

We must now confront a crucial implication of the argument for inclusive language that appeals to God's genderlessness: it takes the doctrine of God's genderlessness and makes it the basic criterion in our language for God. Some inclusivists use this doctrine as an argument for gender-inclusive "translations" of Scripture. Others refrain from tampering with Scripture but promote inclusive language in all other areas of Christian worship and life. Either way, the doctrine of divine genderlessness, not the language of Jesus Christ and Holy Scripture, is made the fundamental criterion by which the Christian church is to shape its living language for God. Whether they realize it or not, inclusivists make divine genderlessness more definitive than the particularities of God's self-revelation.

Even inclusivists who affirm a high view of Scripture make this move. Southern Baptist Paul Smith writes: "There is widespread agreement among Christian theologians that God transcends gender. . . . How will anyone believe us when . . . we talk as if God is only male?"[40] It is also the strategy of Presbyterian Old Testament scholar Johanna van Wijk-Bos: "In our search for language about God that is other than masculine, we look first for models in Scripture that emphasize a God

40. Smith, *Is It Okay to Call God "Mother"?* 39.

who transcends male and female."[41] She then considers the exalted view of God in Isaiah 40–55, and concludes by asking: "Are we willing to say that whether we call God 'father' or 'mother,' 'he' or 'she,' we are both right and wrong, for as we speak we know that our words are only a stammering approximation of the reality that is God?" And again: "If God indeed transcends sexuality, . . . God is referred to no more accurately with 'he' than with 'she.'"[42] The logic of this standard inclusivist argument is clear: God is transcendent and thus beyond gender; our human language is inadequate; therefore the pattern of the biblical text can be augmented so that God is both father and mother, he and she.

Traditionalists also affirm that God in himself is not gendered, but they do not use this doctrine to overturn the language of Scripture. So we are faced with a fundamental question: what should take precedence in shaping our language for God, the doctrine of God's genderlessness or the biblical pattern? Most Christians are inclined to confess Scripture as the basic standard and to regard theological doctrine as derivative and secondary. To appreciate why this is also the actual and proper order for determining our language for God, let's examine Scripture and its relationship to the doctrine that God in himself is ungendered.

Some observations and questions focus the issue. We know the biblical pattern of language for God, culminating in the triune name, *Father, Son, and Holy Spirit*. It is clear, pervasive, and undeniable. But how do we know that God in himself is ungendered? Where do we obtain this information? Is it such a basic or certain truth that it ought to have more authority than the Bible in shaping the living language of the Christian faith? Is it clearly taught by the Bible itself, as clearly as the triune name of God, *Father, Son, and Holy Spirit*? Is it a self-evidently true proposition of reason, like 1+1=2? Is it a universal human religious intuition? What is the status of the doctrine of God's genderlessness that justifies inclusivists in giving it final authority?

In the following sections it becomes evident that the Christian doctrine of God's genderlessness is not as clear or basic as the Bible's naming of God. That doctrine is not stated in Scripture. It has a substantial biblical basis, but its derivation involves some debatable cultural and philosophical assumptions about sex, gender, body, and spirit. It also involves philosophical conclusions about the attributes of the divine nature. Divine genderlessness does not have a status in Christian doctrine equal to or greater than Scripture's presentation of God.

---

41. van Wijk-Bos, *Reimagining God*, 11–12.

42. Ibid., 22, 25. Recall from chap. 3 and 4 that in the latter part of Isaiah the feminine and maternal references to God are similes, but God is *Yahweh the King* and *father* is used as an appellative. The transcendence of God does not equalize the genders in Isaiah.

I strongly affirm the Christian doctrine that God himself is beyond gender. But I also conclude that because this doctrine is derived from Scripture and relies on extrabiblical assumptions, it ought not to be placed prior to or above Scripture in shaping the language of the Christian faith. Instead it ought to be used to interpret the meaning of the biblical presentation of God and the language of the faith, as has been done throughout the history of the Christian church and its theology.

God beyond Gender in Scripture

We have seen that the biblical text consistently and pervasively speaks of God anthropomorphically as a masculine person, primarily as King and Father. *El*, the high God in the ancient Near East, was a male deity. *Yahweh* means *He Who Is*. Nevertheless, most commentators believe that the Bible writers themselves did not intend to attribute sexuality or gender to God. And Christian theologians virtually all hold that God is beyond gender. There are several indications in Scripture that these conclusions are correct.

First, although God is spoken of as masculine and even as having body parts, such as a face, eyes, ears, arms, and hands, he is never said to have reproductive organs (as Baal and other gods have). He has no wife or consort, except that he is "married" to Israel. He does not produce the world or his covenant people by emanation or procreation, but by creation and election. God is therefore not a reproductive, sexual being, a fact that distinguishes him from the pagan gods.

Second, there are a number of texts in Scripture that suggest that God is beyond the male–female polarity of creation. Most basic is the account in Genesis 1:26–28 of the creation of humanity in the image of God.[43] God creates humans, male and female, in his image. Both genders together thus image God. But this imaging does not imply that God in himself is both male and female. In fact, Genesis 1 implies that sex or gender, though created by God, is not part of the image of God in humans. The reason is this: like humans, the animals are created as male and female and blessed "to be fruitful and multiply," but they are not created in the image of God. Thus sex and gender are not part of the image of God. By good and necessary inference, therefore, we conclude that the image of God in Genesis 1 does not include sexual differentiation. Both human males and females image God, but it does not follow that God is male and female or gendered in any sense. And since God created male and female, he must transcend them. This is a widely held traditional argument from Scripture.

43. Achtemeier, "Exchanging God for 'No Gods,'" in *Speaking the Christian God*, 2–4; and van Wijk-Bos, *Reimagining God*, 23–26.

Other biblical texts warn against identifying God with human males and females. Numbers 23:19 points out that "God is not a man [*ish*: male human], that he should lie, nor a son of man [*adam*: human], that he should change his mind." The issue here is God's character and behavior, not his gender. But the text does prohibit thinking of God as a man. Hosea 11:9b is similar: "For I am God, and not man [*ish*]—the Holy One among you, I will not come in wrath." Perhaps most pointed is Deuteronomy 4:15–16: "You saw no form of any kind the day the LORD spoke to you at Horeb out of the fire. Therefore watch yourselves very carefully, so that you do not become corrupt and make for yourselves an idol, an image of any shape, whether formed like a man or a woman." Imaging God to be like a man or woman is proscribed as idolatry. This suggests strongly that biblical religion is inclined against attributing gender to God even though Scripture speaks of God with language befitting a masculine person. A final text frequently quoted is John 4:24, "God is spirit." Sexuality and gender are characteristics of bodily creatures, the argument goes. But God has no body. Therefore God has neither sex nor gender. These are the main biblical sources of the almost universally held doctrine of God's genderlessness.

God beyond Gender in Culture and Philosophy

God's ungenderedness is not as straightforwardly taught in Scripture as it might first seem, however. For the exegesis of the biblical texts given above depends on an assumption about gender not explicitly taught in Scripture and not self-evidently true. It is the assumption that gender is necessarily connected to sexuality and bodiliness, and thus that a nonbodily spiritual being could not have gender. Closer scrutiny shows that none of the biblical texts quoted above says that God is not masculine. In fact, they speak of him as though he is masculine. What they say is that God is not like a human male (or female) in form, character, or behavior. Without the assumption that gender is tied to sexuality, however, it is possible to hold that God could be a purely spiritual masculine person and could still forbid imaging himself as a human male. In fact, God could conceivably be masculine and still create both human males and females in his image, as proclaimed in Genesis 1. For the image of God in humans does not include gender or sex, as shown above. From Scripture as a whole we know that the image of God consists in true righteousness, knowledge, and holiness, in covenantal love and faithfulness, and in the capacities necessary for exercising dominion over the earth. In other words, the image of God includes all the personal capacities and excellences that are exemplified by humans of both genders. In traditional theological terminology, the image of God reflects the communicable attributes of God.

Given this understanding of the image of God, *Elohim* in Genesis 1 could be analogically masculine and nevertheless create both male and female in his image. John 4:24 likewise does not deny that God is masculine; it says that God is Spirit. So none of these biblical texts explicitly states that God transcends gender. And they do not imply that God transcends gender without the assumption that gender must be tied to sexuality.

Is that assumption self-evident or universally affirmed? Suppose there is a difference between sex and gender such that sex has to do with anatomy and reproduction whereas gender has to do with personhood. Then it would be possible for personal beings—spirits—who lack bodies to have gender. Is it self-evident that gender is exclusively a quality of bodily beings? The Bible speaks of angels, spirits, and God as gendered (masculine) and the gods of the nations as male and female.[44] Many of the world's religions affirm the existence of gendered gods and spirits. The *jinn* ("genies") of Islamic folklore are both male and female. Thus it is neither a self-evident postulate of reason nor a universal dictate of human common sense that spirits are ungendered. The presence of this assumption in Christian tradition largely reflects the influence of Plato and others in Greco-Roman culture who held that both sex and gender have to do with being embodied, and that human souls in themselves are genderless. This assumption is present in Christian thinking about the human spirit as well as about God. The proposition that gender is not a characteristic of spiritual beings is a cultural-philosophical assumption, true as it may seem to us. It cannot be listed as a teaching of Scripture. And thus the genderlessness of God is less than an absolutely certain teaching of Scripture.

The other crucial source of the doctrine of that God transcends gender is philosophical theology based on both Scripture and general revelation (the nature of God deduced by arguments). Reflection on the attributes of God as understood in terms of classical philosophical categories quickly leads to the conclusion that God is beyond gender, if not beyond personhood as we humans define it. A being who is absolute, eternal, necessary, infinite, simple, wholly good, perfect, complete, and the ground of all relative and contingent attributes without himself having any of those attributes—this is not the sort of being who could be gendered. For masculinity and femininity, no matter how well-formed and inclusive, are are partial, correlative, relational, and contingent attributes. To be masculine but not feminine is to have a cer-

---

44. However, if gender is a *creaturely* characteristic as distinct from a characteristic of *bodily* beings, then angels and spirits could be gendered because they are creatures, but God would not be gendered because he is not a creature.

tain combination of personality characteristics, but not another combination. To have all personal characteristics in maximal combination is to be neither masculine nor feminine. Thus a perfectly complete being by nature could not have one or both genders. In short, God cannot be gendered any more than he can cease to exist or not be all-powerful. This line of argument is strong and has been very influential among Christian theologians.

Thus there is a good philosophical reason that emerges in reflection on God's nature and attributes which leads to the conclusion that God is beyond gender. Taking this reason together with the biblical material, I am in agreement with virtually the entire Christian tradition that God in himself is beyond gender. My purpose here is not to undermine this doctrine, but to demonstrate that it is derived from a less than certain interpretation of Scripture coupled with some extrabiblical cultural and philosophical ideas about the relations among sexuality, gender, and God's attributes. It is not a direct teaching of Scripture.

Properly Ordering Scripture and God's Genderlessness

The logic of the Christian church's arrival at the doctrine of God's genderlessness has a direct bearing on how we should relate it to Scripture in determining how to speak of God. Since God's ontological genderlessness is not directly stated in Scripture, it does not have the same clear and primary status as the teaching that God is *Father* or, more fully, that God is *Father, Son, and Holy Spirit* (Matt. 28:19). And since God's transcendence of gender is deduced from Scripture in combination with some extrabiblical assumptions and philosophical arguments, this doctrine cannot be treated as more certain and definitive than Scripture as a source of our knowledge of God and his names. But this is exactly what inclusivists do.[45]

This illicit move is most blatant in cases where Scripture itself is rendered gender-inclusive by explicitly appealing to God's genderlessness. Examples are the *Inclusive Language Lectionary* and the Oxford *New Testament and Psalms: An Inclusive Language Translation*, which neutralize the primacy of masculine language by balancing it with feminine language and replacing it with ungendered terminology.[46] The illegitimate maneuver is also apparent when inclusivists invoke divine transcendence of gender in order to exegetically side-step the gendered quality of the biblical names of God (e.g. *El, Elohim, Yah-*

45. Garrett Green, "The Gender of God and the Theology of Metaphor," in *Speaking the Christian God*, 44–64, is a penetrating critique of what he calls "genderless theology."
46. See the editors' introductions to both of these works, which explicitly appeal to divine genderlessness as one justification for inclusive language "translations."

weh).[47] In all these cases a doctrine based on Scripture and philosophy functions as a censor of Scripture itself.

Those who refrain from tampering with the biblical text but call for inclusive language throughout the rest of the Christian life reverse doctrine and Scripture in a similar way. They give priority to the doctrine of divine ungenderedness over Scripture in shaping the faith-language of the Christian community. For as shown in chapters 5 and 6, if Scripture is the source and norm for the God-language of the Christian faith, that language will not be gender-inclusive. However, if Christian language must be gender-inclusive, then the doctrine of divine genderless is in fact operating at a more basic and determinative level than Scripture. Once again a doctrine derived from the Bible and extrabiblical conclusions functions to divert the language of the faith from the biblical pattern.

Parallel examples make clear how intolerable this move is. Suppose that hyper-Calvinists used the doctrine of divine predestination to remove all language of human choice from Scripture and from the faith-language of the Christian community. Or what if theologians erased all language about God's seeing, hearing, loving, being angry, repenting, rejoicing, and suffering from the Bible and Christian language on the ground that God in himself has no senses or feelings? What if philosophers who hold that God is eternal and therefore does not really perform particular temporal actions removed from the Bible and from the language of Christian piety all references to God's acts of creating, speaking to Abraham and Moses, punishing Saul and saving David, sending Jesus, raising Jesus, and answering our prayers? If these revisions of Christian language according to philosophical-theological doctrines were implemented, we would be left with the impersonal, detached God of Aristotle, not the living God of Abraham, Isaac, and Jacob. Ordinary Christians and theologians alike rightly resist and condemn this sort of revisionism.

In just the same way we ought to resist the inclusivist use of the doctrine of divine genderlessness to remove, relativize, or neutralize the masculine language for God from the Bible and the living language of the Christian church.

What then should be the relation among Scripture, the language of faith, and the doctrine of divine genderlessness? It should remain as it always has been in the Christian tradition. From the time of the Church Fathers, teachers of the faith have used this doctrine to explain that calling God *Father* does not imply that God is masculine.[48] Thus the

---

47. We have noted this approach, for example, in Johnson's and van Wijk-Bos's discussions of *Yahweh*.

48. Hopko, "Apophatic Theology and the Naming of God," in *Speaking the Christian God*, contains a number of references to writings of the Church Fathers on this issue.

doctrine helps us rightly to interpret Scripture. It prevents us from wrongly inferring from the gendered language in Scripture that God is masculine while we work to understand what this language does mean (the project of the next chapter). But the doctrine that God is beyond gender is no reason for the church's changing from the biblical pattern to gender-egalitarian or gender-neutral language for God.

Back to the Beginning: Revelation

This chapter began where the previous one left off—with the final authority of Scripture. We then considered several topics tied to the assertion that God in himself is not masculine, an assertion that almost invariably turns up in arguments for inclusive language for God. First, we reflected on several theories that attempt to explain how language can communicate truth about a God who far transcends his creatures. It turned out, however, that acceptance or rejection of inclusive language for God does not finally depend on any of these theories, but on one's view of the nature and status of revelation recorded in Scripture. We were back where we started. We therefore considered the relation between Scripture and the doctrine, accepted by almost everyone on both sides, that God in himself has no gender. The sources and assumptions of this doctrine were noted, and it turned out that the doctrine depended on Scripture in such a way that it ought not to be used to alter Scripture or the language of the Christian church in its life of faith. Once again we are back where we began—with the final authority of Scripture in matters of faith and practice, including our language for God.

However, to conclude that Scripture's masculine language for God does not imply that God is masculine is to make a negative judgment. It does not tell us what this language does mean. We must still explain its meaning and state why this meaning depends on the particular language of the biblical text.

8

Inclusive Language
and Christian Truth

If God's self-revelation, fulfilled in Jesus Christ and proclaimed in Scripture, is the final authority for the church, then the doctrine of God embedded in Scripture, properly explicated, is the enduring standard of Christian faith and practice. Gender-inclusive language for God is compatible with biblical Christianity only if it retains the full meaning and specific teachings of biblical revelation and does not diminish, alter, or undermine them.

But it is precisely on these points that defenders of tradition have been most critical. They charge that feminist theology and inclusive language distort Christian doctrine and falsify the faith itself. Elizabeth Achtemeier alleges that feminists are "Exchanging God for 'No Gods.'"[1] Donald Bloesch regards *The Debate over Inclusive God Language* as *The Battle for the Trinity*.[2] The charges that other anti-inclusivists lodge are equally serious. Colin Gunton believes that the choice is "between the gospel and a 'different gospel' which is no gospel at all."[3] Leslie Zeigler charges that "most feminist theologians are presenting us *not* with the Christian faith but with a quite different religion."[4] Defenders of the biblical pattern of language for God are concerned that inclusive language not only departs from orthodox Christian doctrine, but also jeopardizes true piety and the meaning of the gospel itself.

While some inclusivists have quite consciously and intentionally abandoned traditional Christianity as outmoded and irredeemably pa-

---

1. Achtemeier, "Exchanging God for 'No Gods'," in *Speaking the Christian God*.
2. Donald Bloesch, *The Battle for the Trinity* (Ann Arbor: Servant, 1985). I have reversed the title and subtitle.
3. Colin Gunton, "Proteus and Procrustes," in *Speaking the Christian God*, 80.
4. Zeigler, "Christianity or Feminism," in *Speaking the Christian God*, 313.

triarchal, others claim that gender-egalitarian language for God is fully compatible with doctrinal orthodoxy—the entire truth content of biblical Christianity—and authentic Christian piety.[5]

The purpose of this chapter is to work through issues connected to the truth of the Christian faith, leaving the question of Christian piety to the next chapter. The chapter is divided into three main sections. The first observes that biblical-traditional language and gender-inclusive language are complete, structured patterns of meaning that express particular understandings of God's identity, nature, and relationship with his creatures. The meanings of these distinct linguistic practices as integrated wholes must be compared, not just individual words for God. The second section deals with biblical truth. In particular, it explores whether the biblical identification of God and his acts in history can be truly preserved when recast in fully gender-inclusive language. The third section is devoted to the truth content of particular doctrines central to the faith: the Creator–creature relation, the Trinity, the person of Jesus Christ, and the atonement.

If it is really equivalent to biblical-traditional language, inclusive language, taken on its own, should be able to duplicate the essential meaning-content of the biblical presentation of God without alteration or significant distortion. If it cannot, inclusive-language Christianity is in a real dilemma: either it expresses heterodox or non-Christian religious teaching, or else it is not really equal in meaning and status to traditional language, for it remains dependent upon and governed by the masculine language of Scripture for definition and legitimation. If this dilemma is genuine, "inclusivist Christianity" turns out to be an oxymoron, and those who are inclined to embrace it must choose between true Christianity and inclusivism.

A couple of important caveats are in order. First, recall that we are dealing with standard inclusvism—egalitarianism and/or neutrality of gendered language for God. We are not discussing those who wish to use feminine language for God according to the biblical pattern. Second, the discussion is about two kinds of language and linguistic practice, not about persons, their integrity, or their veracity. There are sincere Christians who believe the Bible and the doctrines of the church and who nevertheless use inclusive language for God. I wish to show that there is a tension or incompatibility between what they believe and

5. For example, Margo Houts, "Is God Also Our Mother?" *Perspectives*, June/July 1997, 12, challenges the claim "that *mother* and other instances of the divine feminine, when presented in linguistically privileged forms, necessarily import aberrant meanings of sexuality, birthing, immanence, pantheism, and Gnosticism into our understanding of God." Nancy Hardesty, Paul Smith, and Aída Besançon Spencer would also defend this view.

their linguistic practice. I do not wish to question the sincerity or authenticity of their faith.

Two Distinct Linguistic Practices

The Language of Biblical Christianity

Traditional Christian language is not just the mummified carcass of an archaic religious vocabulary. It is a living practice, the Christian church's continuing proclamation of a communal narrative that has grown through telling and retelling since the people of Israel. To be sure, there are variations in the accents and styles of speech among different traditions and eras, but the basic vocabulary, syntax, and semantics—the "players" and "rules" of the Christian "language game"[6]—are fairly constant and universal because they are nourished and guided by the fixed written text of Holy Scripture. The liturgies, musical texts, doctrinal statements, educational materials, and evangelistic communications of the various Christian churches trace their language back to the Bible. Their vocabulary has certainly been enriched by extrabiblical sources. But the basic terms, grammar, and core meaning of Christian language have remained the same.

The language of the biblical tradition, which narrates God's self-disclosure in his work of creation and salvation, is highly complex and intricately interwoven. The views of God, Jesus Christ, the Holy Spirit, creation, fall, sin, grace, the way of salvation, the church, the will of God for life, and hope for the life to come that are presented in Scripture gradually emerge and come into focus as we read and reread the Bible as a whole. Each book contributes its purposes, themes, and perspectives on God, his work, and his will. The books of the Bible each play their own role in the historical unfolding of divine revelation. The message of Scripture as a whole has been constituted by the Holy Spirit, consolidating the contributions of each part into a single, complex, seamless, coherent unity.

The church has been working since earliest times to discern, clarify, and reflect the teachings of the grand message of Scripture in an orderly, coherent summary of doctrine. The Apostles' and Nicene Creeds are the best-known results of this work. The many confessions and catechisms of the various branches of Christianity are other significant

---

6. "Language game" is a term coined by the philosopher Ludwig Wittgenstein to suggest that the meaning of language is determined by the way it is actually used by people in life. The expression has been taken up by theologians for use in interpreting religious language, especially by those of the so-called Yale School associated with Hans Frei and George Lindbeck, as well as other proponents of "narrative theology." It is common in discussions of inclusive language.

products of doctrinal reflection on Scripture.[7] Of a more technical nature are the great works of dogmatic and systematic theology written by the doctors of the church.

Christian doctrine is not frozen or finished. There are of course debates among traditions and theologians on every point. In addition, the inexhaustible richness of biblical revelation, combined with the various historical attempts to understand it, means that this work will never be done before Christ returns. There is always more to learn, received formulations to revise, intra-Christian debates to continue, new questions to consider, and new challenges from the world to meet.

But underlying these debates and framing these developments, a general consensus about the basic structure and core teachings of the Christian faith has been achieved by the ecumenical Christian church. There is widespread commitment to the normativity of the language and teaching of the Bible. This is evident in the universal affirmation of the Apostles' and Nicene Creeds, which are organized according to the triune name of God: *Father, Son, and Holy Spirit*.[8] Further, there is ecumenical acceptance of the view that Christian doctrine is to be formulated on the basis of everything taught in Scripture as a whole, and each doctrine should be defined in terms of its place within the unified body of Christian truth in its entirety.[9] In spite of the fractures within historic Christianity and the concessions of some to modern rationalism, naturalism, or relativism, it is not pure idealism to say that there is a biblically-based, ecumenically affirmed understanding of the Christian gospel. Never before has the cultural and denominational diversity of the historical Christian church generated a movement to alter the basic biblical terminology for God.

7. See John Leith, ed., *Creeds of the Churches: A Reader in Christian Doctrine from the Bible to the Present* (Garden City, N.Y.: Doubleday Anchor, 1963) and *Catechism of the Catholic Church* (Mahwah, N.J.: Paulist, 1994).

8. See, for example, *Confessing the One Faith: An Ecumenical Explication of the Apostolic Faith As It Is Confessed in the Nicene-Constantinopolitan Creed (381)* (Geneva: World Council of Churches, 1991), the authors of which are Protestant, Roman Catholic, and Eastern Orthodox. The major creedal disagreement between the Western and Eastern churches after Nicea is whether the Holy Spirit proceeds from the Father or from the Father and the Son.

9. Grant Osborne, *The Hermeneutical Spiral* (Downers Grove: InterVarsity, 1991) and V. Philips Long, Tremper Longman III, Richard Muller, Vern Poythress, and Moisés Silva, *Foundations of Contemporary Interpretation* (Grand Rapids: Zondervan, 1996), are two evangelical Protestant accounts tracing the process of formulating Christian doctrine from Scripture. For the Roman Catholic view, see *Catechism of the Catholic Church* (Mahwah, N.J.: Paulist, 1995) prologue and chaps. 1–3. In contrast, see Sandra Schneiders, "The Bible and Feminism: Biblical Theology," in *Freeing Theology: The Essentials of Theology in Feminist Perspective*, ed. C. M. LaCugna (San Francisco: Harper, 1993), for a Roman Catholic feminist perspective.

Gender-Inclusive Language for God

The contemporary promotion of gender-inclusive language for God is precisely this sort of movement for basic historical innovation. It therefore deserves scrutiny. Proponents should neither be surprised nor offended that it is receiving careful critical examination. Given the nature of these innovations, it is only fair to ask whether inclusivist Christianity is an expression of "the faith that was once for all entrusted to the saints" (Jude 3) or an aberration. It clearly bears the burden of proof.

The essential nature of gender-inclusive language for God makes it a complete, integral, standard linguistic practice in the same way that the use of biblical-traditional language is.[10] Inclusivism cannot be content with mixing occasional feminine images with the masculine names and titles of God, as in the biblical pattern. It cannot be satisfied by praying to God as *Mother* occasionally if prayer to the *Father* is regular. It cannot accept relegation of feminine language for God to hymns and prayers when blessings and sacraments are exclusively reserved for Father, Son, and Holy Spirit. It cannot accept the use of inclusive language in worship while acknowledging that the masculine language of Scripture is privileged. For none of these arrangements is egalitarian.

Gender-egalitarianism is the ruling value. Gender-equality is crucial. That is what *inclusive* means: not excluding one from anything that the other is or has. Thus gender-equality of language pertains not only to frequency of terminology, but also to its form and function. Obviously there should not be more masculine than feminine terms for God. But there should also be feminine names, titles, and pronouns for God, if there are masculine ones. And feminine terms should be used in all the same genres and venues as masculine ones: in Scripture, the creeds and doctrinal statements, in worship, including blessings and the sacraments, in Christian education, devotions, and in the faith-language of the Christian life. The whole point of inclusive language is to eliminate the primacy and exclusive authority of masculine language for God. Inclusive language for God is precisely analogous to inclusive language for humans. It is totalistic.[11]

---

10. See "What Exactly Is Inclusive Language for God?" in chap. 1.

11. Johnson, *She Who Is*, 48–49, rejects all proposals that feminine language be included in less than equal ways. "Inequality is not redressed but subtly furthered as the androcentric image of God remains in place, made more appealing through the subordinate inclusion of feminine traits." Similarly Margo Houts, "Is God Also Our Mother?" *Perspectives* June/July 1997, rejects "hierarchical inclusivism," in which feminine language is included but subordinated to masculine language, in favor of "gender-equivalent inclusivism."

Thus inclusivists who stop short of full equality of language for God are inconsistent with the inner logic of their position. For if there are any ways in which feminine or ungendered language cannot function that masculine language does function, then they are not equal, and language for God is not inclusive after all. In the end there would still be something properly and exclusively privileged about the Bible's masculine language for God.

As noted in chapter 1, gender-inclusive language can be achieved in several ways. The first is by balancing masculine and feminine terms.[12] Thus God is *Father and Mother*, or *the Father-Mother*, or sometimes *Father, he* and sometimes *Mother, she* in equal proportions. The second strategy is to use ungendered personal terms so that neither gender is favored.[13] Instead of *Lord, King,* and *Father*, God is *Ruler, Monarch,* and *Parent*. *Lord, King,* and *Father* are replaced by *Eternal Light, Keeper of the Nations, Hope of the World,* and dozens of other ungendered references to God. In place of masculine pronouns, the term *God* is simply repeated or substitutes such as *Godself* are devised.[14] The third strategy is to combine gender-equal and gender-neutral language: an occasional *Father-Mother* with *God, Sovereign, Holy One, Eternal Light,* and other mostly gender-neutral references. Most inclusivists favor the third approach as most flexible, least monotonous, and best able to "bring many names to God."

When we compare gender-inclusive language for God with the language of Scripture, therefore, we must juxtapose two complete practices to see whether they are equivalent or compatible in meaning. Of course there is one crucial sense in which inclusivists openly admit to changing the meaning of traditional biblical language for God. They believe that the tradition is sexist both with respect to its depiction of God and with respect to the message that this view of God sends to men, women, and children. The whole point of gender-inclusivism is to eliminate this alleged sexism and patriarchalism from the language of the faith.

12. Duck, Mollenkott, Ruether, Wren, Johnson, van Wijk-Bos, and most inclusivists we have considered favor gender-egalitarian language, provided it does not perpetuate unequal stereotypes of mothers and fathers.

13. Ramshaw, *God beyond Gender*, urges that we move toward ungendered language for God rather than gender-egalitarian language.

14. The term *God* is currently considered gender-neutral and not the masculine correlate of *goddess*. Even in some traditional Christian churches there is a subtly increasing use of *God* without the other traditional masculine terms *Father, Lord,* and *King*. Incidentally, this practice is not only promoted by gender-inclusivists; it is also favored by religious-inclusivists. It is much easier to avoid offending Jews, Muslims, Deists, Spiritists, and Pantheists by speaking of *God* than using distinctively Christian language, such as *the Father of our Lord Jesus Christ*.

Are Biblical Language and Inclusive Language for God Equivalent?

The Identity of the God of Scripture

Above we characterized biblical-traditional language for God as a complete, integrated linguistic practice. The identity of God is disclosed through the entire biblical narrative, from the beginning of Genesis to the end of Revelation. The outline of God's self-identification in Scripture was traced in chapter 4. El reveals himself as Yahweh, the God of the covenant with Israel, the Great King who fulfills that covenant in his messianic Son, Jesus, and who through him is disclosed as his Father and our Father. He sends us to baptize and disciple the nations into the name of the Father and of the Son and of the Holy Spirit, proclaiming salvation through Jesus Christ and announcing his coming kingdom. In the Old Testament the basic idea or "root metaphor" of God is the Great King. In the New Testament the central and distinctive presentation of God is as Father in relation to Jesus the Son.

The identity of God in the biblical narrative is the entire web of meaning constituted by the development and interplay of the basic themes of Yahweh the Father-King and his Messiah. That web is enriched by hundreds of strands provided by other ways the Bible speaks of God. But the web's basic structure, central strands, and anchor points are distinct and stable. God's identity in history is a unique identity, at least as unique as any human person's whose identity is disclosed by his or her life-history.

A Formal Linguistic Difference of Meaning

If the text of Scripture is rendered gender-inclusively, the particularity of this narrative and the web of meaning it embodies are unavoidably altered. This distortion is an obvious consequence of linguistic factors connected with the meaning of words and figures of speech.

Different words almost never have exactly the same meanings. Consider words for parents. Fathers and mothers are both parents, and as such they share many characteristics and functions. But they have different reproductive roles and kinds of relationships with their children. A parent is either a father or mother, but *parent* is a generic term. It is not a person-specific term like *father* and *mother* are. These three words are very closely related and largely overlap in meaning. But they are not equal or equivalent.

Individual differences of meaning are compounded when words are combined into linguistic constructions such as figures of speech. Modern linguists insist that the meaning of a metaphor is unique, that it

often cannot be translated fully into literal language or captured precisely by another metaphor. It is difficult, for example, to unpack fully
what it means that "life is just a bowl of cherries." Baskets of oranges or
trays of bananas won't do it. Even an extended explanation that life includes a lot of fun, good times, good feelings, good things, freedom
from care, and so forth seems to fall short. But even if metaphors can
be replaced or translated, the issue remains whether the translation or
replacement retains or alters the meaning of the original.

Concerns about altering the meaning-content of biblical language by
altering words and figures of speech are often expressed by defenders
of the biblical pattern. According to Roland Frye, a professor of English, the fact that biblical language for God is figurative "should not de-
lude any of us into assuming that we can therefore change the biblical
figures for others that we may prefer. . . . The fundamental literary principle is that figures cannot be abandoned, symbols cannot be substituted, images cannot be altered without changing the meaning they
convey."[15] The blurring and alteration of the biblical presentation of
God generated by inclusivist substitutions are pointed out in subsequent sections of this chapter.

But the entire project seems problematic at its foundations. Frye
points out that revising the text of Scripture, as done in the *Inclusive
Language Lectionary* or the new inclusive God-language Bible translations, lacks simple integrity. "Even in secular literature, such violations
are regarded by responsible students as the cardinal sin of literary criticism, interpretation, and translation." He characterizes gender-inclusive translations as a form of "bowdlerization." As Thomas Bowdler attempted to edit Shakespeare to conform to Victorian standards of
propriety, so inclusivists politically correct Scripture and Christian language to conform to gender-egalitarian norms.[16] The article "I believe
in the Holy Spirit, who proceeds from the Father-Mother and from the
Child," from the Inclusive Language Nicene Creed, has the aura of
Bowdlerian silliness about it. Such alterations, no matter how well-mo-
tivated, inevitably violate the texts and distort their meaning. They sel-
dom improve on the author. The question remains, however, how sub-
stantive and serious the changes are.

A Difference of Historical Truthfulness

Immediately there is a serious problem: The gender-inclusive Bible
falsifies the account of God's self-involvement in history. It does not tell

15. Frye, "Language for God and Feminist Language," in *Speaking the Christian
God*, 33.
16. Ibid., 23–24.

God's "story" the way God brought it about. The Bible is not a complex metaphorical fiction attempting to symbolize a transcendent God. If it were, perhaps we could devise another metaphorical fiction that did roughly the same job. But at its core the Bible narrates the history of God's involvement with the world from creation to the new creation. It is "God's story" not in a fictional sense but the sense that my life history is "my story." Perhaps God's involvement in history might have been different if he had so willed. Perhaps God could have chosen to reveal himself as *Mother* or *Father-Mother* without misrepresentation and still have accomplished his redemptive purposes in the world. But he didn't. He revealed himself as *Elohim*, the King of Creation, and gave *Yahweh—He Who Is*—as his name. In Jesus Christ he showed himself to be *Our Father in Heaven*, the God who is *Father, Son, and Holy Spirit*. This is a straightforward matter of fact. Whatever their theological meanings, the biblical names and titles of God are integral to the history of God's mighty acts in the world. Changing the terms that identify God changes the account of what happened. It changes the historical record from true to false. For God did not reveal himself as *She Who Is* and the *Father-Mother*. When Aída Besançon Spencer writes, "Jesus taught us to pray, 'Our Parent who art in heaven,'" she asserts a straightforward falsehood.[17]

If inclusive language cannot preserve the truthful character of the history of God's mighty acts, it is not equivalent to biblical-traditional language.[18] Pannenberg puts the point this way: "As we have to accept other contingencies of the historical incarnation, we have to realize that the word *father* in Jesus' own language functioned not as an exchangeable image, but as the name he used in addressing the God he proclaimed. Therefore, in the Christian church the name father, and its use as Jesus used it, belongs to the identity of the Christian faith. It cannot be changed without abandoning that identity."[19]

A Difference in Reliability of Reference

A related problem follows: inclusive language no longer provides certainty of the identity of the God about and to whom we speak.[20] In chap-

---

17. Spencer, *The Goddess Revival*, 183.

18. Virtually all defenders of biblical-traditional language appeal to the biblical narrative as definitive of the meaning of our terminology for God, a meaning that Mother-language cannot duplicate or maintain. I have benefited on this point from most of the authors in *Speaking the Christian God*.

19. Wolfhart Pannenberg, "Feminine Language About God?" *Asbury Theological Journal* 48, no. 2 (1993): 29.

20. Donald Hook and Alvin Kimel Jr., "Calling God 'Father': A Theolinguistic Analysis," *Faith and Philosophy* 12 (1995): 207–22, is an excellent technical discussion of this problem.

ters 4 and 5 we identified *Father* as a basic and central New Testament term for God, part of the triune name. In the New Testament *Father* is a kinship-title that functions like a proper name (title and proper name are the first two meanings of *name of God* we considered) in that it has a unique personal referent. *Mother* is a figure of speech for God in the Bible and is not a title or name. Since *Mother* is not functionally equivalent to *Father* as a biblical term for God, it is not even a candidate for adequate substitution. When praying to *Our Mother in Heaven* (thereby elevating *Mother* to the status of a title), therefore, we could only know that we were addressing the God of the Bible if we intended or specified that we were praying to the God who is the Father of our Lord Jesus Christ, his historical-biblical designation. Otherwise we might be praying to the *Great Mother*, *Sophia* or *Ishtar*, or the Hindu divine Mother, *Kali*. Similarly, prayer to the Father-Mother might be invoking the deity of ancient Gnosticism, modern Christian Science, or some other dual-dimensional Force, not the God of the Bible.

Even prayer to God as Father, if taken out of the New Testament context of Jesus as the messianic Son and of the triune name, *Father, Son, and Holy Spirit*, fails explicitly to address the God of the Bible.[21] There is nothing inherently special about the word *Father* by itself. Other religions address God as father. The point is that the designation of God as Father, with the entire web of meaning that *Father* has in the Bible, is the definitive specification of who God is. Alternatives, including *Mother*, *Father-Mother*, or *Parent*, do not on their own clearly refer to that God. Thus they either fail to pick out the true God, referring instead to a false god or perhaps to nothing at all, or otherwise they depend upon the biblical designation of God to identify the One addressed as *Mother, Father-Mother*, or *Parent*. In neither case are the gender-inclusive alternatives equivalent to the biblical *Father* as a reliable referent to God.

This inequality of reliability can be illustrated from human history. We typically refer to historical persons by clear terms of identification, usually names and titles—Julius Caesar and President George Washington, for example. Sometimes we can also pick them out by descriptive terms such as "the Roman ruler who crossed the Rubicon," "the first executive officer of the U.S.A.," and "the general who prayed at Valley Forge." But in the final analysis, the specific identifiers, the designations by name and title, are what nail down who we are talking about. For if someone changed *Julius Caesar* to *Julius the Ruler* and *President*

---

21. Adolf von Harnack's liberal Christianity proclaimed the fatherhood of God and the brotherhood of man, but without the biblical doctrine of the Trinity. See Johnson, *She Who Is*, 118–20, for examples of other religions besides Christianity which invoke God as father.

George Washington to *George the First of the United States*, we would not be sure that these were the people who crossed the Rubicon and prayed at Valley Forge, respectively. We might wonder whether there were, unknown to us, other historical figures with similar designations who also fit these descriptions. Or probably we would suspect that these puzzling yet strangely familiar designations were confused and mistaken. The point is that we need a clear and correct personal designation in order to pick out historical figures accurately and reliably. For there is a causal connection between their identities and our ability to refer to them: the historical tradition of referring to them which transmits their identity verbally to us.[22] Those who knew about Julius Caesar and George Washington spoke and wrote about them, eventually passing that knowledge on to us.

It is no different for our knowledge of God. He has shown himself to us in history. The witness of the apostles and Scripture with the continuous tradition of the church based on them together provide the historical link that guarantees that our language still refers to the God who showed himself to Abraham, Moses, and fully in Jesus Christ. As Pannenberg points out, "Where the word 'Father' is replaced by something else, there can be no warrant anymore that we are talking about and addressing the same God as Jesus did."[23] To change the basic terms of that linguistic tradition either leaves the object of our reference uncertain or otherwise makes those terms depend on biblical-traditional language for God to guarantee the accuracy of their reference.

To sum up this section, gender-inclusive language for God is not synonymous in meaning or equivalent in authority to the biblical pattern of language for God. Without tacitly depending on the biblical pattern, inclusive language cannot retain the meaning of the biblical presentation of God, it cannot truthfully retell the history of God's self-revelation, and it cannot reliably distinguish the God of Scripture from false gods. But if inclusive language must be subjected to biblical language, then inclusivists should be consistent and submit fully to the norms of the biblical pattern.

Inclusive Language for God and Basic Christian Orthodoxy

Doctrine and theology are not abstact human speculations antithetical to the biblical narrative and irrelevant or harmful to a vital, fruitful Christian faith. They are ordered summaries of the teachings of Scrip-

22. Hook and Kimel, "Calling God 'Father,'" 217–18.
23. Wolfhart Pannenberg, *An Introduction to Systematic Theology* (Grand Rapids: Eerdmans, 1991), 31–32.

ture, most of which are directly about God, his mighty acts of salvation, and his will for Christian living. The church has always been concerned to teach true doctrine, because heresies often lead to idolatry, false gospels, and dishonor to God. False doctrines may not merely be mistaken conceptualizations but may promote religions other than what God through Scripture calls us to.[24]

In this section we consider four doctrines: the Creator–creature relation, the Trinity, the deity of Jesus Christ, and the atonement. In the end it is clear that inclusive-language Christianity is in the same dilemma with respect to doctrine as it faced above. Either it presupposes biblical-Christian orthodoxy, in which case it is not equal in authority and should be abandoned, or else, standing on its own, it confuses or alters the meaning of Christian orthodoxy.

The God–World Relation

Traditional theologians have repeatedly expressed concern over inclusivism's inability to preserve an orthodox biblical view of the relationship between God and the world. It is well known that the mother goddesses of the world religions typically imply continuity of being between the divine and the world, since they are thought to give birth to the world and humans.[25] This relationship implies that the divine is an integral part of the world or that the world is an extension of the divine, in other words, either paganism or pantheism. It is also well known that some forms of contemporary feminist spirituality, such as Wicca, are returning to the ancient worship of the feminine divine principle of life supposedly implicit in and animating all things.[26] The concern of Christian theologians is that feminine language for God, apart from its place in the biblical pattern, promotes or falls prey to an immanent view of the divine in nature like these.

Biblical Christianity affirms an absolute Creator–creature distinction. God is completely distinct from the world and in no sense dependent on it for his existence, fulfillment, or glory. The world is completely distinct from God, although it depends absolutely on God for its existence, both its beginning and its continuation. Yet God is also im-

---

24. Mormons, Jehovah's Witnesses, and the Unification Church (Moonies) speak of God, Jesus Christ, and salvation, but these religions are not versions of biblical Christianity because of the doctrinal meaning they give these terms. See Ruth Tucker, *Another Gospel: Alternative Religions and the New Age Movement* (Grand Rapids: Zondervan, 1989).

25. James Livingston, "Mother Goddesses, " *Anatomy of the Sacred*, 174–81.

26. Achtemeier; "Exchanging God for 'No Gods'," in *Speaking the Christian God*; Spencer, "God as Female," in *The Goddess Revival*; *Womanspirit Rising: A Feminist Reader in Religion*, ed. C. P. Christ and J. Plaskow. A few leaders at the Re-Imagining God Conference in 1993 were promoting this kind of spirituality.

manent. He is omnipresent throughout creation, fully involved with the world and present at every spatiotemporal point in it as creator and sustainer, as well as savior or judge. In sum, God is completely distinct from and transcendent of the creation, yet fully immanent in and involved with it as God.[27]

Inclusivist theologians hold a variety of views on the Creator–creature relation. Some straightforwardly affirm the classical theistic position. In other words, they accept the doctrine of creation as presented in Scripture and associated with God the Father in the Apostles' and Nicene Creeds. They endorse fully inclusive language but want to give it the meaning that comes from the Bible and its tradition. They intend *Mother* as a synonym for what Scripture means by *Father*.[28] These inclusivists reject paganism or pantheism by privileging the biblical-confessional tradition of Christianity. (Our question for them remains: if Scripture is privileged, isn't full gender-inclusivism illegitimate?)

Many others have taken inclusive language on its own terms and have found it most compatible with a contemporary form of panentheism, the view that God and the world, though distinct, are essentially and mutually interrelated. The panentheistic God is or is becoming part of the world, and the world is or is becoming part of God. Both are growing and changing in the process. Panentheism is a third option between orthodox theism and pantheism (belief that the world is divine because it is identical with God or is an extension of God).[29]

There is an identifiable linguistic connection between inclusivism and panentheism. Gender-inclusive language balances masculine and feminine attributions to God. Given the (stereotypical?) correlation of masculinity with separation or transcendence and femininity with continunity or immanence, a gender-inclusive God is both distinct from creation and ontologically bonded with it.[30] Inclusivism neither stresses the immanence of God by using feminine language exclusively nor divine transcendence by using only masculine language.

27. See Bavinck, *The Doctrine of God*, 156–64, for a classic Reformed discussion of God's immanence and omnipresence in creation in relation to his transcendence.

28. Houts, "Is God Also Our Mother?" takes this position.

29. Much modern panentheism is the legacy of German Idealism and Romanticism, especially Hegel's philosophical theology. Different kinds of panentheism are found in Paul Tillich's notion of God as the Ground of Being in all beings but not itself a being, in the process theology of Alfred North Whitehead and Charles Hartshore, and in the cosmic-evolutionary spiritualism of Teilhard de Chardin. Many feminist theologians explicitly associate themselves with one or more of these perspectives.

30. John Cobb and David Griffin, *Process Theology: An Introductory Exposition* (Philadelphia: Westminster, 1976), 61–62: "The positive aspects of these 'masculine' attributes can be retained...if they are incorporated into a revolutionized concept of God into which the stereotypically feminine traits are integrated."

Since traditional theism also attributes both transcendence and immanence to God, what is the problem with panentheism? It is its understanding of divine immanence. Orthodoxy affirms immanence without ontological continuity. But the Mother-womb-birth language of panentheistic inclusivism implies that the mode of God's immanence is some kind of ontological continuity or symbiosis, not merely the omnipresent activity of God, as in traditional theology. For the child comes out of the Mother, having grown within her body from her very substance. Perhaps it is still growing in her divine-cosmic womb. The connection between birth imagery and ontological continuity is not logically necessary. It can be resisted. But it is an almost universal human association, as is evident from the history of the world's religions and current feminist spirituality. Apart from biblical orthodoxy the dynamic of birth-Mother-God imagery pushes strongly in the direction of ontological continuity between Creator and creature. This is the concern of orthodox Christian theologians.

Gender-inclusive panentheists are not hard to find. Ruether's "God/ess" invokes Teilhard de Chardin and Tillich's Ground of Being. "Here the divine is not 'up there' as abstracted ego, but beneath and around us as encompassing source of life and renewal of life; spirit and matter are not split hierarchically. That which is most basic, matter (mother, matrix), is also most powerfully imbued with the powers of life and spirit." Indeed God/ess is "the Primal Matrix" for Ruether, a kind of divine womb.[31] Sally McFague appeals to Whitehead and Teilhard in developing her model of the world as "God's Body."[32] God and the world are distinct but inseparably integrated, as she believes the human soul and body to be. Perhaps less intentionally panentheistic, Virginia Mollenkott nevertheless refers to our natural environment as "The Divine Milieu."[33]

Brian Wren rejects the traditional notion of God as Almighty and Omnipotent, associated with the masculine biblical language of Father-Kingship.[34] He substitutes the panentheistic notion that God is in some sense limited in knowledge and power and is in a mutually influential growth relationship with his creation. Wren's well-known hymn, "Bring Many Names," the unofficial anthem of the inclusivist movement, is marbled with this language. It not only names God equivalently as Father and Mother, but goes on to intone that the "Old, aching God, grey with endless care" "is glad of good surprises." Age-inclusive, it also

31. Ruether, *Sexism and God-Talk*, 48–49; see also 86–92.
32. McFague, "God and the World," *Models of God*, 59–90.
33. Mollenkott, *The Divine Feminine*, chap. 18.
34. Wren, *What Language Shall I Borrow?* 129.

hymns the "Young, growing God, eager still to know, willing to be changed by what you started."[35]

It is true that Scripture speaks of God as the Ancient of Days and says that he sometimes changes his mind. But the God of the Bible does not suffer the pains of aging from caring for creation. He does not learn new things, take risks, become surprised, or grow in stature from interacting with his creatures. Wren's catchy metaphors express modern panentheism.

If Mother-Father language for God is arbitrarily given orthodox biblical meaning, its intended use does not imply heresy. We cannot say categorically that any use whatsoever of Mother-language for God necessarily and inevitably contradicts the biblical doctrine of the Creator-creatures relation. This issue by itself is not sufficient to reject inclusive language as heterdox, as some critics of Mother-language apparently contend.[36] But then gender-inclusive language is not really a self-sufficient, self-validating alternative equal to biblical language. It remains under the "patriarchy" of Scripture.

If, however, biblical-confessional theology is set aside and the nuances almost universally associated with Mother-Father language are given free rein, some form of panentheistic theology is most likely to emerge and crystallize. But then the worries of traditionalists seem well-founded: standard use of inclusive language for God as a self-defining practice would likely lead the Christian community to a more immanentistic, correlativistic theology than is taught in Scripture.

The Creator–creature distinction may indeed be one of the nongendered meanings of the Bible's masculine language for God alluded to in chapter 7. Perhaps *father* is a better parent image for creation and election than *mother*, given universal human experience, because it more readily suggests a relationship between two distinct beings instead of an emanation by birth of one from the other. Perhaps this is why God chose to designate himself as father and only to liken himself to a mother. And perhaps, having chosen the masculine figure of father, he chose masculine figures for other purposes as well, since persons in human experience have only one gender. The basic metaphor of King would work best to represent God's absolute power and authority over creation.

35. Ibid., 137–38.
36. For example, Achtemeier in "Exchanging God for 'No Gods'" hangs a great deal on Creator–creature distinction as God's primary purpose for using masculine language and seems to argue that any use of Mother-language obliterates this distinction. While her concern is valid, this argument can backfire. For if this is the basic objection to inclusivism, it can be circumvented by defining Mother-language in terms of the biblical Creator–creature distinction.

All of this is of course no more than theological speculation. It is a plausible suggestion based on Scripture, religious language, and our knowledge of world religions. But it is guesswork. We do not know whether the Creator–creature distinction is why God chose masculine language for himself. But even if we knew that this was God's reason, and even if we could come up with an orthodoxy-preserving inclusive substitute, we would still retain the language of Scripture, because that is the way God has personally introduced himself to us.

The Trinity

What Is Definitive, the Bible or Theology?

The doctrine of the Trinity as confessed in the Nicene Creed and elaborated in subsequent Christian theology was formulated historically out of the New Testament's presentation of God as Father, Jesus Christ as the divine Son of God, and the Holy Spirit, synthesized and focused in the triune name, Father, Son, and Holy Spirit, invoked by Jesus himself (Matt. 28:19).[37] The doctrine affirms that there is one God who exists as three distinct persons, each of whom is fully God and essentially interrelated with the other two.

The logical and historical order of the formulation of the doctrine of the Trinity is crucial to recognize. The Bible is the source and norm for the doctrine, not the reverse. God as Father, Son, and Holy Spirit is the self-given reality, the datum to be received, worshiped, and contemplated. The term *Trinity* has no standing except as an extrabiblical Latinate term for "threeness." The doctrinal formulations "three in one" and "three persons in one God" are human attempts to summarize and describe the biblical revelation of God. They have no independent meaning or foundational status as Christian truth. The human doctrines have no validity apart from their reference to and accurate reflection of the biblical witness to God.

Inclusivists unavoidably reverse this relationship. By substituting *Father-Mother, Child, and Spirit* or *Creator, Redeemer, and Sanctifier* for *Father, Son, and Holy Spirit*, they take the abstract doctrine of the Trinity to be the irreducible substance of Christian knowledge of God and

---

37. The New Testament material was summarized in chap. 4. A classical Reformed account is Herman Bavinck, "The Divine Trinity" in *Our Reasonable Faith*. Catherine LaCugna, "God in Communion With Us: The Trinity," in *Freeing Theology*, 83–114, is a feminist Roman Catholic treatment. Wren discusses the Trinity and linguistic variations for it in chap. 8 of *What Language Shall I Borrow*? Duck, *Gender and the Names of God*, chaps. 6 and 7, discusses the triune name in conjunction with baptism. Many inclusivists believe that the Nicene Creed reflects more of Roman imperialistic political ideology than the New Testament: see Ruether, *Sexism and God-Talk*, 124–25.

relegate the triune name to secondary, incidental status. This is a bait-and-switch. They take the idea of a three-in-one God derived from *Father, Son, and Holy Spirit,* eliminate the triune name, and then substitute other terminological triads for it. The triadic idea is made the constant, the names variable. A theological formula, not the revealed name of God, becomes definitive. Scripture and doctrine are reversed. The abiding presence of God's name is traded for an abstraction.

Consider an analogy. We notice that our three friends, Bill, Jim, and Ray, regularly play ball together. So we refer to them as the *Tri-Team,* but no longer mention their names. We substitute other references for them, like *Forward, Guard, and Center,* or *Numbers 1, 2, and 3.* In this example the personal identities of our three friends, the primary reality from which we began, have gotten lost. Surely *Tri-Team* and the replacement terms, valid descriptions though they be, are not equivalent to the names of our friends. They are abstractions and designations we have made. In the same way, the term *Trinity* and the various gender-inclusive substitutions do not have the primary reality and status of *Father, Son, and Holy Spirit,* the culmination of the entire historical revelation of God's name.

This point is crucial because most inclusivist theologians take pains to affirm orthodox trinitarian doctrinal formulas: God is three-in-one, they insist. But they eliminate or completely relativize the triune name *Father, Son, and Holy Spirit.* Brian Wren works with the terms *Trinity* and *Three-in-One* as constants, offering a variety of names. But his hymn entitled "How Wonderful the Three-in-One" does not even mention *Father, Son, and Holy Spirit.*[38] Ruth Duck operates with the term *Trinity* and "the triadic formula." She considers a great variety of alternatives to *Father, Son, and Holy Spirit,* which she does recognize as "the strong name of the Trinity." Her reversal of Scripture and doctrine is evident in her claim that the church's practice of baptism into the name of the Father, Son, and Holy Spirit "has been a shorthand affirmation of classical trinitarian doctrine."[39] While it is true that baptism affirms the Trinity, Duck makes it sound as though the point of using the triune name is to preserve trinitarian doctrine instead of to obey Matthew 28:19, from which the doctrine was derived.

Elizabeth Johnson presents the most elaborate, sophisticated case for alternatives. She works "from below" through *Spirit-Sophia, Jesus-Sophia,* and *Mother-Sophia* to establish a "tripersonal mystery of love" in God. She then discusses the "triune symbol" in the sophisticated terminology of scholastic theology. It is this trinitarian concept that she

---

38. Wren, *What Language Shall I Borrow?* chap. 8 and 215.
39. Duck, *Gender and the Name of God,* chaps. 7–9, quote from 150.

considers crucial to Christian orthodoxy. She concludes that "different metaphor systems are needed to show the mutuality, equality, and reciprocal dynamism of trinitarian relations." Her own preferred system is "God as Holy Wisdom:" "unoriginate Mother, her beloved Child, and the Spirit of their mutual love."[40] In Johnson's case it is clear that a refined analysis of a doctrine, not the triune name of God given in Scripture, is the irreducible touchstone of Christian truth.

It is ironic that, after so many twentieth-century complaints against "scholasticism" and "doctrinalism" and during a time when many theologians are returning to the particularity of the biblical narrative, inclusivists are adopting medieval categories and abstract formulations to rationalize their revisions of language for God. The God they acknowledge is the Transcendental Triad, not the living Father, Son, and Holy Spirit. They move from the God of Scripture toward the God of the philosophers. This retreat from the particularity of Scripture into theological abstraction is the same pattern we encountered in chapter 7 with respect to divine transcendence and the limitations of human language. There too we noticed that the triune name of God was marginalized or jettisoned by sophisticated philosophical appeals to the otherness of the divine nature and the impossiblity of any real analogy of being.

Gender-Egalitarian Alternatives Are Inadequate

The fact that none of the proposed alternatives is an adequate expression of the triune name can be demonstrated by comparing them. Since it is impossible to examine every suggestion, we test a few prominent examples: first masculine-feminine egalitarian alternatives, then gender-neutral alternatives.[41]

A modest strategy for balancing masculine and feminine language is to regard the Holy Spirit as feminine, using the pronoun *she*.[42] Traditionalists might not object to this in principle as contrary to Scripture. We saw, however, that there is significant doubt whether *Spirit* in the Old Testament is personally as well as grammatically feminine. In

40. Johnson, *She Who Is*, chaps. 7–10, quotes from 192, 197, and 215. See also Ramshaw, "The Language of Trinitarian Doctrine," in *God beyond Gender*.

41. I have benefited from the essays of Achtemeier, Frye, Robert Jenson, Green, Gunton, Kimel, DiNoia, and Wainwright in *Speaking the Christian God*, and from Bloesch's *Battle for the Trinity*, as well as many others in evaluating the aptness and orthodoxy of inclusive-language substitutions for the divine name.

42. Chap. 3 discussed the feminine grammatical gender of the Hebrew word *ruaḥ*. Hopko, "Apophatic Theology and the Naming of God," in *Speaking the Christian God*, 160–61, notes some openness to the femininity of the Spirit in Eastern Orthodoxy based mainly on the grammatical gender of the term in vernacular languages.

addition, the Greek New Testament uses grammatically neuter language for the Holy Spirit. And since both Testaments contain a few masculine references to the Spirit, there is a small toehold for the tradition of referring to the Holy Spirit as *he*. In the end the Bible does not specify the anthropomorphic gender of the Holy Spirit. So there is some possible biblical basis for the Spirit as feminine, but far less than a mandate.

Perhaps surprisingly, inclusivists are also quick to register objections. Taking the Spirit as feminine is problematic because it leaves the Father and Son, two-thirds of the Trinity, masculine, they say. Futhermore, it reinforces stereotypes of women as subordinate and servile. For the Father and Son are the dominant persons who send the Spirit. The Spirit is self-effacing and does their bidding. This solution is not egalitarian but reinforces patriarchalism.[43]

Introducing *Mother* into the trinitarian formula is another strategy. This can be done in several ways: *Father and Mother* or *Father-Mother* as the name of the first person, or *Mother* predicated of the entire triune name.[44]

Father and Mother is hardly adequate because it suggests that the first person is really two persons, a couple of divine parents. That is surely what this expression means in language about humans. Thus it implicitly introduces a fourth person into the Trinity.[45] Furthermore, it readily suggests that the Son is somehow the offspring of the Father and Mother. But this would be to reactivate a version of the ancient heresy of Arianism, rejected by the Nicene and Athanasian Creeds. The Arians thought that the Son is literally an offspring of the eternal God, somehow a creation or procreation of God. Against this view the Nicene Creed teaches that the Son is of the same fully divine nature as the Father, begotten but not made. Begottenness is an eternal relationship, not a process of generation. Although Father-Son language can also be misconstrued, introducing a Mother into the picture greatly increases the likelihood of distortion.

Father-Mother does not suggest two persons, but one bisexual person, "a grotesque hermaphrodite god or androgynous divinity."[46] Its masculine–feminine polarity thus introduces gender into the first person in a way that traditional language of *Father* does not. It also shares the Arian

43. LaCugna, "God in Communion With Us," in *Freeing Theology*, 105.

44. Replacements like McFague's *Mother, Lover, Friend* are not considered, because they eliminate masculine terms in a noninclusive way. Nevertheless, their inherent inadequacy is apparent from the discussion of the egalitarian revisions.

45. Frye, "Language for God and Feminist Language," in *Speaking the Christian God*, 24.

46. Ibid., 25.

tendency to attribute a reproductivity to God that procreates the Son. In this case it is self-fertilization by a male-female being. *Father-Mother*, like *Father and Mother*, is reminiscent of ancient Gnosticism, which posited a masculine-feminine God in various forms.[47] Some Gnostics held God in himself to be beyond gender, but in relation to the world to be both masculine and feminine. Others held an essentially dyadic male-female God. The current Christian proposals combining Father and Mother are inadequate, confusing, and almost inevitably distorting, not only because they deviate from the triune name as given, but also because they tend to promote heresies like Arianism and Gnosticism.

Another suggested alternative is to attach *Mother* to the entire triune name: *Father, Son, and Holy Spirit, One God, Mother of us all.*[48] This formula has been used for baptism by William Sloane Coffin at Riverside Church in New York. Initially it may seem less theologically confusing and less prone toward heresy than the previous suggestions. But its problem is that it is not egalitarian. For *Father* is only the name of the first person, whereas *Mother* is the title-name of the entire Godhead. So *the Mother* is *Father, Son, Holy Spirit*. But Scripture uses *Father* to speak of the one God, so this designation breaks continuity with the identification of God in the biblical tradition. In addition, leaving *Father* out of *One God* is not exactly inclusive. So the formula should be *Father, Son, and Holy Spirit, One God, Father and Mother of us all*. But now we have another problem: it is a bit heavy on *Father*-language and *Mother* is beginning to be dominated again. To fix that we could perhaps introduce *Mother* among the persons of the Trinity. But then we are back to the previous suggestions with all their problems. It soon becomes apparent that there is no good way to fix the formula by adding *Mother* so that it preserves the identification of the true God, Christian orthodoxy, and egalitarian language. This conclusion can be generalized to the many other suggestions for balanced masculine-feminine language for the Trinity.

Gender-Neutral Alternatives Are Inadequate

Gender-neutral replacements for the triune name are suggested more frequently than gender-equal alternatives. *Creator, Redeemer, and Sanctifier; Source, Word, and Comforter; God, Christ, and Spirit; Lover, Beloved, and Love;* and *Parent, Child, and Spirit* are among the more

47. Elaine Pagels, "What Became of God the Mother? Conflicting Images of God in Early Christianity," *Signs: Journal of Women in Culture and Society* 2 (1976): 293–303; Pagels, *The Gnostic Gospels* (New York: Random House, 1979), 48–70; and Ruether, *Sexism and God-Talk*, 59–60.
48. Duck, *Gender and the Name of God*, 163–66. It is mentioned as a possible innovation by Hardesty, *Inclusive Language in the Church*, 96.

popular.[49] Because feminine language is avoided, these suggestions are initially less controversial. In addition, many of them are straightforwardly biblical. They therefore deserve careful consideration.

Assuming that the triune name can be replaced, candidates for adequate substitution must be able to preserve the personal identity of the three persons in one name of God. *Father, Son, and Holy Spirit* are the biblical title-names of the persons of the Trinity, names in the sense of unique, primary personal identifiers, whose identity must be preserved. Furthermore, since God is one, these title-names together actually constitute one complex triune name.[50] The identity of each person is inextricably tied to the other two: the Father is Father in relation to the Son, and vice versa. Thus their identity is constituted eternally in relation to each other. It does not derive from their relation to creation or their work of redemption (although it is only through their relation to creation and redemption that we know them).

Creator, Redeemer, and Sanctifier fails to meet these requirements for several reasons. One is that this formula refers to distinct functions or roles, not to distinct persons, and therefore is not equivalent to naming three persons. Second, the activities of creating, redeeming, and sanctifying do not belong exclusively to distinct persons of the Trinity, even though the Apostles' and Nicene Creeds make this correlation. For in Scripture Father, Son, and Holy Spirit are together involved in creation, redemption, and sanctification. Apart from biblical and credal language for God, therefore, the proper correlation of the functions of creating, redeeming, and sanctifying with divine persons is unclear. Third, creating, redeeming, and sanctifying are God's relations to creation. Thus the formula fails to identify the persons in relation to each other, as the triune name does.[51] Fourth, a unitarian (one who believes that God is one but not three distinct persons) could easily speak of God as creator, redeemer, and sanctifier, which demonstrates that this triadic terminology is not necessarily trinitarian or Christian. Identifying the three persons of the Godhead as equivalent with three modes of activity toward the world is really a modern variant of the heresy of modalism, which was rejected by the councils of the early church.

The only way that *Creator, Redeemer, and Sanctifier* retains orthodox trinitarian meaning is if it is defined in relation to the biblical triune

49. Duck, *Gender and the Name of God*, chap. 8, and Ramshaw, *God beyond Gender*, chap. 7, consider a number of gender-neutral suggestions. Ramshaw (82) favors neutral language because "the language of the Trinity is on life-support and *Father* an embarrassment, as well as the unlikelihood that *Mother* can meet current expectations."

50. These claims were defended in chaps. 4 and 5.

51. Stated in theological language, the relations of Father, Son, and Spirit are within God (*ad intra*), not just toward creation (*ad extra*); they are *ontological*, not just *economic*.

name, *Father, Son, and Holy Spirit*. Given this dependence, the substitute is not equivalent in meaning or authority to the triune name. There is no objection to its occasional use, but it cannot stand on its own as a standard replacement. Used independently, it fails to preserve trinitarian orthodoxy.

Source, Word, and Comforter are likewise unobjectionable for use by Christians, for these terms come from the Gospel of John. But John's Gospel is full of the language of the Father, Son, and Spirit. Apart from that context we do not know that the Father is the Souce, the Son is the Word, and the Spirit is the Comforter. In fact we do not even know that they are divine persons.[52] It is the language of Father, Son, and Spirit that constitutes the rich trinitarianism of John's Gospel. For these reasons *Source, Word, and Comforter*, biblical as this triad is, is not equivalent to the triune name and therefore cannot replace it to achieve inclusive language for God.

God, Christ, and Spirit is also impeccably biblical (cf. 2 Cor. 13:14). Moreover, this formula uses personal names or titles. But it is not equivalent to the triune name. For taken on its own, it seems to imply that Christ and the Spirit are not God. That implication might not be disastrous for *Christ* as a referent to the human nature of Jesus. But it still leaves the Holy Spirit out of the Godhead. It also juxtaposes God with the humanity of Jesus, failing to communicate that Jesus is God the Son. Though this trio of terms is biblical, it is not even close to the meaning of the triune name. Like the other formulas, it depends on the triune name to be understood in a trinitarian sense.

Lover, Beloved, and Love is a formula derived from Augustine, who used it as an illustration of the Trinity but not as a replacement for the triune name. The problem with this candidate is that it seems to present two persons, an active lover and a passive beloved, and one act of relating, the lover's love for the beloved. That is something less than three mutual persons in one God.

Least acceptable is the triad *Parent, Child, and Spirit*. The first two of these terms are neither biblical nor personal. Of course it is obvious that a father is a parent and a son might be a child. So in an abstract sense this formula is not necessarily false. But *parent* and *child* are generic terms referring to classes of persons in familial relationships, not terms for specific persons, as are *father* and *mother, son* and *daughter*. *Parent* and *Child* thus suffer from the impersonal distance of much gender-neutral language. Doctrinally one still needs biblical information about God the Father and the Son to know who the Parent and Child

---

52. Duck, *Gender and the Name of God*, 182, exhibits confusion over the meaning of *name* in asserting that *Source* is a theologically acceptable name for the first person.

alluded to in this formula are. And the personal-spiritual distance this impersonal aura creates makes these terms unsuitable for the language of worship. Finally, *Child* inappropriately connotes a kind of immaturity that *Son* does not have.[53] Surely this triad cannot replace the triune name of God.

Conclusion: The Irreplaceability of the Triune Name

We have examined the most prominent gender-egalitarian and gender-neutral replacements for the triune name of God, *Father, Son, and Holy Spirit*. None of them is capable of meeting all the necessary criteria: reliable identification of the divine persons, preservation of orthodox trinitarian doctrine, and gender-inclusiveness. This result does not prove that such a formula could never be devised, but it tends to diminish optimism about the success of the search.

Even if a fully equivalent alternative were found, the problem would remain precisely that it is an *alternative*. If *Father, Son, and Holy Spirit* is truly the definitive culmination of God's self-naming, spoken by the incarnate Son and witnessed by the Spirit in Holy Scripture, then it is unique and nothing can substitute for it. That is the end of the matter.

In the triunity of God we encounter a second ungendered significance of the Bible's masculine language for God, the question left by chapter 7. In Scripture God presents himself as Father, Son, and Holy Spirit. The title-names of the first two persons are masculine, but the divine persons to whom they refer are not ontologically masculine. The meaning of these terms is their status as divine names and the glimpse at the triune nature of God that they afford.

We have found that this terminology is religiously and theologically irreplaceable. It is possible to speculate further about whether God in himself is "really" Father, Son, and Holy Spirit or whether this is just an accommodation to us. We can wonder whether God could have revealed himself with other names. But the fact is that God has introduced himself this way. We humans, especially those who through Jesus Christ have been adopted as his children, are in no position and have no right to revise or reject his personal names and titles.

In conclusion, we have discovered the same pattern for the Trinity as we did above for the historical identification of the biblical God and the Creator–creature relation. On its own, gender-inclusive language either fails to preserve or actually changes the meaning of biblical language. Only if defined by the language of Scripture and the doctrine it teaches can inclusive language be made to fit biblical Christianity. But then in-

---

53. Bloesch, *The Battle for the Trinity*, 46; DiNoia, "Knowing and Naming the Triune God," in *Speaking the Christian God*, 185.

clusive language is not equal in status. It remains under the authority and legitimation of the (anthropomorphically masculine) language of Scripture. But if it is under the authority of Scripture, inclusive language must yield where it transgresses the biblical pattern or else be declared a religious renegade.

Sophia Christology

Inclusive language not only involves God; it also affects our understanding of Jesus Christ. This may seem surprising, since Jesus was a human male. Feminists have debated whether Jesus' maleness is a barrier to women, most of them concluding that it is not.[54] But it is not possible to speak of Jesus in other than masculine terms.

However, the gender equality inclusivism seeks is in Jesus' divine nature. In Scripture he is called *the Son of God*. Understood in terms of the biblical triune name, he is therefore also God the Son, co-eternal with the Father and the Holy Spirit. It is as God the Son that he takes on our human nature in the incarnation.[55] So the Son is not merely male in his human nature; he is linguistically masculine in his eternal identity. Thus inclusivists allege that the Bible is sexist not only with respect to the one God and the first person of the Trinity. It is also sexist in its presentation of the divinity of Jesus Christ.

Inclusivists enlist the biblical idea of God's wisdom as a means of achieving a gender-balanced account of the deity of Christ. They note that the New Testament speaks of Jesus as the wisdom (Greek: *sophia*) of God (1 Cor. 1:24, 31), that it attributes deity to him, and that it acknowledges his role in the creation of the world (Col. 1:15–17), a role also associated with the *word* of God (*logos* in John 1:3, *rhema* in Heb. 1:1–3). Sophia Christologists point out that a significant Old Testament background of these teachings is Proverbs 8, where the wisdom of God by which he created the universe and through whom we have life is personified as a female figure. These observations are thoroughly biblical and equally affirmed by traditional Christianity.

On this basis two strategies for a gender-inclusive Christology are proposed. The first correlates *wisdom*, a grammatically feminine term in Hebrew and Greek, with *word*, a grammatically masculine term in those languages. Assuming that wisdom is a feminine quality and word (rational order) is a masculine trait, this approach views Jesus Christ,

---

54. Ruether, "Christology: Can a Male Savior Save Women?" *Sexism and God-Talk*, chap. 5.

55. Bavinck, *Our Reasonable Faith*, chap. 16, is a classical Reformed presentation of the person and natures of Jesus Christ as taught in Scripture and the creeds.

the Word and Wisdom of God, as incarnating both the masculine and feminine aspects of God. This is a modest kind of inclusivism that gender-balances our understanding of how Jesus exemplifies the nature of God. It does not directly challenge the exclusivity of *Son* as the primary title of the second person of the Trinity.

The problem with this Christology is not its orthodoxy but its understanding of language. Scripture certainly teaches that Jesus Christ is the Word and Wisdom of God. But as shown in chapter 3,[56] it is a mistake simply to extrapolate the grammatical gender of nonpersonal words into personal gender. In Hebrew *wisdom* and and *folly* are not feminine personality traits because they are feminine in gender any more than *breast* and *womb* are male characteristics because the words for them are grammatically masculine. As we saw, the fact that wisdom is personified as a woman in Proverbs probably does follow a literary convention based on grammatical gender, as *Justitia* is a female in the imagery of Roman law because *justice* is feminine in Latin. But it is a mistake to suppose that ascribing grammatically gendered attributes to someone thereby predicates personal gender characteristics of that person. Saying "the Lord is wise" in Hebrew no more attributes femininity to the Lord than saying "the King is wise" highlights the feminine side of the King. Therefore neither God's word nor God's wisdom connotes gender characteristics of God in Jesus Christ.

The second inclusivist strategy is more fully developed Sophia Christology. Appealing to the Wisdom Goddess in the religious background of the Old Testament and to later Jewish tradition, this approach interprets Woman Wisdom in Proverbs 8 not just as the personification of God's attribute of wisdom, but as a personification of God. God is Wisdom (*Sophia*); she is a female person.[57] When Paul says that Jesus is the wisdom of God, on this interpretation he implies that divine *Sophia*, a feminine persona, has become incarnate in him. This then becomes the explanation of the deity of Jesus Christ, the personal presence of God in Christ, implied by the Nicene Creed and explicitly formulated by the Council of Chalcedon (451), that Jesus Christ is true God and true human. He is *Sophia's Child*[58] or *Jesus-Sophia*.[59] Since the word of God,

56. See "Proverbs 8," "*Spirit of God,*" and "Psalm 103:13, *compassion* and other words related to *womb*."

57. Claudia Camp, "Sophia/Wisdom," in *Dictionary of Feminist Theologies*, 268–70; Virginia Mollenkott, *The Divine Feminine*, chap. 17; Gale Ramshaw, "God as Sophia," in *God beyond Gender*, 44–46; Ruether, *Sexism and God-Talk*, 57–59; van Wijk-Bos, *Reimagining God*, 78–85.

58. Elizabeth Schüssler Fiorenza, *Jesus: Miriam's Child, Sophia's Prophet* (New York: Continuum, 1994).

59. Johnson, *She Who Is*, chap. 8.

unlike wisdom, is not personified in the Old Testament, Sophia Christology gives Wisdom precedence over Word in designating the divine personhood of Jesus. In this way *Wisdom* and *Son* are given equal status as personal designators of the preincarnate Word, thus achieving a fully gender-inclusive Christology.[60]

Sophia Christology attempts to identify with biblical Christianity by affirming the deity of Jesus Christ. But it is crucial to look more closely at how it does this. We argued above that confusing an attribute of God with God is a basic mistake. God has wisdom; he is wise. But that does not make wisdom God. Therefore personification of a divine attribute is not personification of God. It is clear in Proverbs 8 that wisdom is an attribute that *Yahweh* possesses; they are not equated. In fact Proverbs 8 is most likely a polemic against worshiping the Wisdom manifest in creation as itself divine, a practice in the cults of the female deities *Maat, Ishtar, Isis,* and later *Sophia*.[61] Sophia Christology mistakenly identifies God and Wisdom.[62]

This leaves it with an insoluble dilemma. If it straightens out the confusion and admits that Wisdom is not God but an attribute of God, it is not orthodox. For then Jesus is not the incarnation of a divine person, but only of the divine attribute of wisdom (along with love, truth, justice, and the other communicable divine attributes). But this falls far short of orthodoxy. For the formula of Chalcedon (451) insists that the incarnate Lord is one person with two natures. And the Nicene Creed teaches that the person who took on our human nature as Jesus Christ is divine, the Son who is consubstantial with the Father. According to this version of Sophia Christology, however, Jesus Christ is a human person whose divinity consists in his special endowment with the attribute of wisdom. Although this sort of Christology was condemned by Chalcedon, it has reappeared in modern theology and in this form of Sophia Christology.

The other half of the dilemma is to continue the confusion between God's wisdom and God himself in order to maintain that Jesus Christ is the incarnation of a divine person. This sounds more orthodox. A ques-

60. Some feminists go further, arguing thate *Son* in the New Testament refers only to Jesus in his role as Messiah, a role incorporated into the triune name and later divinized by the church. This leaves *Wisdom* alone as the basic designator of the personal presence of God in Christ: the feminine is most definitive.

61. Fiorenza, *In Memory of Her,* 133, sees it instead as assimilation: "Divine Sophia is Israel's God in the language and *gestalt* of the goddess."

62. The traditional theological doctrine of divine simplicity holds that God is identical with each and all of his attributes, thus implying the identity of God and Wisdom. This is a puzzling, controversial claim and does not pertain to the debate about Proverbs 8, which deals with the language of the biblical text, not philosophical theology.

tion immediately arises, however: which divine person? The New Testament and the creeds of the church clearly state that the divine person who took on our human nature is the Son, the second person of the Trinity. If Sophia Christology simply identifies Wisdom with the person of Yahweh and then affirms Yahweh as the divine person incarnate in Jesus, it fails to be trinitarian.[63] It does not assert that the Word and Wisdom spoken of in the New Testament is the Second Person. Similarly, Sophia Christologies claiming that Jesus is divine because he is indwelt by the *Spirit of Wisdom* either fail to be trinitarian or else they assert that Jesus is the third person, the Holy Spirit, incarnate. These heretical implications are fatal flaws.

In order to assert clearly that Jesus is the Second Person of the Trinity incarnate, Sophia Christology must rely on the whole New Testament presentation of Jesus as Lord and as the Son of God, which, taken together with God as Father and the triune name, entails that Jesus is God the Son. But then Sophia Christology would merely be affirming historic Christology. It would not be elevating *Wisdom* to a status correlative with *the Son*. And so it would fail to provide a gender-inclusive Christology.

In sum, Sophia Christology taken on its own terms either fails to affirm that Jesus Christ is a divine person or that he is the Second Person of the Trinity. If it is to present an account of Jesus' deity faithful to Scripture, Sophia Christology must rely on the masculine language of the *Father* and the *Son*. Here again is the same pattern we have encountered with respect to other issues of true Christianity: gender-inclusive language on its own is deficient or distorted as an expression of the faith. Furthermore, here we have encountered another nongendered meaning of the Bible's gendered language for God: the identity of the Second Person of the Godhead.

The Atonement

Inclusivist worries about the patriarchal presentation of God in Scripture and traditional Christianity are not limited specifically to gender, but also include issues of power and the abuse of power. The doctrine of the atonement is a foundational confession of the Christian church that has been criticized and revisioned by inclusivists out of these concerns. Their treatment of this doctrine deserves brief consideration because it clearly illustrates the inherent dynamic of the inclusivist approach to the entire Christian faith.

---

63. Traditional Christology, if it understood the wisdom of Proverbs 8 to be personification of a divine person, always took this as an implicit reference to the preincarnate Son.

The Bible characterizes Jesus' death on the cross in a variety of ways: as the result of human hate and injustice, as a manifestation of divine love, as a victory over the power of evil, and as a model for us to emulate. But a central motif, based in the sacrificial rites of the Old Testament, is that Jesus is the Lamb of God whose death removes the guilt of sin from God's people by suffering for them the punishment that they deserved.[64]

Many inclusivists have an insurmountable problem with this view of the atonement because they claim that it represents an angry Father punishing his Son with death for something he did not do. It makes the abuse of an innocent child the way of salvation. Child abuse is elevated to the level of a divine principle. Let me not put words into their mouths. Elizabeth Johnson is quite blunt: "feminist theology repudiates an interpretation of the death of Jesus as required by God in repayment for sin. Such a view today is virtually inseparable from an underlying image of God as an angry, bloodthirsty, violent, and sadistic father, reflecting the very worst kind of male behavior."[65] Ruth Duck supplies the rationale: "Calling God 'the Father Almighty,' who demands the death of his child as a sacrifice for human sin, may unintentionally and unconsciously encourage fathers to use their power over children in harmful ways, and may encourage children to accept this lot."[66] So the doctrine is summarily dismissed.

There are genuine issues here. Thoughtful Christians wrestle with questions about the meaning of substitutionary punishment.[67] Evangelical pastors should be sensitive to how abused children understand and respond to the crucifixion of Jesus.

But the inclusivists cited here do not exert themselves to understand and apply this doctrine properly. Instead they present caricatures that fail to acknowledge the complexity and redemptive implications of the biblical data. Scripture teaches that God's deepest motivation in offering his Son is love (John 3:16) and that Jesus is not a helpless victim of uncontrolled rage, but lovingly and voluntarily accepts his atoning role as the Lamb of God who takes away the sin of the world. These feminist

---

64. Bavinck, *Our Reasonable Faith*, chap. 17, presents a classic Reformed account of the atonement derived from Scripture and the creeds.

65. Johnson, *She Who Is*, 158. See also JoAnne Brown and Rebecca Parker, "God So Loved the World," in *Christianity, Patriarchy, and Abuse*, ed. J. Brown and C. Bohn (New York: Pilgrim, 1989), and Patricia Wilson-Kastner, "Theological Perspectives on Sexual Violence," in *Sexual Assault and Abuse*, ed. M. Pellaur (San Francisco: Harper & Row, 1987).

66. Duck, *Gender and the Name of God*, 54.

67. See, for example, Philip Quinn, "Aquinas on Atonement" and Eleonore Stump, "Atonement and Justification" in *Trinity, Incarnation, and Atonement*, ed. R. Feenstra and C. Plantinga (Notre Dame, Ind.: Notre Dame Press, 1989).

and inclusivist theologians prefer to ridicule and jettison a crucial biblical understanding of the atonement and the Father-language that goes with it because they suspect that it somehow promotes patriarchalism and child abuse. Thus they give more weight to their own prescriptions for social dysfunctionalities than to the teaching of Scripture.

But the priority of a social agenda over the content of Scripture is the operative assumption of the entire movement for inclusive language for God. In the words of Elizabeth Johnson, "the one criterion of truth and adequacy" in matters of religion and theology is "the emancipation of women toward human flourishing."[68] This treatment of the atonement illustrates again why inclusivism is fundamentally unreliable as an expression of Christian truth.

Conclusion

We have completed an extensive tour. We set out to determine whether inclusive language for God, taken as a self-defining linguistic practice, preserves the truth of the biblical-Christian faith or departs from it. We surveyed a variety of ways in which dissimilarities to the language of the Bible raise questions about the meaning of inclusive language for God, about truth in reporting historical revelation, and about the identity of God. Then we turned to specific topics in Christian doctrine: the relation of God to creation, the Trinity, the deity of Jesus Christ, and the atonement.

The same pattern was repeatedly found in all of these discussions: a dilemma for inclusivism emerged. If inclusive language for God was taken on its own as a standard expression of Christianity equal in status to traditional biblical language, it either failed to state Christian truth with full adequacy, or else it actually changed the meaning. The only way inclusive language could express the faith with fidelity and reliability is if it were assigned the references and meanings of biblical-traditional language. But then inclusive language would not have the status of equality with biblical language. It would still be subject to the text of Scripture as written for its meaning and validity. But this would be to admit that, after all, Scripture is the final norm, as we argued in chapters 6 and 7. And if Scripture is the final norm, serious doubts about the validity of inclusive language for God arise. This is a real dilemma for those who wish to affirm both biblical Christianity and inclusive language for God.

In the process of taking this tour, we have also tentatively identified at least three nongendered meanings of the Bible's masculine language

---

68. Johnson, *She Who Is*, 30.

for God (there may be more). Chapter 7 raised a question from inclusivists: If God in himself is beyond gender, what difference does the masculine language of the Bible make? This chapter has shown that it makes an important difference for our view of God's relation to creation, for the Trinity, and for the deity of Jesus Christ. Thus, although we acknowledge Scripture as the final norm simply because of its status as divine revelation, there are additional reasons to believe that its pattern of language for God is neither arbitrary nor replaceable.

9

Inclusivism and Christian Piety

Spiritual Dangers of Inclusivism

It has become obvious that in order to justify itself, gender-inclusive Christianity must take distance from the text of Holy Scripture and its naming of God. Chapter 8 demonstrated how this distance renders inclusive language for God unreliable as a vehicle for expressing accurately the central truths of God's self-revelation as preserved in Scripture and summarized in the historic Christian confessions.

But now an even more basic issue arises: the dynamics of one's relationship with God. If God has acted and shown himself as Scripture testifies, if the Bible reliably witnesses the fullest, most gracious self-manifestation of God as our Father through his Son, Jesus Christ, then taking distance from the God of the biblical text amounts to taking distance from God himself. For this reason inclusive language for God is not just a matter of orthodoxy, the truth content of what one believes. It touches the character of one's relationship with God: true piety, worship, love, faith, humble submission, and obedience.

This chapter explores some of the spiritual temptations and dangers, the threats to true piety, lurking around the trend toward gender-inclusive language for God. We expose some of them by considering the first three of the Ten Commandments, which forbid apostasy, idolatry, and misusing the name of God. Rejecting God as revealed in Scripture and worshiping a deity that has been reimagined and renamed certainly have the potential for transgressing these commandments. Additional spiritual dangers accompany inclusivism's distant, critical attitude toward Scripture as well. This attitude gives new voice to the serpent's question to Eve, "Did God really say?" If the Bible is not our final authority on the unique identity of God, is it the final authority on the way of salvation and on the specific norms of God's will for our lives, including the proper relationship between men and women? Relativizing Scripture for the sake of gender-inclusive language not only threatens orthodoxy, it also endangers true piety and godly practice as well.

Several disclaimers must immediately be made, however: two about inclusivism and two about traditionalism. With respect to inclusivism, first, I do not claim that endorsing gender-inclusivism for God automatically involves impiety or false religion. I claim that these spiritual dangers accompany inclusivism. Second, therefore I do not make blanket judgments about the spiritual motives of inclusivists in general. Some may promote inclusive language out of conscious rejection of the biblical God, an attitude they openly express, while others may believe (mistakenly) that inclusivism is more faithful to the God of Scripture than traditionalism. Only God can judge people's hearts. But the dangers remain.

My first caveat regarding defenders of biblical-traditional language is a truism: we are not perfect in piety or free from sin. Defense of tradition is no guarantee of true faith or a Christ-like life. Some traditionalists may indeed make an idol of masculine views of God. Some may use biblical views of God unbiblically to justify sinful patriarchal power structures in human social relations or to rationalize their own advantages over women. Some may be hateful toward inclusivists or unreasonably rigid in their attachment to tradition. These temptations are real and are rightly rejected by inclusivists.

Second, we must recognize that traditional biblical language itself can occasion spiritual distress. Some faithful, pious Christians have real emotional difficulties relating to the linguistically-anthropomorphically masculine God of Scripture as a consequence of the sinful effects of patriarchalism or abuse by their fathers. Thus there is a genuine issue of spiritual health connected with the use of biblical language for God. This is one of the main motives for adopting inclusive language, as we saw in chapter 1. We will address it in a final chapter.

These disclaimers are necessary to guard against the fallacy of guilt (or innocence) by association.[1] We do not suggest or assume that all inclusivists are implicitly impious or that all traditionalists are free of spiritual defects. What is intended is an honest exploration of the threats to true piety and spiritual health associated with the zealous promotion of inclusive language for God.

---

1. See Rebecca Merrill Groothuis, "Guilt by Association: Liberalism, Gnosticism, and Feminism," in *Women Caught in the Conflict: The Culture War Between Traditionalism and Feminism* (Grand Rapids: Baker, 1994), chap. 12.

The First Commandment: Dangers of False Gods and Apostasy

When God covenanted with his people at Mount Sinai, he said "I am the Lord [*Yahweh*] your God, who brought you out of Egypt. . . . You shall have no other gods before me" (Exod. 20:2–3). The first element in keeping covenant with God is recognizing that he, the one who introduced himself as Yahweh to Moses and rescued Israel from Pharaoh, is the only God. There is no other God. The gods worshiped by other nations are idols, counterfeit products of the human imagination (Ps. 115:3–8; Isa. 44:6–20). Worshiping something else instead of the true God is false religion, serving a false god, even when people do not know the true God (Rom. 1:21–23). Even worse, turning one's back on the true God after having encountered him is apostasy—rejection of and rebellion against the One who spoke at Sinai and revealed himself as the Father of Jesus Christ. Scripture likens apostasy to spiritual adultery. It leads to spiritual death.

Single-minded pursuit of the advancement of women does sometimes lead people to reject the God of Scripture for some other god. A well-known, self-proclaimed example is Mary Daly, a former Roman Catholic and leading radical feminist. Her journey away from Christianity can be traced in her writings. In 1968 she wrote *The Church and the Second Sex*, a critical response to statements of the Second Vatican Council on the role of women in church and society.[2] *Beyond God the Father* appeared in 1973.[3] In this book she repudiates the patriarchal God of Scripture and tradition as irredeemably implicated in and responsible for the sexism and patriarchalism of the societies influenced by Christianity. She judges that God the Father and the Son of the Bible are simply incompatible with the liberation of women, and she chooses for liberation.[4] She does not become an atheist or reject spirituality altogether, however. Instead she develops a notion of deity that is much more immanent in the cosmos and conducive to the feminist liberation she envisions. Her new religion, theology, and philosophical worldview are further spelled out in her books, *Gyn/Ecology* and *Pure Lust*.[5]

2. Mary Daly, *The Church and the Second Sex* (New York, 1968; Boston: Beacon, 1985). Notice the allusion to *The Second Sex*, the title of a 1949 book by French existentialist feminist Simone de Beauvoir.

3. Mary Daly, *Beyond God the Father: Toward a Philosophy of Women's Liberation* (Boston: Beacon, 1973).

4. The vitriol of her rejection of the faith is evident in the title of her article, "Theology after the Demise of God the Father: A Call for the Castration of Sexist Religion," in *Sexist Religion and Women in the Church,* ed. Alice Hageman (New York: Association Press, 1974).

5. Mary Daly, *Gyn/Ecology: The Metaethics of Radical Feminism* (Boston: Beacon, 1978) and *Pure Lust: Elemental Feminist Philosophy* (Boston: Beacon, 1984).

Since she is a radical feminist, perhaps it is unfair to link Mary Daly with inclusivism, which does not absolutize the feminine aspect of reality exclusively. However, she is clearly an example of someone whose rage against sexism is aimed at the God of the Bible, whom she repudiates with animus and sarcasm. Some inclusivists do share her anger against the God who is exclusively Father even though they do not share her feminist spirituality or theology. But therein lies a danger.

Somewhat more irenic is Daphne Hampson, a former member of the Church of England. She too struggled to reconcile full affirmation of the rights of women with the God of the Bible. But she eventually concluded that the masculine God of Christianity and the liberation of women are incompatible. She criticizes Christian feminists and inclusivist theologians for engaging in what she regards as a hopeless attempt to salvage a version of Christianity that is hospitable to femininism. For she recognizes that the particular identity of God as expressed in Scripture is essential to Christianity as a distinctive religion. She agrees with traditionalists that to relativize the designations of God as the King of Israel and the Father of Jesus Christ is to abandon Christianity as a particular revealed religion for a more generic form of theism or deism. But she also insists that it is impossible to reconcile full equality, dignity, and rights for women with the patriarchal God essential to Christianity. So she opts to keep her feminism and to adopt a more generic and genderless God instead of the God of biblical-traditional Christianity. She sets forth her position in *Theology and Feminism*.[6]

Other post-Judeo-Christian feminists have gone over to neo-pagan nature religions associated with the Goddess, whether known as *Gaia* or *Sophia* or by some other name.[7] In these religions the divine is identified with the life-force that permeates the cosmos and animates all living things. Since it is immanent, inclusive of all things, and nurturing rather than transcendent, distinct from all things, and in hierarchical control, the deity is (stereotypically) regarded as feminine rather than masculine. Whether explicitly associated with Wicca or the New Age movements, such religious practices are clearly substitutes for worshiping the true God. They very much resemble the ancient pagan religions against which the Bible polemicizes.

Another god placed before the true God is women themselves, whether their femaleness, humanity, dignity, or rights. This rival religion

6. Daphne Hampson, *Theology and Feminism* (Oxford: Basil Blackwell, 1990).

7. See Miriam Starhawk, *The Spiral Dance: A Rebirth of the Ancient Religion of the Great Goddess* (San Francisco: Harper & Row, 1979) and Carol Christ, *Laughter of Aphrodite: Reflections on a Journey to the Goddess* (San Francisco: Harper & Row, 1987).

is simply another species of the humanism that people have practiced since Adam and Eve tried to become like God (Gen. 3:5). It deifies humans themselves or aspects of human nature in place of God. Whereas traditional humanism was typically androcentric—male-oriented—in the vision of humanity it worshiped, inclusivistic humanism divinizes a view of humanity that includes both genders in mutuality. In contrast to both androcentrism and inclusivism, radical feminist humanism deifies the female gender or the feminine aspect of humanity exclusively.

Having other gods instead of the God of the Bible is a sin against the First Commandment and is the heart of the human problem. It is spiritual death, especially when apostasy from the true God is knowledgeable and intentional. The fact that there are many people who want to affirm both inclusivism and the Christian God, as we have repeatedly recognized, indicates that inclusivism and apostasy are not necessarily connected. However, there is sufficient evidence from the lives of real people that other gods hover around the movement for inclusive language for God. Commitment to the humanity of women and resentment against the "masculine" God of the Christian faith have moved too many people to reject God for a more generic, genderless theistic God, for a dual-gender neo-Gnostic God, for neo-pagan pantheism, or even for inclusivist secular humanism. In the words of Elizabeth Achtemeier's essay, these people have exchanged God for "no gods."[8] They practice "a quite different religion."[9] They offer "a 'different gospel,' which is no gospel at all."[10] Their spiritual journies are evidence that temptations and threats to true faith and spiritual health do lurk among some of the strongest motives for inclusive language for God. In no way does this conclusion imply that all or most or a significant proportion of inclusivists are apostate, however.

The Second Commandment: The Danger of Idolatry

The First Commandment warns against worshiping false gods. The Second Commandment warns against making and worshiping false representations of the true God. It is ironic that inclusivists so often accuse traditionalists of idolatry.[11] For if idolatry is putting the image of a creature in place of the Creator, then the reimagined God, the off-

8. Achtemeier, "Exchanging God for 'No Gods,'" in *Speaking the Christian God.*
9. Zeigler, "Christianity or Feminism," in *Speaking the Christian God*, 315.
10. Colin Gunton, "Proteus and Procrustes: A Discussion in the Dialectic of Language in Disaagreement with Sally McFague," in *Speaking the Christian God*, 80.
11. See "Exclusively Masculine Language Is Idolatry" in chap. 2.

spring of inclusivist spirituality and theology, is an obvious candidate to become an idol. But inclusivists insist that the tradition's privileging of a few masculine terms for God, like *Father, Lord*, and *King*, is tantamount to idolatry. In the words of Virginia Mollenkott, "our almost exclusive focus on male God-imagery has resulted in an idolatry of the male."[12] How can we sort this out?

It all depends on what idolatry is. The Second Commandment begins: "You shall not make for yourself an idol in the form of anything in heaven above or on the earth beneath or in the waters below" (Exod. 20:4). If, as some inclusivists assume, this prohibits using all creaturely categories for identifying God, then, as we saw in chapter 7, no true religious language is possible, for we can only speak of God using human language. If, as other inclusivists argue, this commandment means that all creatures are equal as sources of "forms" for God, that all human language for God is therefore equally valid, and thus that no words are more "privileged" or appropriate for God than any other, the commandment could have been stated more clearly. For this interpretation seems to be opposite of what the Second Commandment literally states, that no creatures should be made into images of God. But taken in biblical context it cannot mean any of these things, for God himself gave special status to some terms, such as *Yahweh* and *Father*, even though they also have creaturely meanings.[13]

Defenders of Scripture and tradition define idolatry differently. According to the Heidelberg Catechism, Answer 96, the Second Commandment requires "that we in no way make any image of God nor worship him in any other way than he has commanded in his Word." The key is in the last phrase, "in any other way than he has commanded in his Word." God himself has chosen to make us humans in his image. We do not make him in our image. God-imaging is his prerogative. Therefore we are to worship him as he has revealed himself in his Word. In his Word he has revealed himself primarily as the King, the Lord, and the God and Father of our Lord Jesus Christ.[14] Worshiping him as such is therefore not to commit idolatry, but to accept him as he has come to us. Worshiping him as the Mother or Sophia or the Goddess or the Primal Matrix is attempting to access God in some other way than he has revealed himself. It is in fact substituting a creature-image for the Creator—not an image of a creature made by God and placed in nature, but a creature of the human religious imagination, a product of inclusivist ideology.

12. Mollenkott, *The Divine Feminine*, 114.
13. Chap. 7 discusses how creaturely language applies to the Creator.
14. Chap. 4.

Notice that once again the particularity of special revelation as attested in Scripture is the issue. If the Bible contains merely human or sexist cultural representations of the divine, then taking them too exclusively or definitively is idolizing something creaturely. But if the biblical language for God is God's self-designation, and if Scripture is the final authority, then replacement of its linguistic depiction and designation of God with inclusive language is to idolize something creaturely, which breaks the Second Commandment.

But are all deviations from the biblical presentation of God forms of idolatry? Don't all of us, traditionalists and inclusivists alike, work with our own misrepresentations of God? Surely no human being fully or perfectly comprehends and restates God's revelation. Of course this is true. But although no human understanding of God is adequate, there is a crucial difference between those that attempt faithfully to explicate Scripture and those that revise it inclusively, as shown in chapter 8. When inclusivism is given free rein, the line between the First and Second Commandments, between idolatry and worshiping a false god, between having a distorted view of the true God and having an ersatz god, is easily transgressed. A human illustration makes this clear.

Bill Clinton is currently president of the United States. George Bush and Ronald Reagan are former presidents. Suppose someone who knew nothing of Clinton as a person and little of the American form of government pieced together enough information to conclude that the most politically powerful person in the United States lives in Washington, D.C., that this person is a former governor of California, and that he is called *Commander-in-Chief George Clinton*. Here is the question: Does this conclusion offer a poor and distorted though partially correct representation of the real President Clinton? Or is it a construct that combines bits of Presidents Clinton, Bush, and Reagan into an imaginary person whose title, though accurate in the abstract, misrepresents the president as a military figure? Is this construct a poor account of fact, or is it fiction?

The same question is fairly asked of inclusivist theologies. Is *Sophia* an inept representation of the true God that confuses him with a personification of his wisdom? Or is it really capitulation to the Goddess, a false god? It may be one, the other, or both, depending upon the particular beliefs of different *Sophia*-worshipers.[15] Another example: Is Ruether's *Primal Matrix*—the panentheistic Ground of Being in whom we live, move, and have our being—a distorted account of the true God? Or is it so different from the true God that, like Commander-in-Chief

---

15. Schüssler Fiorenza, *In Memory of Her*, 133, stresses continuity with the Goddess, whereas Ramshaw, *God beyond Gender*, 44–46, warns against syncretism.

George Clinton, we are actually dealing with a human construct that has no referent in reality. Again, is the Father-Mother God of Neo-Gnosticism merely an altered picture of the true God? Or is it a piece of theological fiction, an image that "suppresses the truth," "exhanges the truth of God for a lie, and worships and serves created things rather than the Creator" (Rom. 1:18, 25)? Whether distortion of reality or sheer fiction, these theologies are idols because they intentionally do not represent God the way he has revealed himself. They are very different from theologies that strive for complete faithfulness to Scripture but fall short.

Faithfulness to biblical revelation with its primarily masculine language for God is not idolatry, for it accepts God as he has introduced himself. There is no other, more accurate way to know and speak of God. Biblical Christianity does not commit idolatry for any of the reasons that inclusivists allege.[16] First, it does not confuse God with a man, a king, a father, or any human being. It does not make masculinity absolute. It recognizes that God in himself is not male. Second, it does not take language for God literally. It recognizes the analogical or metaphorical nature of all language for God, even God's basic names and titles. Third, biblical Christianity does not speak of God exclusively as King, Lord, and Father. It does not privilege these terms any more than Scripture does. It simply follows the biblical pattern. It emphasizes that no human term defines or fully reveals God. It recognizes that in addition to the primary titles and names for God there are hundreds of other biblical depictions and locutions for God, including feminine ones (although it has not given the feminine ones their due). Further, it affirms that everything in creation—God's general revelation—reflects the nature and name of God. The tradition is replete with varied and interesting language for God within the framework of the primary biblical terms for God. In the end, a judicious examination of the inclusivist charges of idolatry conclusively results in the exoneration of biblical Christianity.

Of course this does not mean that Christians have always avoided the kinds of idolatry inclusivists allege. We all have a tendency to identify God with our own mental pictures and theological definitions of him. *But if inclusivist accusations against the Christian tradition as a whole are valid, then the Bible itself is an idolatrous document.* What an awful allegation! For the tradition is only following Scripture in its massively masculine primary language for God. Inclusivists are in far greater danger of idolatry than traditionalists in following their religious linguistic practices.

16. See "Exclusively Masculine Language Is Idolatry" in chap. 2.

The Third Commandment:
The Danger of Dishonoring God's Name

The Third Commandment forbids us from misusing the name of the Lord (Exod. 20:7). For centuries Christian teachers have been unpacking everything that this means. Ultimately it requires that we must, in the words of the Heidelberg Catechism's Answer 99, "praise him in everything we do and say," not just in our use of words that name God. As "Christians," people who bear the name of Jesus Christ, nothing we do should dishonor his name or the name of the God whose Son he is.

But this broad interpretation surely includes our language for God. Indeed in post–Old Testament Judaism the special name, *Yahweh*, was no longer used at all in order to avoid breaking this commandment inadvertently. While *Yahweh* is the name explicitly mentioned in the Commandment, all the biblical names and titles that designate who *Yahweh* is are covered by association with the divine name. For example, Christians have always regarded the name of Jesus Christ as protected by the Third Commandment. Carelessly using the name of Jesus as an expletive is as sinful as doing so with the word *God*. In chapter 4 we saw that the biblical revelation of God's name in the technical sense of title-name begins with *Elohim* and culminates in *Father, Son, and Holy Spirit*, which means that the triune name likewise is covered by the commandment.[17] Trifling with the name of God is no light matter in Scripture. Inclusivist eagerness to "bring many names" to God while suppressing others ought to be tempered by the Third Commandment.

But the commandment does not specifically rule out bringing new names. It merely enjoins reverence for God. As the Heidelberg Catechism summarizes, "it requires that we use the holy name of God only with reverence and awe, so that we may properly confess him, pray to him, and praise him in everything we do and say." Why is it not possible to fulfill these obligations while calling God *Father-Mother, Mother*, or *Parent*?

The problem is not merely with revising our terminology for God, but also with the assumptions and implications of doing so. We are commanded to reverence, honor, and worship the God whose name is *Yahweh*, who through Jesus Christ names himself as *Father, Son, and Holy Spirit*. Inclusivism is not satisfied with these names for God, or with the entire complex of the biblical names for God, because they are primarily masculine. So it wishes to change, augment, or delete the biblical names for God. It can reverence and worship God only after it has first revised his names. Dissatisfaction and the desire to rename embody two great potentials for transgressing the Third Commandment.

---

17. Bavinck, *The Doctrine of God*, 110.

First, there is dissatisfaction and critique. The biblical presentation of God is said to be inadequate if taken at face value. It is alleged to be gender-imbalanced, harmful to women, or unacceptable to people in our egalitarian culture. Anger is not the only manifestation of this dissatisfaction. Some inclusivists express sadness that the Christian tradition has remained so biblical in its language. Others state their acceptance of the culturally limited nature of Scripture's patriarchal representation of God and move beyond it. A few even betray a condescending or patronizing attitude toward the biblical God's limitations.[18] But whatever its emotional tone, inclusivism is critical of and dissatisfied with the Bible as written. It cannot accept Scripture as providing the definitive linguistic framework of the Christian faith. It must change that framework before it can worship God "with reverence and awe."

But recall that in Scripture God's name is ultimately equivalent to God himself.[19] It is God who revealed himself in history and inspired Scripture as he did. Thus dissatisfaction and criticism of the biblical pattern of language for God are dissatisfaction with and criticism of God himself. Apart from this judgmental attitude toward biblical-traditional language, inclusive language for God lacks a motive. Why change what is not unsatisfactory? With this attitude, however, it is hard to see how inclusivism can "use the holy name of God only with reverence and awe." This is one danger of breaking the Third Commandment.

Another danger permeates inclusivists' wish to reconfigure the name of God. Out of dissatisfaction and critique of biblical-traditional language for God arise new proposals for gender-balanced and gender-neutral names. This is the whole point of inclusive language for God. *Yahweh* becomes *She Who Is*, *the Father* is replaced by *the Father-Mother* or *the Parent* or just *God*. Inclusivism creatively names and renames God to conform to its notion of correct human gender relations.

In Scripture, however, naming is an act that presupposes the authority to name.[20] It is a right that superiors have over those under their jurisdiction. In Scripture only God names himself. And only God has the right to name himself. No human may name God by imposing language on him because no human has authority over God. No human can name God because none has knowledge of God independent of his revelation. Humans can rightly name God only by recognizing and repeating the names God has revealed in creation as interpreted by Scrip-

18. It is difficult to read the First Act of Ruether's "The Kenosis of the Father: A Feminist Midrash on the Gospel," *Sexism and God-Talk*, 1–3, as anything but sarcastic, patronizing blasphemy.
19. See "The Biblical Understanding of Names and Naming" in chap. 6.
20. See ibid.

ture.[21] Inclusivism's zeal to "bring many names to God" in order to reconfigure the biblical-traditional pattern is tantamount to attempting an assertion of authority over God. It is an illegitimate attempt to seize a divine right. However we characterize this act—as spiritual *hubris*, religious insurrection, reversal of the Creator–creature relation, or violation of our status as vassals of God's covenant—it is hard to see how it can be an expression of reverence and awe for the holy name of God. It looks more akin to the sin of our first parents, who coveted divine authority to define good and evil (Gen. 3:5). Whether aware of it or not, inclusivism is in danger of breaking the Third Commandment, not just because it changes theological vocabulary, but because of the attitude and stance toward God that this act implies.

Dangers of Relativizing Scripture

Loss of Confidence in Scripture

The historic Christian church confesses that Holy Scripture is the Word of God. Ordinary Christians believe that by reading Scripture they hear God speak. Of course it is necessary that the Bible be rightly interpreted. Subjective readings that distort the meaning of the text frustrate the hearing of God's Word. The general message of Scripture is clear and readily available. People with ordinary intelligence and education can read and understand it. However, it is also true that a more technically correct understanding of Scripture and what it teaches usually requires familiarity with appropriate methods of interpretation. So the church has often adopted standard readings of Scripture that have been presented to the people through preaching and religious education in order to guide their own private reading of Scripture. However this has been done in the different ecclesiastical traditions, Christians are encouraged to read Scripture, which makes plain to them redemptive history, the way of salvation, and the manner of life pleasing to God. Confidence that Scripture speaks God's truth is essential to historic Christianity.

The theology of gender-inclusive Christianity requires taking distance from Scripture, however. There is nothing clearer in Scripture than the presentation of God in masculine language. The thousands of instances of masculine personal terms for God are far more numerous and far less debatable than the particularities of the Bible's teaching on sin, the nature of Christ's atonement, or God's will for particular aspects of human life. If Scripture's masculine language for God is not normative for the church today, what in Scripture is normative? And

---

21. This is a major conclusion of chap. 6.

how can we tell? Thus inclusivism's approach to the Bible inevitably raises serious questions about the status of the content of Scripture. The confidence of Christians in the Bible as the Word of God is undermined. Chapter 8 explored this problem with respect to its historical reliability and doctrinal truth content. Now we explore how incluvism's distance from Scripture can adversely affect faith, piety, and humble obedience to God.

Loss of Intimacy with God

It is the heart of the gospel that, through Jesus Christ, the God who is creator of the world is our Father: "You received the Spirit of sonship. And by him we cry, '*Abba*, Father.' The Spirit himself testifies with our spirit that we are God's children" (Rom. 8:15–16). Jesus' Father is also our Father (John 20:17). This intimate, loving, Father–children relationship is a marvelous gift of grace and comfort to us, given the great distance between God and us both ontologically and spiritually.

Ontologically there is unimaginable distance between our finite, dependent, fallible, creaturely existence and God's self-sufficient being with its fullness of goodness, power, knowledge, and perfection. Although the Lord is nearer than hands and feet as the omnipresent creator and upholder of the universe, we humans sense the great distance from the divine nature that is manifest in our inability to perceive or comprehend him. Though creation reveals its Creator, without special revelation his presence among us remains mostly a mystery.

Morally and spiritually there is also an infinite difference between us and God, because he is perfectly good and holy, whereas we are sinners, polluted by the fallen nature we have inherited and stained by our own sins. We are spiritually alienated from God, morally removed from him a distance far too great for us to travel.

In his grace God has come close to us, overcoming the distance and bringing us into a relationship of personal intimacy with him. In Jesus Christ he has bridged the moral-spiritual chasm caused by our unholiness, reconciling us to himself by the blood of Christ's cross (Col. 1:20) and adopting us as his children (Eph. 1:5). No longer are we alienated by sin like prodigal sons and daughters. Calling God *Father* through Jesus Christ and living in the name of the Father and of the Son and of the Holy Spirit we are receiving the gracious, intimate, personal presence of God himself as his beloved children.[22] "Because you are sons,

---

22. DiNoia, "Knowing and Naming the Triune God," in *Speaking the Christian God*, 162–87, defends the triune name from revision because God in grace "gifts us with his very self," "his personal presence " as Father, Son, and Holy Spirit. We can take it or leave it, not change it.

God sent the Spirit of his Son into our hearts, the Spirit who calls out 'Abba, Father'" (Gal. 4:6). Addressing him as *our Father* expresses our gratitude for the gracious, loving intimacy into which he has drawn us.

The familial intimacy of our salvation is at the same time intimacy with God the Creator. In the Old Testament Israel knew that *Yahweh*, who saved them from Egypt, was *Elohim*, the King of Creation and the Lord of all the nations. In the New Testament likewise the Father of Jesus Christ is also the Creator God. "There is but one God, the Father, from whom all things come" (1 Cor. 8:6), "the Father, from whom his whole family in heaven and on earth derives its name" (Eph. 3:14–15). We can address the God of the universe as our heavenly Father, for in Jesus Christ that is who he is. The Absolute and Transcendent Ground is our Father. No longer are we distanced by our finitude. Thus, calling God *Father* acknowledges that we gratefully receive the intimacy with which he has bridged both our ontological and spiritual distances from him.

The danger with inclusive language for God is that it widens the gap that God has closed. Using other names for God, ones selected or devised by humans, is not receiving God on his own terms, but distancing ourselves by placing linguistic conditions on God. We attempt to meet God on our terms. We place a linguistic mask over the self-named presence of God. We insert linguistic filters between us to strain out the alleged patriarchalism of the language he has chosen. We hold God at arm's length until we dress him in linguistic clothing pleasing to us.

There is a place for feminine and genderless language for God. Scripture does teach that God is like a mother to us, giving us life, loving, caring, nurturing, and protecting us. Scripture does use impersonal and gender-neutral terms for God. And in a conceptual sense, he is our Parent if he is our Father. But Scripture does not give *Mother* or impersonal, gender-neutral terms, such as *Parent*, as divine names or titles. The Bible says that God is our Lord, King, and, most intimately, our Father. That is how he has introduced himself and how Jesus taught us to pray. Demanding that we pray to him as *Father-Mother*, as *Mother*, or as *Parent* equivalent to *Father* is to refuse to relate to God in the loving, intimate terms he has provided. This problem is most obvious with the gender-neutral term *Parent*. It is a generic term for a mother or father, not a specific personal term of warmth and closeness. Thus inclusive language for God, whether gender-egalitarian or gender-neutral, is incapable of participating in the God-initiated close fellowship with himself into which he has lovingly brought us.

A human parallel is an adopted child who is invited to call his warm and loving step-father "Dad," but who refuses and instead calls him "Mother's New Husband" or "Mr. Bill" or "Sir." Even if these alternatives were accurate and respectful, they would signal a resistance to the intimacy offered. Our adoption as children of God though Christ makes this illustration apt. Jesus warned, "If you really knew me, you would know my Father as well" (John 14:7a). Those who regularly practice speaking of and to God inclusively are in danger of resisting intimacy with God in this way.

Loss of Jesus as Savior

In chapter 8 we noted that some inclusivists reject the doctrine that Jesus is the eternal Son incarnate, whose death, among other accomplishments, atoned for the sins of the world by suffering the penalty that humans justly deserve.[23] The values of our culture, colored by gender-egalitarianism, have led some inclusivists to think of Jesus as a good, compassionate, inclusive human being especially empowered by the Spirit and Wisdom of God to promote liberation of people from all sorts of oppression. As they tell it, his ministry ran afoul of the patriarchal Jewish religious establishment, who manipulated the Roman political authorities into executing him. In their view, the resurrection and heavenly reign of Jesus Christ mean that his spirit—his love for all people and his passion for justice, liberation, and true community—lives on in Christians, continuing to inspire them with the same self-sacrificial devotion to the liberation of all people that he practiced.[24]

Inclusivists did not invent this view of Jesus, and they are not the only people to hold it. In fact, it is typical of the "modernist" or "liberal" branch of Christianity that has grown since the Enlightenment.[25] Currently it is being popularized by the *Jesus Seminar*. The basic issue is whether the faith taught in the Bible—including the deity, incarnation, teachings, miracles, sacrificial atonement, bodily resurrection, actual ascension into heaven, and current rule of the living person, Jesus Christ—is to be taught and lived by the church, or whether the faith of the church must be "re-understood" in conformity to the developments of scientific naturalism, liberal ethics, and modern cultural values, including gender-inclusiveness.[26]

Feminist and inclusivist theologies that depart from the historic doctrines of the deity of Christ and the atonement merely continue the tradition of liberal or modernistic Christianity. What makes them in-

---

23. See "Sophia Christology" and "The Atonement" in chap. 8.

24. Ruether's view of Jesus in *Sexism and God-Talk* is very much like this.

25. A classic statement of the differences between historic and modernist Christianity is J. Gresham Machen, *Christianity and Liberalism* (Grand Rapids: Eerdmans, 1923, 1983).

26. This controversy continues, as we are reminded by the 11 August 1997 issue of *Christianity Today*, which devotes several articles to "The Struggle for the Soul of Mainline Denominations."

novative is that they criticize and reinterpret the historic faith specifically from the standpoint of antipatriarchalism. The danger for gender-inclusivists is therefore the same as the danger for modernistic Christianity in general, that Jesus the Savior is lost and what is preached is actually "another gospel."

This strong statement requires two qualifications. First, I make no final judgment about the salvation of modernistic Christians, including modernistic inclusivists. Salvation is by God's sovereign grace, not by works, not even by holding the right beliefs. Although Scripture makes clear what we must believe to be saved, God alone is Savior and Judge. Second, I do not imply that all or most inclusivists are modernistic Christians or that all or most fail to believe the true gospel. Chapter 8 repeatedly pointed to inclusivists who affirm the new language for God but selectively (and inconsistently) understand it in terms of the old language. To the extent that their faith is defined by the biblical paradigm, it does embrace the true gospel. Most inclusivists may in fact occupy this position. I do not judge their faith. I do point out the spiritual danger that lies in taking inclusivism on its own terms, that is, defined by its own inherent meaning and not by Scripture.

Loss of Obedience to God's Will

The distance from Scripture required for the promotion of inclusive language for God not only relativizes the biblical presentation of God, Jesus Christ, and the way of salvation. It also relativizes specifically biblical teachings on ethical matters—God's will for our thoughts, words, and deeds as we live our lives. Issues such as abortion and homosexuality divide people in the church, as they divide the general population. What must be faced is the correlation between Christians' views on these ethical issues and their views of Scripture, which is the same general correlation that holds between their views of Scripture and their attitude toward inclusive language for God. In inclusivism's approach to Scripture, therefore, lurk threats to another aspect of true faith and healthy piety—acknowledgment of and obedience to the will of God.

In a recent article James Edwards points to the emergence of two movements within most mainline denominations. "The one camp inclines toward the conservative side of the spectrum, committed to recovering the biblical and theological basis of the church. The other camp leans to the liberal side of the spectrum and defines the nature of the church in terms of pluralism and inclusiveness."[27] The anecdote

27. James R. Edwards, "At the Crossroads: The Battle for a Denomination's Soul," *Christianity Today*, 11 August 1997, 21.

with which he sets up this observation is striking. It relates a conversation among an interdenominational group of people who had been enthusiastic participants at the Re-Imagining God conference. These people, many of them non-Presbyterians, were now strategizing about how to influence the vote of the Presbyterian General Assembly of 1996 in favor of ordaining practicing homosexuals.

This anecdote is not in the least surprising. For it is very difficult consistently to elevate the cultural norm of gender-inclusivism and the liberty of interpretion over Scripture's revelation of God and at the same time not to elevate the cultural norms of sexual-orientation-inclusivism and sexual liberty over Scripture's prohibition of sexual activity outside of heterosexual marriage. Those who favor inclusive language are likely to favor progressive views on other ethical issues. Those who hold traditional positions on the ethical questions are also much more likely to oppose inclusive language for God. The common denominator is their views of Scripture and how properly to interpret it.

This judgment regarding the connections among Scripture, inclusivism, and other ethical issues is not based on the empirical research of opinion polls. It is not an illegitimate generalization based on Edwards' single anecdote. And it is not the fallacy of guilt by association, poisoning the wells, or any other rhetorical dirty trick. It is a theological judgment regarding biblical hermeneutics. The same distance from Scripture and cultural accommodation required by inclusive language for God, if consistently applied, will likely result in inclusivism of ethical positions. One can promote inclusive language for God and retain the church's historic position on matters of sexual ethics and the sanctity of life only by practicing an inconsistent hermeneutics. So another spiritual danger of inclusivism is that it undermines Christian orthopraxis—right action—obedience to the will of God. More than orthodoxy is at stake.

Loss of Foundation for True Gender-Inclusiveness

Perhaps the greatest irony of the inclusivist approach to Scripture is that, if consistently applied, it unwittingly undermines the biblical basis and thus the clear divine mandate for true gender equality among humans. The Bible expresses God's will for healthy and just relations between the sexes, but inclusivists relativize the normativity of the Bible.

The claim that Scripture supports the equality of women may appear startling to some readers, because many traditionalists and inclusivists alike assume that biblical Christianity is patriarchal in its view of men and women. Given the patriarchal (male-governed) social order everywhere reflected in the Bible, as well as its teachings about the subordination of women in marriage and in the church, and given the strong patriarchalism of the Christian tradition, this assumption is understandable. At this point I beg the reader's indulgence. The charge that God the Father and the Bible teach, promote, and inevitably generate unjust, hierarchical, sexist relationships is answered in chapter 10. There, we consider the case for the view that Scripture as a whole teaches the mutuality and equality of men and women in creation and redemption. For the present we anticipate the outcome of that discussion and assert without argument that the will of God expressed in Scripture requires healthy, loving, just, and mutually fulfilling relationships among men and women. (More debatable are the nature of headship in marriage and whether Scripture permits female leadership in Christian worship or the ordination of women to ecclesiastical office.)

Christians who take Scripture as the final authority for faith and practice, therefore, have a sure foundation for the view that women are equal to men in dignity, worth, inherent human rights, and giftedness by the Holy Spirit. This view is the basis for a Christian view of love, mutuality, and justice for women and men in marriage and family, as well as in the social, economic, political, cultural, and ecclesiastical spheres (whether or not women may be ordained). Scripture is a sure foundation from which to judge all the forms of sexism, oppression, abuse, injustice, and marginalization from which women, children, and many men suffer. It is the beacon on the path toward healing and overcoming these sins and evils.

The irony of inclusivism is that its view of Scripture really does not acknowledge this solid foundation for the well-being of women. No doubt inclusivists agree with everything in Scripture that affirms their position. But the distance and culturally relative view of Scripture they must take in order to justify inclusive language for God, if consistently applied, would not allow them to take the texts supporting the equality of women as providing a universally normative, transcultural statement of the will of God. When they appeal to the Bible as sanctioning their views, they typically apply a double standard: they find a canon of agreeable, liberating material within the patriarchal canon of Scripture as a whole, which they relativize.

But then the inclusivist commitment to women's dignity and rights must be based on women's experience, reason, or conscience—values known independent of Scripture. For there must be a criterion of truth other than Scripture in order to judge which parts of Scripture constitute the true, liberating canon and which are the false, patriarchal canon. The foundation for inclusivist claims about the equality of men and women must therefore be based in conscience and experience, not primarily in Scripture.

But there is the rub. Given the relativism and pragmatism of our postmodern, post-Christian culture, are experience and conscience sure foundations for women's rights? Most Christian traditions affirm that by God's grace unregenerate humans retain some ability apart from Scripture to know the general requirements of the moral order (Rom. 2:14–15), including the inherent value and dignity of every human being. But Christian tradition also recognizes that human consciences are dulled by sin, so that Scripture is the final and certain authority for specific knowledge of our duties to others.

Modern philosophy attempted to ground moral knowledge apart from revelation in reason alone, and it eventually failed. Moral law and inalienable human rights are neither demonstrable by deductive proof nor are they verifiable from experience. They do not amount to objective truth according to modernistic notions of rationality. To many modernists, therefore, moral norms appear to be subjective cultural preferences or perhaps pragmatic necessities required to make social life possible. But preferences and practical necessities such as these can vary among societies, cultures, and different historical epochs. So in this line of thought there appear to be no universal moral laws or essential humans rights, including the equal rights of women. Some cultures recognize them; some don't. And that is the end of the matter in much contemporary thought.

This sort of moral relativism is a strong current in our postmodern society. It continues to do battle with the moral intuition that all humans, including women, have equal basic rights and dignity. But this polemical situation does not provide a very secure basis for the well-being of women. If the moral universalists win, then women's rights will be recognized. If the moral relativists win, then women's rights are up for grabs. Women have equal ability and rights if they can get a particular society to say that they do; they don't if they can't. Does world history make us optimistic that women will win their rights permanently? Or will contemporary feminism be swept away by the resurgent patriarchalism of a future dark age?

Here then is the problem fully spelled out: Scripture provides a sure foundation for women's equality and rights, rooting them in the will of God himself, who made women in his own image and gave them equality in Christ. Inclusivism, however, has chosen to relativize Scripture in terms of certain cultural patterns and values. But those cultural patterns and values may in the end undermine the foundations of the rights and dignity of women. In that case, inclusivism would be without a reliable basis and authorization for the very thing that it prizes most. Therefore, taking the approach to Scripture needed to justify inclusive language for God endangers inclusivist claims about the equality of women. That is indeed ironic, not to mention self-defeating. A traditional reading of Scripture yields male–female mutuality, harmony, and justice as the ultimate will of God. But it also yields the enduring pattern of masculine language for God.

Conclusion

In this chapter we have focused on a number of dangers to authentic Christian piety and spirituality associated with the promotion of inclusive language for God. Some of them threaten sin and rebellion against God himself—the dangers of false religion, idolatry, and dishonoring the name of God. Others threaten diminishment of biblical religion due to the distance taken from Scripture—loss of confidence in the Bible as God's Word, loss of intimacy with God the Father, loss of trust in Jesus as Savior, loss of biblical obedience, and even loss of a firm foundation for the equality of women.

Throughout the chapter we have been careful not to condemn inclusivists as a group for being guilty of these kinds of impiety and diminishment of authentic Christianity. While some appear to be guilty according to their own words, many inclusivists seem fully intent on professing the historical, biblical, Christian faith. The intention of this chapter is to point out the sometimes hidden spiritual tensions and incompatibilities between their Christian piety and their practice of inclusive language for God. Good intentions notwithstanding, inclusivism is spiritually dangerous.

At the beginning of the chapter we also acknowledged that there are spiritual dangers for traditionalists as well. Traditionalists can make idols of maleness or of tradition itself. They can misuse the Fatherhood of God to promote sexism and illegitimate power relations over women. They can be close-minded and nasty in the debate about inclusive language for God. This chapter is not about the virtue and sincerity of individuals but about the intrinsic dynamics of Christian piety and language for God.

10

Is the God of the Bible a Sexist?

The Basic Charge of Inclusivism

We have argued that inclusivism and its language for God are in tension with both biblical truth and biblical piety. But we have not yet engaged the fundamental assumption that motivates inclusivism, its belief that the biblical presentation of God is sexist. Inclusivists proceed from the allegations that exclusively masculine language for God gives a distorted picture of who God really is and that this picture exacerbates many sorts of harm and injustice, especially to women.[1] The famous shot of Mary Daly hits the bull's-eye for inclusivists: "If God is male, then the male is God." It galvanizes them into action. Inclusivism isn't just another fad in academic theology. It is part of a broad movement with an agenda for the rights and well-being of women in church, home, and society at large. Inclusivism is animated by the assumption that the privileged status of God the Father in historic Christianity is the root of much evil, especially for women. The God of Scripture is not just old-fashioned and irrelevant; he is actually harmful.

These charges are serious. They are persuasive to many in our culture and even to some in our churches. Thus it is not sufficient for defenders of biblical language merely to urge faithfulness to Scripture. We must also show that the charges of sexism and patriarchalism leveled against biblical-traditional language for God are not true.

We begin by examining the alleged sexism of the Bible and its presentation of God as Father, King, and Lord. Just what is it about the God of Scripture that diminishes women? Does he put them down, or fail to raise them up, or is it simply unfair to women that God reveals himself in masculine language? When these charges are examined, it

---

1. See the section on "Inclusive Language for God and the Women's Liberation Movement" in chap. 1.

turns out that the anthropomorphically masculine God of Scripture and the welfare of women are not only compatible, but that God actually promotes and guarantees women's welfare and equality.

The equality of male and female in the Bible involves a second topic, the doctrine of the image of God. Since both men and women equally image God, inclusivists reason, God must be imaged equally in male and female terms. But this argument suffers from several flaws. In exposing them we refute the inclusivist axiom that promotion of gender justice for humans requires inclusive language for God.

Finally, we confront the charge that even if the masculine language for God in Scripture is not harmful, it is outmoded and culturally irrelevant. Fathers nowadays are very different from those in biblical times, according to inclusivists. Powerful lords and kings don't exist in our culture. So they urge us to adopt new language so that the Bible can be understood.

Throughout this discussion we must remain clear about the real issue. We are defending the integrity of what Scripture teaches about God and human gender relations. We are not obligated to defend the behavior of Christians down through the centuries. Some beliefs and practices of many Christians and of the church itself may be sinfully sexist, patriarchal, and harmful to human well-being. If we are faithful to Scripture, we will confess and repent of these sins. But the failures of Christians do not invalidate biblical language for God any more than failure to love invalidates Jesus' love command. This chapter defends the biblical presentation of God from charges of sexism and irrelevance. The next chapter suggests ways in which the historic Christian church can use feminine language for God as part of its ministry and response to problems caused by unbiblical patriarchalism and sexism.

God the Father and Patriarchalism

The Patriarchal Pattern of Scripture and Tradition

Before defending the Bible from charges of sexism, we must admit the fact of male primacy in Scripture and Christian tradition. In addition to its overwhelmingly masculine language for God, there is no doubt that the Bible reflects the patriarchal culture in which it was written. Authority and leadership in family, society, government, and religious institutions are almost always held by men: husbands, fathers, prophets, priests, and kings. Girl children seem less desired and important than boys in the Old Testament. "Sons are a heritage from the Lord," says Psalm 127:3–4, but it does not mention daughters. Some passages of Scripture intended for all persons seem to address only men or to address women through their men. "I appeal to you, brothers," writes Paul repeatedly in 1 Corinthians 1 and elsewhere. The pattern of male primacy in the Bible cannot be denied.

Furthermore, the patriarchalism of Christian tradition is also impossible to hide. Male authority or "headship" has been affirmed both in the private spheres of marriage and family and in the public domains of the economy, education, culture, politics, and church. Biblical and theological explanations for the inferiority and legitimate subordination of women have been widely accepted. Male leadership has taken different forms in different cultures, but it has been virtually universal in Christendom.

It would be dishonest and detrimental to our credibility not to acknowledge the apparently inevitable correlation between the anthropomorphic masculinity of God and male primacy in Scripture and tradition. Inclusivist charges are not frivolous but are based on a lot of apparently good evidence. We must demonstrate that they misinterpret the evidence.

Inclusivist Complaints against the Father

The prominence of God as *the Father Almighty* is a basic problem for inclusivists. *Father* is a culturally current and emotionally significant word, they point out. It has been at the center of the Christian understanding of God because of its frequency in Scripture, prayer, and worship. The key difficulty is that the term is strikingly gendered: fathers are male; mothers are female. If God is *our Father* but not in an equal sense *our Mother*, according to inclusivists, then in an emotionally and religiously compelling way, masculine power is ensconced in the highest, most venerable reality. God is a Patriarch, a father figure with unlimited power and authority who rules over all. Thus the Absolute Reality is Exclusively Masculine Power.

We are already somewhat familiar with the evils that inclusivists blame on the traditional view of God as Father. Ruth Duck's summary is broadly representative: "The patriarchal order, articulated as *patria potestas* in Rome and continued in other Western societies, makes some social groups dominant over others: men over women, adults over children, free men and women over slaves, clergy over laity, and humanity over nature. God, when portrayed as 'omnipotent Father/King,' rules at the top of the pyramid." According to this scenario, the Christian doctrine of God the Father is responsible for an unjust hierarchical social order which, among other evils, subordinates and marginalizes women and makes them feel inferior. But that is not the worst of it, according to Duck. "The tradition of *patria potestas* . . . encourages abuse of children by their fathers." In particular, "the overwhelming use of masculine language for God contributes to male dominance, which in turn leads to domestic violence."[2] So there it is: if the church does not "dethrone" the Father/King (to use Brian Wren's phrase) and stop privileging masculine language for God, we are guilty of perpetuating social injustice and promoting child abuse.

What is wrong with this picture? In the following sections we will show that it is false, confused, in danger of spiritual insubordination, and self-defeating. First, it is false that the predominant use of masculine language for God promotes social injustice and the oppression of women and children, for the God of the Bible forbids these things and demands the well-being of the weak and oppressed. Second, the picture is confused, for it rejects the biblical revelation of God on the basis of human failure to obey that revelation. Thus it fallaciously rejects the use of biblical language because it can be abused. Third, some versions of this picture are in danger of religious insubordination, for they not only reject the Bible's masculine language for God, but also its language of God's hierarchical rule. Finally, rejecting God's power and authority to rule is self-defeating for inclusivists, for only a superhuman power can bring about gender justice, equality, and harmony.

The God of Scripture Promotes Well-Being, Not Injustice

On the first point, it is simply false that the Father-King God of the Bible promotes injustice and abuse. In the Old Testament Yahweh, the great King, is just and the source of justice for all. His covenantal laws with Israel, repeatedly stated, are full of concern for the protection of widows, orphans, and strangers. In fact the Lord's compassion and justice are important reasons for praise, as in Psalm 146:7–9: "He upholds the cause of the oppressed . . . the Lord lifts up those who are bowed down. . . . The Lord watches over the alien and sustains the fatherless and the widow, but he frustrates the ways of the wicked."

To be sure, there are "texts of terror" in which women are horribly abused.[3] Think of Judges 19, where the Levite's concubine is raped and butchered. But these texts do not endorse or encourage such behavior. They illustrate the degeneration, depravity, and evil that result when people are not faithful to God's law. In fact the honor and protection of women sexually, socially, in marriage, and even in divorce demanded by Yahweh the King gave women in Israel a status superior to the status of women in most other ancient Near Eastern cultures.

---

2. Duck, *Gender and the Name of God*, 47. The chapter is entitled "Beyond the Father's Fearful Mask."

3. Phyllis Trible, *Texts of Terror* (Philadelphia: Fortress, 1984).

Of course this legislation regulates the patriarchal culture of that historical setting and does not fully overturn it. Full social equality with men is not provided in the Old Testament. But its dynamic and direction are toward fuller justice and well-being for women. A striking illustration of this is the story of the daughters of Zelophehad (Num. 27:1–11). Although women did not have property rights, these daughters were allowed to inherit their father's right to property in the Promised Land because there was no male heir. Yahweh lifts women up.

Father is not a prominent title of God in the Old Testament. But when it does occur, it is always expressive of God's powerful compassion and protective love. Most familiar is Psalm 103:13: "as a father has compassion on his children, so the LORD has compassion on those who fear him." God's love, nurture, protection, and faithfulness to his people are the connotations of his fatherliness in the Old Testament.[4] It is never associated with wrath, punishment, or anything harmful to his people.

Yahweh explicitly presents himself as Father-King in giving the messianic covenant to David, guaranteeing that his royal son will always rule over his people in a kingdom of justice and peace (2 Sam. 7). The idea that the Father-King of the Old Testament is an abusive tyrant who by nature frustrates the flourishing of women and children, who commands, encourages, tolerates, or takes no action against injustice, abuse, and neglect of women and children is absurd. It is difficult to see how anyone who has read the Bible could make such a claim.

In the New Testament women are accorded even higher standing. Striking evidence of this is Paul's modification of the messianic covenant in 2 Corinthians 6:18: "I will be a Father to you, and you will be my sons and daughters, says the Lord Almighty." Paul reiterates *Father* to identify God. But instead of using *sons* exclusively, Paul picks up *sons and daughters* from Isaiah 43:6.[5] The implication is that both men and women share the messianic, kingly office—the authority to rule in God's kingdom—of Jesus the Messiah. Paul further declares that in Christ the traditional human classifications that have created divisions among people are no longer valid: "There is neither Jew nor Greek, slave nor free, male nor female, for you are all one in Christ Jesus" (Gal. 3:28). While this declaration of unity is surely not a prooftext for social egalitarianism or the ordination of women, it does have implications for how men, women, and even children should relate.

4. Recall the section on *Father* in chap. 4.
5. I owe this insight to Carl Bosma, a colleague who teaches Old Testament.

We see these implications drawn in Ephesians 5:21–6:9, after Paul has elaborated the themes of unity in Christ and unity in the church. While the husband is identified as the head of the wife, he is not granted absolute authority or hierarchical rule over her. He is to love her as Christ the Savior loves the church. Thus he is to give himself to her and for her, loving her equally as he loves himself. She is likewise to submit to this Christ-like headship. As a result there is mutual submission even if the relationship between husband and wife is not exactly symmetrical (Eph. 5:21–33). The relation between parents and children is also one of mutual subjection within a structure of authority. While children must respect and obey their parents, parents do not have absolute power. They are to raise their children to love and obey the Lord so that it goes well with them. Fathers are explicitly commanded not to "exasperate" their children (Eph. 6:1–4).

This then is what the Father God of the New Testament wants for men, women, and children: love, justice, and mutual respect within legitimate relations of authority. Thus it is patently false that the Bible, including its exclusively masculine-language presentation of God, endorses or promotes the *patria potestas* model of patriarchy, which allegedly gives the father absolute arbitrary authority over his wife and family and thereby encourages their abuse.

But Are Women Equal?

So far we have only shown that women should not be harmed by men. We have not yet demonstrated that Scripture accords women equality with men. Unless that be done, inclusivists can still argue that the Bible is sexist both in its vision of human society and in its view of God.

Defending the equality of women from Scripture is a genuine challenge. For until recently all major Christian traditions appealed to Scripture for the subordination of women.[6] Some traditions held that women are subordinate to men because they were not created with quite as full a measure of the image of God as men. Others held that women were created equal but lost equality as a result of Eve's role in the fall. The Reformed tradition taught the basic human equality of men and women in creation and in redemption, but also held that God in his sovereign wisdom has given women different (and subordinate) roles in marriage, family, church, and society.

Some Christians still affirm certain kinds of limitation and subordination for women, although they also tend to emphasize the spiritual

---

6. Ruether, "Patriarchal Anthropology," in *Sexism and God-Talk*, 94-99.

and human equality of men and women more than the tradition did.[7] However, there is also a lot of recent Christian scholarship that emphasizes the spiritual and functional equality of men and women. Evangelicals have argued for this equality from the Bible, using the same traditional methods of interpretation that were endorsed in chapter 6.[8]

A brief overview of a biblical case for equality runs as follows: Male and female equally image God in Genesis 1. Together they are equally blessed with fruitfulness and dominion (authority) over the earth. Adam is created first in Genesis 2, but as the first among equals. Woman is taken from his side to stand with him, not under him, as together they care for the garden. The fact that she is called a *helper* does not make her subordinate, for God is also the *Helper of Israel* in the Old Testament. Further, Genesis 2 speaks about marriage, not the universal relationship between all males and all females. It does not teach universal social subjection. Furthermore, the hierarchical subordination of wife to husband is not found in the order of creation, but is a consequence of the curse after the fall (Gen. 3:16). Thus the strong patriarchalism that we see in the Old Testament is actually a result of the fall, not an exemplification of the universal will of God. The social legislation given by God through Moses provisionally accommodates this fallen patriarchal order while it consistently promotes the elevation of women to greater inclusion and mutuality with men. Patriarchalism and polygamy are both accommodated by God in the Old Testament, although neither is his final will.

The New Testament proclaims that the negative divisions of male and female caused by the fall are removed in Jesus Christ (Gal. 3:28). The restoration of creational equality begins already now in the lives of God's people. The Holy Spirit is poured out on men and women (Acts 2:17–18 from Joel 2:28–29), thus anointing them all with the offices of Jesus Christ: prophet, priest, and king. The gifts of the Spirit, which are

7. See, for example, John Piper and Wayne Grudem, eds., *Recovering Biblical Manhood and Womanhood: A Response to Evangelical Feminism* (Wheaton: Crossway, 1991).

8. A few of the books that promote gender equality and mutuality on the basis of a high view of Scripture and general theological orthodoxy are Gilbert Bilezikian, *Beyond Sex Roles: What the Bible Says about a Woman's Place in Church and Family*, 2nd ed. (Grand Rapids: Baker, 1986); Elaine Storkey, *What's Right with Feminism* (Grand Rapids: Eerdmans, 1985); Mary Stewart Van Leeuwen, *Gender and Grace: Love, Work, and Parenting in a Changing World* (Downers Grove: InterVarsity, 1990); Ruth Tucker, *Women in the Maze: Questions and Answers on Biblical Equality* (Downers Grove: InterVarsity, 1992); V. Norskov Olsen, *The New Relatedness for Man and Woman in Christ: A Mirror of the Divine* (Loma Linda, Calif.: Loma Linda University, 1993); and Rebecca Merrill Groothuis, *Women Caught in the Conflict: The Culture War Between Traditionalism and Feminism* (Grand Rapids: Baker, 1994).

concretized into positions of service and leadership in the church, are given to men and women alike (1 Cor. 12). In the New Jerusalem, the saints, presumably both male and female, will reign with Christ (Rev. 22:5). So in the end, the original correlative image of God in male and female, an image actualized in having dominion in covenant faithfulness with God, is restored.

This summarizes a biblical account of male–female equality and mutuality. It interprets the hierarchical subordination and marginalization of women in Scripture, like slavery and polygamy, as God's provisional accommodation of human fallenness. It identifies the equality and mutuality, though not the sameness, of male and female in creation and in Christ as the fundamental theme of Scripture from Genesis 1 to Revelation 22 and thus as God's abiding will.

While many contemporary Christians, conservative and progressive alike, agree that Scripture does not universally subordinate women to men, reserve cultural leadership for men, or make motherhood a commandment for women, there are areas of continuing disagreement regarding marriage and female leadership in the church. Some Christians hold that there is a kind of authority of husband over wife connected with "headship" (Eph. 5:22), while others believe in biblical equality and argue that Paul was accommodating his culture.[9] Some Christians believe that women may serve in the offices of the church, while others strenuously disagree.[10] The important point here is that Christians must seek to formulate their views of gender and gender-roles by acknowledging Scripture as the final authority. We may not set Scripture aside or twist it to conform to the egalitarianism of our culture.

However the disagreements about marriage and ordination turn out, there is strong consensus that the Bible generates a high view of

9. My own view is that headship in marriage is permanently valid because it is taught by Paul and never qualified by other passages of Scripture. But straightforward exegesis of Ephesians 5 in my view yields the conclusion that headship is not about a chain of command but about taking primary responsibility in marriage for showing Christ-like love, as pointed out a few paragraphs above. Authority comes with this responsibility, but it is "servant leadership" rather than hierarchical authority. Headship is limited to marriage (Gen. 2) and therefore it does not make all men heads of all women or limit women from leadership in society.

10. I believe that Scripture permits women to be ministers, elders, and deacons, provided that this does not undermine marriage, cause trouble in the church, or give it a bad reputation. However, I came to this view only through careful study of Scripture using traditional methods of interpretation. My belief is not a consequence of contemporary social dynamics that have been adopted in spite of what Scripture teaches. See my *A Cause for Division? Women in Office and the Unity of the Church* (Grand Rapids: Calvin Theological Seminary, 1991).

women, considers them naturally and spiritually equal to men, insists on their well-being, and provides the foundation for healthy and just relations between the genders. Thus we come to a curious conclusion: The Bible progressively elevates the status of women as it progressively reveals God as Father. God the Father loves women and provides for them as much as men. Therefore the inclusivist charge that the Bible, especially its predominantly masculine presentation of God, promotes the devaluation and oppression of women is false.

Inclusivism against Itself

Inclusivists should know better than to perpetuate this false allegation. For the point that the Father God whom Jesus introduces is not the distant, domineering patriarch, but our strong, loving *abba* has frequently been made.[11] Such prominent nonfeminist scholars as Paul Ricoeur[12] and Jürgen Moltmann[13] have argued that the problem is not with God as Father per se, but with negative patriarchalistic understandings of God the Father. Even feminist theologians, such as Elizabeth Schüssler-Fiorenza, have made this point, although they downplay the term *Father* to avoid the patriarchalist misunderstanding.[14] So inclusivists themselves recognize that the biblical presentation of God is not inherently sexist, patriarchalistic, or harmful.

Inclusivist scholars should be able to arrive at the same conclusion in another way. A controversy within feminist theology has been whether Jesus' maleness is an impediment to women. Some argue that worshiping Jesus as Lord and Savior simply perpetuates female subordination to a male authority figure. Women are sick and tired of being rescued by men and having to serve them. But Christianity makes these dependencies sacred and permanent. Those who argue this way conclude that Christianity is essentially hostile to women.

In response, however, most femininst theologians have argued that Jesus' maleness is incidental. It is not his gender, but his teachings,

11. The works of Robert Hamerton-Kelly, *God the Father: Theology and Patriarch in the Teaching of Jesus* (Philadelphia: Fortress, 1979) and "God the Father in the Bible and in the Experience of Jesus," in *God as Father?* ed. J. B. Metz and E. Schillebeeckx (New York: Seabury, 1981), 95–102, are regularly referred to by inclusivists.

12. P. Ricoeur, "Fatherhood: From Phantasm to Symbol," in *The Conflict of Interpretations: Essays in Hermeneutics*, ed. D. Ihde (Evanston: Northwestern University Press, 1974).

13. J. Moltmann, "The Motherly Father: Is Trinitarian Patripassionism Replacing Theological Patriarchalism?" in *God as Father?*

14. E. Schüssler-Fiorenza, *In Memory of Her* (New York: Crossroads, 1983) 150–51. See also R. Duck, "Jesus' Language About God," in *Gender and the Name of God*, 59–72, and Janet Martin Soskice, "Can a Feminist Call God 'Father'?" in *Speaking the Christian God*, 81–94.

love, and example that are normative for the Christian faith. In the words of Rosemary Ruether, Jesus' "ability to speak as liberator does not reside in his maleness. . . . Theologically speaking, then, we might say that the maleness of Jesus has no ultimate significance."[15] Thus feminist theologians come to terms with a male Savior.

But the point Ruether makes about Jesus can also be made about God. If God the Father-King stands for justice and the abundant life for women, isn't his anthropomorphic masculinity incidental? Why is it an insurmountable problem for women? If women can relate to Jesus, who is a human male, they can surely relate to God the Father, who is neither male nor masculine. The point is that inclusivist theology contains sufficient resources of its own to recognize that the gendered quality of the biblical presentation of God need not be problematic for women.

Confusion: Judging the Use by the Abuse

Why then do inclusivists persist in charging the biblical presentation of God with promoting unjust and harmful patriarchalism? Sometimes it is because of an easy but illegitimate equivocation on the word *patriarchy*. If patriarchy is simply a social organization under a male authority figure, then God the Father is a patriarchal figure, Paul's ideal husband and father is a patriarch, and the father of the Roman family is a patriarch. But these are very different kinds of patriarchy. To incriminate the biblical model by association with the evils of the Roman model under cover of the common term *patriarchy* is simply unfair and untrue. It is like banning all police or all forms of marriage because some are abusive. But this sort of guilt by association is a fairly common tactic of inclusivists.[16] They appeal to historical abuses in order to disqualify the biblical use of patriarchal power, which is an obvious fallacy.

But perhaps some inclusivists are more fair and sophisticated. Perhaps they are only protesting the fact that Christians in history have interpreted Scripture as endorsing the Roman model, thereby baptizing harmful unbiblical notions of authority and gender relations. Perhaps inclusivists are merely complaining about the ways in which Scripture and God the Father have been abused historically to rationalize domineering versions of theological and social patriarchalism, with their terrible consequences for many people, not just women.

15. Ruether, "Christology: Can A Male Savior Save Women?" in *Sexism and God-Talk*, 137.

16. Ruth Duck very quickly associates the Roman and biblical models of patriarchy in *Gender and the Name of God*, 47, quoted above at the beginning of this section.

If that is their charge, it has merit. Conscientious Christians must acknowledge the sins of the tradition. Some great theologians did hold unbiblical and distorted views of women.[17] Christian civilization was male-dominated. Women were often regarded demeaningly and treated terribly. Christians did burn witches, most of them female.[18] These things are evil, lamentable, and we ought to be profoundly sorry about them. At the same time, we must defend the integrity of the tradition from false charges. Not all the allegations made by femininsts against historic Christianity are valid.[19] Furthermore, compared to many other religious cultures, the place of women in traditional Christian society was high.

We must confess the sins of patriarchalism and sexism in Christian tradition. However, the fact that Christians did not live up to the teachings of the Bible does not imply that the Bible itself commands or encourages injustice or abuse toward women. It surely does not imply that the masculine language for God or the central doctrine of the Fatherhood of God caused such evils. We have shown that the Bible teaches otherwise. So when inclusivists urge that we replace biblical language for God because of the evils of patriarchalism, they are confused. They reject something good because it has been abused.

But perhaps some things that may be good in themselves, such as guns and radioactive chemicals, should be banned because they often do lead to harm or abuse. This is the sort of argument that many inclusivists press against the biblical God. He may be okay in principle, they say, but in practice he leads to no good. Notice again the carefully chosen language of Ruth Duck: "the overwhelming use of masculine language for God contributes to male dominance, which in turn leads to domestic violence."[20] One thing leads to another.

But this argument is flimsy. We have already shown that masculine language for God should not and does not necessarily lead to male dominance. But important questions remain. Does it usually lead to dominance? If so, is that because of the language itself or because of other factors? And even if masculine language in Scripture is correlated with male dominance, as for example in a strongly traditional patriarchal Christian family, does it always lead to domestic violence? Usually? Does it do so in more cases than in the non-Christian population? In more cases than it would if the same family used inclusive language for God? Lots of questions remain.

17. Ruether, *Sexism and God-Talk*, 95-96.
18. Ibid., 170–72.
19. Francis Martin, *The Feminist Question: Feminist Theology in the Light of Christian Tradition* (Grand Rapids: Eerdmans, 1994), chaps. 3 and 4, provides a fine overview of the role of women in Christian history and some evaluation of feminist views of this history.
20. Duck, *Gender and the Name of God*, 47.

I have not taken the time to check on reliable, well-structured statistical studies, if there are any. But I seriously doubt that, in situations where God the Father of the Bible is sincerely worshiped and conscientiously obeyed, there is a higher rate of domestic violence than where some other god or no god at all is worshiped. Of course in a large traditional Christian population there will be many men who worship God the Father and mistakenly believe that God is masculine. They may also believe that God has given them patriarchal power because they are male, power that some of them use to abuse their wives and children. But there is no empirical evidence that their masculine view of God was a significant motive for the abuse, much less the decisive one. Most likely the problem is an emotional disorder not caused by theology at all. And if they do mistakenly believe that God has authorized their misuse of power, they did not get these ideas from the teachings of the Bible or the historic church.

This inclusivist allegation against traditional language for God is tenuously perched on a series of weak associations: one thing might lead to another, and that might lead to something bad. By this sort of argument it would be easy to get many things banned. Cars contribute to accidents, which hurt people. Away with cars. Music at high school parties leads to dancing, and you know what that can lead to. So much for music at high school parties. We simply do not and cannot live by this kind of "stop the use because of possible abuse" policy. So we ought not to eliminate biblical language for God because of possible abuses. Instead we ought to conform fully to Scripture, both its language for God and its teachings about gender relations.

A Danger of Spiritual Insubordination

For some inclusivists the core of the problem with the Bible's language for God is not that it is masculine, but that it is hierarchical. What really bothers them is not God the Father as much as God the Lord and King, not the *patri* (father) as much as the *archy* (rule). It is bad enough that biblical language favors one gender over the other, they complain. What is worse is that it places all of us, male and female, in a perpetual master–slave relationship.

Rosemary Ruether urges us "to rethink the whole Western theological tradition of the hierarchical chain of being and chain of command."[21] This is the source of all domination and oppression, even of humans over the earth. Although Ruether believes hierarchicalism and exclusive masculinity go together, she does not find a solution in

21. Ruether, *Sexism and God-Talk*, 85.

gender-balanced or gender-inclusive language. For unless the hierarchy is abolished, the problems continue. She certainly prefers inclusive language to masculine language, but not as a final solution. "Mother-Father God has the virtue of concreteness, evoking both parental images rather than moving to an abstraction (Parent) . . . But the parent model . . . suggests a kind of permanent parent-child relationship to God." Ruether instead wants "autonomy and assertion of free will."[22]

What we encounter here is a theme that has already surfaced in the last chapter, the spiritual danger of rebelling against our covenantal relationship with the all-powerful God of Scripture. Ruether's God/ess is a panentheistic dynamism, immanent in the world and therefore limited in power and knowledge. What she rejects is not just masculine language for God, but God's absolute power and authority. Scripture's use of parent-child and even of master-servant language to describe our relationship with God must be eliminated, for it impedes our maturation and self-determination.

The same theme is voiced in Brian Wren's *What Language Shall I Borrow?* though a bit less stridently. With scant argumentation Wren asserts that the randomness of subatomic particles, the reality of great evil in history, and the love of Jesus are irreconcilable with God as Almighty King and Father. We have a different worldview than the Bible writers, he claims, and a God in ultimate control does not fit into it. "The KINGFAP metaphor system cannot deal with this new reality; we need new language to express God's love and human autonomy."[23] Wren, too, prefers a more limited view of the divine nature than the theological tradition has articulated.

Sally McFague is another proponent of a limited deity. She frankly asserts that belief in "the guidance of a benevolent but absolute deity" is the remnant of "a bygone world." "But this is not *our* world, and to continue doing theology on its assumptions is hurtful."[24] With Ruether and Wren, she views power, not gender, as the real problem with biblical language for God.

To their credit, some inclusivists do not challenge God's absolute authority. Although Gail Ramshaw agrees with Wren that we must "break the myth of the crown"[25] and likewise wants to get beyond the language of the Father-King and his kingdom, she warns against giving up what that language symbolized: God's right to rule and power to save. Ramshaw prefers gender-neutral to gender-egalitarian language. So she rec-

22. Ibid., 69.
23. Wren, *What Language Shall I Borrow?* 126.
24. McFague, *Models of God*, 3.
25. Ramshaw, *God beyond Gender*, chap. 6, "The Myth of the Crown."

ommends that *King* and *Lord* be rendered as *Sovereign* and that we speak of God's *realm, dominion,* or *commonwealth* instead of his *kingdom.* She champions language that eliminates gender but not God's sovereignty.

In sum, there are inclusivists whose main charge against biblical Christianity is that its God slights human autonomy, not the feminine gender. What they reject about patriarchy, literally "father-rule," is more the *rule* than the *father.* They are challenging not merely language for God, but God himself, given that he is the Almighty Creator of heaven and earth that Scripture presents him to be.[26]

Limiting the Almighty Is Self-Defeating

Freedom-from-God inclusivists need to see that, in addition to the spiritual danger of their position, it is self-defeating. Their God/ess cannot be counted on for the salvation they desire. Whatever questions the phenomena of human freedom and evil raise for the traditional doctrine of God, the God of Scripture is always able to carry out his plan to put a stop to this evil, to save the world from it, and to create a new heaven and earth in which righteousness dwells. He has the power and goodness to save. The agonizing question for believers is why God apparently does not act more quickly and decisively to eliminate evil in history.

In contrast, the panentheistic God/ess of many inclusivists is on a journey with his/her creatures, immanently nurturing us, cooperating with us, and striving for the same just, peaceful, ecologically sound, and nuclear-free community that we all desire. God/ess does not have absolute power and thus does not control or compete with human self-determination. That explains why God/ess does not prevent people from doing bad things: he/she is not coercive (patriarchal). Thus the evil in the world cannot be blamed on God/ess' failure to act.

But this theodicy also raises a crucial question: Does God/ess have enough power and foresight to bring about the wonderful, inclusive world we all long for?[27] The irony is that the traditional God, because he has patriarchal power, has the ability to bring about the inclusive commonwealth, whereas God/ess as conceived by many inclusivists actually lacks that power. Uncooperative creatures may have the ability forever to frustrate the realization of the peaceable realm. Given the predominance of patriarchalism throughout human history, there is every reason to believe that it will continue in spite of the efforts and

---

26. Chap. 9 addressed the danger of rebellion against God.
27. See Ruether, *Sexism and God-Talk*, chap. 10 and postscript for a vision of inclusive eschatology.

temporary gains of inclusivists. Thus inclusivists should prefer the God of biblical tradition over his modern surrogates if they realistically hope for the community of mutual love and justice. It is self-defeating for inclusivist theology to limit the power of God.

Here we conclude our response to the charge that the biblical pattern of language for God promotes patriarchalism and abuse in human relationships. We have shown that this charge is false, is based on confusions, and that in some forms it expresses a self-defeating spiritual insubordination to the God of Scripture. The allegation of sexism is best consigned to the oblivion it deserves. For in fact the Father God of the Bible wills a community of males and females characterized by love and justice. Through Jesus Christ and the Holy Spirit he is making it an everlasting reality.

Inclusive Language, the Image of God, and Justice

It is a fundamental axiom of inclusivism that language for humans and language for God run parallel: Using masculine language for God inevitably privileges men, they argue. By the same token, promoting equality between men and women requires gender-inclusive language for God. If the parallel axiom is not true, most of the rationale for inclusive language collapses.

We have already challenged one support for the axiom, the notion that the Bible's masculine language for God privileges males and harms females. Two additional arguments for the parallel language axiom are often made. One is based on the image of God: since God created both male and female equally in his image, God should be imaged equally as male and female. The other argument is more often assumed than explicitly voiced: there is something unfair or unjust about language that features one gender more prominently than the other.

The Image of God

"If women are created in the image of God, then God can be spoken of in female metaphors in as full and as limited a way as God is imaged in male ones," according to Elizabeth Johnson.[28] While Johnson is careful not to project gender into God, Virginia Mollenkott throws caution to the wind. She claims that "the biblical authors did move the feminine principle into the Godhead."[29] Each in her own way uses the image of God to justify inclusive language for God.[30]

---

28. Johnson, *She Who Is*, 54.
29. Mollenkott, *The Divine Feminine*, 4.
30. See "Both Male and Female Image God" in chap. 2.

Johnson is correct when she argues that since both male and female image God, both can provide verbal images for God. The doctrine of general revelation led us to conclude in chapter 6 that all creatures reflect God's eternal deity and power, thus providing "names" for God. Furthermore, Scripture uses both male and female language for God. It can do so because both male and female humans image the God of heaven (Gen. 1:26–28).

But Johnson goes wrong when she slips from *can* to *must*. It might be true that God *could have* chosen either males, females, or both as ways of revealing himself. But it does not follow that God *must have* done so. And therefore it does not follow that he must have done so equally, or that we must do so equally. Instead we must affirm that God is sovereign, free, wise, and good. He chose to reveal himself in nature, history, Scripture, and in Jesus Christ just as he did. Though both males and females image him, he revealed himself as the Lord and Father whose excellences are also motherlike. There is nothing in the doctrine of the image of God that conflicts with the particularity of the Bible's presentation of God.

Mollenkott actually does project masculinity and femininity into God. Her inference seems to be that if the image of God is both masculine and feminine, then the God who is imaged is both masculine and feminine. But this conclusion is fundamentally mistaken.

In the first place, it cannot be assumed that all the characteristics of an image are found in its prototype. Many blue and red Volkswagon Beetles were made in the image of the archetypal Beetle. But the archetypal Beetle is not necessarily blue and red. In fact it probably has no color at all. In the same way, it cannot be assumed that the divine prototype has gender because the humans who image him are gendered. But Mollenkott's argument depends on the assumption that gender is part of the image of God.

Scripture, however, implies just the opposite, that gender is not part of the image of God. In Genesis 1 we read that God made male and female animals as well as male and female humans. But only humans are made in the image of God. So the image of God pertains to what is uniquely human. Since maleness and femaleness are not uniquely human, they are not part of the image of God. This straightforward argument has been accepted by theologians for many centuries. It is a serious mistake to endorse inclusive language for God on the ground that God must somehow be both male and female because we humans are.

If the image of God does not include gender, then it is perfectly understandable that *Elohim*, the King of Heaven and Earth, could create both males and females equally in his image. The fact that he chose to reveal himself as anthropomorphic masculinity has nothing to do with the image of God. As an illustration, both my son and my daughter are the "spittin' image" of their father.[31] Gender is not an issue. In an analogous way both men and women are the image of their heavenly Father. There is nothing mysterious or illogical about this.

Justice and Inclusive Language

A deep sense of injustice and unfairness overtakes some people when they contemplate biblical-traditional language for God. As it is not fair that women have been subordinated and marginalized in society and church, so it is not fair that our language for God is predominantly masculine.[32] If both male and female image God, and if God is good and just, and if God wants people of both genders to respond to him with love, inclusivists reason, then God must want gender-inclusive language. It would be wrong of him not to. It is surely wrong for the church not to practice inclusive language, they conclude. This complaint is not usually stated outright, but often seems to hover in the background. Inclusivists sense an aura of injustice surrounding the biblical pattern of language for God.

But how is it unjust? What is unfair about the Bible? We have shown that biblical language for God does not promote unjustice toward women. Just the opposite is true. If the Bible actually did teach us to harm or demean women, inclusivists would have a legitimate complaint against it. But their only valid complaint is against the lamentable failure of Christians to live up to the biblical view of women.

Is it unjust of God to choose masculine language to reveal himself? Does he owe us an egalitarian Bible? Justice requires that persons fulfill their obligations, that we render to each what is due, that we be fair. But God has no obligation to us to reveal himself in a certain way. He is subject to no law binding him to do so, and he has not entered any contract that so binds him. We can be sure that God will reveal himself truthfully, faithfully, wisely, and with goodness, for that is his nature. But he is not obligated by his nature or by our nature or by any commitment to us to use masculine and feminine language equally. How then is the Bible's masculine language for God unjust?

Perhaps it violates an aspect of justice. Justice requires that like cases be treated alike, that people receive equal treatment if there are no relevant differences among them. We call this fairness. Perhaps a sense of fairness accounts for the feeling that the biblical pattern of language for God is unjust. If God loves men and women equally, and if language is

---

31. My thanks to Al Wolters for this illustration.
32. See the subsection on "Equality for Women in Church, Theology, and Language for God" in chap. 1.

important to their human flourishing, then it seems that he should have treated both genders alike in choosing language for the Bible.

I understand this apparent unfairness. But it does not justify inclusive language for God. There are many things in human life that seem deeply unfair, things that move us to question God because we do not understand why they have to be the way they are. But in the end, like Job, we either curse God and die or we accept the God who reveals himself to us as our friend, trusting in his goodness and wisdom in doing what he does. In this book we have looked at the biblical pattern of language for God. We have asked whether the masculine names and titles are culturally relative, we have attempted to determine their theological meaning, and we have speculated about why God chose the particular language in which he revealed himself. Perhaps all this analysis has been persuasive, perhaps not. But even if it is not, even if we have no idea why God named himself as he did, we are still called on to take him as he presents himself in spite of our questions. Feelings of unfairness are no basis on which to reject the particularities of God's revelation. It is not our right to redress what in our opinion is a divine injustice with inclusive language for God.

Is the Language of Scripture Still Relevant?

Even if the biblical presentation of God isn't sexist, perhaps it is no longer relevant. Many inclusivists urge revision of Christian language on the ground that contemporary people simply cannot relate to the traditional vocabulary. Kings and lords are relics of a bygone age. Modern fathers are very different from fathers in biblical culture. Thus, inclusivists conclude, these traditional terms simply fail to convey their biblical meaning to modern people. Besides, Christians have used them to death. *Father*, *King*, and *Lord* have been repeated so many times that they no longer communicate any religious meaning. They are simply labels.

In addition, some inclusivists assert, we now recognize that men and women do not think and feel exactly alike, even though they are equal images of God. Since women in our culture have begun to develop their own gifts and validate their own experience, it is more difficult for them to relate to the all-male Bible than when they were treated as inferior versions of males. For all these reasons, inclusivists argue, it is strategically necessary to use contemporary egalitarian language for God instead of the archaic language of the Bible.[33]

---

33. Recall the sections "Women Experience God Differently Than Men," "Traditional Language Is Dead," and "The Gospel Must Be Proclaimed in Contemporary Language," in chap. 2.

Long Live the King

It is obvious that the few constitutional monarchs still around in the twentieth century are mere shadows of the powerful kings of history, such as Henry VIII or Louis XIV. They are nothing at all like the quasi-divine, absolutely powerful male rulers of the biblical world, such as Pharaoh, Nebuchadnezzar, and Caesar. Thus inclusivists are correct that we cannot simply relate the biblical picture of God as the Great King to contemporary monarchs. But why does that make biblical language impossible to use? What better language is there?

In the first place, the contemporary world provides no better categories. It is virtually impossible to put the biblical language for God into twentieth-century political categories. We would need to adopt the terminology of a benevolent dictator who makes and enforces the rules but who delegates significant administrative responsibilities to his subjects. For that is the biblical picture of God as Ruler and us humans as his covenant partners. Presidents and prime ministers are not adequate representations, and neither are Hitler or Stalin, for none are good analogies of divine theocracy in Scripture. Inclusivists end up with terms like *Sovereign* or *Ruler*.[34] It's hard to see that these alternatives are more contemporary than the language of powerful royalty.

Second, it is not true that *King* and *Lord* are out of touch with our experience. From fairy tales and fantasy literature, school book history, television and movies, and the Bible itself, children are quite aware of powerful kings and queens, both historical and fictional. They know of the benefits that good monarchs bring to their people and of the love and loyalty that these subjects feel for their monarchs. The whole world of divine royalty comes to life in C. S. Lewis's *Narnia* series, for example. This imagery strikes a resonant chord someplace deep inside most people. Intuitively we sense that if the world is not like the kingdom of Narnia ruled by Aslan, it should be. There is something universally attractive about life in a good kingdom. Thus it is false that most modern people cannot relate to the biblical message of the kingdom of God. For those who do have experiential difficulty understanding the kingdom, the church must find ways to help, as when a traveler explains snow to jungle-dwellers. But we need not abandon the language of Scripture for modern substitutes.

Since Scripture represents the normative framework of our lives, we Christians must envision ourselves and our culture within the reality it describes. We must not reduce or alter Scripture to fit into our current cultural reality. We are citizens of the Father's kingdom now and for-

34. See Ramshaw, *God beyond Gender*, chap. 6.

ever (Col. 1:12–13). We ought to see ourselves in these terms. To the extent that our culture makes this difficult, so much the worse for our culture. God is King. We are to praise him forever and ever (Ps. 145:1) The biblical language of God's kingdom is irreplaceable.

Biblical scholar Nellie Stienstra identifies three possible options for translating biblical metaphors into modern language when significant cultural shifts in meaning have occurred.[35] Only one can she endorse. The first is to eliminate the metaphor altogether. However, she points out that this tactic would remove many prominent metaphors from the Bible. The second option is to find a contemporary metaphor that communicates the meaning of the biblical metaphor. But this is impossible, Stienstra argues, both because metaphors have unique meanings that are untranslatable and because many biblical metaphors have no near equivalents in our culture. The only other option is to retain the biblical metaphor and do whatever is possible to enable contemporary readers to understand what it meant originally so that they can understand what it means for us today. Stienstra's analysis is penetrating and exhausts the possible approaches. The third option, the one she recommends, is the strategy we have defended throughout this book. All things considered, it is the only viable approach. We must remain faithful to the language of the Bible, especially its language for God.

God Is Still Our Father

God's fatherhood is much less culture-bound than his kingship. For we still have fathers in our society. Of course there have been some cultural shifts. If anything, the typical American Dad is more chummy, informal, and permissive than his ancient Israelite or early Christian counterpart. Our experience of fathers may actually be less likely to inspire reverence for the awesome heavenly Patriarch[36] than the fathers of previous ages.

It is also true that many people in our culture (and others) have difficulty relating to a Father God if they lack experience of a good father. This may be a wrenching emotional and spiritual problem for those who have been abused, neglected, abandoned, or otherwise hurt by their fathers. We must do everything possible to help them. But are they really benefited by eliminating God as Father? There may be some for whom a father-figure is such a negative force that it is better to begin with some other human relationship through which to enable them to

---

35. Nellie Stienstra, *YHWH is the Husband of His People*, 188–90. She works with the marriage and family imagery in Hosea.

36. Duck, *Gender and the Name of God*, chap. 2 is entitled "Beyond the Father's Fearful Mask."

feel love and to trust. But for most people, the need, desire, and ability to relate to a father-figure is still strongly present. Many people who lack good human fathers gladly and readily receive God the Father as their ultimate security and source of healing.[37] Eliminating the Heavenly Father is neither necessary nor helpful for dealing with the sins of their earthly fathers.

In spite of cultural differences or emotional injuries, there is something significant in our experience of human fathers that still resonates deeply with the *Abba Father* of our Lord Jesus. This universal intercultural experience, which binds us to Scripture, is more than enough basis for continuing to love, obey, and pray to our Father who is in heaven.

Male and Female Spirituality

Are the differences between men and women so great that women actually have a distinct feminine experience of God? Some inclusivist theologians say so. Elizabeth Johnson argues that "women's awakening to their own human worth can be interpreted at the same time as a new experience of God. . . . This theological interpretation of female identity is the center of gravity for feminist discourse about the mystery of God."[38] Marchiene Rienstra also stresses the difference between men's and women's spirituality, concluding that God "is as appropriately imaged and named in feminine ways as in masculine ways."[39] Gender-specific spiritual experiences are thus used to justify gender-egalitarian language for God.

But this argument involves a confusion of religious experience with divine revelation. The religious experience of men and women may be different in certain typical ways, although this sort of judgment is always in danger of gender stereotyping. However, there are also female scholars who disagree with the basic premise that male and female spirituality yield different experiences of God. Elizabeth Morelli, a Christian philosopher, asserts a counterthesis: "If, as I have argued, the process of conscious intentionality is not gender-specific, it follows that there is no conscious access to God unique to woman."[40] Thus Mar-

37. Diane Tennis, *Is God the Only Reliable Father?* (Philadelphia: Westminster, 1985). Suggestions for the use of masculine and feminine language in outreach and pastoral counseling are made in chap. 11 of my book.

38. Johnson, *She Who Is*, 62.

39. Rienstra, "Grounded in Gender," *Perspectives*, November 1995, 8–11, an article adapted from her book, *Come to the Feast: Seeking God's Bounty for Our Lives and Souls* (Grand Rapids: Eerdmans, 1995).

40. Morelli, "The Question of Woman's Experience of God," in *Speaking the Christian God*, 235.

chiene Rienstra is claiming way too much when she places "beyond dispute" the assumption that "the nature of our relationship to God, and therefore our spirituality, is grounded in gender." In any case, the quality of women's religious experience is only one issue.

The other issue is the nature and location of divine revelation. Spiritual experience, however genuine, is not revelation in the normative sense that warrants language for God as Scripture does. We Christians do have an authentic, experiential relationship with God through the Holy Spirit. But experience of God's presence in our lives and of his continuing revelation in nature and in Scripture cannot be equated with revelation itself. As noted in chapter 6, there are inclusivists who believe that women's experience is a source of continuing revelation that supersedes the Bible. But that view cannot be held by Christians who confess that God's revelation in Jesus Christ as witnessed in Scripture is the defining authority for the church.

Once we distinguish between religious experience and divine revelation, it is possible to affirm whatever genuine differences there are between men's and women's spirituality. It is also possible to understand that both men and women can feel motherly as well as fatherly love in relationship with God. This experience only confirms what we already know from the Bible, that Yahweh's love is like a mother's and that our heavenly Father has a motherly touch. But religious experience does not reveal that God is our Father-Mother or warrant gender-inclusive language for God.

This conclusion does not invalidate all use of feminine language that arises from religious experience. For the Christian church has adopted many images and terms for God that are not found in Scripture: *the Trinity, the Great Designer,* and *the Hound of Heaven* come to mind. Such language is legitimate in so far as it is consistent with the biblical pattern of language for God and does not undermine it. But that is a topic of the next chapter.

Conclusion

The Chapter: God Is Not Guilty of Sexism

In this chapter we have considered variations on the theme that the Bible's language for God is problematic. Inclusivists charge that it is sexist, promoting injustice and abuse against women. They argue that justice and the image of God require our language for God to be gender-inclusive. They also allege that the biblical vocabulary for God is irrelevant to people in our modern, egalitarian culture, as well as to the religious experience of women.

As it turns out, however, none of these arguments for abandoning Scripture in favor of gender-inclusive language is valid or sound. Some allegations are transparently false. Others require more extensive consideration. But when the jury is in, the defendant is acquitted.

The Book: Christian Inclusivism Is Untenable

Inclusivists have not only brought charges against the biblical presentation of God. They have also undertaken a massive effort to justify their revision of Christian language for God. Their case consists of many kinds of arguments from sociology and psychology, from Scripture, hermeneutics, and theology, as well as philosophy, linguistics, and literary theory. They claim that inclusive language for God preserves everything true in Scripture and historical Christianity while revising them to promote gender justice and a more accurate understanding of God.

Most of this book has prosecuted a case against inclusive language for God. We have examined the relevant biblical texts, the structures of language, the doctrines of revelation and Scripture, the nature and meaning of the Bible's language for God, and related dynamics of Christian piety. We charge that inclusive language for God is guilty beyond a reasonable doubt of deviating from the doctrine and piety of biblical Christianity. Although there are elements of truth in its evidence and arguments, we have found no conceivable way to justify fully gender-inclusive language for God that is compatible with Holy Scripture and the historic Christian faith.

The courtroom analogy is helpful in anticipating reactions to our case. The reader is the jury. Has our prosecution of inclusivism demonstrated its guilt beyond a reasonable doubt? Has our defense of historic Christianity at least shown that inclusivist charges against it are full of reasonable doubt? As the O. J. Simpson trial reminded us, people are not equally reasonable and do not use the same standards of rationality. Some readers therefore may not be persuaded by what I regard as an overwhelming case.

But if the argument of this book is cogent, inclusivists should be honest and openly admit their significant differences with historic Christianity, as many of them have done. Those readers who are committed both to the historic Christian faith and to fully inclusive language for God ought to recognize the internal tension, instability, and spiritual ambiguity of their position. They should return to the biblical paradigm. Readers who are committed to the historic Christian faith but who find themselves attracted to inclusive language for God should resist this temptation. Finally, those readers who feel vindicated because they have agreed with the book all along ought to postpone their celebration for one more chapter.

I hope that all readers will go on. Our treatment of language for God is not yet complete. We must still appropriate the elements of truth in the case for inclusivism. We must still explore the proper use of feminine language for God.

11

The Motherly Touch of Our Heavenly Father: The Language of Biblical Christianity

Although the main purpose of this book has been to challenge the case for inclusive language for God, we have never alleged that all of its claims are false. Simple integrity requires us to recognize the important elements of truth it contains. Defenders of biblical-traditional Christianity may not simply ignore inclusivism or reject it out of hand. The church should not merely continue to speak of God the way it always has with no change whatsoever. We ought to be exploring ways of using feminine language for God that are faithful to biblical Christianity.

While examining inclusivism we have noted that Scripture itself uses feminine imagery for God. We have found that the doctrine of general revelation implies that all creatures, including female creatures, reveal God and thus are sources of legitimate language for him. Human males and females, the living images of God, are the most graphic linguistic resources of all. We have noted that exemplary figures in Christian tradition, including John Calvin, have occasionally spoken of God as our mother. We have also admitted that there are gender-related pastoral problems associated with traditional biblical language for God, problems that the ministry of the church ought to address. For all of these reasons the issue is not whether we ought to use feminine and gender-neutral language for God, but how we should do so. How can we use this language in ways that faithfully express biblical Christianity, avoid the aberrations of contemporary gender-inclusive language for God, and promote justice and well-being for women and men in contemporary culture?

265

This chapter begins to answer these questions. To that end it first recollects conclusions from previous chapters to summarize the pattern of original biblical language for God and address issues of gendered language in Bible translation. The second section formulates rules or guidelines for the use of masculine, feminine, and neuter language for God consistent with the standard, biblically based linguistic practice of historic Christianity. The third section considers circumstances and reasons that bear on the propriety of using feminine language for God. The final section offers concrete suggestions for using feminine language for God in the ministry of the church and in the lives of Christians.

Thus we conclude our examination of inclusive language for God by demonstrating that biblical Christianity can have it both ways. It can use feminine and gender-neutral language for God within the framework of Scripture without endorsing the egalitarian gender-inclusivism that is being promoted in parts of mainline Christianity. We can testify to the motherly qualities of our heavenly Father without redefining God as our Father and Mother.

The Biblical Pattern of Gendered Language for God

The Source and Norm of Our Language for God

In chapter 6 we pondered God's self-revelation—the source of all our language for God—in creation, in the history of his relationship with his people, and in Scripture. We concluded that, while all of creation reveals his eternal deity and power, special revelation is the source of our knowledge of the particularities of God's personal identity. His encounters with Adam and Eve, Abraham, and Moses, with the prophets, priests, and kings of Israel, and with his people in Jesus Christ disclose much more of who God is and what he is doing than general revelation does. This specificity, combined with the sinful human tendency to suppress the truth of general revelation, means that special revelation must interpret general revelation. Because Holy Scripture is special revelation, and because it is the completely truthful and reliable written account of God's special revelation in history and general revelation in creation, it is the definitive source and norm for our knowledge of and language for God. Therefore *theological ideas and verbal references to God that are derived from nature, human nature, religious experience, or intellectual reflection are legitimate to the extent that they conform to and expand upon the biblical revelation of God. But language and conceptions of God that compete with, obscure, or alter the biblical presentation of God are illegitimate.*

The Biblical Pattern as a Whole

Thus the overall pattern or paradigm of Christian language for God is provided and defined by Scripture. We explored the personal-linguistic gender characteristics of this pattern in chapters 3, 4, and 5. It became clear that the Bible from Genesis to Revelation consistently identifies God as Lord, King, and Father with a variety of other titles and subtitles. We noticed that the God of the Bible is an anthropomorphically masculine person and never a feminine person or a nonpersonal being.[1] However, the Bible does contain occasional instances of cross-gender imagery in which it uses feminine and maternal figures of speech to describe the attitudes and actions of the anthropomorphically masculine God. It also uses language for God derived from things that are genderless and inanimate, terms such as *rock, light,* and *fortress.* The cumulative pattern of Scripture's language for God is the linguistic paradigm that the Christian church ought to practice in its worship and propagation of the faith.

Gender in the Translation of Scripture

Just as the Bible was originally written in the common languages of Hebrew- and Greek-speaking believers, so Christians around the world love to read Holy Scripture and to express their faith in their own native languages. That is why the Bible has been translated. Ever since the Old Testament was rendered into the Greek Septuagint, principles of biblical translation have varied somewhat and have been debated, especially recently. Should translations be literally word-for-word, or depart from literalism in order to convey the dynamic equivalent meaning of the original words, or should they actually be paraphrases that highlight the relevance of the biblical message to the reader's context?[2] The debate continues as translations proliferate.

If Christians are to continue using the language of Scripture in speaking of God, we must ask how the gendered character of this language functions in translation. For as we have seen, grammatical gender and personal gender are present to different degrees and related in different ways from language to language. Many languages do not indicate personal gender the way the biblical languages do. How then ought gendered language for God to be translated?

Without engaging the philosophical details of the debate about translation, I affirm the general principle that translations of Scripture

---

1. The possible but unlikely exception of *Spirit of God* in the Old Testament is reviewed later in this chapter.
2. Eugene Nida, *Message and Mission: The Communication of the Christian Faith* (South Pasadena, Calif.: William Carey Library, 1972, 1975, reprint of Harper & Row, 1960), is a classic discussion.

ought to render the original meaning of the biblical text as fully and accurately as is possible in the standard, natural forms of the recipient language. Call this *the fully natural principle* for short. With respect to gender, this principle implies that a particular language should speak of God according to the same rules and conventions that apply to humans, just as the original text of Scripture does.[3] Some languages have gender-specific personal pronouns, adjectives, articles, or verb forms. Others do not. Some have gender-specific terms for male and female persons of equivalent position, for example, *mother* and *father*. Other languages indicate this distinction with specific gender-markers of the same word-root, for example, *actor* and *actress*. It would be rare indeed, however, for a language to speak of persons without ever distinguishing their gender at all. I know of no natural language that completely lacks indicators of personal gender, no language that is completely and naturally gender-neutral. Is there any language that only refers to parents and children, for example, but does not distinguish fathers and mothers or brothers and sisters? Any translation of Scripture, therefore, will preserve the basic biblical pattern that speaks of God as an anthropomorphically masculine person with occasional feminine imagery and gender-neutral descriptions in natural patterns of the recipient language.

But what if the biblical pattern does not fit a cultural pattern? Consider the case of the Peve, a matriarchal tribe in southwestern Chad for whom it just did not naturally work to refer to God as "he." So Bible translators resorted to "she."[4] This unusual example raises the issue of dynamic equivalent translation in a mission setting, a problem similar to translating "white as snow" for desert dwellers who have no knowledge of snow. Although we can debate how best to solve this particular problem, in the final analysis Christians in any culture must conform to the transcultural truth of Scripture, which must be preserved and taught. There are many things in many cultures, including our own, that impede understanding and acceptance of biblical truth. We may not "tone down" or alter the intended message of the Bible in order to accommodate what is out of line with it, although we may educate and disciple people gradually to conform to that message. A few unusual cases that challenge our ingenuity are no basis for rejecting the general principle that full, natural translation is the proper approach to the gendered language of Scripture. The challenge of the Peve language is no justification for wholesale inclusivism.

3. Chaps. 4, 5, and 7 made the point that the original Bible speaks anthropomorphically of God as it does of human males.
4. Rodney Venberg, "The Problem of a Female Deity in Translation," *Bible Translator* 35 (1984). Margo Houts is my source for this reference.

Applied to English, the principle of fully natural translation means that we ought as much as possible to preserve the distinctive masculine character of the biblical terminology for God: *ab, abba*, and *pater* ought to be translated as *Father*, not *Father-Mother* or *Parent. Melek* and *basileus* mean *king*, not just a gender-neutral *monarch* or *ruler*. Grammatically appropriate pronouns ought to be supplied where needed. Thus *God . . . God . . . God* repeated *ad nauseum* and *Godself* or *God's own self*, which are unnatural linguistic novelties invented in order to avoid appropriate gender-specific pronouns, violate the principle of fully natural translation. They also implicitly validate the charge that biblical language is sexist and needs correction.

Inclusivist versions of Scripture are either outright alterations instead of translations, as when they render *Father* as *God* or *Father-Mother*, or else they adhere to the principle of gender-inclusiveness more strongly than to the principle of fully natural translation, as when they choose *Monarch* instead of *King*.[5] Most inclusivists acknowledge that meaning is lost. Brian Wren writes: "It is worth asking what is lost when we depart from KINGAFAP."[6] Ruth Duck is quite candid: "Through the method of translation, I use the words 'offspring of God' to hint at what 'Son of God' has traditionally expressed."[7] She knows that a full translation does more than hint at the original.

The principle of natural translation also means, however, that English versions will be less gender-specific than the original text. Articles, adjectives, verb forms, and some pronouns are parts of speech that attribute masculinity to God in Hebrew and Greek but not in English. In addition, there are many words that are gender-neutral in English but gender-specific in the original: *creator, redeemer, judge*, and *shepherd* are examples. Even the word *God*, which some English speakers now take to be gender-neutral, is always masculine in the original. Since English is naturally much less gender-specific than Hebrew and Greek, it is legitimate for the English Bible to reflect the linguistic masculinity of God to a lesser extent than the original. It is surely not necessary for English translations to devise unconventional ways of explicitly marking the masculinity of Hebrew and Greek words. To illustrate, it would be a bit overdone for the English Bible to specify *male judge* or *male shepherd* as a standard procedure when translating the respective Hebrew

5. Duck, "Method of Translation," *Gender and the Name of God*, 93–100, appeals to Eugene Nida's principle of dynamic equivalence to justify inclusive language for God. But the translations she recommends fail to communicate equivalently the historical-theological meaning of Scripture's masculine language, discussed in chap. 8.

6. Wren, *What Language Shall I Borrow?* 229. KINGAFAP, you recall, is God as King, Almighty, Father, Protector, a metaphor-system he wants to "dethrone."

7. Duck, *Gender and the Name of God*, 189.

words, whether they stand for humans or for God. Faithful English translations clearly preserve the gender pattern of biblical language for God. If they did not, inclusivists would not be complaining about them and publishing new ones.

Principles of the Biblical Pattern of Gendered Language for God

Standard Primary Language for God

What are the principles that implicitly govern the biblically patterned use of gendered language for God, whether in the original or in translation? In this section we identify what is legitimate in principle for biblical Christians. In the next section of the chapter we consider when it is appropriate and edifying to practice what is in principle legitimate.

The fundamental principle, which follows from the status of the Bible as unique revelation, is that *Christians ought to continue as their standard regular practice naming and identifying God primarily with the basic terminology of Scripture.* Just as human beings are identified by a few basic names and titles, although they can be described and referred to in hundreds of ways, so the Bible uses a few primary identifying terms for God, whom it also refers to in hundreds of other ways. It is helpful to recall key points of chapter 4.

The most basic terms are *God, Lord, King,* and *Father. God* is the standard English translation of the biblical terms *El, Elohim,* and *theos. Lord* is the common rendering of *Yahweh,*[8] *adonai,* and *kurios. Lord* and *God* are often used in combination. *King* is the definitive title (or "root metaphor") of *Yahweh Elohim* in the Old Testament, identifying the position and authority from which almost all of his other actions and functions derive. *King* is conjoined with *Father* in the messianic covenant so that when this covenant is fulfilled in Jesus the Messiah, *Father* becomes the distinctive term for the Lord God in the New Testament. *Father* is used regularly by Jesus to speak of God and especially to address him in prayer, a practice he taught his disciples to follow. The status and meaning of the term *Father* is revealed most fully in the triune name of God invoked by Jesus, *Father, Son, and Holy Spirit.*

In addition to these primary terms for God are his basic titles. Some of them are epithets—descriptive adjectives. Often they highlight his elevated status: God is *the Almighty, the Lord of Hosts, the Most High, the Everlasting, the Holy One.* Other primary titles designate God's status

---

8. The Old Testament of the *Jerusalem Bible* retains the Hebrew word *Yahweh,* a practice that may enhance the meaning of Scripture for those who understand the history and significance of this special name of God. Although *Lord* replaces *Yahweh* in the New Testament, it does not preserve its original Old Testament meaning.

through basic kinds of actions in relationship with his creation and his people: God is our *Maker* and *Creator*, our *Savior* and *Redeemer*, and our *Judge*. These terms are primary because they identify God's proactivity in the basic epochs of redemptive history as narrated in Scripture and summarized in the Apostles' and Nicene Creeds: creation, redemption, and consummation.

Scripture's primary names and titles for God, used in conjunction with the standard New Testament language identifying Jesus as Christ, Son of God, Savior and Lord, identifying the Holy Spirit as God's Spirit, sent by the Father and Son, and culminating in the triune name—these names and titles clearly, reliably, and enduringly name and identify the true God in distinction from all distorted and false attempts to invoke deity. *The primary language of Scripture must continue to be the basic linguistic paradigm of historic Christianity.*

We must reiterate that gender is not the central point or meaning of the Bible's identification of God. What is primary is that God is the Sovereign Lord, our King, Father, Creator, and Savior. The particular meaning of the terms for God are what is of primary importance, not the fact that they are masculine. Nevertheless, the masculinity of the Bible's terminology for God does turn out to be a constant, exceptionless feature. All the names, titles, and general appellatives designating God in Scripture are personally masculine terms. In addition, all the inflected parts of speech that indicate personal gender in the original languages—articles, pronouns, adjectives, verb forms—refer to God anthropomorphically as a masculine person. God is never spoken of as though he is a feminine person or a nonperson.

Being presented as an anthropomorphically masculine person turns out to be an essential feature of the historical identity of the God of Scripture. Although it is a secondary characteristic and does not mean that God is ontologically masculine, the gender of this terminology does have an apparently irreplaceable theological significance for the God–creation relation, the Trinity, and the deity of Jesus Christ.[9]

Principles for Using Gendered Language for God

So we come back to our first principle: *Christians should continue to use the basic, primary biblical names and titles for God as their standard practice.* Since definitive biblical language is essentially masculine, a corollary is that *we ought to speak of God as an anthropomorphically masculine person.* We should do so even when using extrabiblical personal language, such as *Master of the Universe.* A second corollary is

---

9. These points were discussed in chap. Eight.

that, since there is no biblical warrant, *we should not use feminine terms as names or primary titles of God*. Specifically, we should not use *Mother* as a regular or standard designation for God.[10] *Mother* lacks the biblical status and thus the liturgical and doctrinal centrality of *Father* as a term for God and should not be used as though it had that status.

Pronouns and other grammatical constructions (in languages where structures such as articles and verb-endings reflect personal gender) should also reflect the fact that biblical language for God is anthropomorphically masculine but never feminine. *He* and *himself* are the appropriate English pronouns for God, for they are grammatically required by their antecedent, the God who is Lord, King, and Father. These pronouns do not imply that God is ontologically masculine. Since pronouns derive their meaning from their antecedents, they have the same analogical-metaphorical-theological meaning as *God, Lord, King,* and *Father*. Perhaps it is permissible in conformity with good style to reduce the number of masculine pronouns used, but they cannot be eliminated or drastically reduced without reducing the intelligibility of the text or tacitly validating inclusivist complaints against them.[11] Since there is no feminine term for the person of God in Scripture, the pronoun *She* is never appropriate as a direct reference to God. Thus *we should use masculine pronouns for God as necessary, but no feminine pronouns*.

Gendered Language and the Holy Spirit

An explanation is in order about pronouns for the *Spirit of God* and the *Holy Spirit*.[12] In English this an issue only for the third-person pronouns *he, she,* and *it*. Given Scripture's uniformly masculine personal language for God, it would be appropriate to refer to the Spirit of God in the Old Testament as *She* only if we had sufficient reason to believe that *Spirit of God* is a feminine personal reference to God himself. But we lack sufficient reason, since this reference is in fact unlikely. It is noteworthy that the Old Testament never uses a feminine pronoun to refer to the Spirit of God even in texts where *Spirit* is grammatically feminine. Furthermore, in about a quarter of the cases, *Spirit of God* is grammatically masculine. For all these reasons we can best refer to the Spirit of God in the Old Testament with the pronoun *it*, as we would refer to God's heart, mind, power, and glory, or to the spirit of Moses.

---

10. Below we suggest ways in which it is permissible to speak of God as Mother.

11. Robert Jenson, "The Father, He . . .'" in *Speaking the Christian God*, 95–109; Donald Hook and Alvin Kimel, "The Pronouns of Deity: A Theolinguistic Critique of Feminist Proposals," *Scottish Journal of Theology*, 1993, 46:297–323.

12. See the relevant sections in chaps. 3 and 4.

In the New Testament, however, the *Holy Spirit* is a divine person. The Greek term is grammatically neuter, although the Holy Spirit is the direct or indirect antecedent of masculine pronouns at least three times. In the final analysis, therefore, the anthropomorphic personal gender of the Holy Spirit is unclear from the biblical text. As an impersonal pronoun in English, *it* is not appropriate. *She* has no linguistic basis at all in the New Testament, even if feminine Old Testament imagery hovers in its background. That leaves either *he* or no pronoun at all. There is a slim textual footing for *he*, since *Spirit* is sometimes masculine in the Old Testament and a few times in the New. Furthermore, since *God, Father*, and *Son* all require *he*, it can be argued that *he* is the appropriate pronoun for the Holy Spirit as well. Thus there is some justification for the tradition of referring to the Holy Spirit as *he*. But it is not nearly as strongly warranted by Scripture as the other masculine language for God.

So if we are careful not to generate rules beyond biblical justification, perhaps it is best to conclude that *it is permissible as a standard practice in English either to use he or to avoid using pronouns for the Holy Spirit.* Given the maternal imagery of the Spirit in the Bible, *she* as an occasional secondary, figurative reference cannot be completely ruled out. (See below for the use of feminine pronouns in figures of speech.) In fact, this has been a practice in parts of the Christian tradition, especially where *spirit* is grammatically feminine in the language of translation.[13] But *She* should not be a standard pronoun for the Holy Spirit in English.

Secondary Language for God

Language from Scripture

Although human beings are typically identified by a few basic names and titles, they can be identified, described, and referred to in an almost infinite variety of ways. Queen Elizabeth is the husband of Prince Philip, the mother of her children, and the owner of property. Her physical appearance, moral character, and personality can be described. All of her actions and accomplishments can be recited. She is a rider of horses, a lover of dogs, a believer in God, a sometime resident of Balmoral Castle, and much more. But *Queen Elizabeth* is the basic title-name by which we identify her.

Similarly, the Bible speaks in hundreds of different ways of the God whom it identifies with a few primary names and titles. Some terms

13. Hopko, "Apophatic Theology and the Naming of God," in *Speaking the Christian God*, 160–61, gives examples from Eastern Orthodoxy and mentions Old Syriac as a language where *spirit* is feminine.

simply use human occupations to designate who he is in terms of a particular thing he does: God is a warrior, a gardener, a potter, and a builder and maker (of the City of God). Other references are impersonal and more figurative, taken from the realm of nature or human artifacts: God is a rock, a shield and fortress, a light, and a consuming fire. Varieties of verbs are used to describe his actions, some of them straightforward, others more obviously figurative: God sees, hears, knows, loves, remembers, gets angry, laughs, forgets, and has regrets.[14]

None of these references to God are basic names and titles, but without them we would not know very much about the biblical God, what he is like, what he does, and how he regards us. Our faith and worship would not be very rich or informed. These allusions shed light from hundreds of different angles on the Lord God, our Almighty King and loving Father. In their own ways, these secondary references are as important for revealing God as the primary terms of designation, but their place and role are different. They elaborate, characterize, and describe. They function to enrich our understanding of God and thereby to increase our love, worship, and service of him. They are an inexhaustible source of spiritual nourishment—worthy of theological reflection, devotional meditation, and regular use in the liturgy and hymnody of the church. But they do not provide basic identification. Thus *the variety of secondary biblical references to God should be used regularly, but they should not be given the status of the basic names and titles of God or be used to relativize or diminish them.*

Feminine and Maternal Imagery for God

Feminine images, especially maternal figures of speech, are part of the Bible's secondary language for God, its rich description of God's attitudes and actions. Some feminine images are similes that explicitly liken God to a mother: "as a mother comforts her child, so will I comfort you" (Isa. 66:13). The metaphors are mainly verbs that depict the action of God in creating the world or in saving his people as giving birth. The work of the Holy Spirit in regeneration is likewise spoken of as "new birth." There are as many as two dozen instances in the Bible where God is figuratively represented in terms of human or animal females, mostly mothers.

For Christians who believe the Reformation motto *tota Scriptura,* "the whole of Scripture," it is imperative to use and benefit from the Bible's feminine language for God in personal meditation, public worship, and Christian teaching and witness. Intentionally or unintentionally, this language has largely been neglected in Christian tradition, and

14. Ramshaw, "Verbs for a Lively God," chap. 10 in *God beyond Gender.*

thereby the fullness of God's verbal revelation has been diminished. In fact, this neglect has lent inclusivist critiques of historic Christianity some aura of plausibility.

All of Scripture's feminine references to God are imagery. They figuratively attribute feminine characteristics to a linguistically masculine person—cross-gender imagery. No feminine term is used as a general appellative ("God is a mother"), title ("God the Mother"), or proper name ("Mother") for God. To speak of God as Scripture does in general means, therefore, that *we should occasionally use feminine and maternal imagery for God, but not as frequent references or standard titles and names for God.*

IS GOD OUR MOTHER? JOHN CALVIN AND JULIAN OF NORWICH

At this point, however, we must address a complex matter that is easily misunderstood: May we ever say "God is our mother"? Although the Bible uses maternal imagery, it never directly says that "God is our mother," even as a predicate metaphor parallel to "the Lord is our shepherd." If we follow the pattern of Scripture strictly, therefore, we will never refer to God as mother. Many people who have agreed with my argument thus far will insist that we adhere to this pattern, going no further. They regard "God is our mother" as illegitimate, a capitulation that leads over the edge of the slippery slope toward wholesale inclusivism.

It is my view, however, that *it can be permissible occasionally to say "God is our mother," provided that it is properly intended and done in appropriate circumstances.* I will explain the circumstantial conditions below. But if it is never permissible, then John Calvin was wrong. For as we have noted, he felt no barrier to writing about Israel in his *Commentary on Isaiah* 46:3 that "God, who has manifested himself to be both their Father and their Mother, will always assist them."[15] Calvin does not make this a regular practice and does not address God as Mother. But he does not consider the mere assertion that God is our mother to be inconsistent with Scripture.

A closer look is instructive. Calvin interprets Isaiah 46:3, which speaks of God's upholding the people of Israel since conception and carrying them since birth, as a maternal figure of speech.[16] He explicitly uses the terms *figure of speech* and *metaphor*. He simply extends the figurative maternal verbs into a figurative noun: God's giving birth

---

15. Calvin, *Commentary on the Book of the Prophet Isaiah*, trans. William Pringle, 3:436–37. Capitalization of *Father* and *Mother* are the translator's choice; they are not in the original.

16. In chap. 3 we concluded that it is uncertain whether this text is a maternal image for God.

means figuratively that God is a mother. Thus Calvin's commentary is completely consistent with the biblical paradigm, linguistic categories, and rules for gendered language that we have set forth in this book. His use of *mother* is a predicate metaphor, not a title or name for God. In saying that God is our father and mother, he may likewise be using *father* as an image parallel to *mother*, which the Bible also does (Deut. 32:18; Job 38:28–29). On the other hand, Calvin might be using *father* as a title and *mother* as a figure of speech, so that they do not have the same status even though they are parallel in structure. In either case, Calvin knows the status of *Father* in Scripture. In this passage he explicitly identifies the term as a *title*. "If it be objected, that God is everywhere called 'a Father,' and that this title is more appropriate to him, I reply that no figures of speech can describe God's extraordinary affection toward us." So Calvin here classifies *father* as a title as well as a figure of speech. He does not identify *mother* as a title, but only as a figure of speech. Thus his exegesis is the same as ours: *Father* is a title that has metaphorical meaning. His statement that God is father and mother is wholly consistent with the biblical pattern, which speaks of the Lord with paternal and maternal figures of speech.

What can be confusing is the fact that predicate metaphors and predicate appellatives have the same linguistic form. A brief review of material from chapter 5 at this point is helpful. *Bill is a teacher* and *Bill is a bear* are identical in structure but not in function or meaning. The former is an appellative whereas the latter is a figure of speech. We need linguistic cues to help us distinguish one from the other. The same is true if we are to say "the Lord is our mother." But as a metaphor, this is a legitimate statement in conformity with Scripture. For the Bible does use maternal metaphors for God, and "God is our mother" can be a metaphor. Thus with Calvin we may occasionally use this expression in the context of the standard biblical pattern of language.

We have also mentioned Dame Julian of Norwich, who in her *Showings, (Revelations of Divine Love)* wrote of God and especially of Jesus as Mother. Dame Julian is frequently enlisted as a historical precursor of inclusive language for God.[17] It is quite clear, however, that she used *Mother* in obviously figurative senses, that she did not use *Mother* as equivalent to *Father*, where *Father* is the title-name of God or of the first person of the Trinity, and that she did not use female pronouns directly

---

17. Jennifer Perone Heimmel, *"God Is Our Mother": Julian of Norwich and the Medieval Image of Christian Feminine Divinity* (St. John's University Doctoral Dissertation, 1980), makes her out to be a protoinclusivist. So does Mollenkott in *The Divine Feminine*, chaps. 2 and 5.

of God.[18] Thus she did not practice egalitarian inclusive language. I have not studied her work in enough detail to identify the principles implicit in her maternal language for God or to compare her practice with the biblical paradigm. Thus I render no judgment about the specific ways in which she spoke of God as Mother.

But even if Julian and other prominent Christians of the past did use fully gender-inclusive language, that would lend no legitimacy to the current practice.[19] Instead it would raise questions about the propriety of their language for God. Not everything done during the history of the church is consistent with the faith, as both the Reformation and Counter-Reformation recognized. Current aberrations are not justified by aberrant precedents.

MAY WE ADDRESS GOD AS MOTHER?

If it is permissible with Calvin and Julian to assert that God is our mother, may we ever pray to God as our Mother? It is true that there are no examples of this in Scripture. But I believe that, clearly understood and carefully practiced, *it can be biblically legitimate occasionally to address God using feminine imagery, including the term* Mother.

My justification is an appeal to the permissibility of occasionally using secondary biblical references to God as forms of address in prayer and song even though they are not used that way in Scripture. For example, Job 41 speaks of God's lordship and power over creation by poetically presenting him as the one who controls and plays with the great sea monster, Leviathan. Is it inappropriate to address God in prayer as the "Tamer of Leviathan" even though no one in Scripture ever prayed this way? Deuteronomy 4:24 and Hebrews 12:29 speak of God as a consuming fire, but this metaphor is never used in the Bible to address God. Does this mean that we may never pray "O Consuming Fire, purify us"? There are many instances in traditional Christian liturgy, hymnody, and prayers where biblical imagery for God is used to address God: a figure of speech is employed as a vocative, a term of address. Is this practice wrong?

If these instances are permissible, then the use of feminine imagery to address God is also permissible in principle. If Psalm 90:2 poetically refers to God's creation of the mountains as giving birth, is it wrong

---

18. Geoffrey Wainwright, "Trinitarian Worship," in *Speaking the Christian God*, 216. These points were thoroughly defended by Douglas Felch in an excellent unpublished research paper, "A Woman for All Times: A Critique of Jennifer Heimmel's Femininst Interpretation of the Writings of the Anchoress Julian of Norwich," for the feminist theology course at Calvin Seminary, Fall 1992. I have also benefited from the work of Susan Felch of Calvin College.

19. See "Inclusive Language for God Is Part of Christian Tradition," in chap. 2.

while camping in the Rockies to address God figuratively as *Mother of the Mountains*? And if Deuteronomy 32:18 speaks of God as giving birth to Israel, then it may not be inappropriate in principle to address God as *Mother of Israel*. Likewise, it is surely not impious to pray *O motherly God* if in Isaiah 66:13 God explicitly states that he is like a mother to his people. Perhaps even the term *Mother* is permissible as a form of address if it used infrequently and is understood as a figure of speech, not as a standard title or name.[20] If we may pray *Father God* on the basis of the paternal simile in Psalm 103:13, may we not occasionally pray *Mother God* on the basis of the maternal similes in Isaiah? Of course prayer to God as *Father* in the full New Testament sense would remain the standard practice.

In sum, *there are various ways of using the Bible's feminine imagery to speak to and about God that conform to the biblical paradigm if their use is figurative and occasional, and as a secondary reference or invocation.* Employed this way, feminine references would not function as standard primary names and titles, confusing or competing with the basic biblical-Christian identification of God.

FIGURATIVE FEMININE PRONOUNS

Nonmasculine pronouns are legitimate within figures of speech for God. God is a mighty fortress in the Psalms and in Luther's great hymn, and *it* is the correct pronoun for *fortress*. Thus we would say "God is (like) a fortress immovable on its foundation." In the same way, a feminine figure of speech can include a feminine pronoun: "God is (like) a mother nursing *her* child." This does not contradict the rule stated above, that feminine pronouns for God ought never to be used. For in the figurative use of pronouns, God is never the direct antecedent. The antecedent is always the noun that stands as a figure of speech for God, and thus the pronoun is figurative. We should never directly refer to God as *She* or *Her*. But cross-gender imagery allows feminine pronouns to be used of masculine persons indirectly. Jesus could say of himself that he is like a hen gathering *her* chicks (Matt. 23:37). So we may say of God that he is (like) a mother nursing *her* child. Feminine pronouns can have a legitimate role in secondary language for God. But this is nothing like inclusive language for God, which insists that masculine and feminine pronouns must have equal status and equal frequency.

---

20. The problem here, of course, is that this form of address is ambiguous. One person may understand it as imagery while another takes it as fully equivalent to *Father*. This places significant limitations on the actual use of such ambiguous expressions, as discussed below.

Extrabiblical Language for God

CHRISTIAN TRADITION

Throughout this book we have recognized the legitimacy of referring to God in ways that Scripture does not model. That is because of our affirmation of the doctrine of general revelation, that nature and human nature manifest the power and deity of their Creator. On the basis of general revelation, poets, preachers, theologians, and philosophers have coined terms and imagined illustrations of God not found in the Bible. Theologians have designated Father, Son, and Holy Spirit as *persons* and called them *the Trinity*. Philosophers have called God *the Necessary Being, the First and Final Cause,* and *the Great Designer.* These technical terms are not just metaphors but function as titles. Preachers down through the centuries have likened God to thousands of earthly things, including a corporate executive, a floodlight, an umpire, and a computer program designer, to mention a few contemporary examples. Artists too have allowed their imaginations to work. I have mentioned a favorite example: Francis Thompson's poem, *The Hound of Heaven,* which represents Christ in his sovereign grace as a great English hunting hound tirelessly and relentlessly tracking his quarry. *Hound of Heaven* is not just an image, but functions as a title of sorts.

While these terms can function linguistically as titles, it would be wrong to use them as equivalent to the standard primary names and titles of God found in Scripture. They do not come from Scripture and most are not even uniquely Christian references. Based in general revelation, they do not identify who God is as accurately or definitively as the Bible does. However, they may be used to elaborate who the God of Scripture is.

The key issue for extrabiblical language for God is whether it illuminates or obscures the biblical presentation of God. The word *Trinity,* for example, comes from a Latin term that means "threeness." It simply stands for the threeness of the Father, Son, and Holy Spirit. Although it is not found in Scripture, it does not alter or confuse biblical revelation. It was chosen precisely because it clearly pointed to the threeness of the Godhead. Thus there is no problem with this term. There have been debates, however, about the adequacy of various images or models that seek to elaborate the triunity of God: Are Father, Son, and Holy Spirit like a three-person family, like Siamese triplets, like a triangle or clover, like a person with three masks, three roles, or three capacities such as love, thought, and will? The question the church's theologians have asked is whether these images clarify the teaching of Scripture or distort it. Their final criterion is sound doctrine based in divine revelation.

Thus *it is permissible for biblical Christians to refer to God with extra-biblical terms, even as titles, as long as such references do not undermine or compete with the biblical pattern of language for God and its meaning.* It might even be permissible on occasion in a context where the biblical pattern of language for God is the standard practice to pray to God as *the Great Designer* or the *Hound of Heaven*, as the Calvinist preacher of my youth did.

Extrabiblical Feminine Language for God

In the same way *it is in principle permissible to use extrabiblical feminine language for God in ways that are consistent with the biblical pattern.* Although *Mother* cannot be classified as a biblical title for God, it can have the same status as *Great Designer, Hound of Heaven*, and other extrabiblical terms that sometimes function as secondary titles and terms of address for God. Poets and preachers might find occasion to use a female teacher, nurse, scoutmistress, or farm laborer as an effective illustration of an attitude or action of the God of Scripture.

But there are feminine images that do alter or confuse the biblical presentation of God instead of unpacking it. Ready examples are found in some kinds of contemporary inclusivist spirituality: God as *the Primal Womb* or *the Soul of the World*. These expressions are more representative of contemporary panentheism or neo-pagan notions of deity than of the Creator of heaven and earth who reveals himself in Scripture. Thus they ought to be avoided.

The relationship of special and general revelation means that *extrabiblical language for God, including feminine language, may be used provided that it faithfully reflects and promotes understanding of the biblical presentation of God and does not transgress its subordinate status.* It should not be used as regular standard religious language for God.[21] Surely it should not be used to correct, relativize, or replace biblical language, as inclusive language would do.

Summary of the Biblical Pattern

If Christians continue to speak of God as the church has done since New Testament times, we will continue to use the Bible's primary names and titles for God as our standard and regular terms of reference and address, with appropriate pronouns. None of these are feminine. We will enrich our religious vocabulary with the many secondary bibli-

---

21. Obviously philosophers of religion will use more philosophical than biblical terminology for God in the practice of their trade. But Christian philosophers of religion will understand the relationship between biblical and philosophical language in disclosing the living God of faith.

cal terms and descriptions of God, including feminine and maternal ones. And we will further explain and illustrate the biblical presentation of God with extrabiblical language, including feminine language. Perhaps we will occasionally even address God in prayer and song using language, including feminine language, in ways not directly modeled in Scripture as long as such uses are consistent with the pattern and meaning of biblical language for God.

We will not use feminine language as standard terminology for God, elevating it to a status equivalent to the primary language of Scripture. Thus it will not be used for standard names, titles, and other basic designations of God. It will be used regularly, but occasionally, not frequently. Thus its secondary status will be preserved, both qualitatively and quantitatively.

There is a rule of thumb: *in principle we may speak of God using feminine and gender neutral language in any way that we* may *use them of a human male*, since the biblical pattern represents God anthropomorphically as a masculine person. Thus if we can say that King David was a mother to his people, and if we might have had occasion to address him as such, then we may also speak of God this way on occasion. But just as such mother imagery is not common and does not warrant making *Queen* a standard title or *she* a proper pronoun for David, so the motherliness of our Heavenly Father does not warrant frequent use of Mother imagery or make *She* and *Heavenly Mother* primary terms for God. This rule of thumb is consistent with the anthropomorphic character of biblical language for God and the doctrine that God is ungendered.

In sum, *we should retain the traditional language of the church and enrich it by the occasional use of appropriate figurative feminine language for God*. We should speak out about "the motherly touch of our Heavenly Father."

Prudent Use of Feminine Language for God

Consider Motives and Consequences

We have affirmed that it is necessary to use feminine imagery for God to conform fully to Scripture. We have pointed out that it may even be permissible in principle to use feminine language for God in ways not found in the Bible, provided that they are consistent with the teaching and meaning of Scripture. We ought to aim at reforming our Christian vocabulary in this direction.

But what is permissible in principle and necessary in general may not be right in a specific situation or for a particular person. Not everything that is permissible is beneficial or constructive, according to Paul

(1 Cor. 10:23). There are other factors to consider when deciding how and when to use feminine language for God. There are personal motives for doing so. And there are consequences as well: benefits and harms to oneself and to others that are likely to result from its use. So the internal and external contexts must be considered when Christians use feminine language for God.

Consider personal motives. Using feminine language for God out of negativity toward the Bible's presentation of God is not a good reason, as indicated in chapter 9. Feeling resentment against religious authority, or asserting one's rights to theological creativity, or desiring to "correct" the inadequacies of the scriptural pattern can be spiritually dangerous. People ought to be wary of these motives if they use feminine language for God. (People who defend traditional language ought to be wary of their motives as well.)

The same caution applies to the personal consequences of this use. If employing feminine language contributes to an increasing sense of distance from the biblical God or to the loss of feeling at home in Scripture, one ought to consider reducing or eliminating its use. We ought to employ feminine imagery because it is part of how God has revealed himself and because using it will draw us closer to him. If other motives and outcomes are involved, we must be careful even though the practice is in principle good.

The motives and consequences for other people must also be considered in context. Using feminine imagery for God might be edifying in one setting but problematic in another. It would not be right to use it, for example, in a worship setting where people will take it as affirming contemporary inclusivist religion, as a necessary improvement on the Bible, or as a critique of the historic Christian church.

In fact, one could argue that, given the gender-egalitarian, politically correct ethos of our culture and the inclusivist theology flourishing in some mainline churches, the late twentieth century is not a good time for Christians to be adopting feminine imagery for God. Julian of Norwich and John Calvin did not live in a culture where speaking of God as *our Mother* would promote false spirituality, heresy, or rejection of Scripture. But we do. While I am not persuaded by this argument, there is truth in it. I urge caution and prudence in how biblical Christians begin to utilize feminine language for God.

The consequences for traditional Christians must also be considered. Many do not understand that there are legitimate ways of using feminine language for God. Any use of it would suggest to them a wholesale capitulation to pagan feminism. While I believe we ought to use feminine imagery for God because Scripture does, it may take time, patience, understanding, and education before many sincere Christians are able to tolerate it, much less experience the reality of God's presence through language that likens him to a mother. It would not be edifying to start wars in families or churches by the abrupt introduction of feminine language for God. At the same time, we must recognize that some defenders of the biblical pattern may be attached to masculine language for God for sexist or traditionalistic reasons, and not merely out of loyalty to the God of Scripture. Those motives, too, must be confronted. The right approach is to consult, dialogue, educate, and pray until the time is right. Then appropriate feminine language should be introduced gently and with clear explanation of its role and meaning.

In sum, feminine imagery properly fits within the biblical pattern of language for God. But legitimacy in principle is not sufficient to determine whether it is appropriate in our personal lives or our churches. We must also pay attention to our motives for using it and to the consequences it will have for ourselves and for other people. *Ecclesia reformata semper reformanda*. The church has been reformed and must always be reforming (according to the Word of God).

Avoid Subtle Inclusivism

Care should be taken so that legitimate feminine and gender-neutral language for God does not inadvertently and subtly promote inclusivism. By *subtle inclusivism* I mean alterations in language for God that are tacitly used to promote inclusive language for God even though that goal is not stated and the results are incomplete. Inclusivism by definition requires both qualitative and quantitative equality of masculine and feminine language. But most inclusivists are tactically willing to settle for half a loaf rather than none. Inclusivist strategies for achieving greater gender balance in our language for God can be subtle and gradual, co-opting the legitimate use of feminine and neutral language for God. Consider the following examples of subtle inclusivism.

A standard tactic is gradually to reduce the frequency with which masculine terms like *Lord* and *Father* are used while gradually increasing the proportion of feminine and neuter references to God. Thus, for example, inclusivists may not overtly place *Mother* beside *Father* in the Lord's Prayer or the triune name. They may not balance each instance of *Father* and *He* with equal numbers of *Mother* and *She*. But they will reduce the frequency and role of *Father* until it is "neutralized." As Ruth Duck advises, "Occasionally calling God 'Father' is not necessarily a patriarchal practice, but *usually* calling God 'Father' does reflect patriarchal values."[22] If this strategy of relativizing the Bible's primary lan-

---

22. Duck, *Gender and the Name of God*, 71.

guage for God to secondary language becomes the regular pattern of worship and the common religious language of the Christian community, the eventual result will be the functional equalization of these terms in the consciousness of worshipers. De facto inclusivism will result from subtle inclusivism.

I have a striking visual example of how this sort of subtle inclusivism works: a bookmark entitled "God of Many Names."[23] Toward the middle of the bookmark is the word *God* in large bold letters. Surrounding it are dozens of other terms for God in various sizes, letter fonts, and colors: *Eternal One, Healer, Friend of the Poor, Wisdom, Shepherd, Holy Mystery, Midwife*, just to mention a few. Among them are *Father* and *Mother*, positioned randomly. *Father* and *Mother* are exactly the same size and color as one another to guarantee equality with each other, but they are smaller and less prominent than several other terms. *Lord* and *King* are nowhere to be found, but their absence is noticed only if one looks for them. The practical effect of this visual pattern is that the basic biblical terms of identification and address to God are lost in the verbal crowd of other biblical and extrabiblical terms. That is precisely how subtle inclusivism is supposed to work. It seems biblical, but it is not.

Another opportunity for subtle inclusivism is provided by the ambiguities of linguistic forms. Above we noted, for example, that *God is our Father* and *God is our Mother* have parallel structures even though they do not have parallel significance. Properly understood, the former is a title-name, whereas the latter is a figure of speech. But this distinction is lost on most people who read both sentences side by side. And it is impossible to tell the difference when both are spoken with the same expression. So it is possible to use feminine language in referring or addressing God that is strategically ambiguous: it can be interpreted as a figure of speech and as a basic title-name. Referring to God as *our Mother* or praying to *Mother God* are systematically ambiguous in this way. Without clear explanation or contextual signals, their use can easily promote gender-inclusivism rather than the full, biblical pattern of language for God.

Gender-neutral language can also aid the inclusivist agenda in subtle ways. In my experience, this is the strategy inclusivists employ in conservative and moderate churches, where the introduction of regular feminine language for God would not be acceptable. Masculine pronouns are avoided. The word *God* is used a lot, sometimes with irritating frequency, but *Lord* and *Father* are not. God is a *Monarch* or *Sover-*

23. Produced by The General Council Committee on Sexism of The United Church of Canada, 3250 Bloor St. West, Etobicoke, Ontario.

eign, but rarely *King*. He presides over a *realm*, not a *kingdom*. The triune name is rarely invoked, whereas other allegedly trinitarian terms like *Creator, Redeemer, and Sanctifier* or *Source, Word, and Comforter* are frequently used instead. Words from the original biblical languages are sometimes substituted in order to hide the masculinity of their English translations: *Yahweh* replaces *Lord*, and *Father* becomes *Abba*.[24] These gender-neutral strategies, or various combinations of them, are used to promote inclusivism even where a *Father-Mother God* is officially opposed.

What enhances the subtlety of these gender-inclusive and gender-neutral tactics is the fact that the masculine terminology of biblical-traditional language is not wholly eliminated. It is still used occasionally. But it is so relativized and marginalized that the overall pattern of the language for God actually practiced, with its equalized quantities of masculine, feminine, and neuter language, is inclusivist. The safeguard against subtle inclusivism is attention to the regular practice of using the biblical-traditional pattern of language for God as the context within which legitimate feminine and gender-neutral references to God are made and understood.

Suggestions for the Use of Feminine Language for God

Public Worship

Since Scripture is the standard of faith and practice, it is the source from which to begin using and validating feminine language for God. An obvious step is occasionally to include passages that contain such language in the reading of Scripture during public worship. This practice has been neglected in most churches. Although the texts containing feminine imagery for God are few, one would expect that the regular and systematic reading of Scripture would include them more frequently than it does. This is true in my experience, although I have attended church all my life.

Occasionally preaching sermons on these texts is a more powerful means of impressing their contents into the souls of the congregants. Mothers' Day provides an excellent opportunity for a message on, say, Isaiah 66:13, where the Lord likens himself to a mother. How edifying it is for those of us who know the love of our mothers to hear from the

---

24. My objection to these original-language substitutions is that their goal is to promote inclusivism. They are not illegitimate in principle, since they merely return to original terms from standard translations of them. In practice, however, such substitutions subvert the communication of Scripture in the standard language of the reader, the whole point of translation.

exposition of Scripture that God's love is like the warm, affirming maternal bond that nourishes us deep down in the core of our beings. How comforting in another way for those who lack a mother's love. I have several times preached on Isaiah 49:15, where God is compared to a mother nursing her child: Is there anything stronger than the love of a mother for her baby? The Lord's love for us is stronger! I also have a sermon entitled "The Motherly Touch of Our Heavenly Father," an exposition of the Heidelberg Catechism's treatment of "Our Father, who is in heaven," the invocation of the Lord's Prayer.[25] The sermon expands on the Catechism from Scripture, pointing out that our Heavenly Father's love is not only like that of our earthly fathers, but also of our mothers. These sermons have been well received in the conservative churches where I have preached them.

Liturgies and litanies, which have traditionally drawn their language from Scripture but seasoned it from extrabiblical sources, can include occasional feminine allusions to God shaped by the appropriate criteria and guidelines. If these liturgical forms were used regularly, then in that way feminine imagery for God could even become a regular part of worship without subverting the standard biblical-Christian paradigm. To preserve that paradigm, feminine and gender-neutral language would not be used in those parts of the liturgy where the triune name *Father, Son, and Holy Spirit* is important, for example, in the invocation of God at the beginning of worship, in the administration of the sacraments, and in the final blessing. *Father* would still be the common term of address in the Lord's Prayer and in most prayers, following the teaching and example of Jesus. Within the traditional pattern of language for God, occasional but regular use of feminine terms for God and alternatives to the triune name are permissible. My examples are merely suggestions, since liturgies vary among traditions, denominations, and congregations.

The music of worship is an especially powerful shaper of souls. Scripture songs based on texts containing feminine imagery are obvious candidates for involving the congregation in using this language. Many traditions have regularly sung the Psalms, several of which (e.g., 123 and 131) contain feminine allusions to God. If suitable versions of these Psalms do not exist, this is a wonderful opportunity for those with the gifts of music and poetry to provide them for Christian worship. Feminine imagery for God is found elsewhere in the Bible. There is currently a great appreciation for tastefully set Scripture songs. Why don't the gifted among us compose songs using these texts with feminine imagery for God?

25. *Partnership*, Spring 1995, 19–23.

The church also possesses well-known hymns that sing of the motherliness of God. A later verse of "My God, How Wonderful You Are"[26] reads: "No earthly father loves like you, no mother half so mild bears and forbears as you have done with me, your sinful child." The old German Lutheran hymn, "Sing Praise to God Who Reigns Above,"[27] includes these lines: "As with a mother's tender hand, He leads His own, his chosen band: To God all praise and glory." The church's traditional hymnody is not totally devoid of feminine imagery for God.

There are also recently composed hymns that use gendered language appropriately. One example is "With a Shepherd's Care" by James Chepponis.[28] Its refrain parallels maternal and paternal imagery: "With a shepherd's care, God leads us. With a father's strength, God guides us. With a mother's love, God nurtures us, and cradles us in gentle arms."

In principle even some hymns that intentionally employ and promote inclusive language for God can be appropriated and reformed within biblical-tradition worship. The gendered language of Brian Wren's "Bring Many Names,"[29] alluded to regularly in this book, can be given an orthodox Christian meaning if used in the context of the clear and explicit practice of the biblical pattern of language for God. Verse 2 addresses "Strong mother God" and verse 3, "Warm father God." In the context of Wren's hymn, intentionally identified and equalized as "names" by the author, these references express inclusivism. Interpreted in the explicit terms of historic Christianity, however, they could be reunderstood as consistent with biblical imagery.[30] Similarly, Wren's hymn "How Wonderful the Three-in-One,"[31] which, true to inclusivism, scrupulously avoids the triune name *Father, Son, and Holy Spirit*, could perhaps be sung in a service where the triune name is properly invoked. After all, the much-loved traditional hymn "Holy, Holy, Holy" sings of "God in three persons, blessed Trinity" without explicitly naming Father, Son, and Holy Spirit. Some contemporary inclusivist hymns can be redeemed.

By mentioning these hymns, I am not necessarily recommending that they be used in biblical-traditional worship. The fact that they are intended to promote inclusivism may be sufficient reason to avoid

26. Frederick W. Faber, 1849.
27. Johann Schütz. I owe this reference to Leroy Christoffels then of Preakness Christian Reformed Church, Wayne, N.J. and to James Culver, St. Peter's Church (ELCA), Stendal, Ind.
28. J. Chepponis, 1992, GIA Publications.
29. Brian Wren, 1989, Hope Publishing.
30. The greater problem with this hymn is its overt commitment to the limited, growing God of contemporary panentheism. See "The God-World Relation" in chap. 8.
31. Brian Wren, 1989, Hope Publishing.

them. In addition, some of them express other doctrinally objectionable opinions. Still other inclusivist hymns are not specifically Christian. They can be sung at interreligious gatherings without making anyone feel uncomfortable. My point is merely to illustrate that, since perceived meaning is influenced by assumptions and contexts, the linguistic ambiguity of some inclusivist hymns leaves them available for orthodox interpretation when placed in the context of traditional biblical worship of God. The same is true, for example, of the statement "God lives in me," which will be understood one way by orthodox Christians and another by New Agers.

While some inclusivist hymns could be reappropriated for historic Christian worship, some cannot be. "Blessed is She," recommended by Wren,[32] simply cannot be rescued, because it is never permissible within the biblical paradigm to refer to God directly with a feminine pronoun, which is to speak of God anthropomorphically as a feminine person.

Church Education

Church education not only provides occasional opportunity for using feminine language for God, but also for discussing the meaning of gendered language for God and its relation to human gender relations.[33] There is probably less opportunity for this in the curriculum for younger children, which is usually based directly on the biblical narrative. Sunday school material ought to use the same language for God as the passages of Scripture it attempts to teach. Subtle inclusivism ought to be avoided. Of course teachers should be sensitive to the possibility that some children might misunderstand or react negatively to the Bible's masculine language for God because their human fathers have not imaged the Fatherhood of God to them.

The curriculum for older children and adults is more likely to focus on non-narrative parts of Scripture, Christian doctrine, and social-cultural issues. These topics offer more opportunities for encountering the Bible's feminine references to God, for understanding their meaning, and for discussing the dissonance between Scripture's language for God and inclusive language for God.

Inclusivists allege that it is no longer possible for most people in our culture to name God as Father and not attribute literal maleness to God.

32. Naomi Janowitz and Maggie Wenig, in *Womanspirit Rising*, 174–78, reprinted in Wren, *What Language Shall I Borrow?* 162.

33. Discussion of editorial guidelines for the use of gendered language for God in the writing of church education material is where the issue first arose in my denomination, the Christian Reformed Church.

But teaching people to avoid simplistic literalism has long been part of Christian education. In the Protestant tradition, for example, we have always instructed our children that Jesus' statement at the Last Supper, "this is my body," is not literally true. We have then explained to them the spiritual sense in which it is true. The very same teaching strategy is available for explaining the Bible's masculine language for God.

In addition, Christian instruction on what it means to be male and female, made in the image of God, and how we should relate to each other as male and female will confront the sinful inclination to use masculine language for God to rationalize the evils of sexism and patriarchalism, including abuse, neglect, and other failures to love and do justice.

Evangelism and Pastoral Counseling

It is upbuilding for all people, whether Christians or not, to hear the good news that the love of God in Jesus Christ is better than the best of our fathers' and our mothers' love. Using feminine imagery for God can make that message more authentic for us all. But use of this feminine language may be especially necessary for those people both in and outside the church who struggle with the truth of the biblical message because of its masculine language and their sensitivity to sexism.

It is difficult to dispute that there is a terrible amount of abuse, neglect, and injustice in our society, much of it the responsibility of males in positions of power. No one should be surprised, therefore, that fear and resentment of male power figures are strong emotions for the victims of these sins and for those who care about them. These emotions can make it difficult for such people to relate positively to the God of the Bible, who is represented as the greatest, most powerful masculine person of all. Ministering to these people with the gospel as proclaimed in Scripture is a pastoral challenge for the church. The use of feminine and neuter language can be of help.[34]

In fact, when evangelizing or counseling such people, it may even be necessary as a temporary tactic to work with more feminine and gender-neutral language than ordinarily occurs in the standard biblical paradigm. This can and should be done without negating or undermining that paradigm, however.

The challenge for pastoral counseling is that there are people already in the church who cannot feel the love of God the Father or pray to him because they have been abused or neglected by their human fathers. Talk of a father's love is either very painful or leaves them cold. These

---

34. I am grateful to Mirth Vos, colleague on the Christian Reformed study committee, and seasoned family counselor, for numerous insights on this topic.

people are not necessarily theological liberals or religious rebels. They may dearly want to relate to the Heavenly Father, but find that they cannot. They may feel terribly guilty about this, even rejected by God. For these people it may be necessary to begin by avoiding talk of God as Father and using other biblical references to him. For people who have had a positive relationship with their mothers or other women, it might be strategically appropriate to begin with those positive feelings and relate them to God's being like a woman or mother, as is done in Scripture. In this way a bridge is constructed between their experience and the message of the gospel. If the Holy Spirit enables emotionally distraught people to relate positively to this presentation of God, healing and growth will occur. Then the positive biblical presentation of God as Father can be introduced. Using this approach we may trust and hope that eventually they will be enabled to experience fully "the grace of our Lord Jesus Christ, the love of God the Father, and the fellowship of the Holy Spirit." In fact we anticipate that such people will eventually discover that their Heavenly Father, who is more than the best earthly father and mother, is the one who fully satisfies all their needs.[35]

Evangelism presents a similar challenge. Many people in our culture are shaped by and wholeheartedly affirm gender egalitarianism. They resonate with inclusivist critiques of biblical language. They find it difficult to take the Bible seriously. Perhaps it is necessary when presenting the gospel to such people that we downplay the masculine terminology a little and use a bit more feminine and gender-neutral language for God. Perhaps we should initially speak of *God* and *Ruler* instead of *Father* and *King*. At the same time, false stereotypes of God as a tyrannical, abusive patriarch must be exposed and refuted. When unbelievers who hate or fear God the Father come to Christ through such a presentation of the gospel, they eventually experience reconciliation with the Father and love him. If they do not come to Christ, antipathy to the Father, not just his title, will remain.

This approach to counseling and evangelism is neither a capitulation to inclusivism nor a justification for it. First, it does not contradict the biblical paradigm but remains within it. It does not use feminine title-names and pronouns for God. It uses selected biblical references to God in order to introduce the rest. Just as we select different texts and doctrines from Scripture when we minister to the sick and dying, the young and wayward, the rich and influential, and the poor and oppressed, so

35. Diane Tennis, *Is God the Only Reliable Father?* (Philadelphia: Westminster, 1985) and John W. Miller, *Biblical Faith and Fathering: Why We Call God "Father"* (New York: Paulist, 1989) are two books that affirm the biblical pattern and contain helpful discussions of the psychological and therapeutic aspects of gendered language for God.

we may select from within Scripture certain ways of speaking about God that will touch those who are sensitive to gender issues. Beginning with texts that include feminine language is perfectly consistent with affirmation of biblical revelation as a whole, as long as the aim and process affirm Scripture and do not replace it.

Second, the intention of this strategy is not to promote inclusivism but to enable the person eventually to be able to relate positively to the God of Scripture, to call God *Father*. By using part of the biblical practice of language for God, it works toward enabling people to use all of Scripture with reverence and spiritual nourishment. It does not attempt to turn a therapeutic or culturally adapted use of language for God into a standard practice for the church, as inclusivism does.

Finally, this approach locates the problem of language where it really is—with the person who cannot relate to God (though not necessarily through his or her own fault), not with Holy Scripture. Inclusivism would change the Bible to accommodate the human inability to accept it, to remove the scandalous and allegedly hurtful particularity of the gospel. The approach we recommend assumes that the inability to respond to the God of Scripture is the result of human fallenness. It trusts God to forgive and sanctify us so that we are conformed to the image of God in Christ as proclaimed in Scripture. Exercised this way, the strategy of temporarily using less masculine and more feminine language for God to reach some people is consistent with commitment to the biblical pattern of language for God.

Personal Devotions

Because they are private and their content is individually chosen, personal devotions provide the most ready opportunity for the use of feminine language for God. If public worship does not include it, or if someone has a greater spiritual need for this language than is met in public worship, personal devotions afford space and opportunity. Reading texts with feminine imagery and offering prayer that focuses on the motherliness of God can take place regularly in devotions that are individual, with a partner, or in small groups. These spiritual exercises can be wholesome and edifying.

It is crucial, however, to engage in such devotions with understanding and the right spirit. The use of feminine language for God is proper only if it is practiced consistent with the biblical pattern, if it is done to worship and be nourished by the God of Scripture, and is not infected with the unbiblical motives, doctrines, and goals of inclusivism. Individuals and small groups who use feminine language for God must discipline themselves to remain faithful in these ways.

Art, Scholarship, and Public Discourse

Scholars, artists, writers, and public speakers who are devoted to the triune God of Scripture may sometimes have good reasons for deviation from the biblical pattern of language for God in the exercise of their callings. Philosophers of religion, for example, usually deal in the abstract terms of their disciple rather than biblical language. As philosophers they use primarily terms like *Great Designer, Necessary Being,* and *Divine Nature* instead of *the Father of our Lord Jesus Christ.* In expressing their basic religious beliefs, however, they do not reduce the special revelation of Scripture to philosophical categories but define their philosophical categories consistent with biblical revelation. They worship the God of Abraham, Isaac, Jacob, and Jesus, not the God of the philosophers or the God of the inclusivists.

A problem scholars and writers in many disciplines face is the fact that most academic professional associations and publishers insist on some form of inclusive language, even in language for God.[36] Using explicitly Christian or exclusively masculine language for God in public presentations or printed publications may draw stiff resistance and hostility. Christian scholars who insist on biblical language may find themselves not invited to give lectures and not getting their articles and books published.

While there are times when Christians ought to stick to principle on language for God and suffer the consequences, it may be necessary and legitimate to conform to moderate kinds of inclusive language in order to have a positive, redemptive witness in one's profession. This accommodation can be permissible provided such language does not overtly contradict the Christian view of God. The sort of inclusivism required in most of these circles is gender-neutral rather than both masculine and feminine. It is usually sufficient simply to use *God* as a genderless term and generally to avoid masculine pronouns. Calling God *Mother* and *She* is typically not required by academic publishing. Christian speakers and writers who strategically adapt to gender-neutral language for professional reasons will surely want to use biblical language for God in worship and in the rest of their lives.

Artists and poets are called to be creative and to explore multiple forms of representation and expression. Thus Christian artists will be motived to discover new ways of portraying the truths and dynamics of the faith. The history of Christianity is a rich treasury of such imagery, including imagery for God. Francis Thompson's poem, "The Hound of Heaven" is an example I have used throughout the book. C. S. Lewis's

36. My·colleague, Ronald Feenstra, pointed out this problem to me.

great lion Aslan, the Christ-figure in his *Narnia* stories, is another of my favorites. In the same way it is possible for poets and artists to use a great variety of feminine and maternal images to represent the attributes, attitudes, and actions of God. My wife, Sylvia, has written a poem in which God's loving, providential care for the details of our lives is represented by the way her mother faithfully braided Sylvia's hair when she was a girl. This wonderful image of God as a mother was crafted by a poet who has no sympathy at all for inclusive language for God.

A more controversial example is *Christa*, Edwina Sandys' 1984 sculpture of a bare-breasted woman hanging on a cross. I have not studied this piece and do not know the intention of the artist in creating it, so my comments are tentative. If *Christa* is intended to suggest that Jesus' maleness renders him inadequate for the salvation of women and that a female Christ is needed, then it is blasphemous. If it is meant to say that women are Christ-figures because they have been crucified by men, it may be an idol. If, on the other hand, it is meant to enable women to see that Jesus shared their humanity, that his incarnation and death incorporates both males and females, that they can identify with him on the cross, then it is a piece of art that expresses important truths of the gospel. It could never move beyond art to become a religious icon, however, for the real Jesus was male.

Art by nature is open to interpretation because it usually has multiple meanings that cannot always be pinned down. Thus it provides great challenges and opportunities for Christian artists and writers to communicate biblical perspectives on God, the world, and human life in the context of creation, evil, and redemption. Creative use of biblical and extrabiblical feminine imagery for God is a legitimate vehicle for faithful expression of this vision. Those who work with feminine imagery may sometimes do so to an extent that is far out of proportion to its role in the standard biblical pattern of language for God. I believe that it is possible for them to do so and still be faithful to the biblical presentation of God in their doctrine, personal spirituality, and the rest of their lives. Given the ambiguity of art, however, they must remain aware that their work is susceptible to interpretation as a statement of inclusivism or feminist spirituality. With artistic freedom comes responsibility.

The End of the Matter

The movement for inclusive language for God in mainline Christianity is a serious challenge to the historic faith that flows from Scripture. Inclusivism ought to be vigilantly resisted. However, it does raise valid concerns about human gender relations that the church must address.

It also reminds us that biblical Christianity can speak of God with feminine language in ways that are faithful to his revelation. We Christians ought to testify to the motherly as well as the fatherly love of our Heavenly Father.

In this chapter I have attempted to state why and how biblical Christians should use feminine language for God and to offer concrete suggestions for actually doing so. These are general rules and examples. While it is necessary to be careful, it is not good to become too legalistic about the use of feminine language for God. Thus I have not formulated a detailed code of laws or established precise numerical quotas. Instead I have tried to identify key features of the biblical pattern of language for God, locate the appropriate place of feminine imagery within the biblical pattern, and warn of ways in which that pattern can be compromised or subverted. I count on the Spirit-led good judgment of biblical Christians to develop uses of feminine and gender-neutral language for God that reaffirm and represent the amazingly gracious revelation of God and the gospel of Jesus Christ presented to us in Holy Scripture.

General Index

Scripture Index

John Cooper (Ph.D., University of Toronto) is professor of philosophical theology at Calvin Theological Seminary and the author of *Body, Soul, and Life Everlasting.* Dr. Cooper served as the reporter for the Christian Reformed Church's committee on inclusive language for God.